SHONEN JUMP ADVANCED MANGA EDITION

Vol. 9

Boy Meets Battle Girl

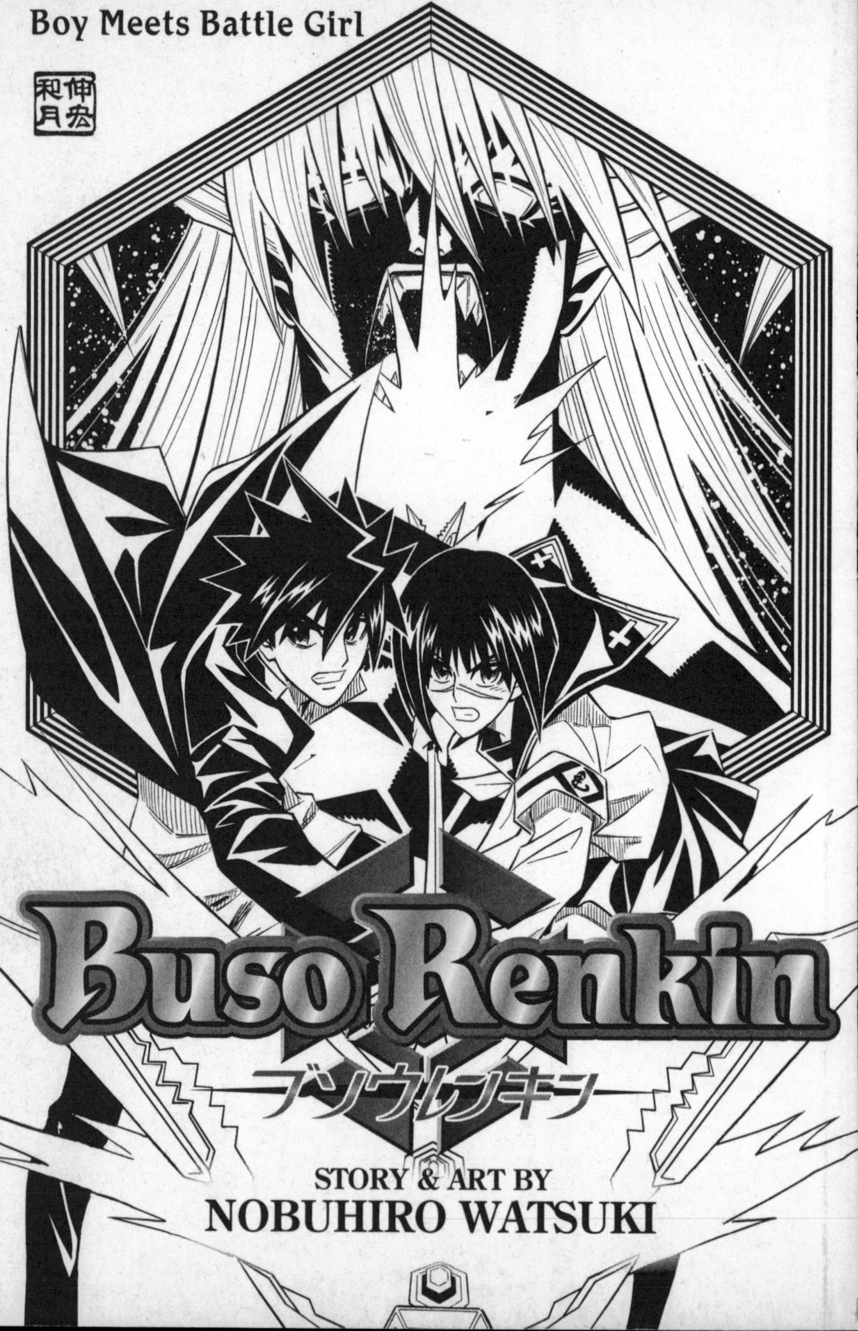
ブソウレンキン

Buso Renkin

STORY & ART BY

NOBUHIRO WATSUKI

Kakugane
The kakugane are forged from a magical alchemic alloy. They are activated by the deepest parts of the human psyche, the basic instincts. Each kakugane can materialize a unique weapon called a Buso Renkin.

Homunculus
An artificial being created by alchemy. The form and powers of the homunculus differ depending on the organism it was based on. Homunculi feed on human flesh and can only be destroyed by the power of alchemy.

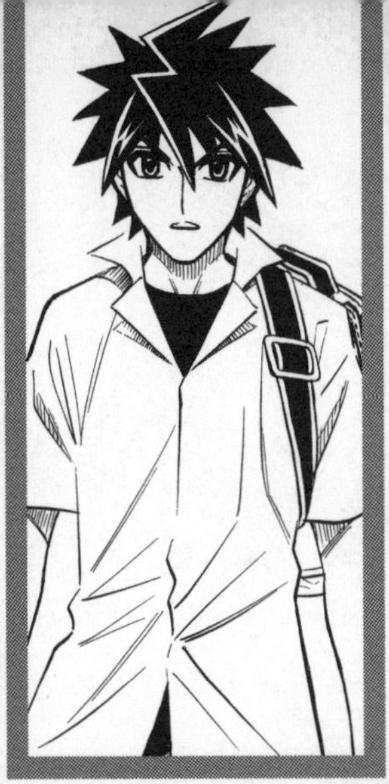

Kazuki Muto

16-year-old Kazuki was killed by a homunculus but was then restored to life by Tokiko, who replaced his heart with a magical talisman called a kakugane. But when it is discovered that he actually has a black kakugane, the Alchemist Army issues a re-extermination order for Kazuki.

武装錬金 CHARACTERS

Alchemist Army
A secret organization started by a guild of alchemists in medieval England. It regulates all things related to alchemy.

Black Kakugane
To facilitate the creation of the Philosopher's Stone, these special kakugane were created a century ago from kakugane with serial numbers I, II, and III. One of the black kakugane was used to revive the injured Great Warrior Victor, transforming him into a monster more terrible than any homunculus; he nearly destroys the Alchemist Army. During this period, the other two black kakugane go missing.

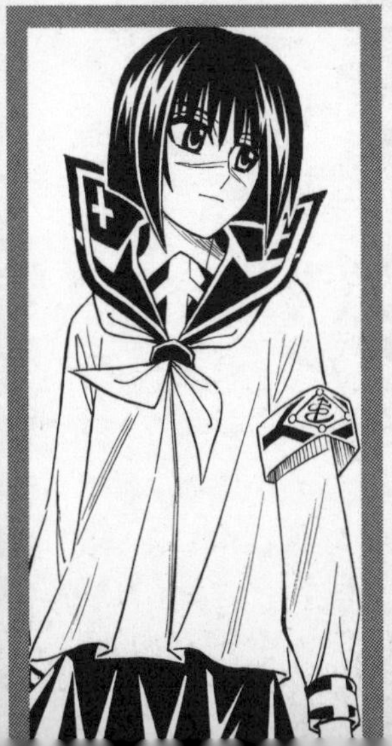

Tokiko Tsumura

Tokiko is an Alchemist Warrior and Buso Renkin expert, but when the Alchemist Army sentences Kazuki to death, she abandons her calling to help him.

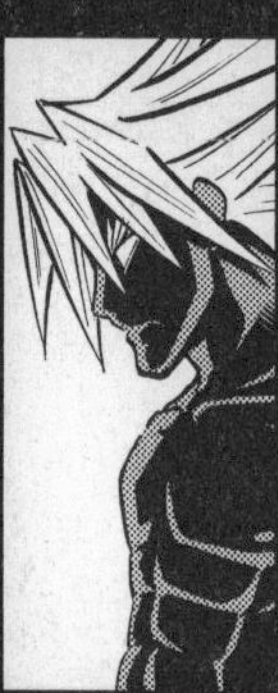
Victor

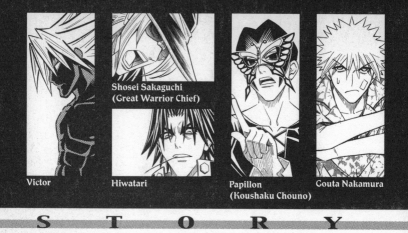

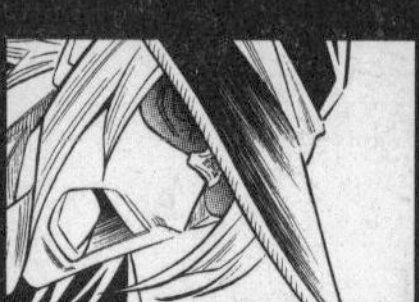
Shosei Sakaguchi
(Great Warrior Chief)

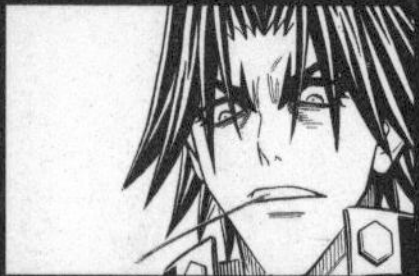
Hiwatari

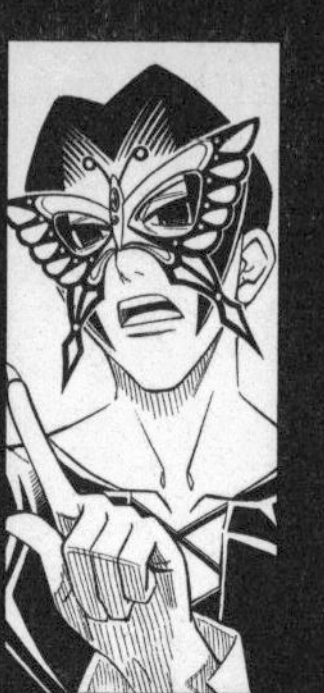
Papillon
(Koushaku Chouno)

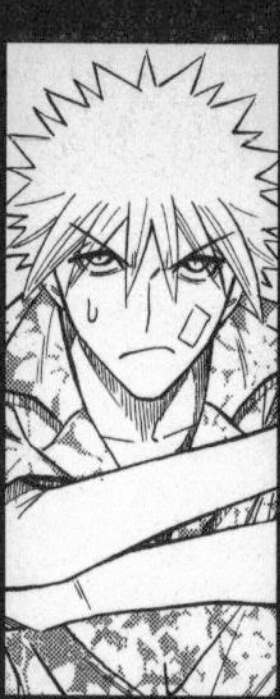
Gouta Nakamura

S T O R Y

Following the destruction of Dr. Butterfly and his League of eXtraordinary Elect, Kazuki learns that he is doomed to become a life-draining creature like Victor because of the black kakugane that serves as his heart. The leaders of the Alchemist Army, fearing that they will soon have two nearly invincible monsters to deal with, order Kazuki's immediate termination. Hunted by friend and foe alike, Kazuki, Tokiko, and Gouta Nakamura make their way toward Newton Apple Academy for Girls where they hope to find a way to reverse Kazuki's condition. They survive attacks by the Re-Extermination Squad and manage to reach Yokohama, where Kazuki once more battles his mentor Captain Bravo. After a fierce battle, Kazuki defeats Bravo, who, touched by Kazuki's willingness to sacrifice himself for others, decides that Kazuki is too valuable an asset to waste. When flame-wielding Hiwatari arrives, Bravo shields the young Alchemist Warriors with his Silver Skin, exposing himself to Hiwatari's fiery attack. Believing that Bravo is dead, Kazuki attacks Hiwatari in a vengeful rage. But before the battle can be decided, it is stopped by the giant hand of the Great Warrior Chief, the highest-ranking officer of the Alchemist Army, who informs them that Victor has been located.

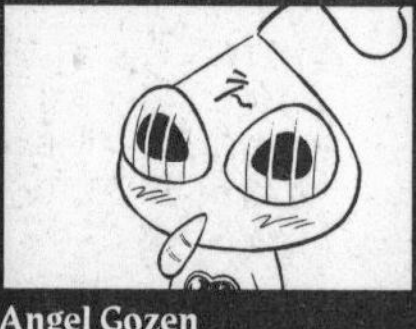
Angel Gozen

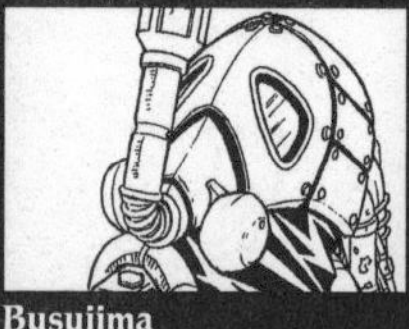
Busujima

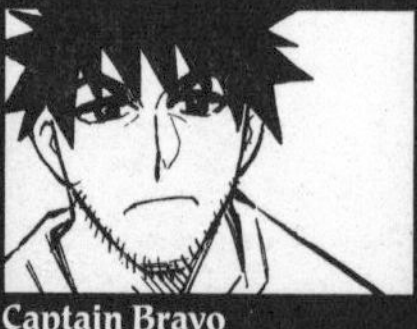
Captain Bravo
(Mamoru Sakimori)

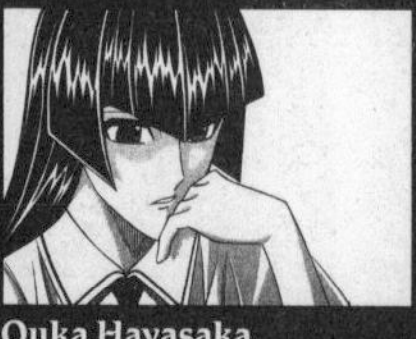
Ouka Hayasaka

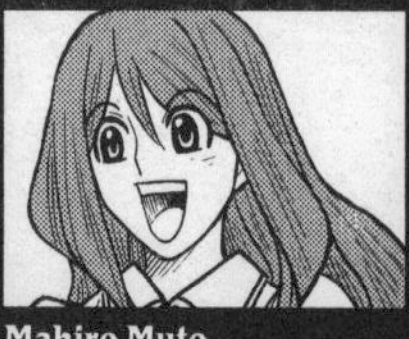
Mahiro Muto

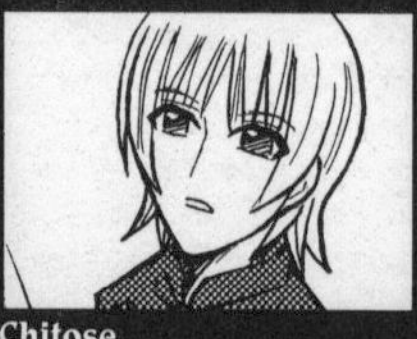
Chitose

BUSO RENKIN
Volume 9: Boy Meets Battle Girl

CONTENTS

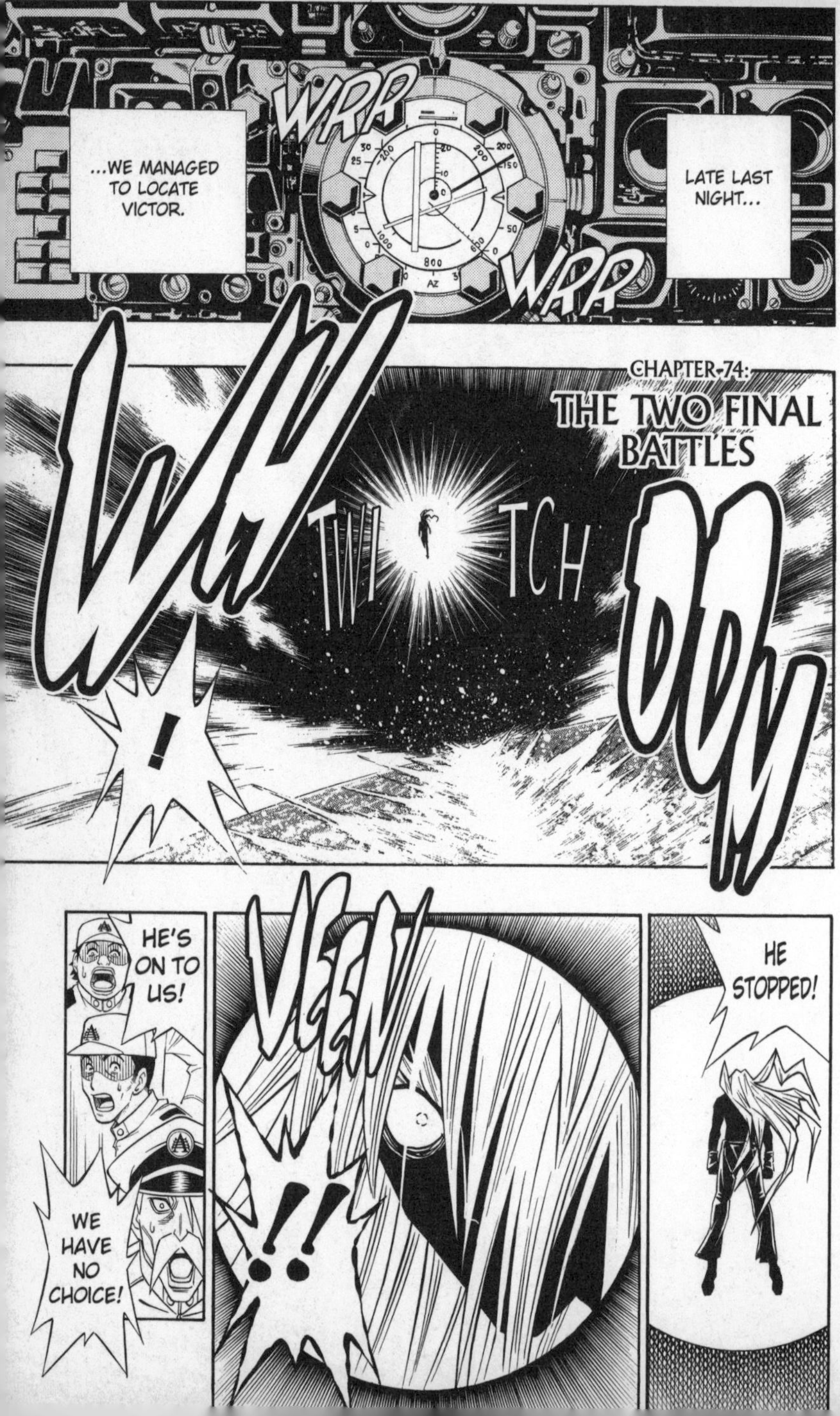
LATE LAST NIGHT...
WRR
WRR
...WE MANAGED TO LOCATE VICTOR.
CHAPTER 74:
THE TWO FINAL BATTLES
TWI TCH
!
HE STOPPED!
!!
HE'S ON TO US!
WE HAVE NO CHOICE!

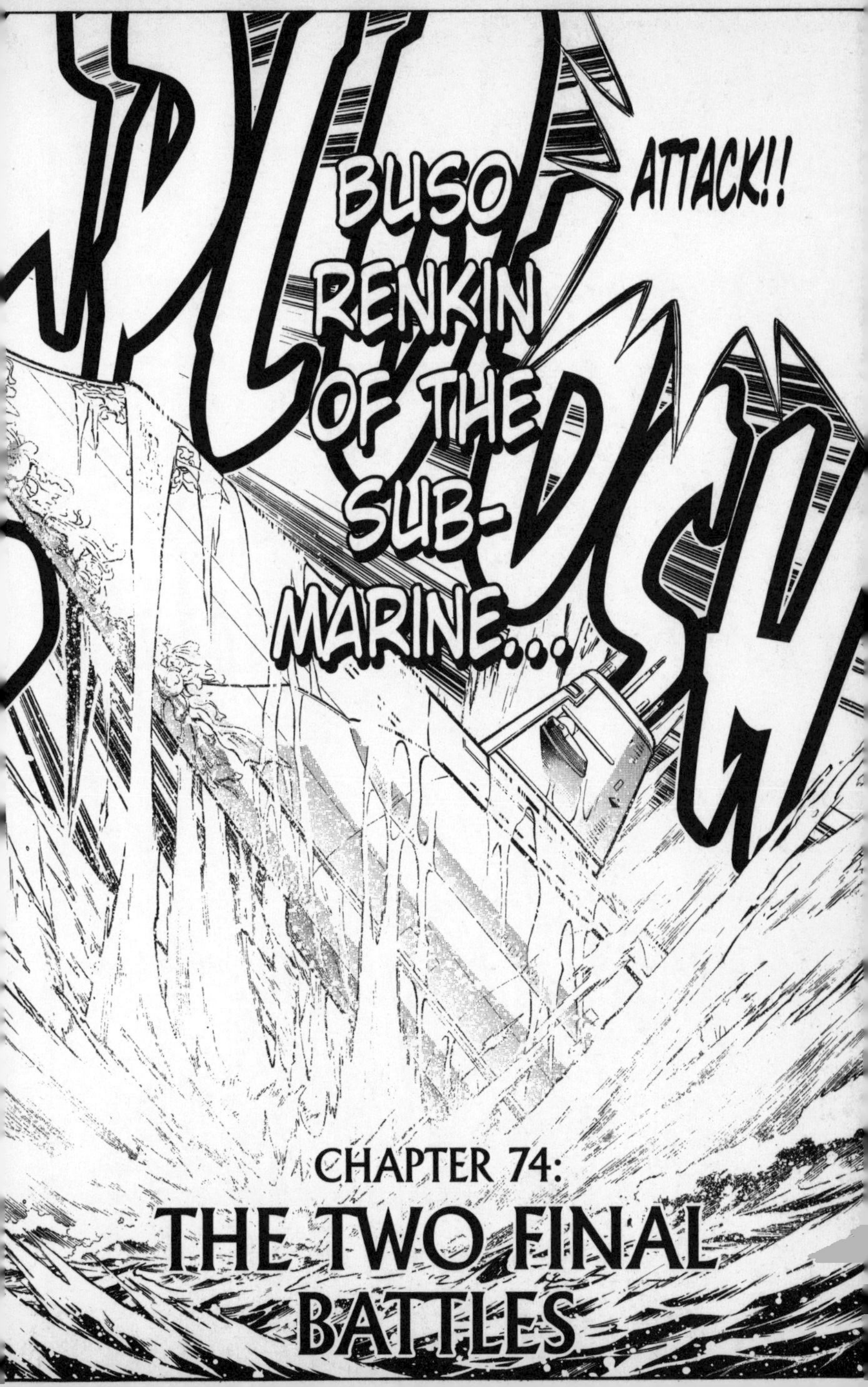
BUSO RENKIN OF THE SUB-MARINE...
ATTACK!!

CHAPTER 74:
THE TWO FINAL BATTLES

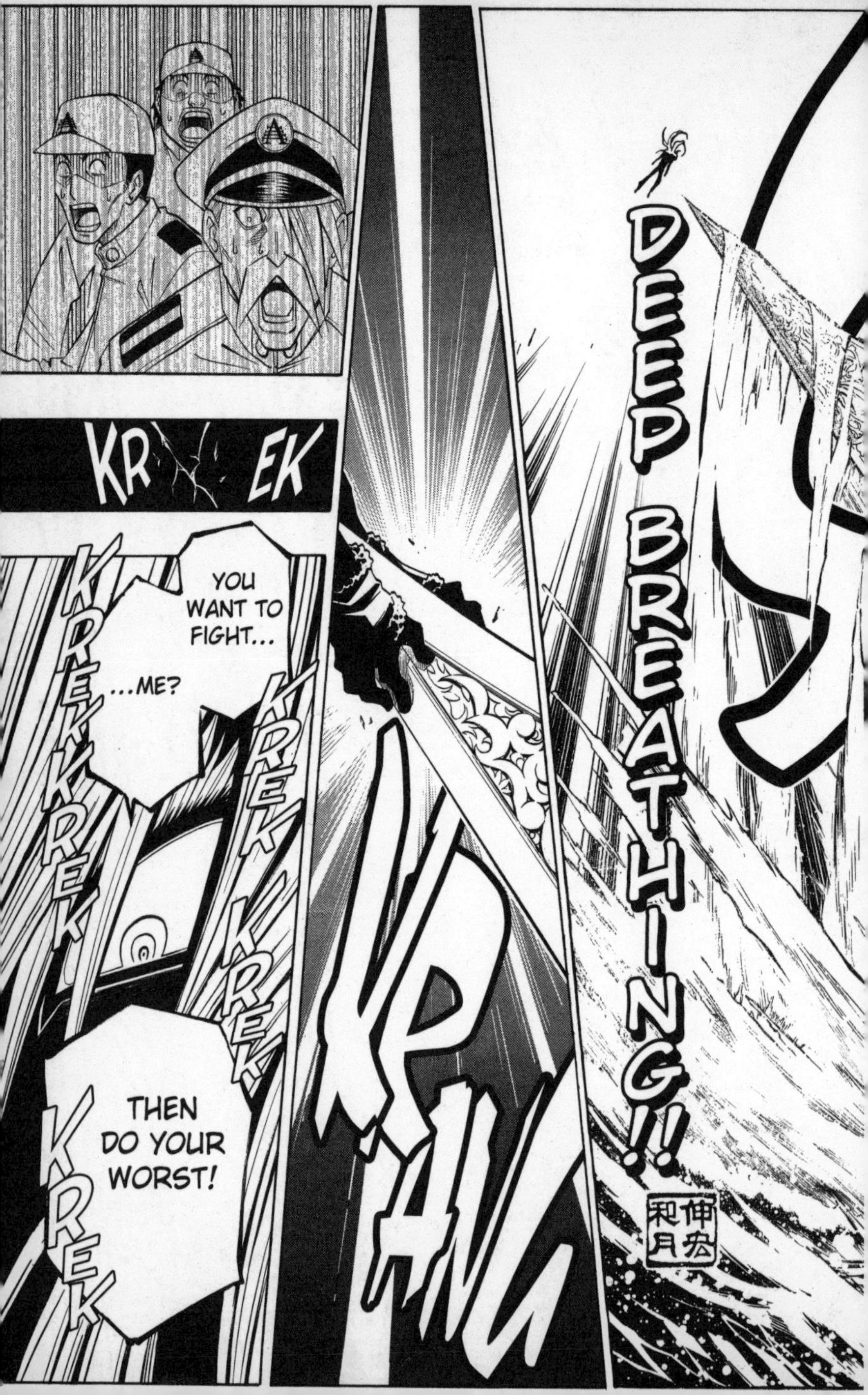
DEEP BREATHING!!
伸宏 和月
KRAN
KR EK
YOU WANT TO FIGHT...
...ME?
KREKKREKKREK
KREK KREK KREK
THEN DO YOUR WORST!
KREK

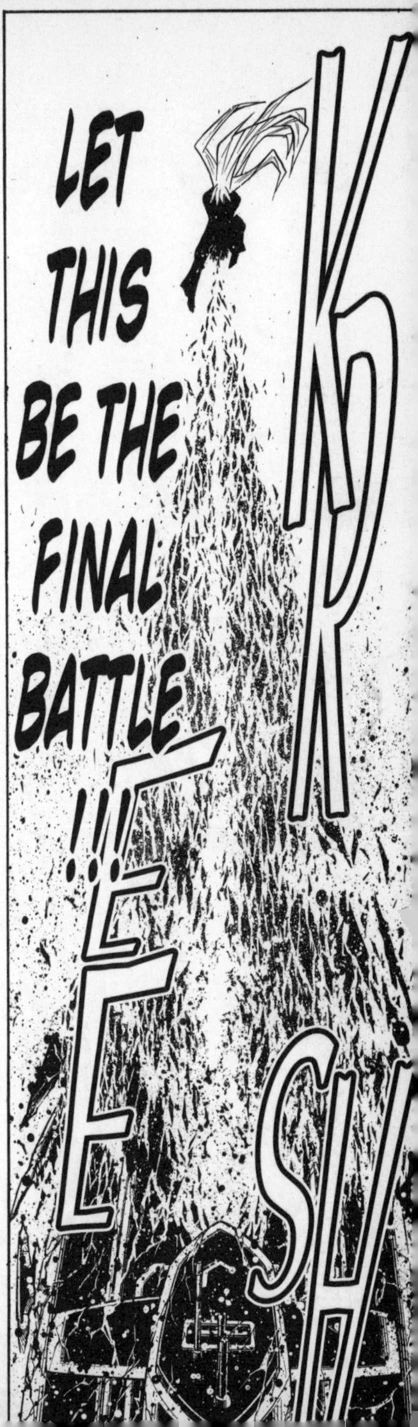
LET THIS BE THE FINAL BATTLE!!!
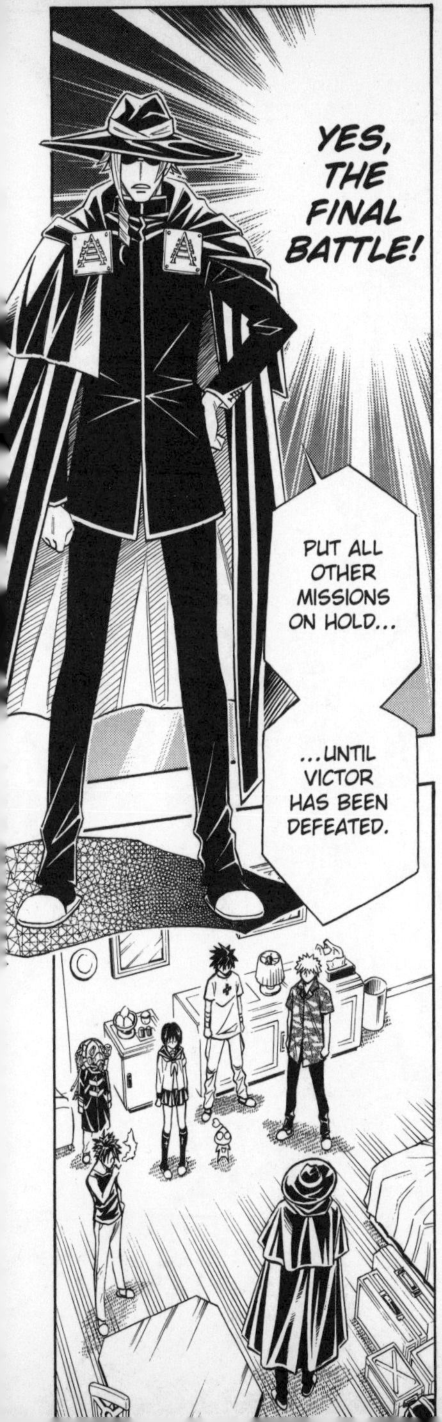
YES, THE FINAL BATTLE!
PUT ALL OTHER MISSIONS ON HOLD...
...UNTIL VICTOR HAS BEEN DEFEATED.

READ THIS WAY

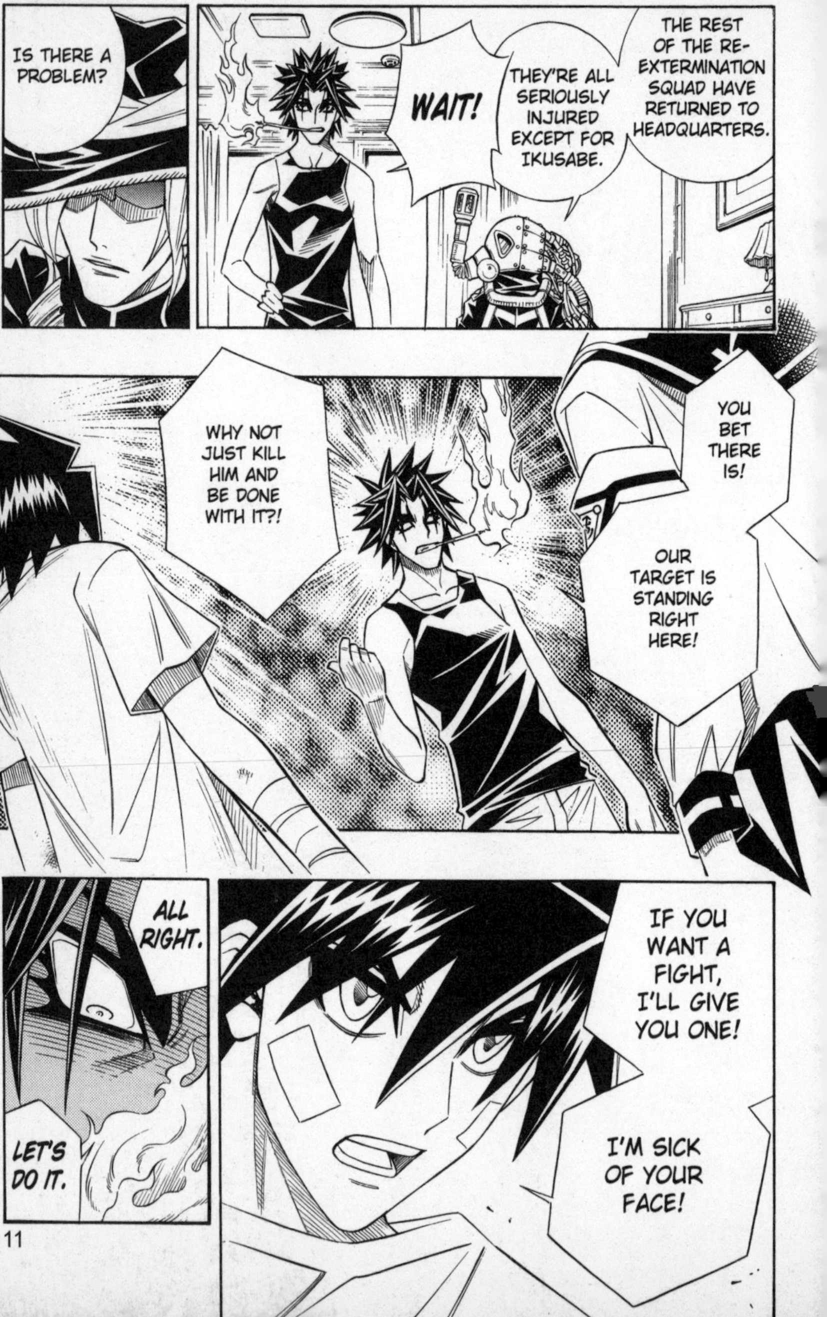
THE REST OF THE RE-EXTERMINATION SQUAD HAVE RETURNED TO HEADQUARTERS.
THEY'RE ALL SERIOUSLY INJURED EXCEPT FOR IKUSABE.
WAIT!
IS THERE A PROBLEM?
YOU BET THERE IS!
OUR TARGET IS STANDING RIGHT HERE!
WHY NOT JUST KILL HIM AND BE DONE WITH IT?!
IF YOU WANT A FIGHT, I'LL GIVE YOU ONE!
I'M SICK OF YOUR FACE!
ALL RIGHT.
LET'S DO IT.

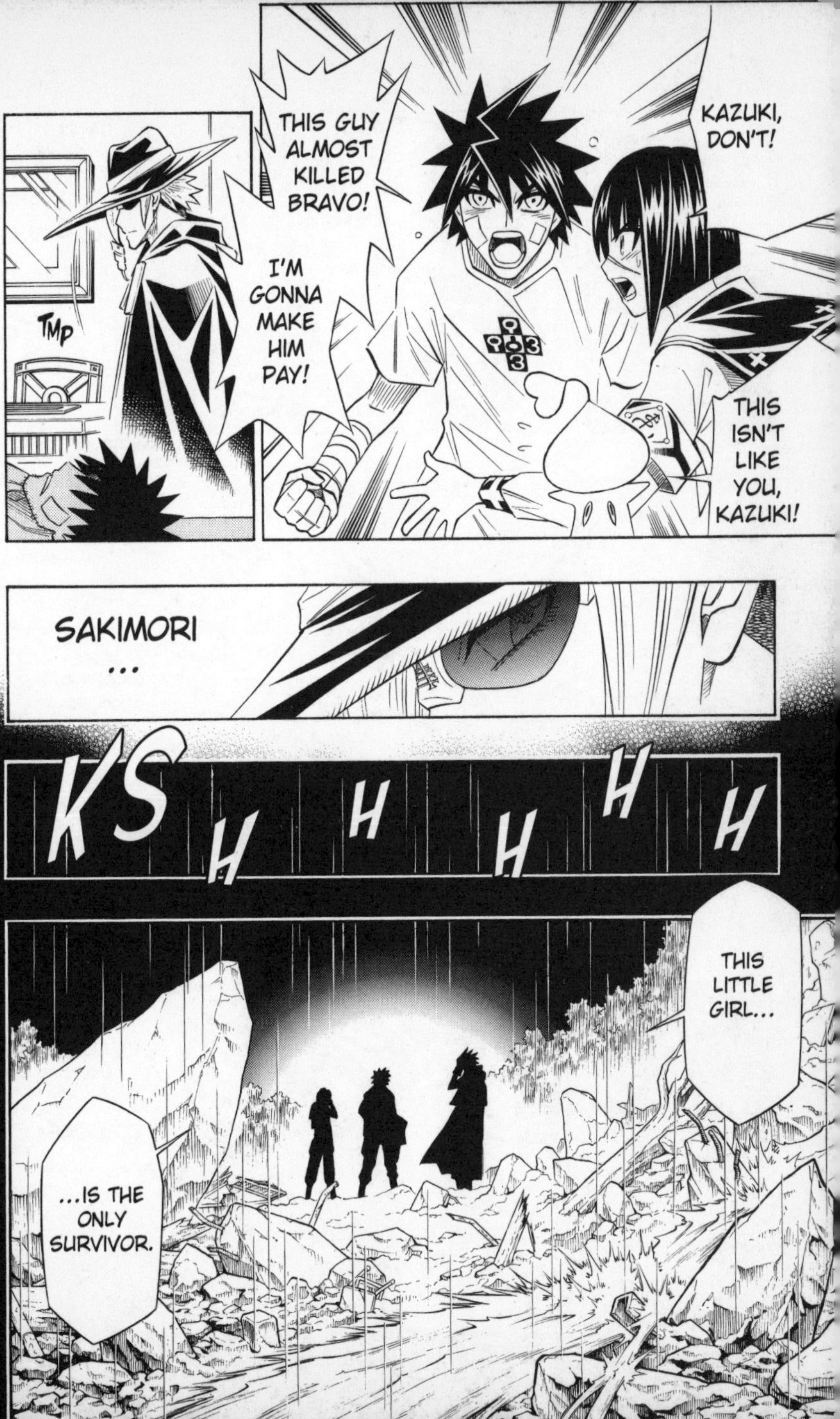
KAZUKI, DON'T!
THIS GUY ALMOST KILLED BRAVO!
I'M GONNA MAKE HIM PAY!
THIS ISN'T LIKE YOU, KAZUKI!
TMP
SAKIMORI ...
KSHHHHHH
THIS LITTLE GIRL...
...IS THE ONLY SURVIVOR.

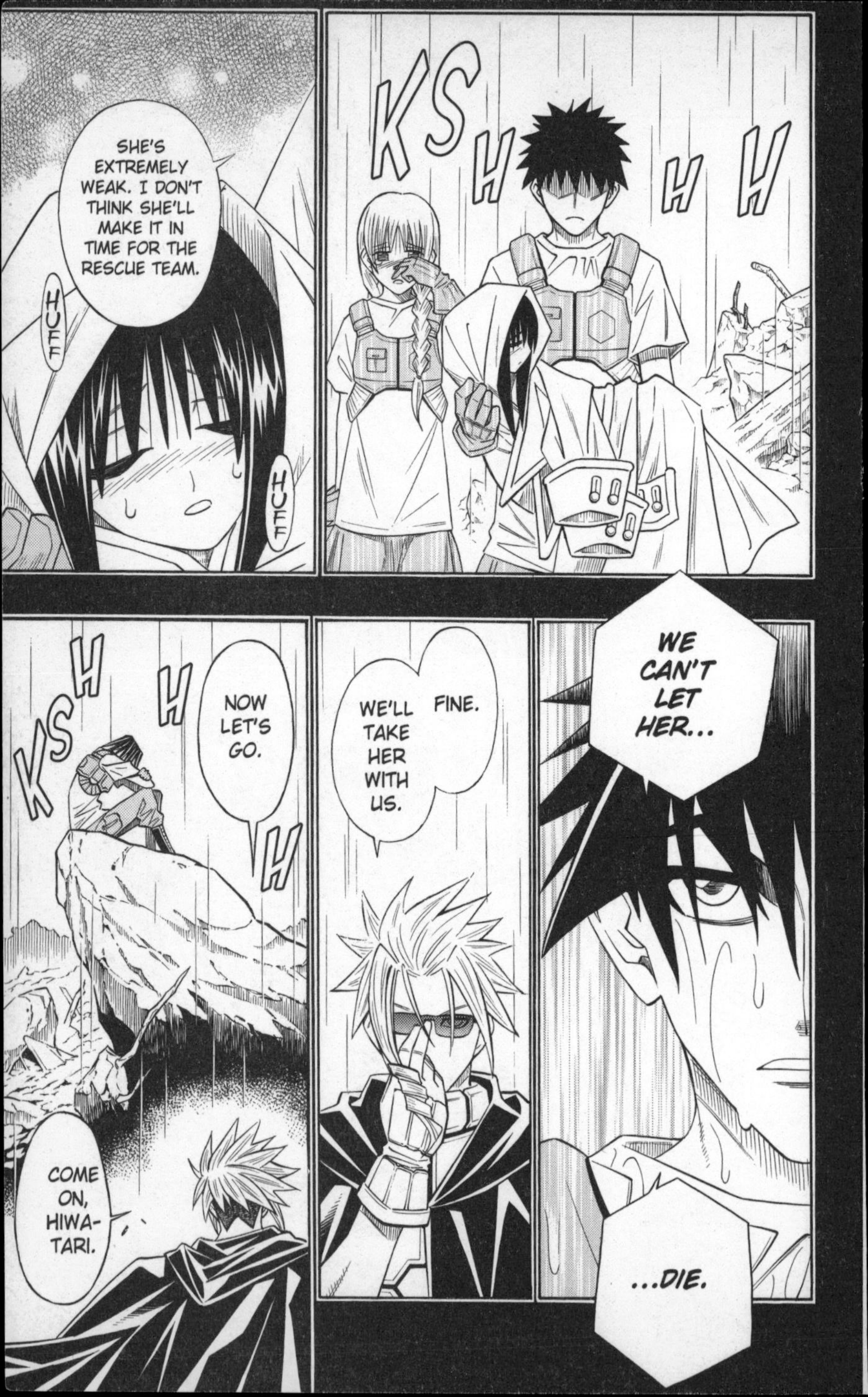
KSHHH
SHE'S EXTREMELY WEAK. I DON'T THINK SHE'LL MAKE IT IN TIME FOR THE RESCUE TEAM.
HUFF
HUFF
WE CAN'T LET HER...
...DIE.
FINE.
WE'LL TAKE HER WITH US.
KSHHH
NOW LET'S GO.
COME ON, HIWATARI.

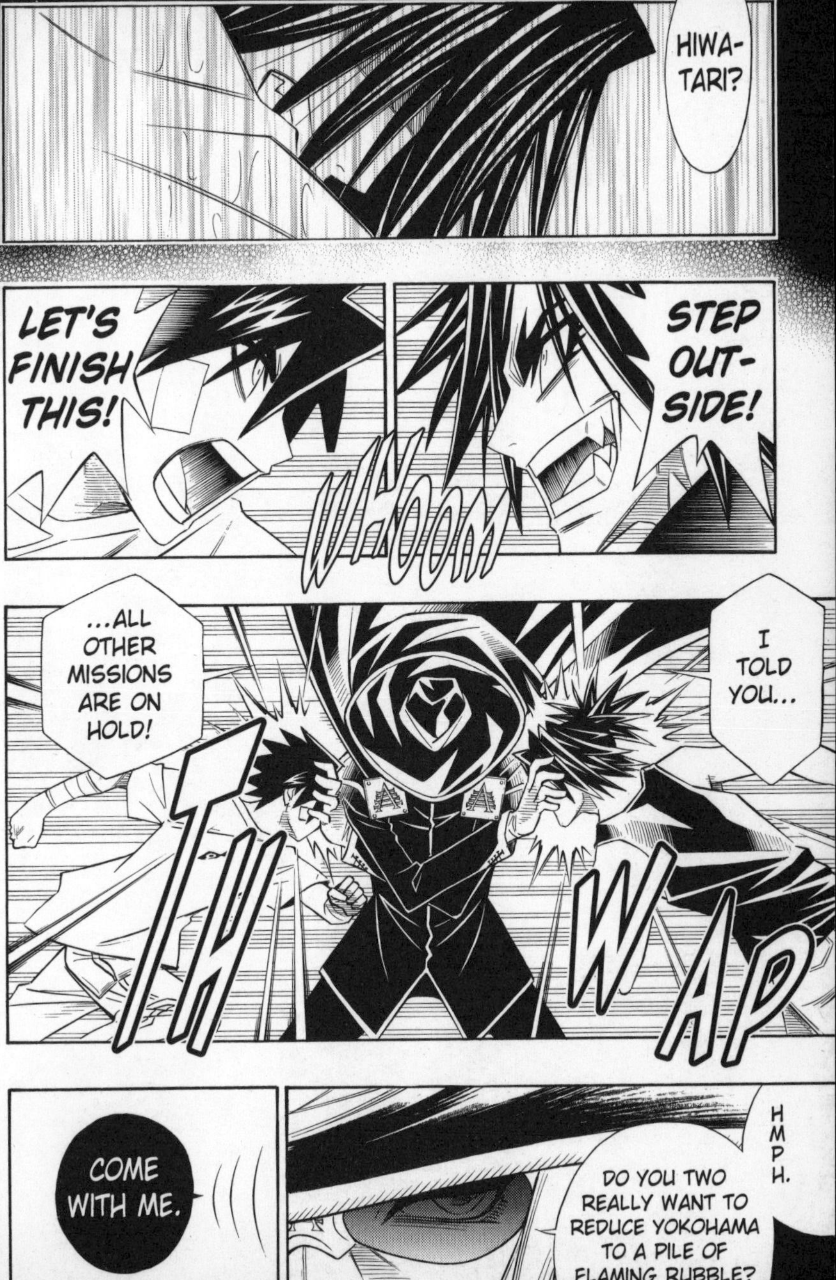
HIWA-TARI?
STEP OUT-SIDE!
LET'S FINISH THIS!
WHOOM
I TOLD YOU...
...ALL OTHER MISSIONS ARE ON HOLD!
THWAP
HMPH.
DO YOU TWO REALLY WANT TO REDUCE YOKOHAMA TO A PILE OF FLAMING RUBBLE?
COME WITH ME.

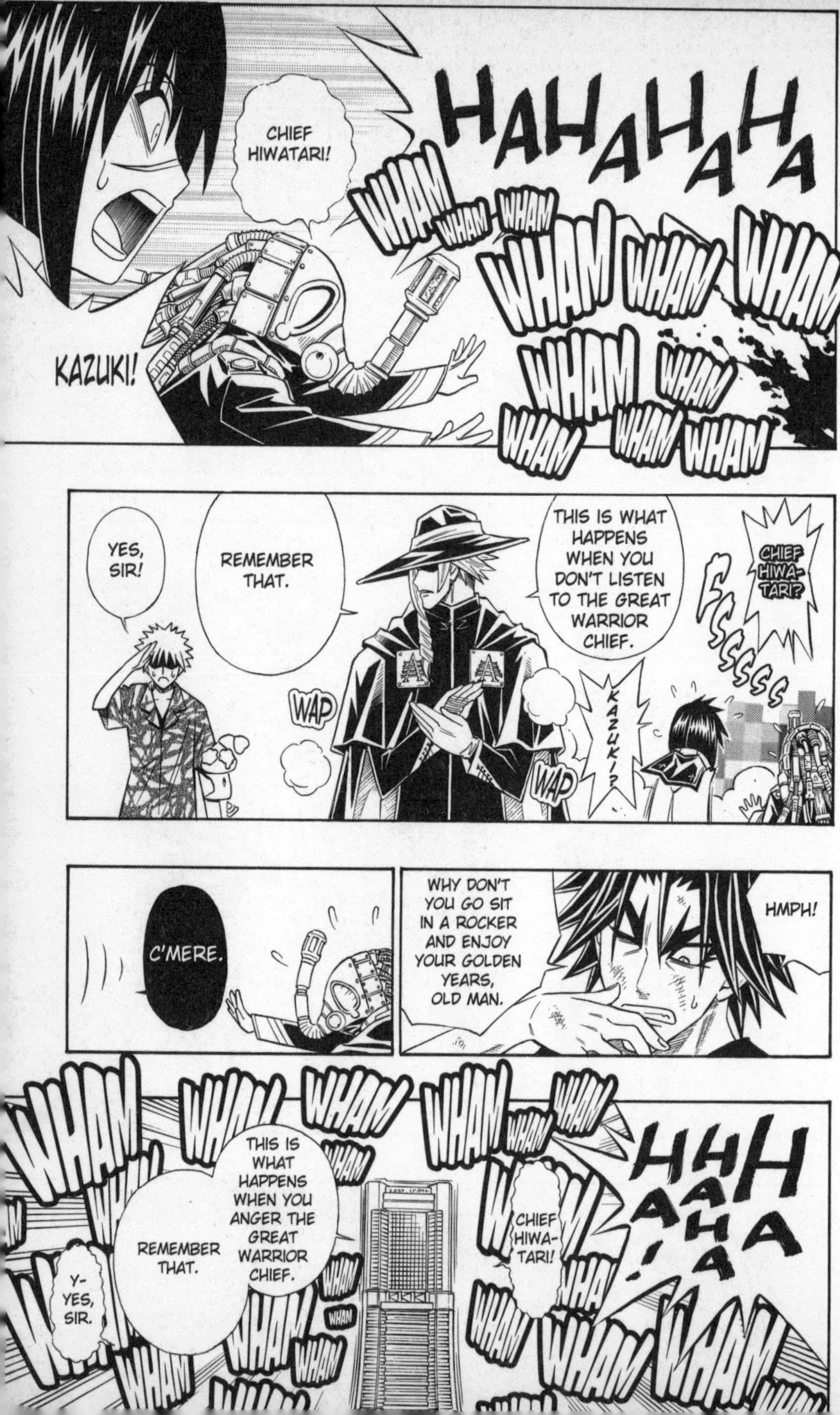
HAHAHAHAA
WHAM WHAM WHAM WHAM WHAM WHAM WHAM WHAM WHAM WHAM WHAM
CHIEF HIWATARI!
KAZUKI!
CHIEF HIWATARI?
FSSSSS
THIS IS WHAT HAPPENS WHEN YOU DON'T LISTEN TO THE GREAT WARRIOR CHIEF.
KAZUKI!?
WAP
REMEMBER THAT.
WAP
YES, SIR!
HMPH!
WHY DON'T YOU GO SIT IN A ROCKER AND ENJOY YOUR GOLDEN YEARS, OLD MAN.
C'MERE.
HAHAHAHA!
WHAM WHAM WHAM WHAM WHAM
CHIEF HIWATARI!
THIS IS WHAT HAPPENS WHEN YOU ANGER THE GREAT WARRIOR CHIEF.
REMEMBER THAT.
Y-YES, SIR.
WHAM WHAM WHAM WHAM WHAM

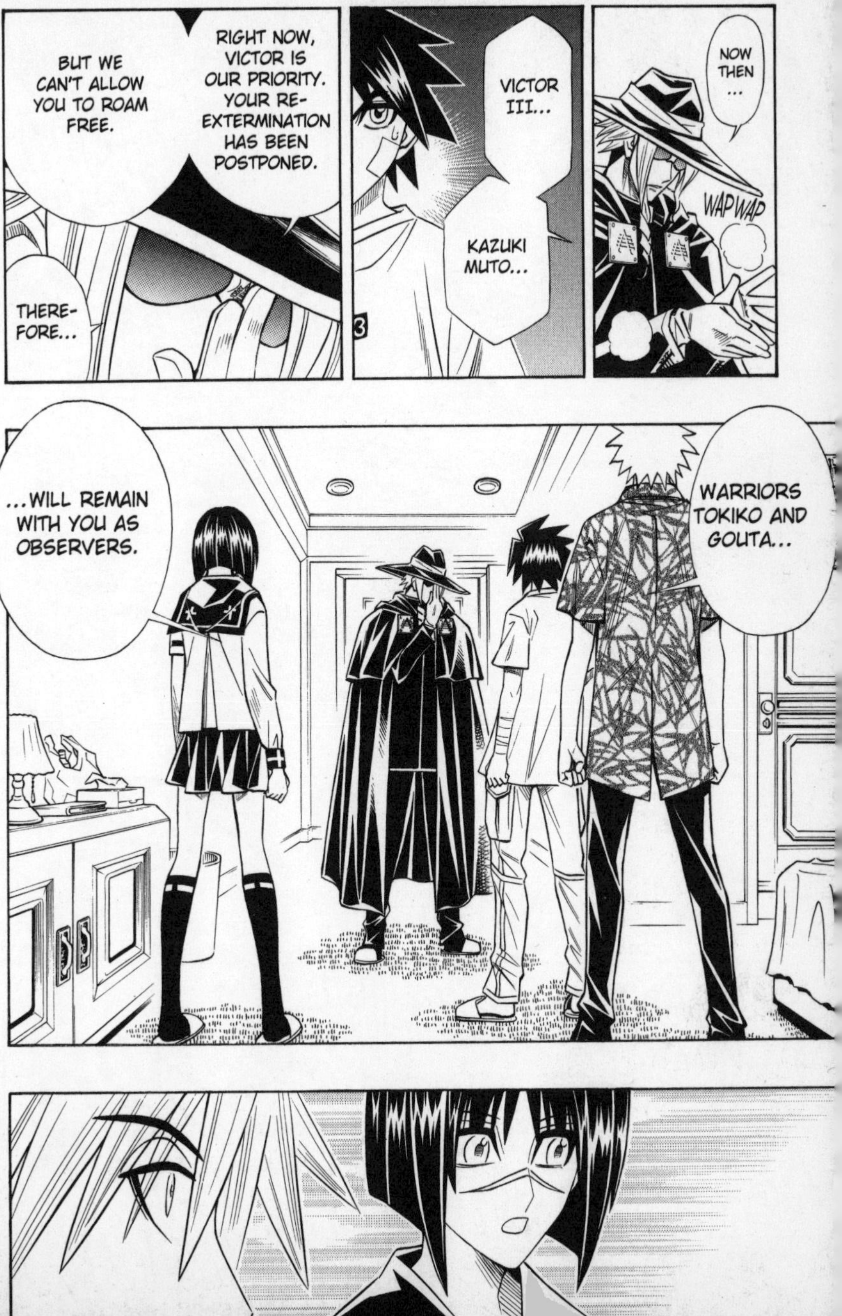
NOW THEN ...
WAP WAP
VICTOR III...
KAZUKI MUTO...
RIGHT NOW, VICTOR IS OUR PRIORITY. YOUR RE-EXTERMINATION HAS BEEN POSTPONED.
BUT WE CAN'T ALLOW YOU TO ROAM FREE.
THERE-FORE...
WARRIORS TOKIKO AND GOUTA...
...WILL REMAIN WITH YOU AS OBSERVERS.

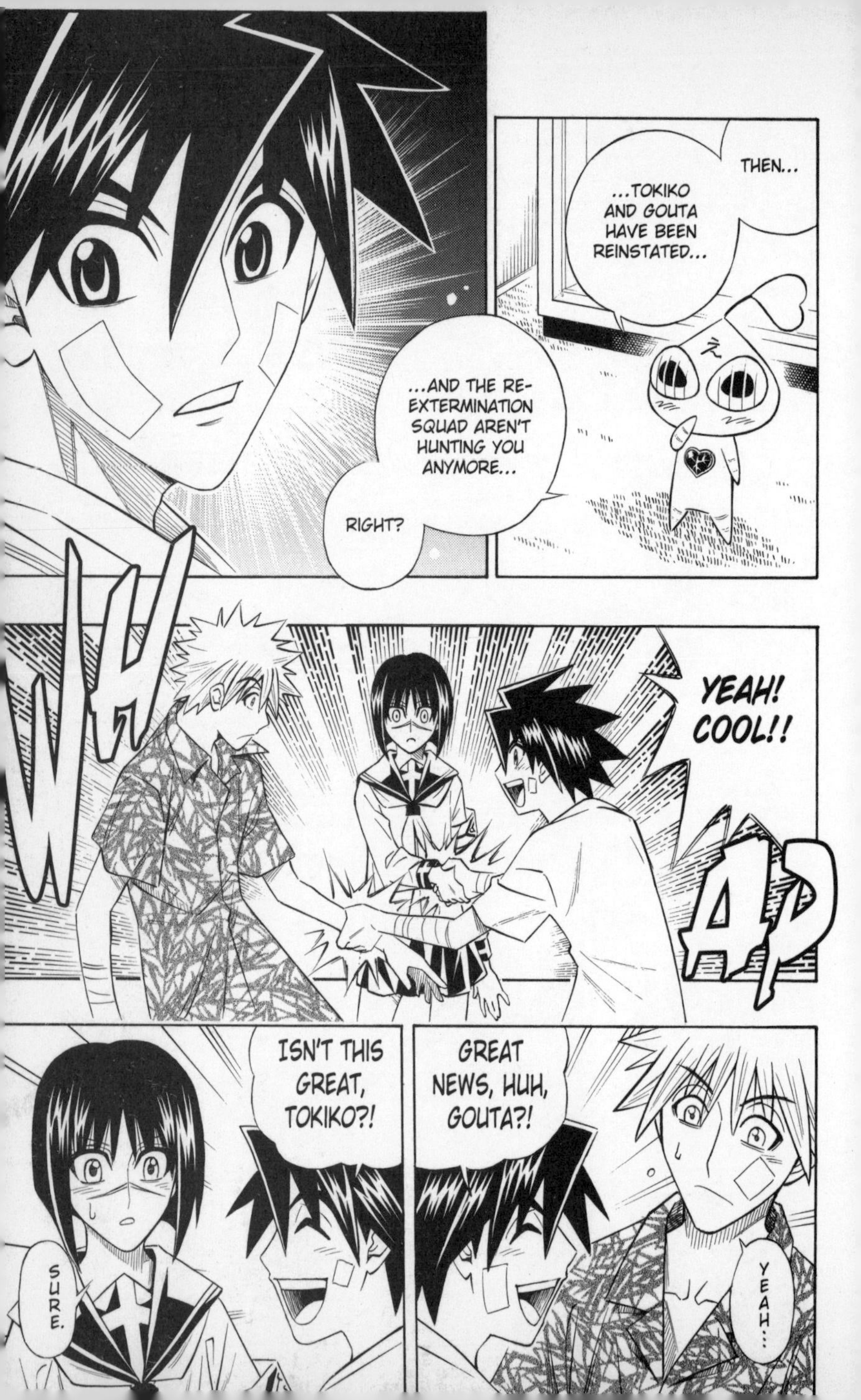
THEN...
...TOKIKO AND GOUTA HAVE BEEN REINSTATED...
...AND THE RE-EXTERMINATION SQUAD AREN'T HUNTING YOU ANYMORE...
RIGHT?
YEAH! COOL!!
WHAP
GREAT NEWS, HUH, GOUTA?!
YEAH...
ISN'T THIS GREAT, TOKIKO?!
SURE.

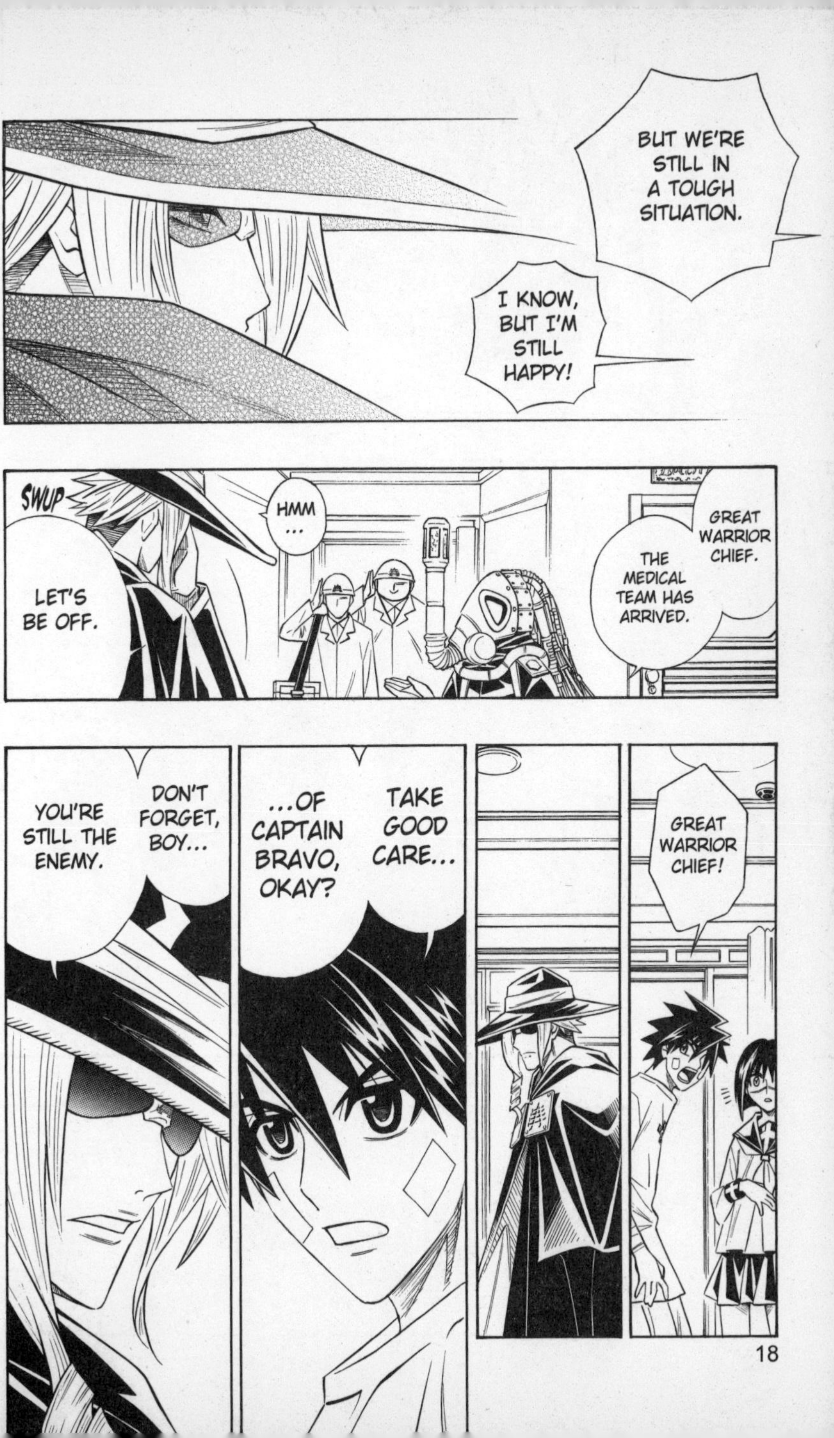
BUT WE'RE STILL IN A TOUGH SITUATION.
I KNOW, BUT I'M STILL HAPPY!
GREAT WARRIOR CHIEF.
THE MEDICAL TEAM HAS ARRIVED.
HMM ...
SWUP
LET'S BE OFF.
GREAT WARRIOR CHIEF!
TAKE GOOD CARE...
...OF CAPTAIN BRAVO, OKAY?
DON'T FORGET, BOY...
YOU'RE STILL THE ENEMY.

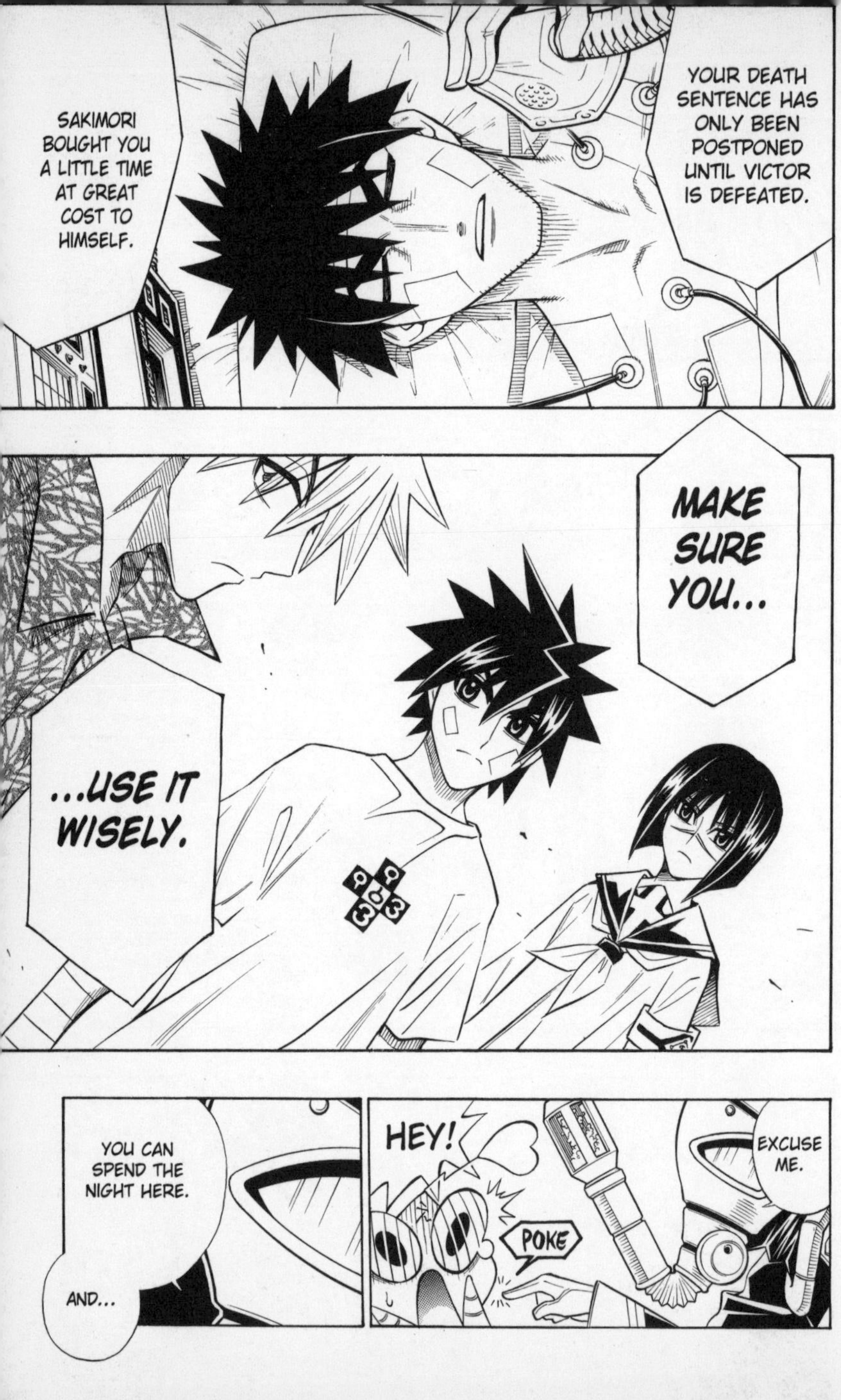
YOUR DEATH SENTENCE HAS ONLY BEEN POSTPONED UNTIL VICTOR IS DEFEATED.
SAKIMORI BOUGHT YOU A LITTLE TIME AT GREAT COST TO HIMSELF.
MAKE SURE YOU...
...USE IT WISELY.
EXCUSE ME.
HEY!
POKE
YOU CAN SPEND THE NIGHT HERE.
AND...

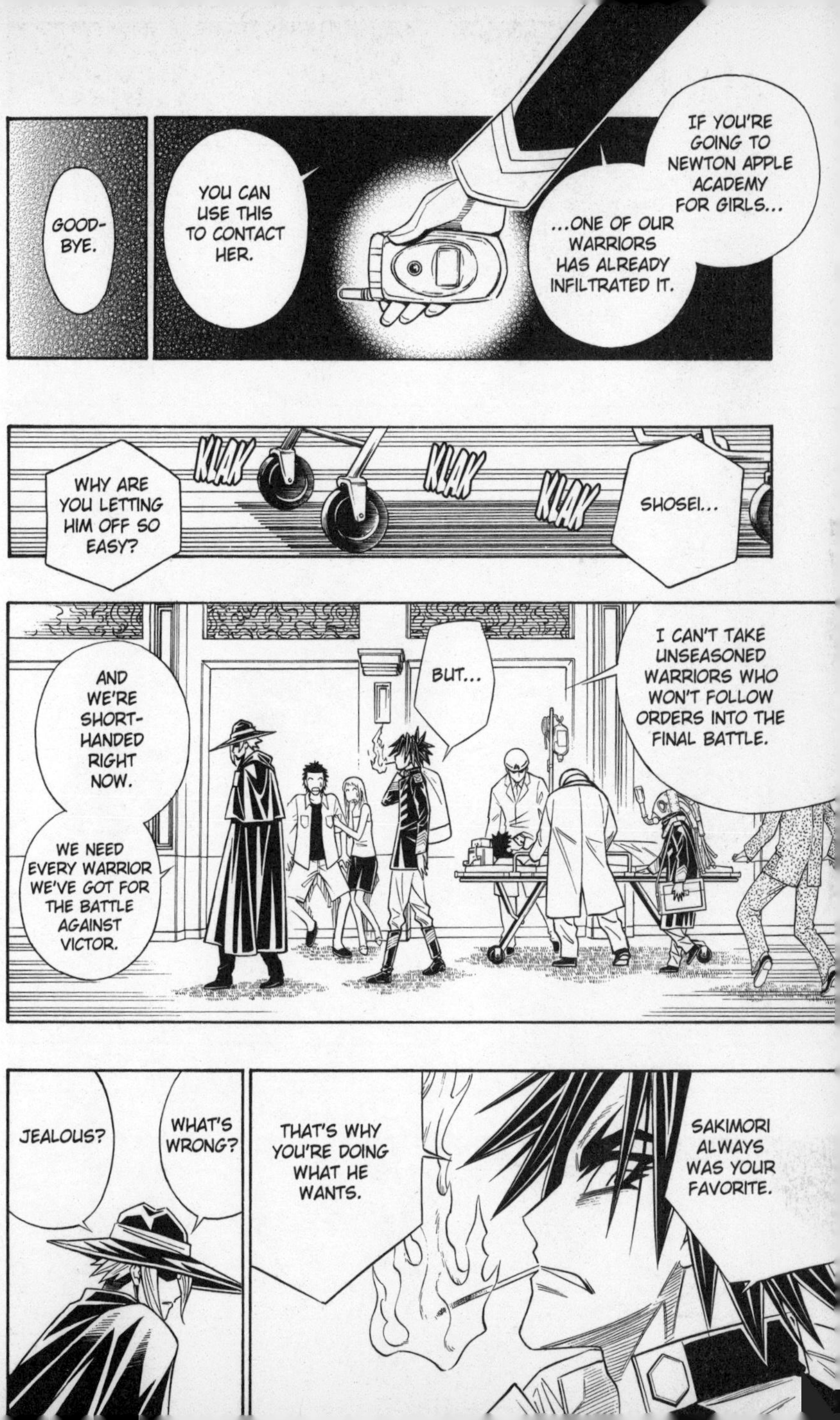
IF YOU'RE GOING TO NEWTON APPLE ACADEMY FOR GIRLS...
...ONE OF OUR WARRIORS HAS ALREADY INFILTRATED IT.
YOU CAN USE THIS TO CONTACT HER.
GOOD-BYE.
SHOSEI...
KLAK
KLAK
KLAK
WHY ARE YOU LETTING HIM OFF SO EASY?
I CAN'T TAKE UNSEASONED WARRIORS WHO WON'T FOLLOW ORDERS INTO THE FINAL BATTLE.
BUT...
AND WE'RE SHORT-HANDED RIGHT NOW.
WE NEED EVERY WARRIOR WE'VE GOT FOR THE BATTLE AGAINST VICTOR.
SAKIMORI ALWAYS WAS YOUR FAVORITE.
THAT'S WHY YOU'RE DOING WHAT HE WANTS.
WHAT'S WRONG?
JEALOUS?

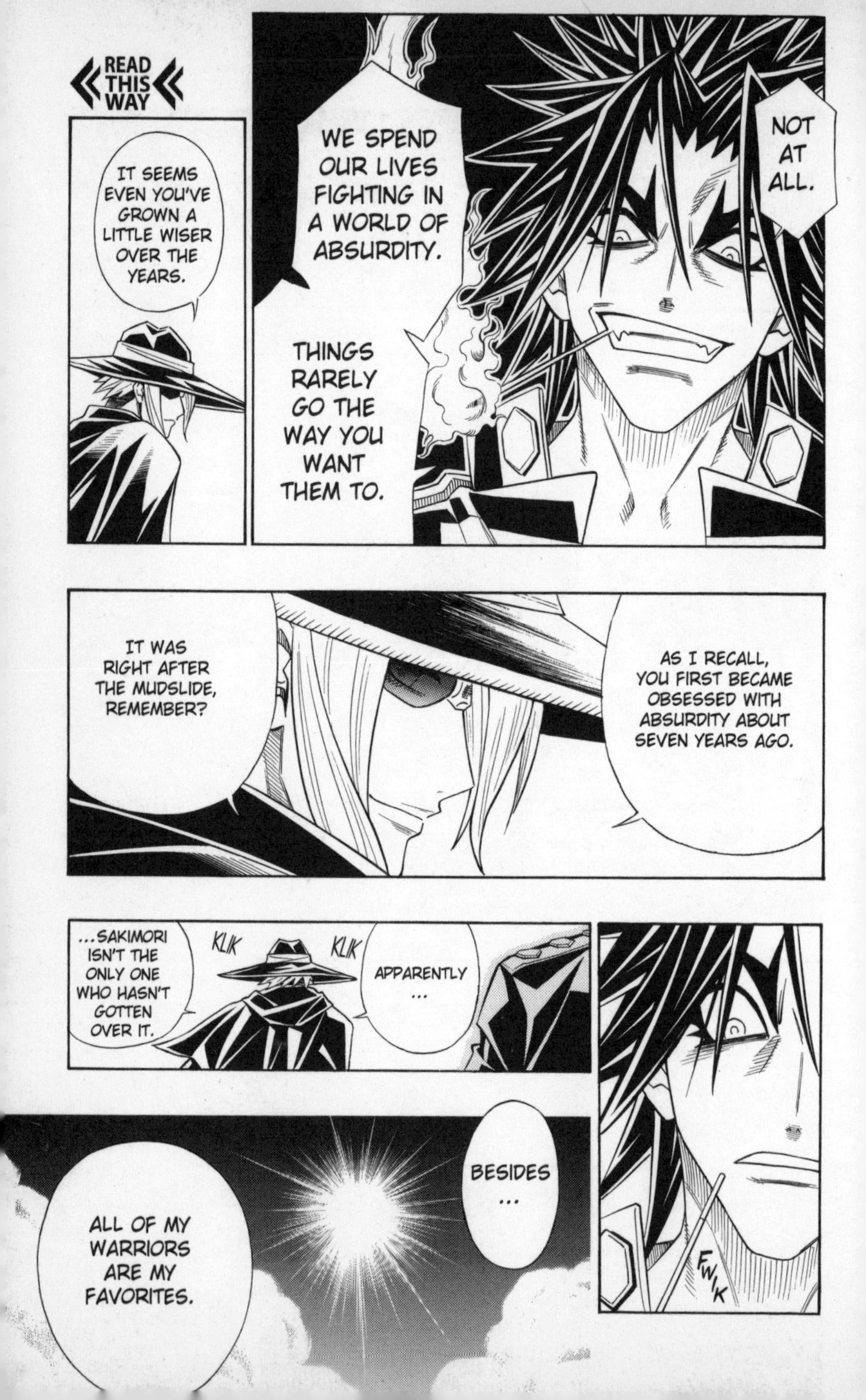
READ THIS WAY
NOT AT ALL.
WE SPEND OUR LIVES FIGHTING IN A WORLD OF ABSURDITY.
THINGS RARELY GO THE WAY YOU WANT THEM TO.
IT SEEMS EVEN YOU'VE GROWN A LITTLE WISER OVER THE YEARS.
AS I RECALL, YOU FIRST BECAME OBSESSED WITH ABSURDITY ABOUT SEVEN YEARS AGO.
IT WAS RIGHT AFTER THE MUDSLIDE, REMEMBER?
FWIK
APPARENTLY ...
KLIK
KLIK
...SAKIMORI ISN'T THE ONLY ONE WHO HASN'T GOTTEN OVER IT.
BESIDES ...
ALL OF MY WARRIORS ARE MY FAVORITES.

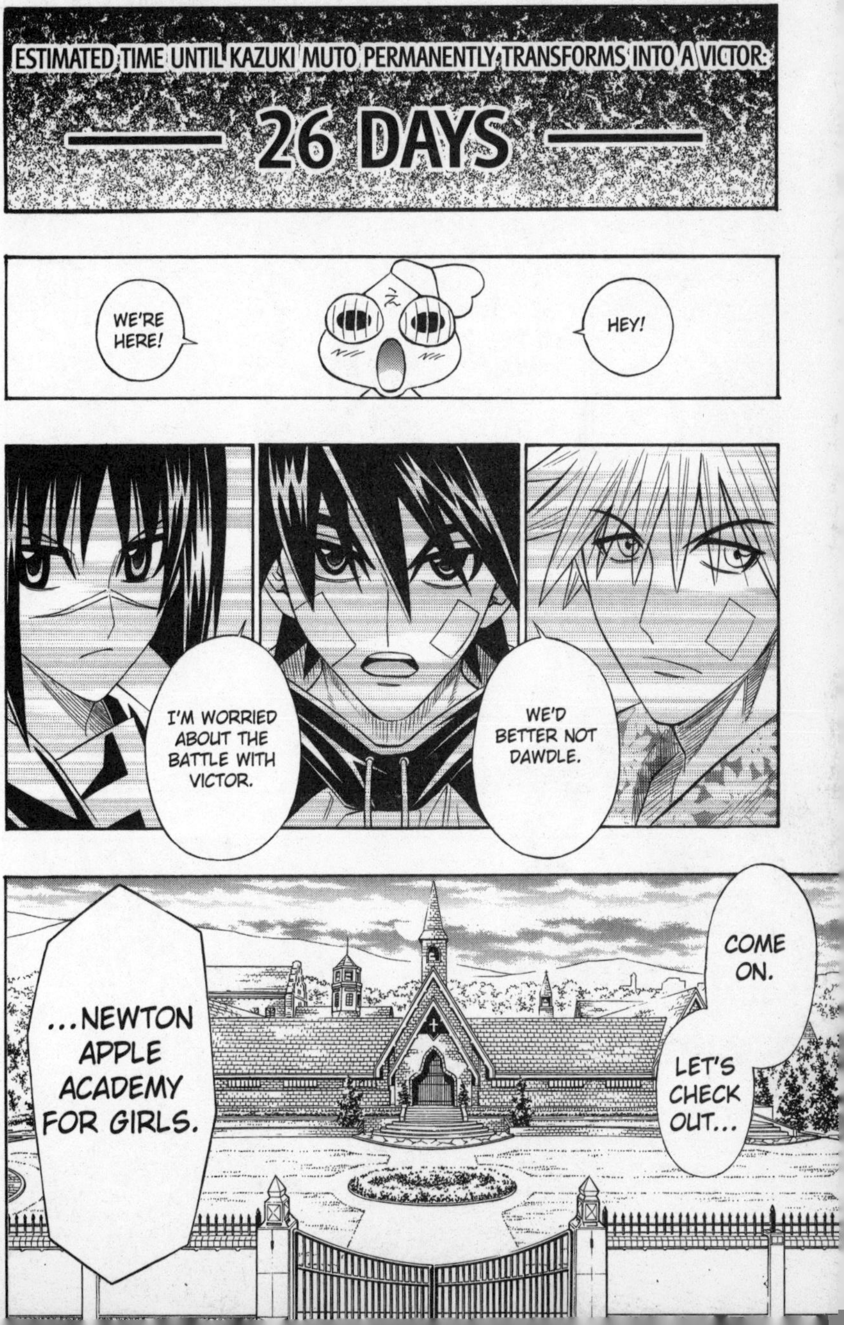
ESTIMATED TIME UNTIL KAZUKI MUTO PERMANENTLY TRANSFORMS INTO A VICTOR:
— 26 DAYS —
HEY!
WE'RE HERE!
WE'D BETTER NOT DAWDLE.
I'M WORRIED ABOUT THE BATTLE WITH VICTOR.
COME ON.
LET'S CHECK OUT...
...NEWTON APPLE ACADEMY FOR GIRLS.

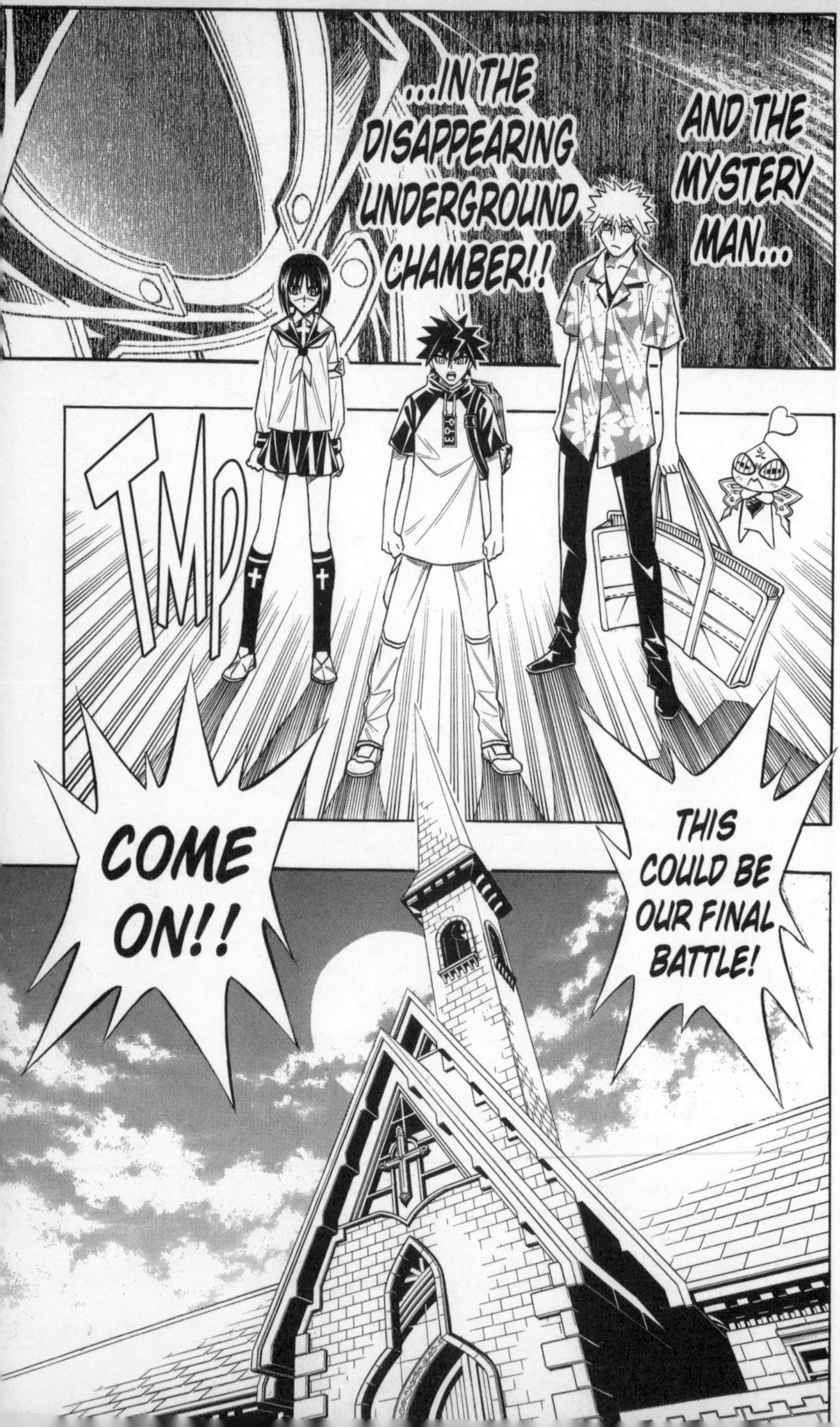
AND THE MYSTERY MAN...
...IN THE DISAPPEARING UNDERGROUND CHAMBER!!
TMP
THIS COULD BE OUR FINAL BATTLE!
COME ON!!

Running and Hiding in the Pathway of the Ninja!

Buso Renkin File No. 16

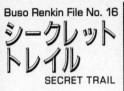

シークレット
トレイル
SECRET TRAIL

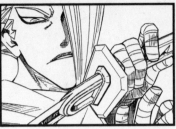

○ Kakugane Serial Number: XIV (14)
○ Creator: Shinobu Negoro
○ Form: Ninja Sword
○ Colors: Moss Green and Gold
○ Special Abilities: · Slices into solid objects to create a pathway to another dimension.
○ Special Traits: · Only the creator of the Ninja Sword can enter the other dimension. However, admittance is triggered by the creator's DNA, so objects that have his hair or blood on them can also pass through.
· The creator can travel to another dimension from anywhere in this one. However, the dimensional opening cannot be created in air or water.

○ Author's Notes:
· I based the design on a typical ninja sword and made it look slightly mechanical. I went with the philosophy that simple is best, like I did with the Sword Samurai X.
· I tried to think of something that fit with a ninja's stealthiness and would be useful in a battle of wits. So, I combined the ability to warp with invisibility.
· But now that I think about it, this is a lot like one of the stands from *JoJo's Bizarre Adventure* called "Diver Down." Araki is a great artist indeed.
· Again, as with Ikusabe's Gekisen, I was left with the problem of how to defeat it. You saw the results in these pages, but I'm afraid it may have been a bit hard to follow.
· The tones I used for the lightning effect when Negoro goes in and out of the other dimension are easy to apply and look really good. I like the way they turned out.

CHAPTER 75: INFILTRATING NEWTON APPLE ACADEMY FOR GIRLS

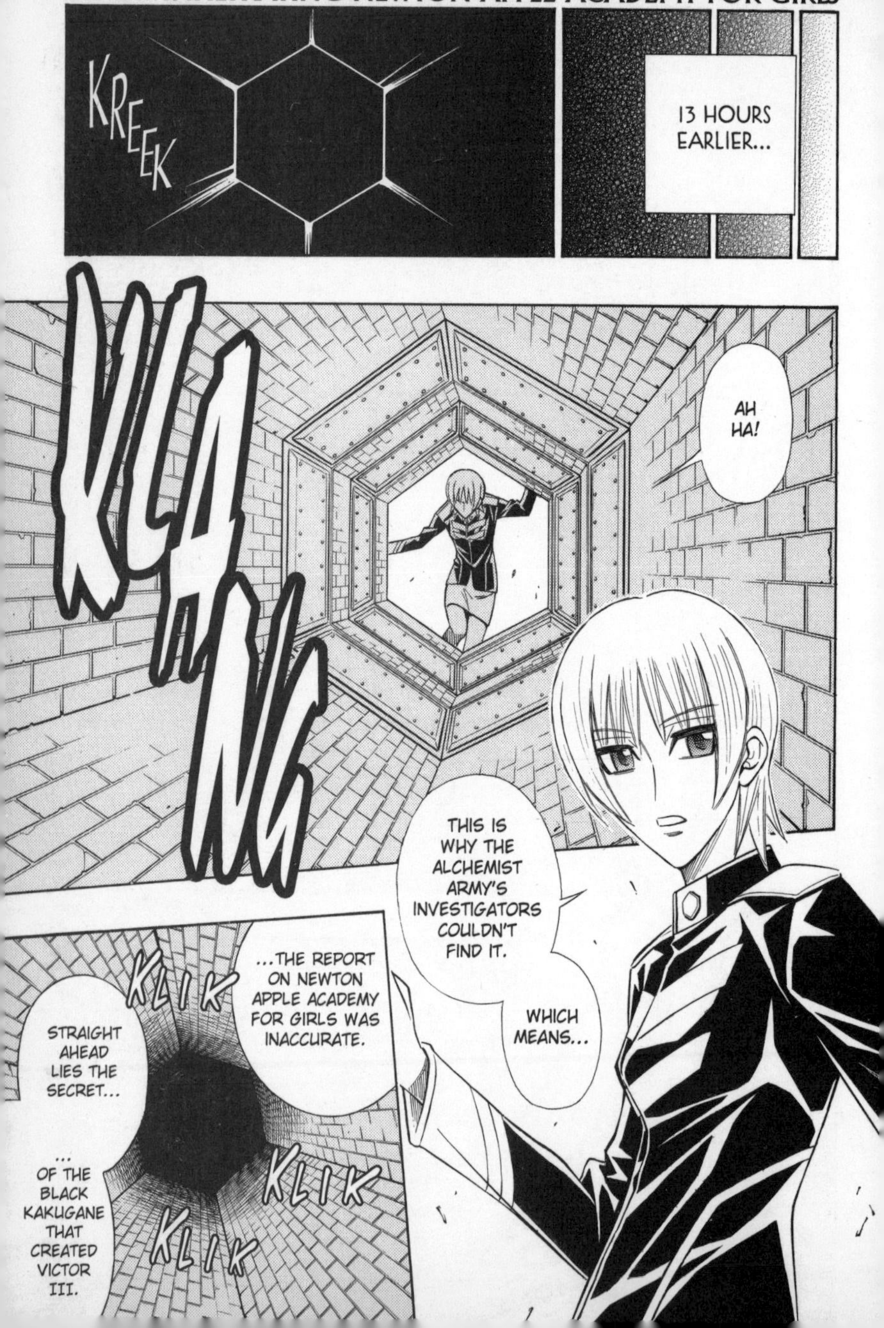
13 HOURS EARLIER...
KREEEK
AH HA!
THIS IS WHY THE ALCHEMIST ARMY'S INVESTIGATORS COULDN'T FIND IT.
KLANG
WHICH MEANS...
...THE REPORT ON NEWTON APPLE ACADEMY FOR GIRLS WAS INACCURATE.
KLIK
STRAIGHT AHEAD LIES THE SECRET...
KLIK
... OF THE BLACK KAKUGANE THAT CREATED VICTOR III.
KLIK

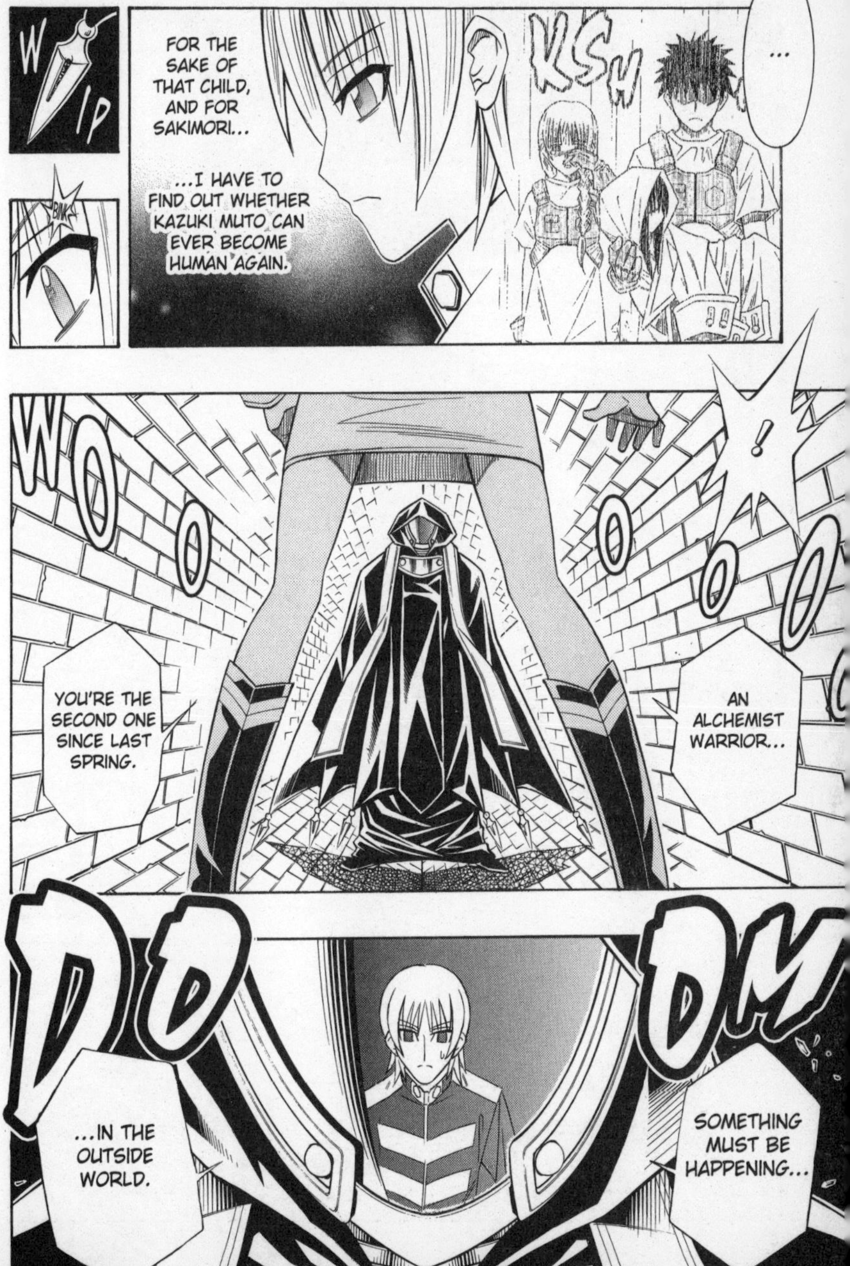
...
KSH
FOR THE SAKE OF THAT CHILD, AND FOR SAKIMORI...
...I HAVE TO FIND OUT WHETHER KAZUKI MUTO CAN EVER BECOME HUMAN AGAIN.
WHIP
BINK
!
WOOOOOO
AN ALCHEMIST WARRIOR...
YOU'RE THE SECOND ONE SINCE LAST SPRING.
DOOM
SOMETHING MUST BE HAPPENING...
...IN THE OUTSIDE WORLD.

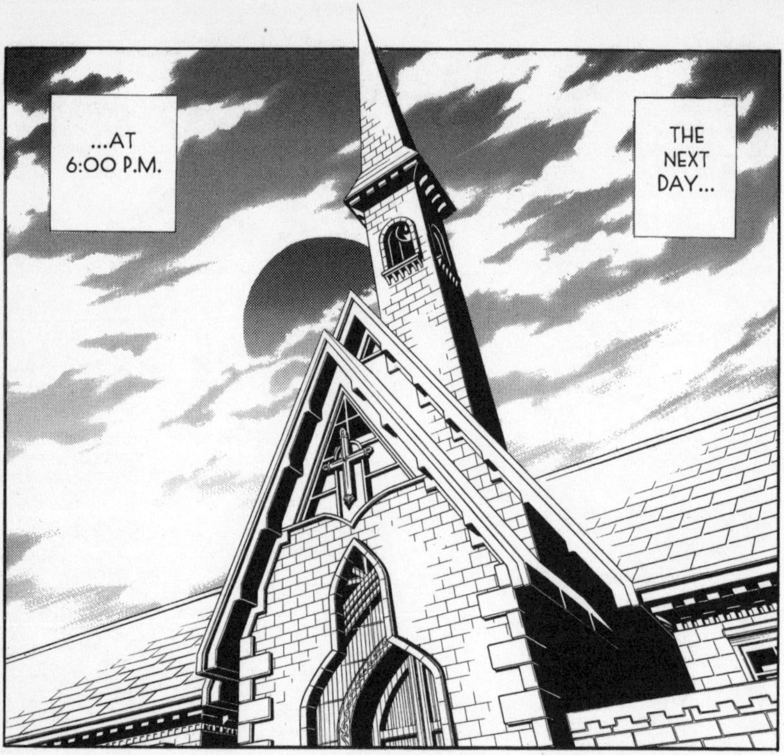
THE NEXT DAY...
...AT 6:00 P.M.

CHAPTER 75:

INFILTRATING NEWTON APPLE ACADEMY FOR GIRLS

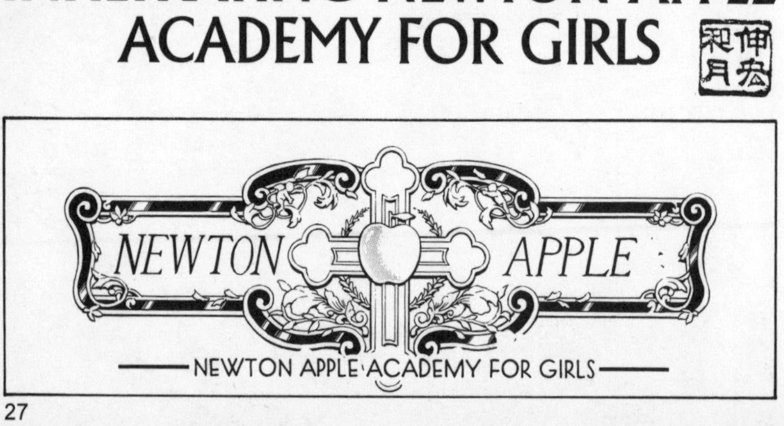
NEWTON APPLE
NEWTON APPLE ACADEMY FOR GIRLS

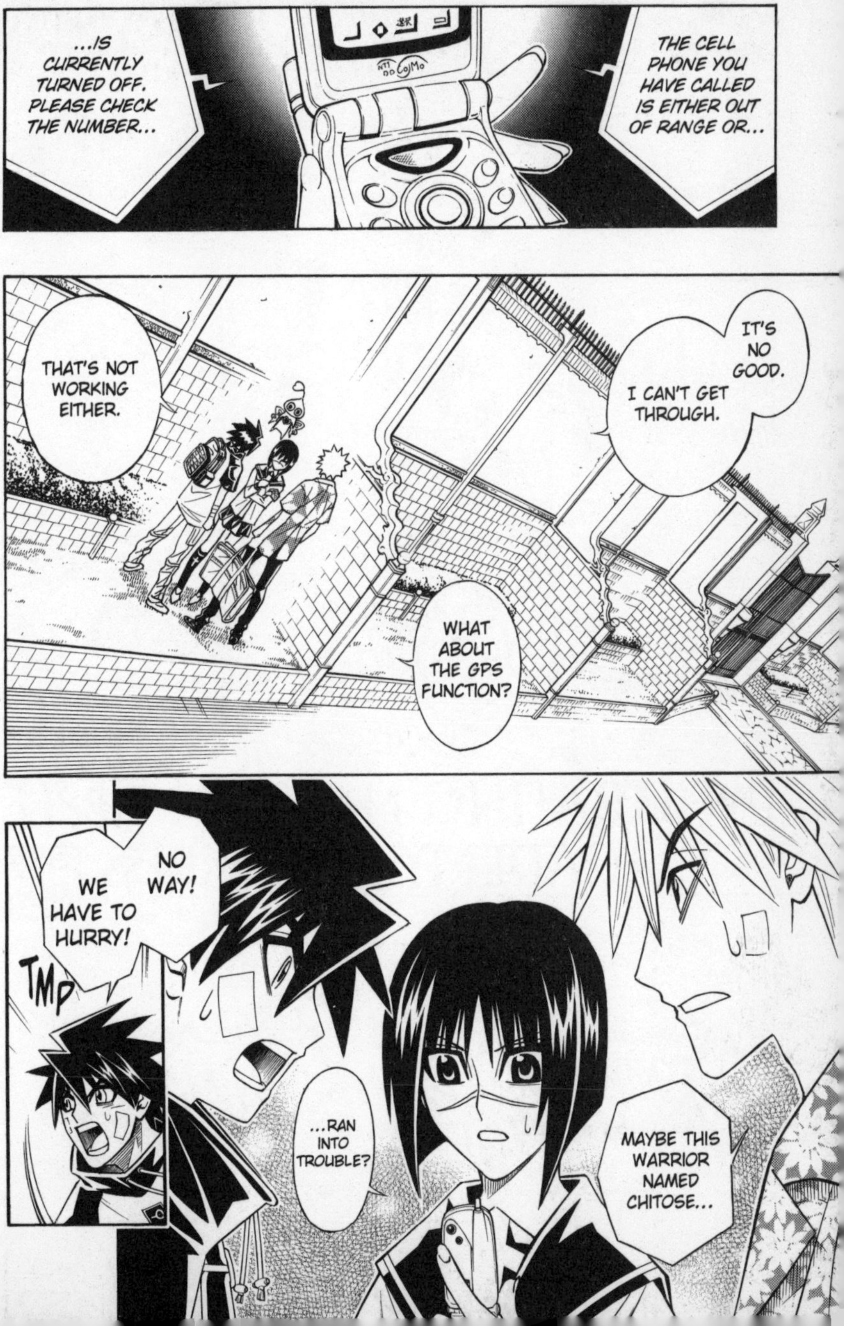
THE CELL PHONE YOU HAVE CALLED IS EITHER OUT OF RANGE OR...
...IS CURRENTLY TURNED OFF. PLEASE CHECK THE NUMBER...
IT'S NO GOOD.
I CAN'T GET THROUGH.
WHAT ABOUT THE GPS FUNCTION?
THAT'S NOT WORKING EITHER.
MAYBE THIS WARRIOR NAMED CHITOSE...
...RAN INTO TROUBLE?
NO WAY!
WE HAVE TO HURRY!
TMP

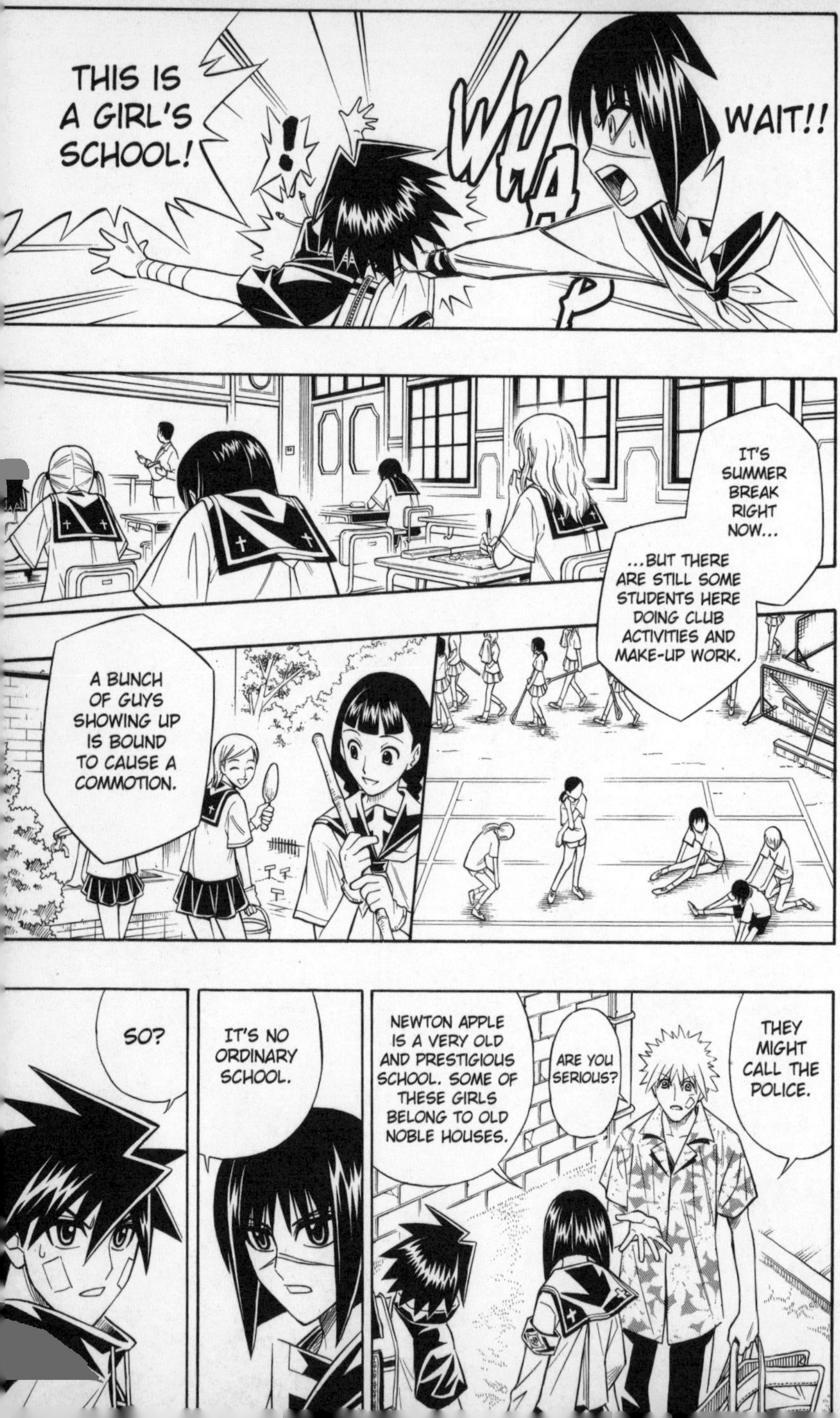
THIS IS A GIRL'S SCHOOL!
!
WHAP
WAIT!!
IT'S SUMMER BREAK RIGHT NOW...
...BUT THERE ARE STILL SOME STUDENTS HERE DOING CLUB ACTIVITIES AND MAKE-UP WORK.
A BUNCH OF GUYS SHOWING UP IS BOUND TO CAUSE A COMMOTION.
SO?
IT'S NO ORDINARY SCHOOL.
NEWTON APPLE IS A VERY OLD AND PRESTIGIOUS SCHOOL. SOME OF THESE GIRLS BELONG TO OLD NOBLE HOUSES.
ARE YOU SERIOUS?
THEY MIGHT CALL THE POLICE.

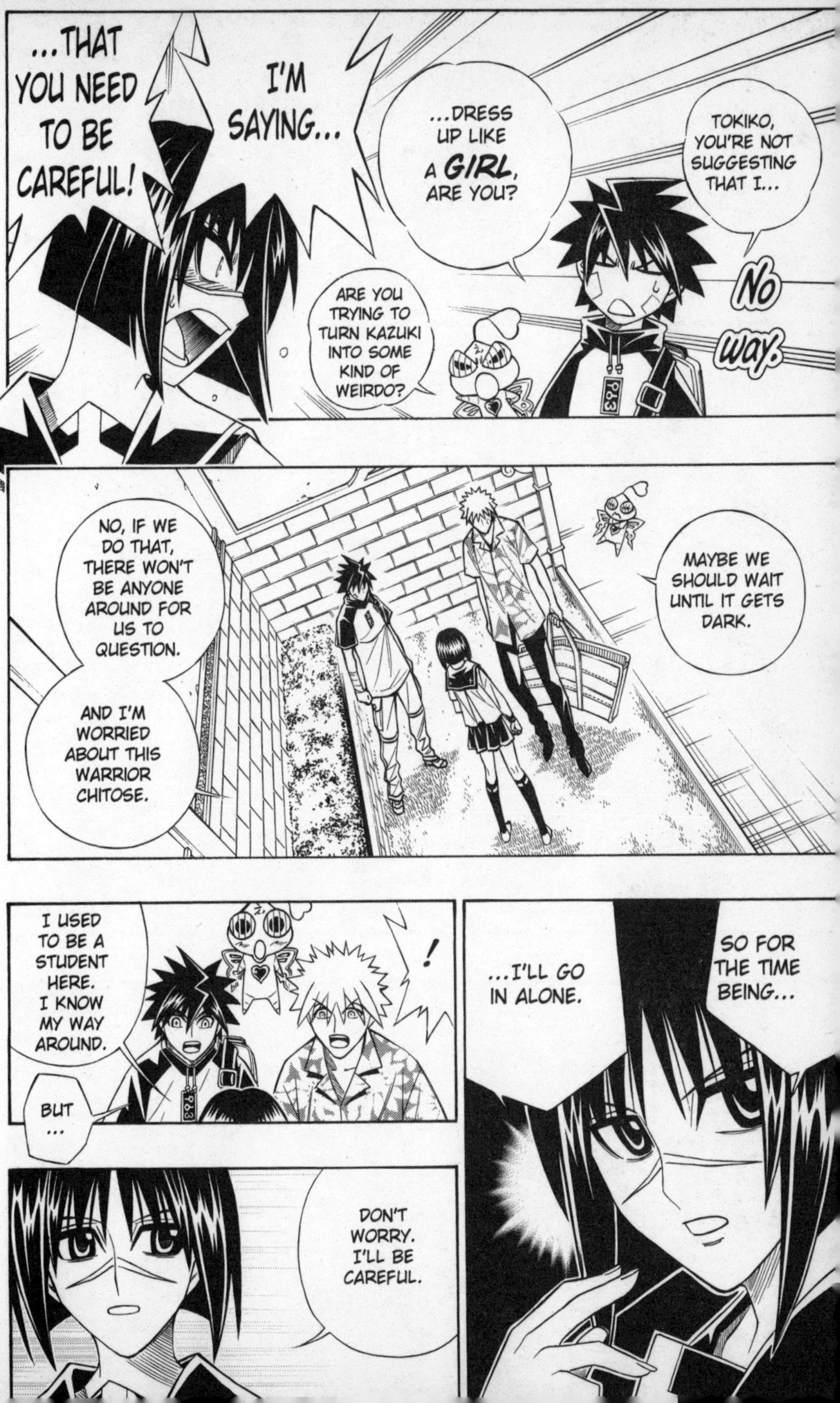
TOKIKO, YOU'RE NOT SUGGESTING THAT I...
...DRESS UP LIKE A GIRL, ARE YOU?
No way.
ARE YOU TRYING TO TURN KAZUKI INTO SOME KIND OF WEIRDO?
I'M SAYING...
...THAT YOU NEED TO BE CAREFUL!
MAYBE WE SHOULD WAIT UNTIL IT GETS DARK.
NO, IF WE DO THAT, THERE WON'T BE ANYONE AROUND FOR US TO QUESTION.
AND I'M WORRIED ABOUT THIS WARRIOR CHITOSE.
SO FOR THE TIME BEING...
...I'LL GO IN ALONE.
!
I USED TO BE A STUDENT HERE. I KNOW MY WAY AROUND.
BUT ...
DON'T WORRY. I'LL BE CAREFUL.

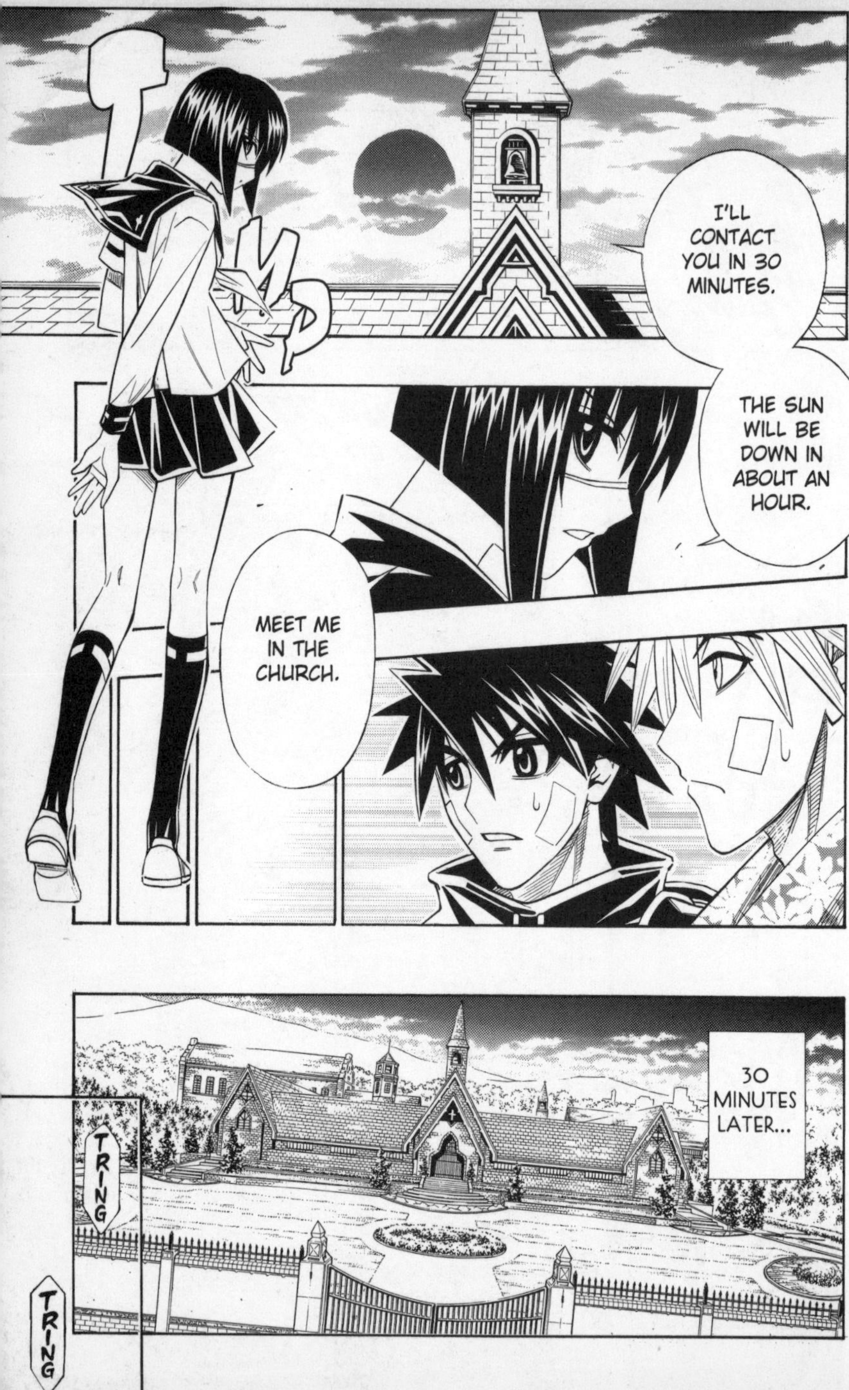
I'LL CONTACT YOU IN 30 MINUTES.
THE SUN WILL BE DOWN IN ABOUT AN HOUR.
MEET ME IN THE CHURCH.
30 MINUTES LATER...
TRING
TRING

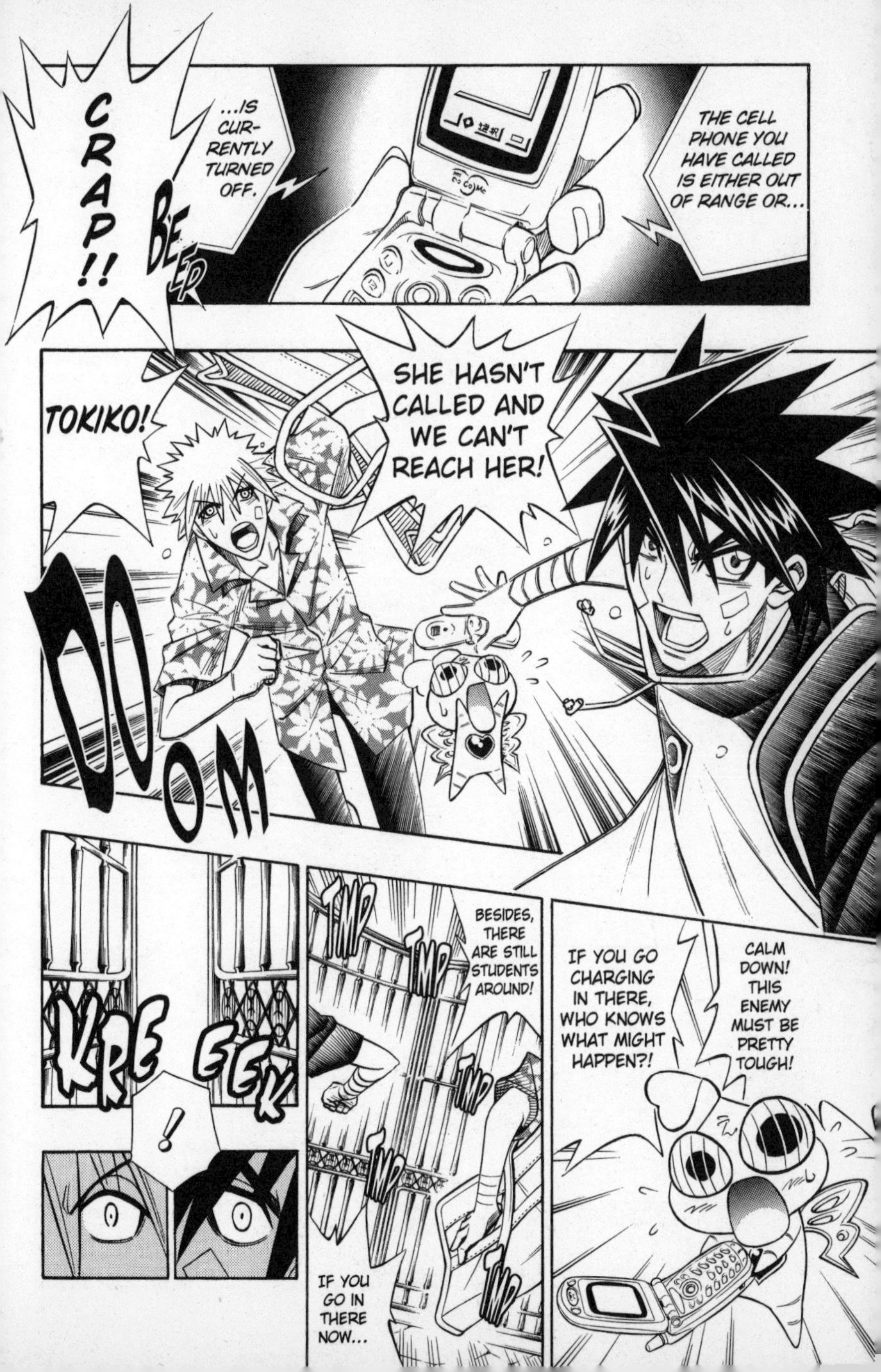
THE CELL PHONE YOU HAVE CALLED IS EITHER OUT OF RANGE OR...
...IS CURRENTLY TURNED OFF.
BEEP
CRAP!!
SHE HASN'T CALLED AND WE CAN'T REACH HER!
TOKIKO!
DOOM
CALM DOWN! THIS ENEMY MUST BE PRETTY TOUGH!
IF YOU GO CHARGING IN THERE, WHO KNOWS WHAT MIGHT HAPPEN?!
BESIDES, THERE ARE STILL STUDENTS AROUND!
TMP TMP TMP TMP TMP
IF YOU GO IN THERE NOW...
KREEEK
!

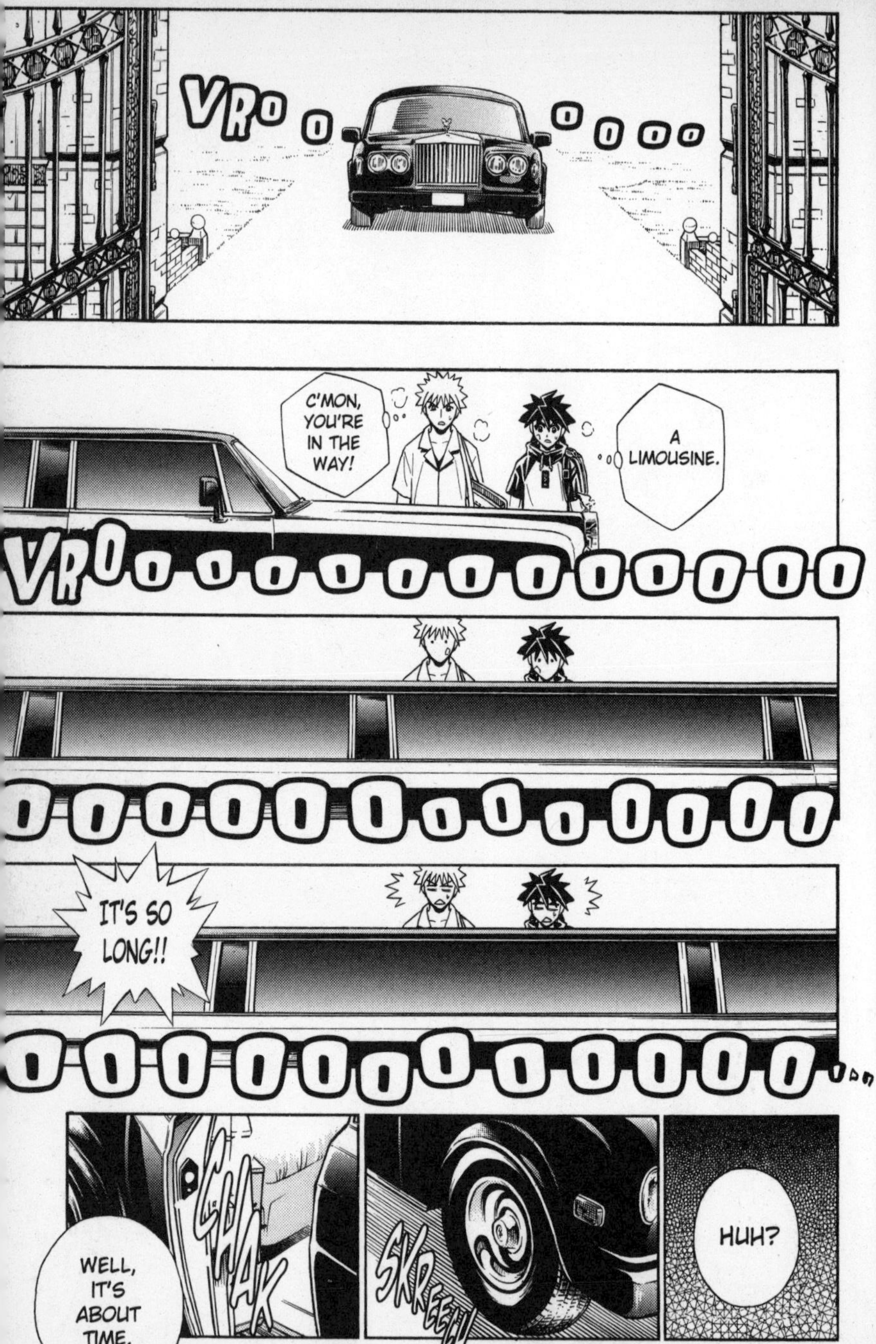
VROOOOO
A LIMOUSINE.
C'MON, YOU'RE IN THE WAY!
VROOOOOOOOOOOOOO
OOOOOOOOOOOOOO
IT'S SO LONG!!
OOOOOOOOOOOOOO
HUH?
SKREEEH
CHAK
WELL, IT'S ABOUT TIME.

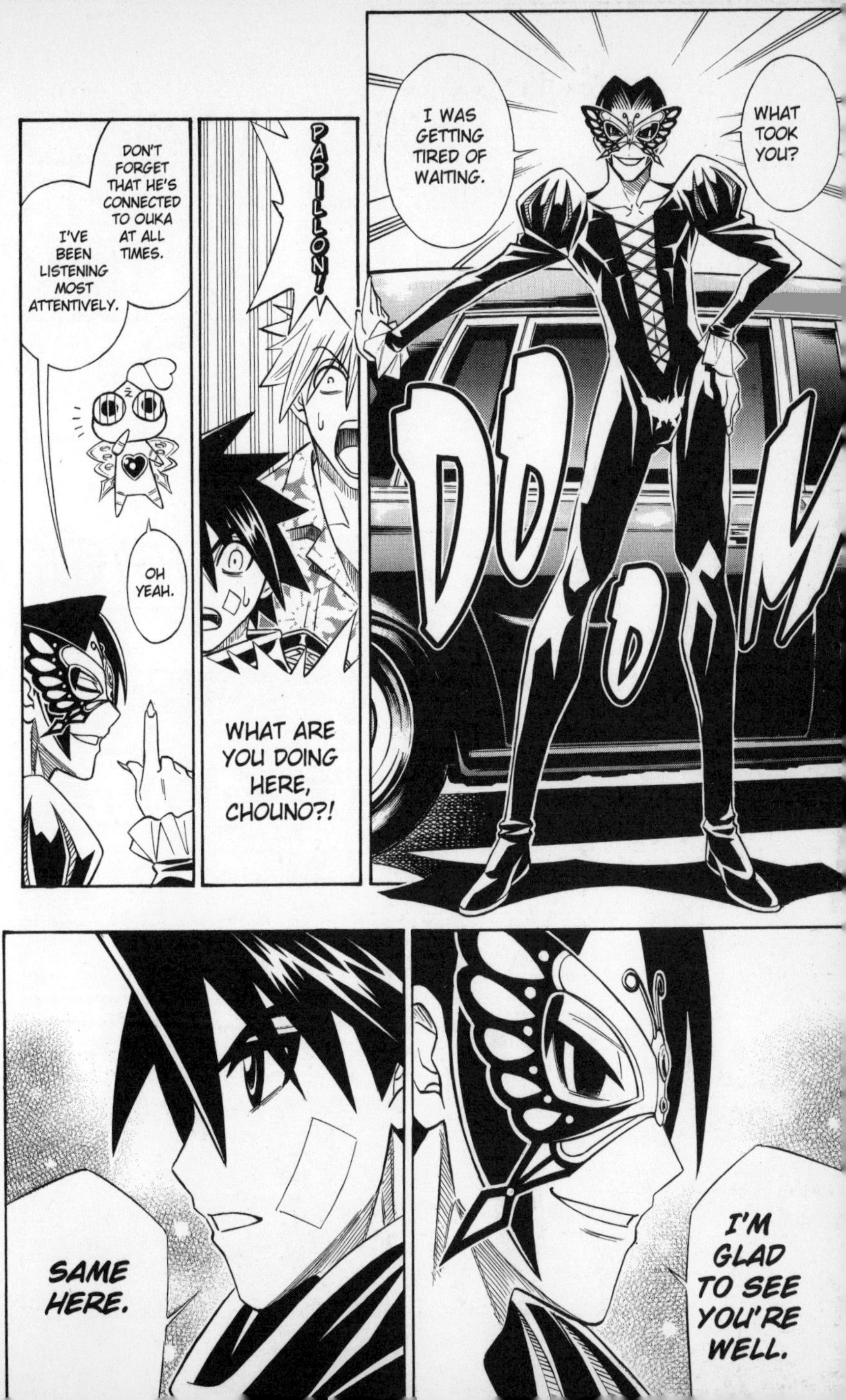
WHAT TOOK YOU?
I WAS GETTING TIRED OF WAITING.
PAPILLON!
WHAT ARE YOU DOING HERE, CHOUNO?!
DON'T FORGET THAT HE'S CONNECTED TO OUKA AT ALL TIMES.
I'VE BEEN LISTENING MOST ATTENTIVELY.
OH YEAH.
I'M GLAD TO SEE YOU'RE WELL.
SAME HERE.

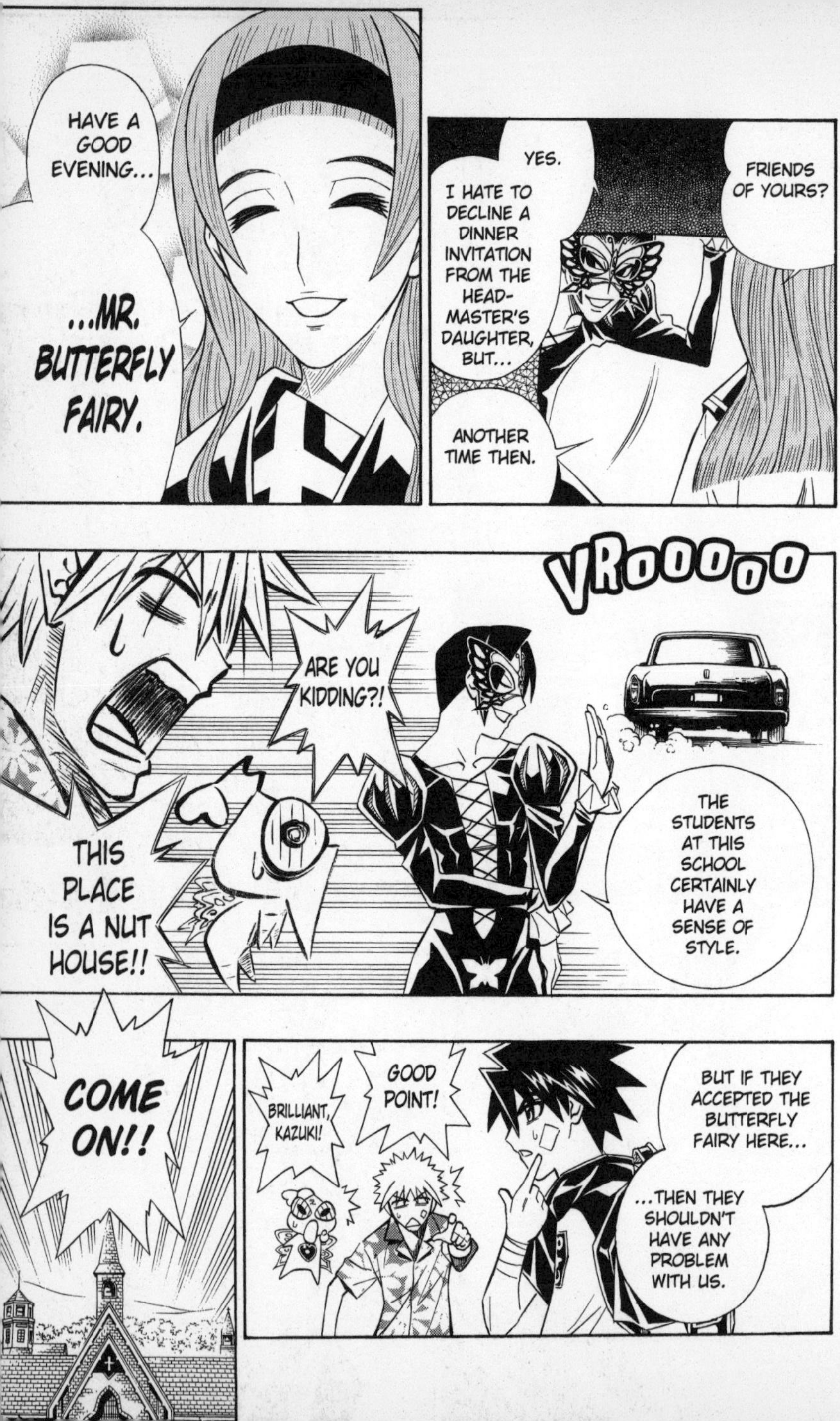
FRIENDS OF YOURS?
YES.
I HATE TO DECLINE A DINNER INVITATION FROM THE HEAD-MASTER'S DAUGHTER, BUT...
ANOTHER TIME THEN.
HAVE A GOOD EVENING...
...MR. BUTTERFLY FAIRY.
VROOOOOO
THE STUDENTS AT THIS SCHOOL CERTAINLY HAVE A SENSE OF STYLE.
ARE YOU KIDDING?!
THIS PLACE IS A NUT HOUSE!!
BUT IF THEY ACCEPTED THE BUTTERFLY FAIRY HERE...
...THEN THEY SHOULDN'T HAVE ANY PROBLEM WITH US.
GOOD POINT!
BRILLIANT, KAZUKI!
COME ON!!

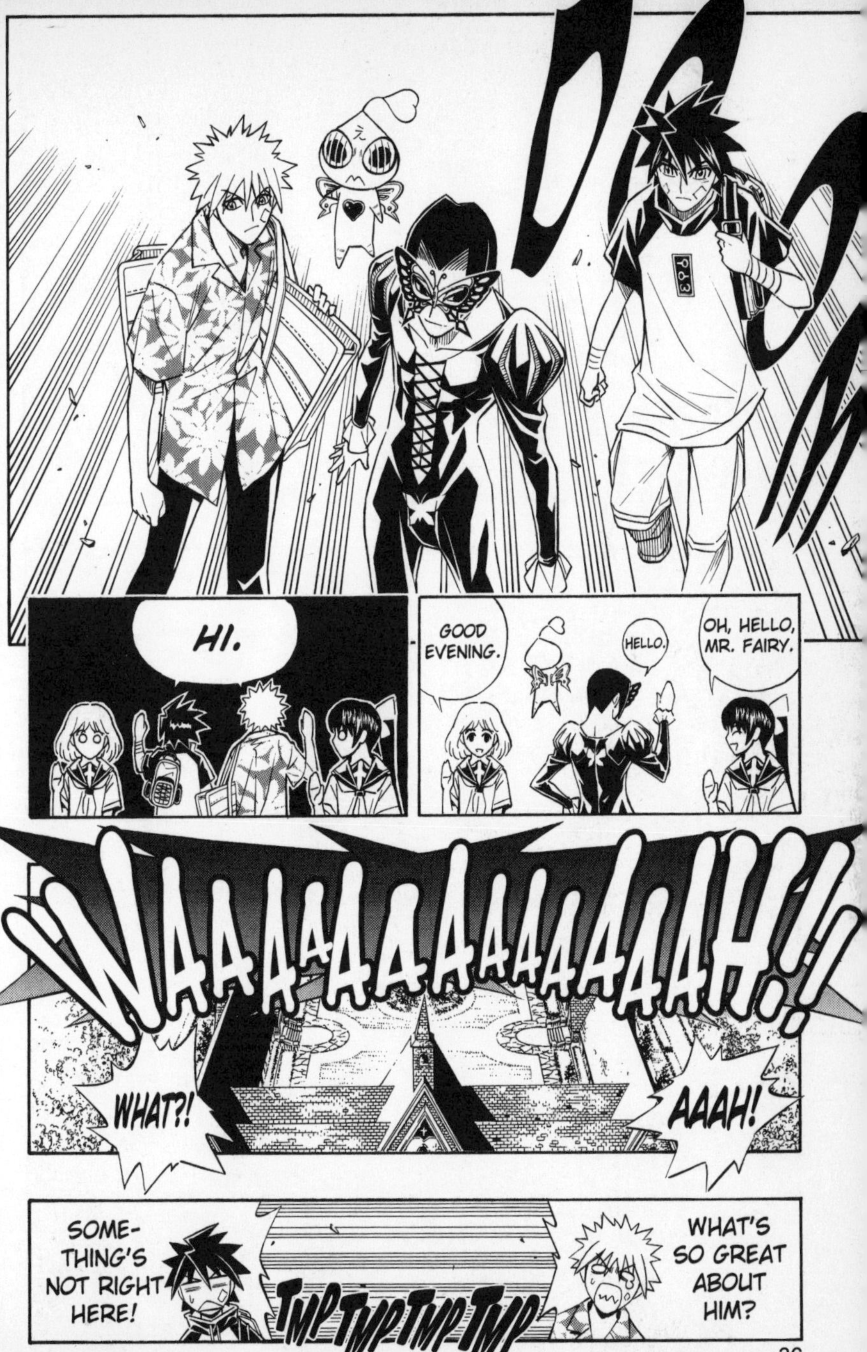
DOOM
OH, HELLO, MR. FAIRY.
HELLO.
GOOD EVENING.
HI.
WAAAAAAAAAAAAAH!!
AAAH!
WHAT?!
WHAT'S SO GREAT ABOUT HIM?
TMP TMP TMP TMP
SOME-THING'S NOT RIGHT HERE!

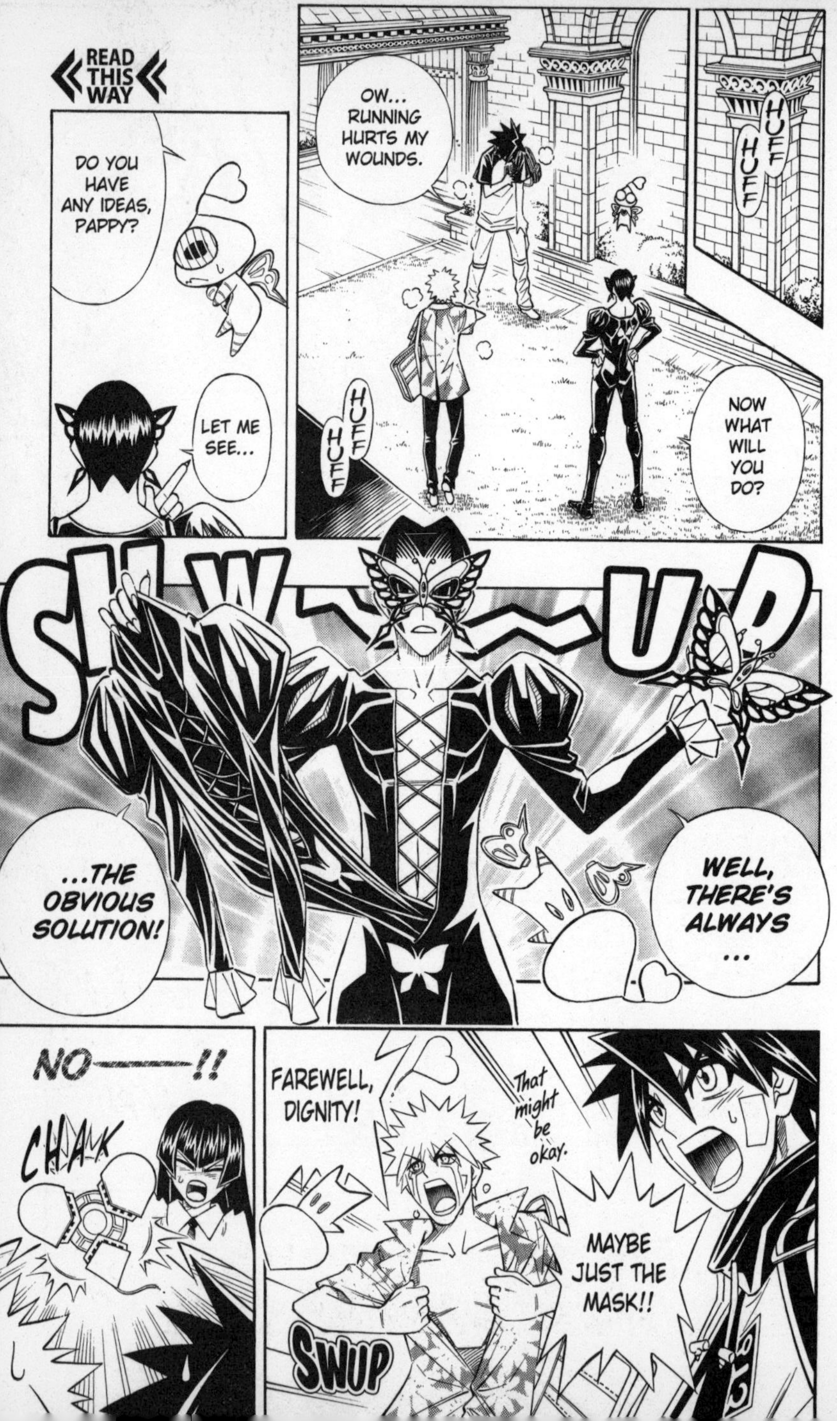
READ THIS WAY
HUFF HUFF
OW... RUNNING HURTS MY WOUNDS.
NOW WHAT WILL YOU DO?
HUFF HUFF
DO YOU HAVE ANY IDEAS, PAPPY?
LET ME SEE...
WELL, THERE'S ALWAYS...
...THE OBVIOUS SOLUTION!
MAYBE JUST THE MASK!!
That might be okay.
FAREWELL, DIGNITY!
SWUP
NO——!!
CHAK

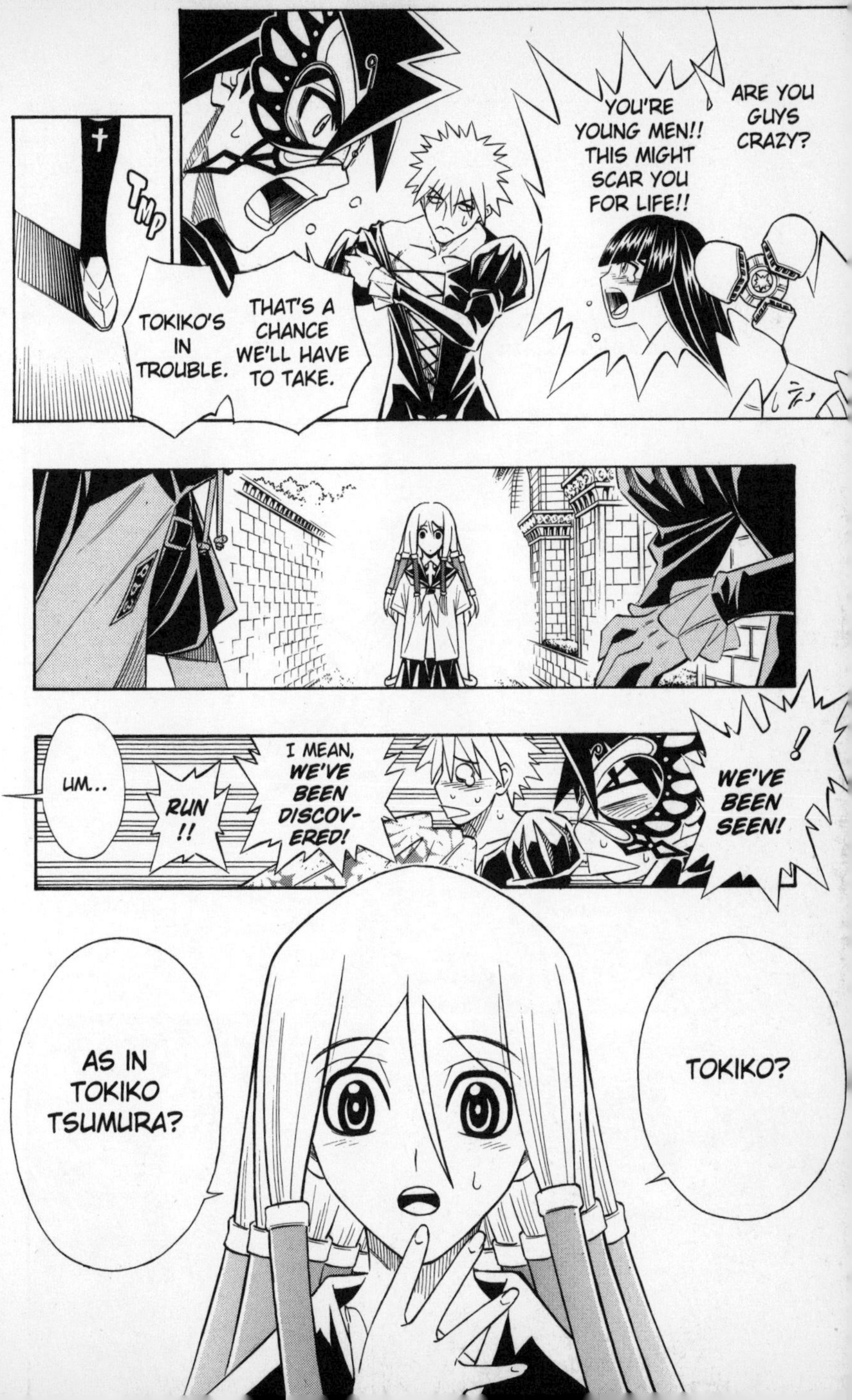
ARE YOU GUYS CRAZY?
YOU'RE YOUNG MEN!! THIS MIGHT SCAR YOU FOR LIFE!!
THAT'S A CHANCE WE'LL HAVE TO TAKE.
TOKIKO'S IN TROUBLE.
TMP
!
WE'VE BEEN SEEN!
I MEAN, WE'VE BEEN DISCOV-ERED!
RUN !!
UM...
TOKIKO?
AS IN TOKIKO TSUMURA?

READ THIS WAY

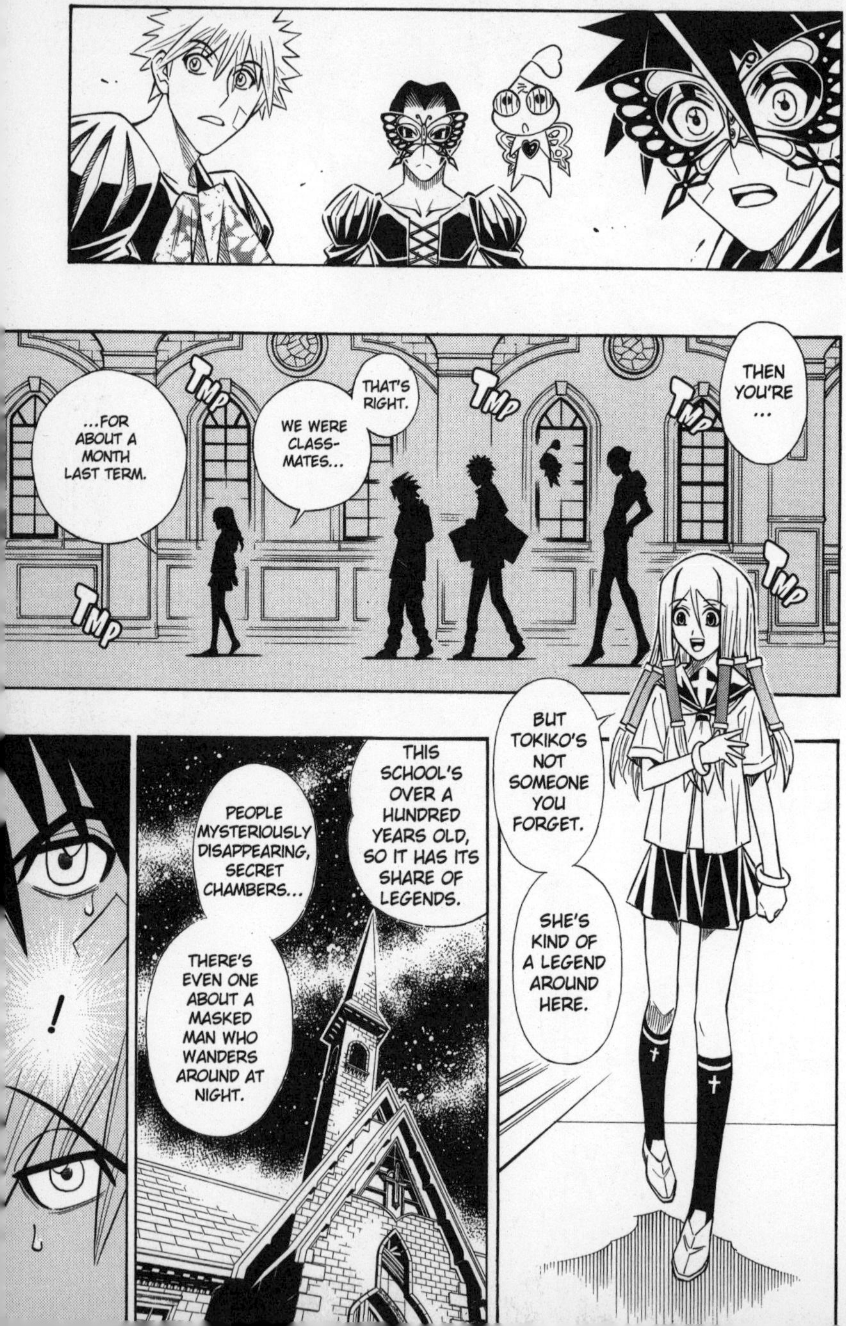
THEN YOU'RE ...
TMP
TMP
THAT'S RIGHT.
WE WERE CLASS-MATES...
...FOR ABOUT A MONTH LAST TERM.
TMP
TMP
BUT TOKIKO'S NOT SOMEONE YOU FORGET.
SHE'S KIND OF A LEGEND AROUND HERE.
THIS SCHOOL'S OVER A HUNDRED YEARS OLD, SO IT HAS ITS SHARE OF LEGENDS.
PEOPLE MYSTERIOUSLY DISAPPEARING, SECRET CHAMBERS...
THERE'S EVEN ONE ABOUT A MASKED MAN WHO WANDERS AROUND AT NIGHT.
!

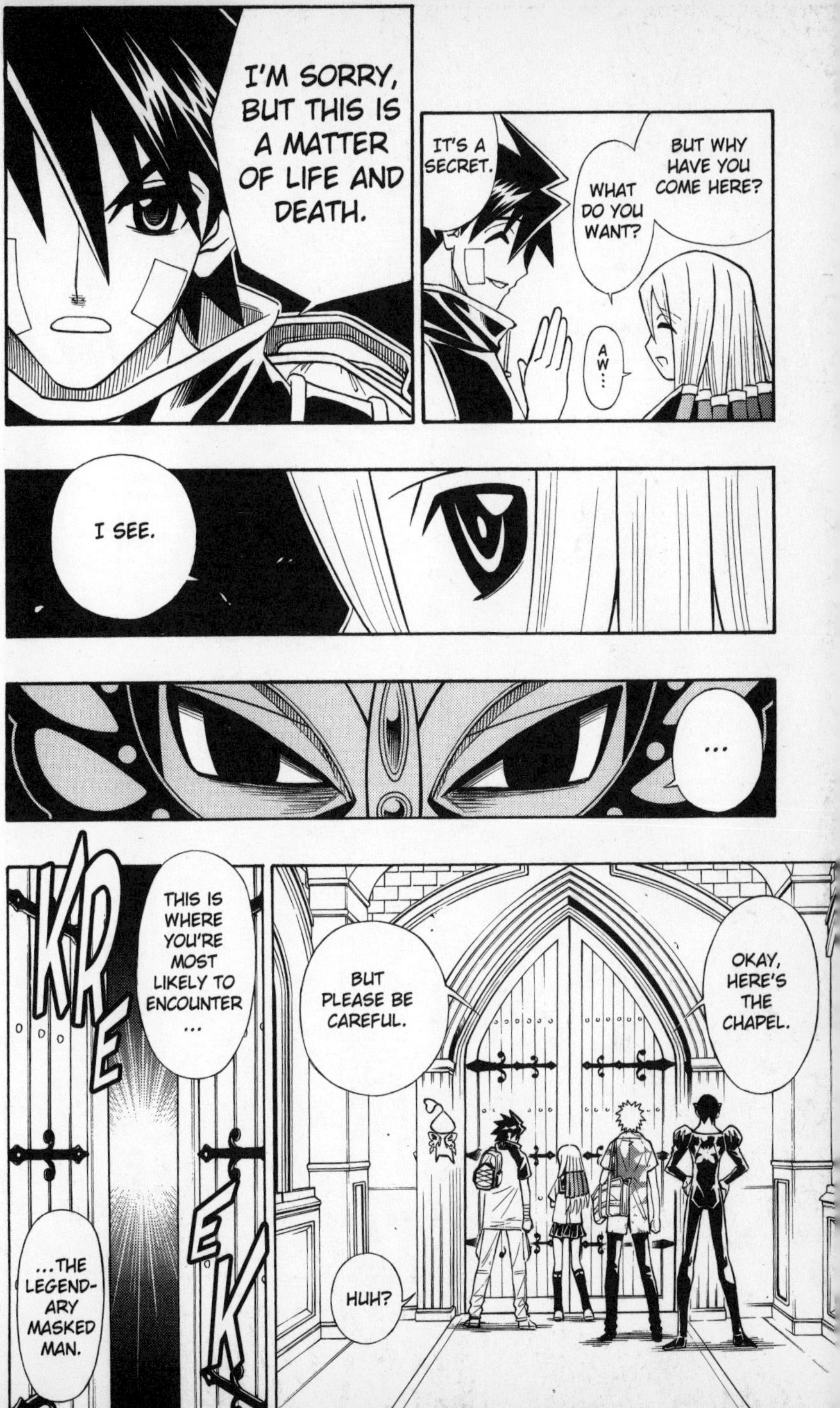
BUT WHY HAVE YOU COME HERE?
WHAT DO YOU WANT?
IT'S A SECRET.
AW...
I'M SORRY, BUT THIS IS A MATTER OF LIFE AND DEATH.
I SEE.
...
OKAY, HERE'S THE CHAPEL.
BUT PLEASE BE CAREFUL.
HUH?
KREEK
THIS IS WHERE YOU'RE MOST LIKELY TO ENCOUNTER...
...THE LEGEND-ARY MASKED MAN.

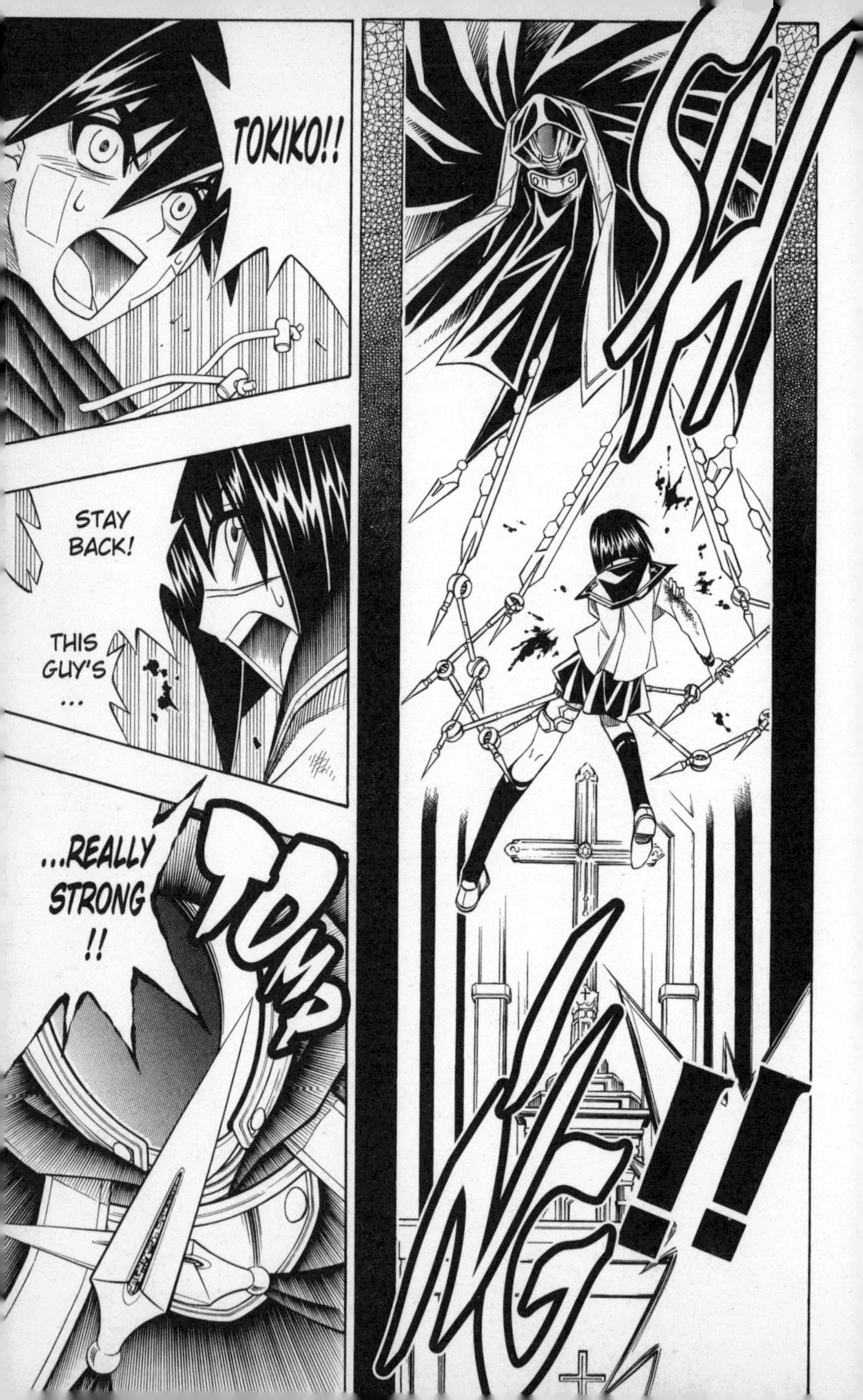
TOKIKO!!
STAY BACK!
THIS GUY'S ...
...REALLY STRONG !!
TUMP

- Height: 168 cm; Weight: 55 kg
- Born: December 22; Capricorn; Blood Type: A; Age: 20
- Likes: Shade, historical ninja
- Dislikes: The sun, American ninja
- Hobby: Reading (mostly books about ninja)
- Special Ability: Able to mask his presence in a crowd and
              blend into the landscape
- Affiliations: The Alchemist Army, Re-Extermination Squad

Character File No. 31

SHINOBU NEGORO

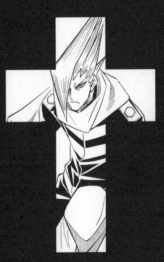

Author's Notes

- His motif is, of course, ninja.
- He was originally supposed to be a stone-cold killing machine, but because of the complexity of his Buso Renkin, he needed to talk so that he could explain how it worked. So overall, he didn't really work the way I wanted him to. When introducing a character like this, you need to have someone around to explain what's going on to the readers. Looking back, it was a mistake on my part.
- For the design, I refined one of my old sketches. He looks very similar to 002 from *Cyborg 009*. I like his blocky shape and jagged hairline. This is one of the characters that I was really pleased with.
- I really like stealthy characters like ninja and spies, people who work in the shadows. I hope to be able to create more of them in the future.

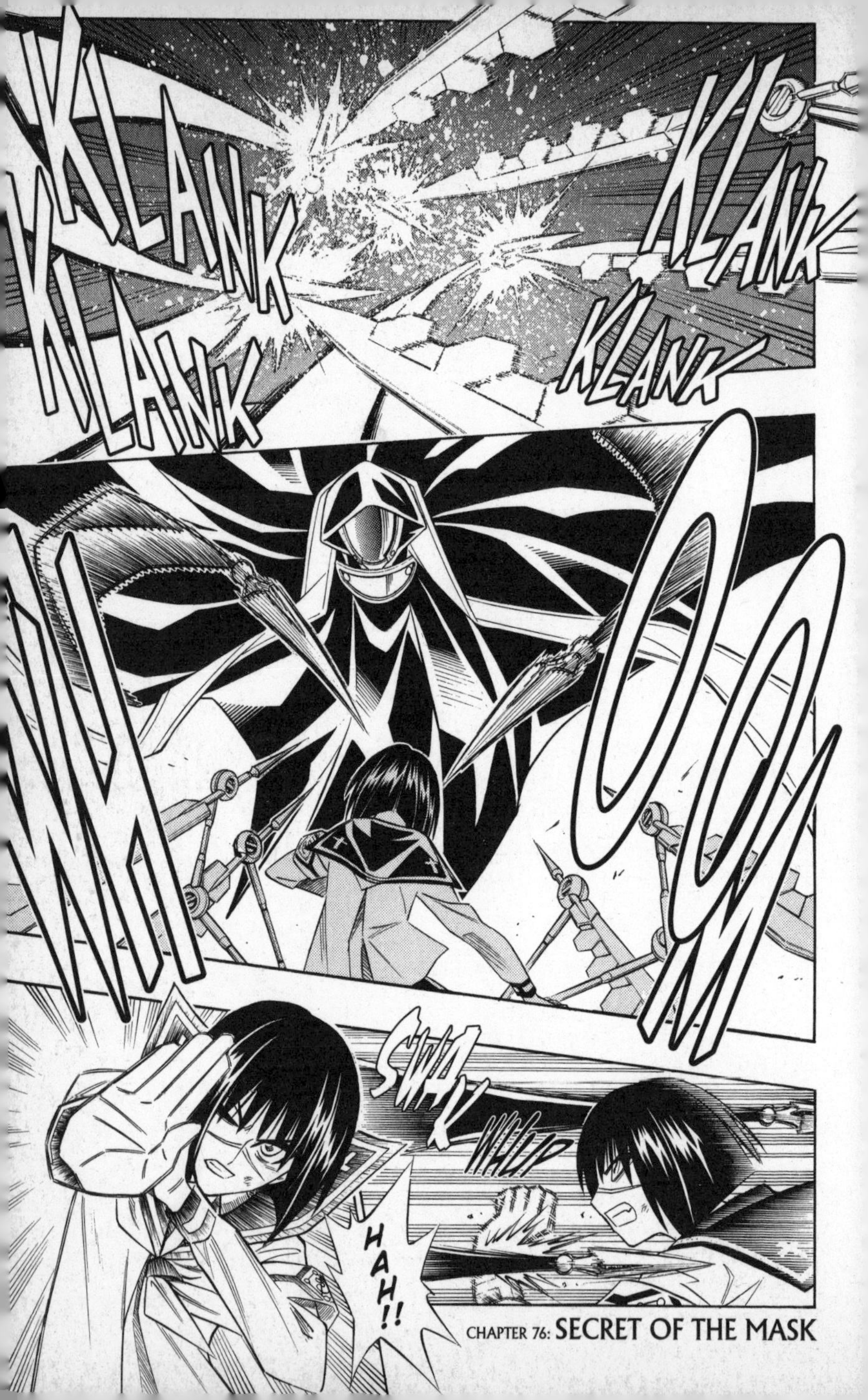
KLANK
KLANK
KLANK
KLANK
WHOOOM
SWAK
WHIP
HAH!!

CHAPTER 76: SECRET OF THE MASK

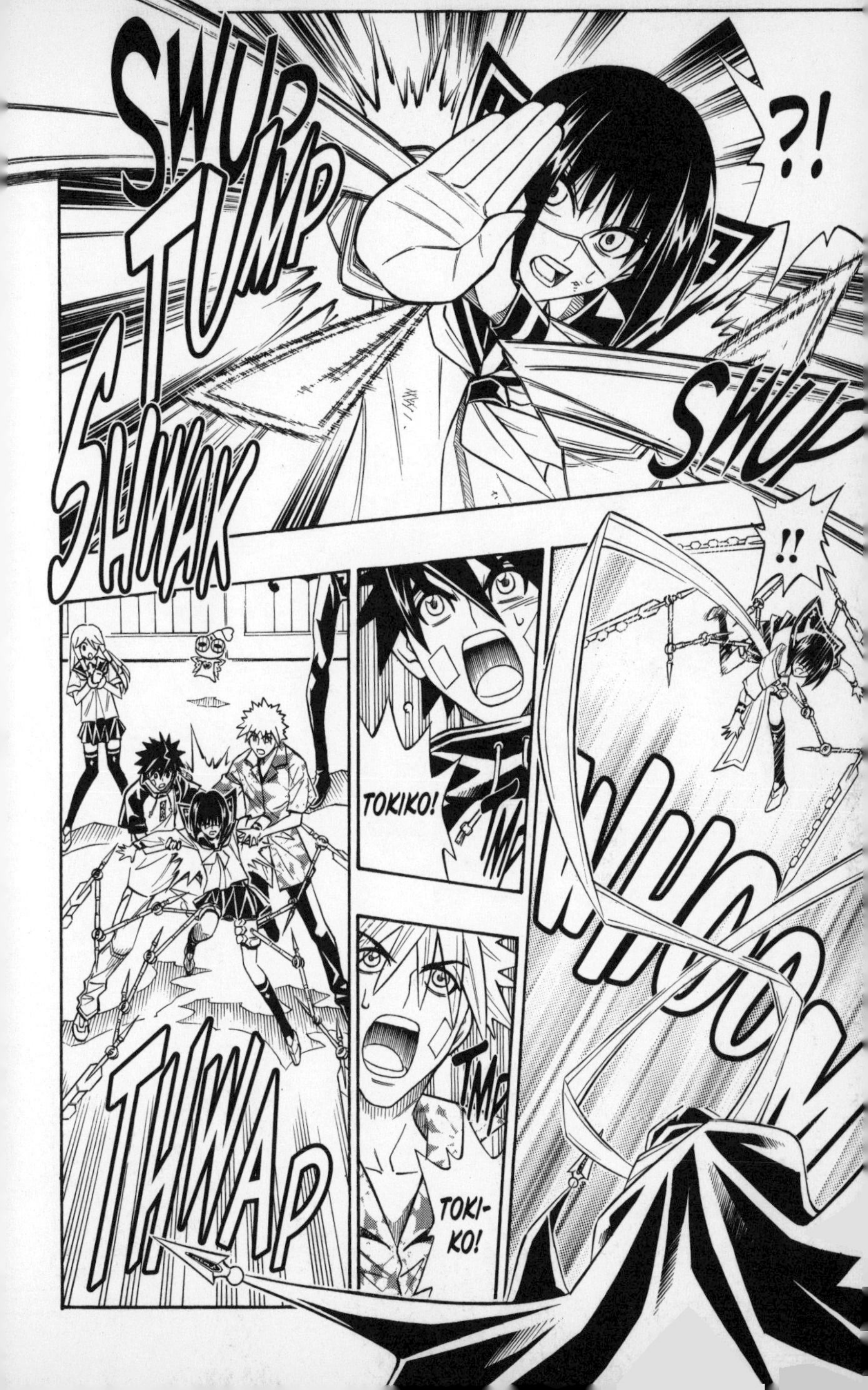

?!
SWUP
SWUP
TUMP
SHWAK
!!
WHOOM
TOKIKO!
TMP
TOKI-KO!
TMP
THWAP

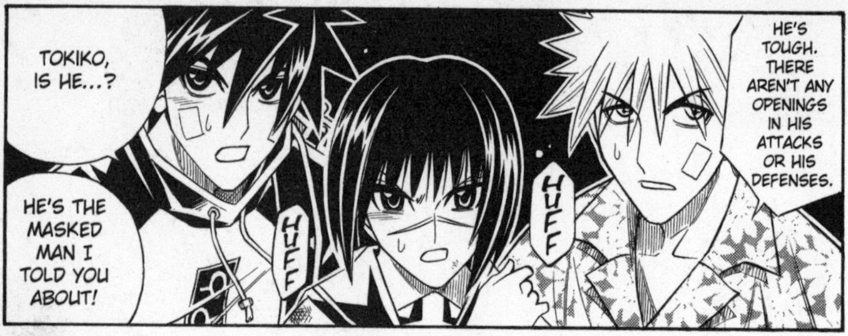
HE'S TOUGH. THERE AREN'T ANY OPENINGS IN HIS ATTACKS OR HIS DEFENSES.
HUFF
HUFF
TOKIKO, IS HE...?
HE'S THE MASKED MAN I TOLD YOU ABOUT!

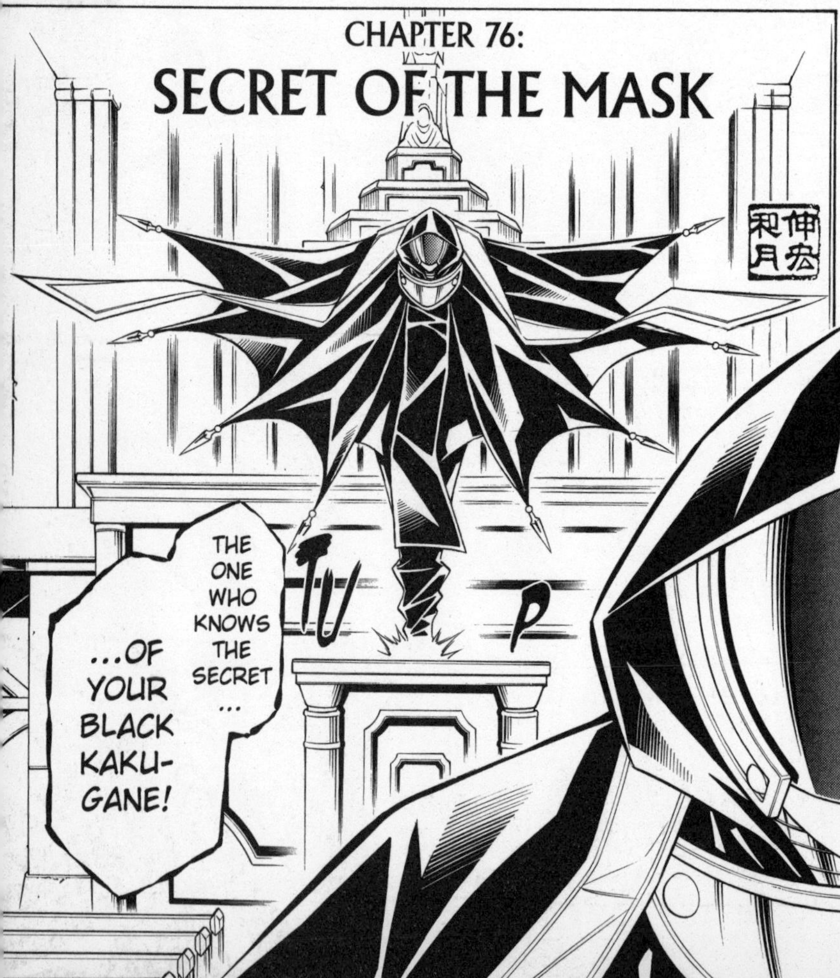
CHAPTER 76:
SECRET OF THE MASK
伸宏
和月
P
TU
THE ONE WHO KNOWS THE SECRET...
...OF YOUR BLACK KAKU-GANE!

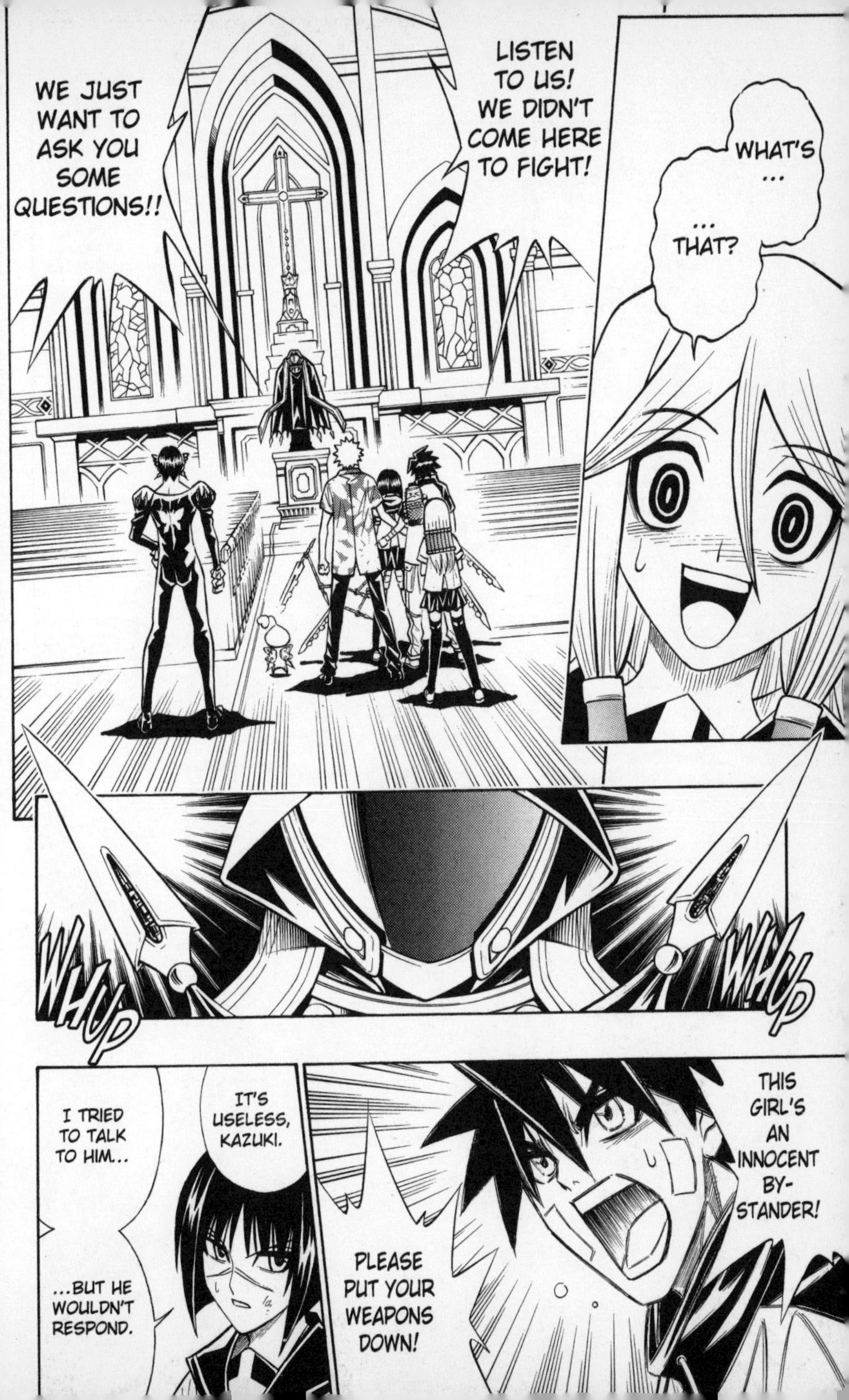
WHAT'S ...
... THAT?
LISTEN TO US! WE DIDN'T COME HERE TO FIGHT!
WE JUST WANT TO ASK YOU SOME QUESTIONS!!
WHUP
WHUP
THIS GIRL'S AN INNOCENT BY-STANDER!
PLEASE PUT YOUR WEAPONS DOWN!
IT'S USELESS, KAZUKI.
I TRIED TO TALK TO HIM...
...BUT HE WOULDN'T RESPOND.

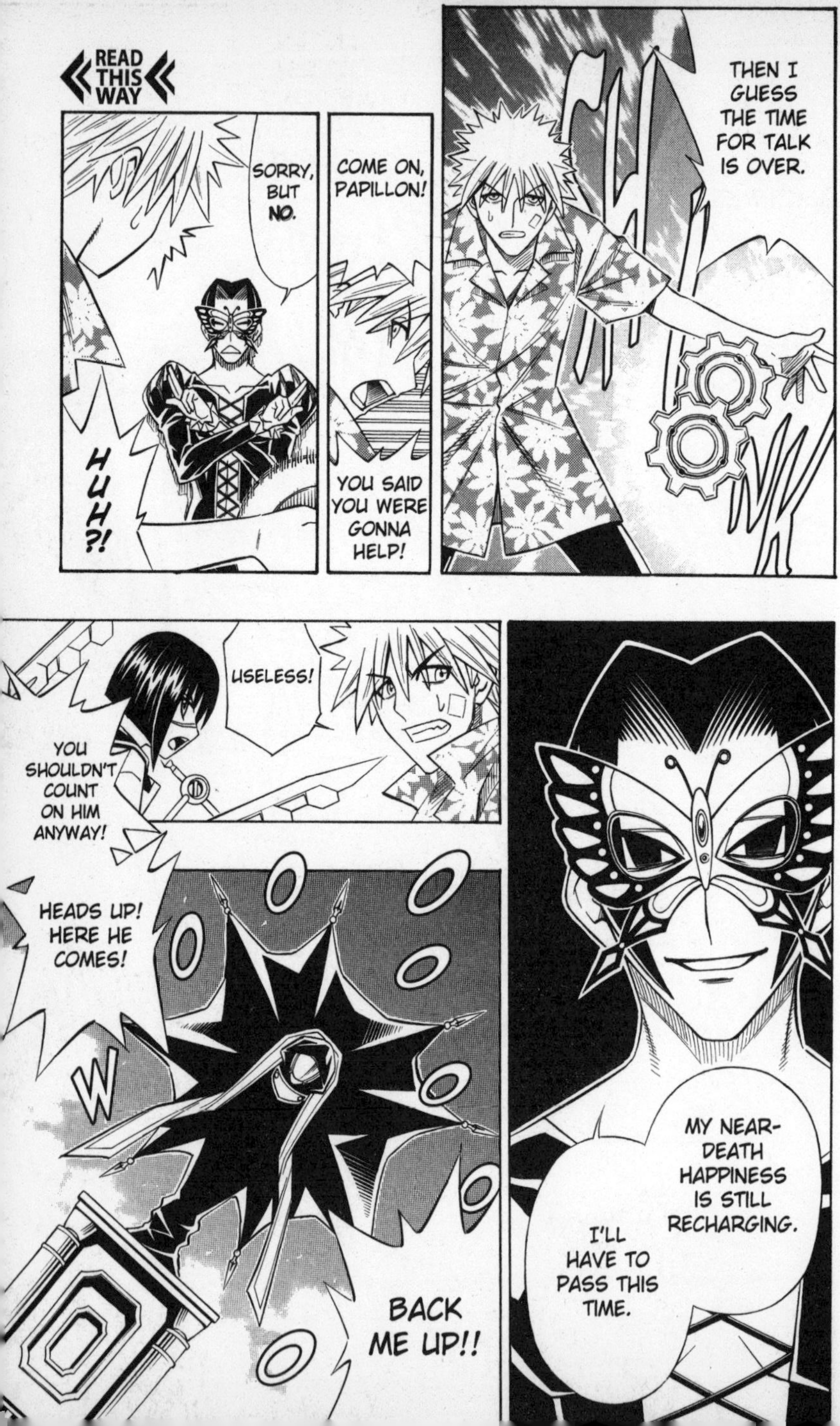

READ THIS WAY
THEN I GUESS THE TIME FOR TALK IS OVER.
COME ON, PAPILLON!
YOU SAID YOU WERE GONNA HELP!
SORRY, BUT NO.
HUH?!
MY NEAR-DEATH HAPPINESS IS STILL RECHARGING.
I'LL HAVE TO PASS THIS TIME.
USELESS!
YOU SHOULDN'T COUNT ON HIM ANYWAY!
HEADS UP! HERE HE COMES!
W
BACK ME UP!!

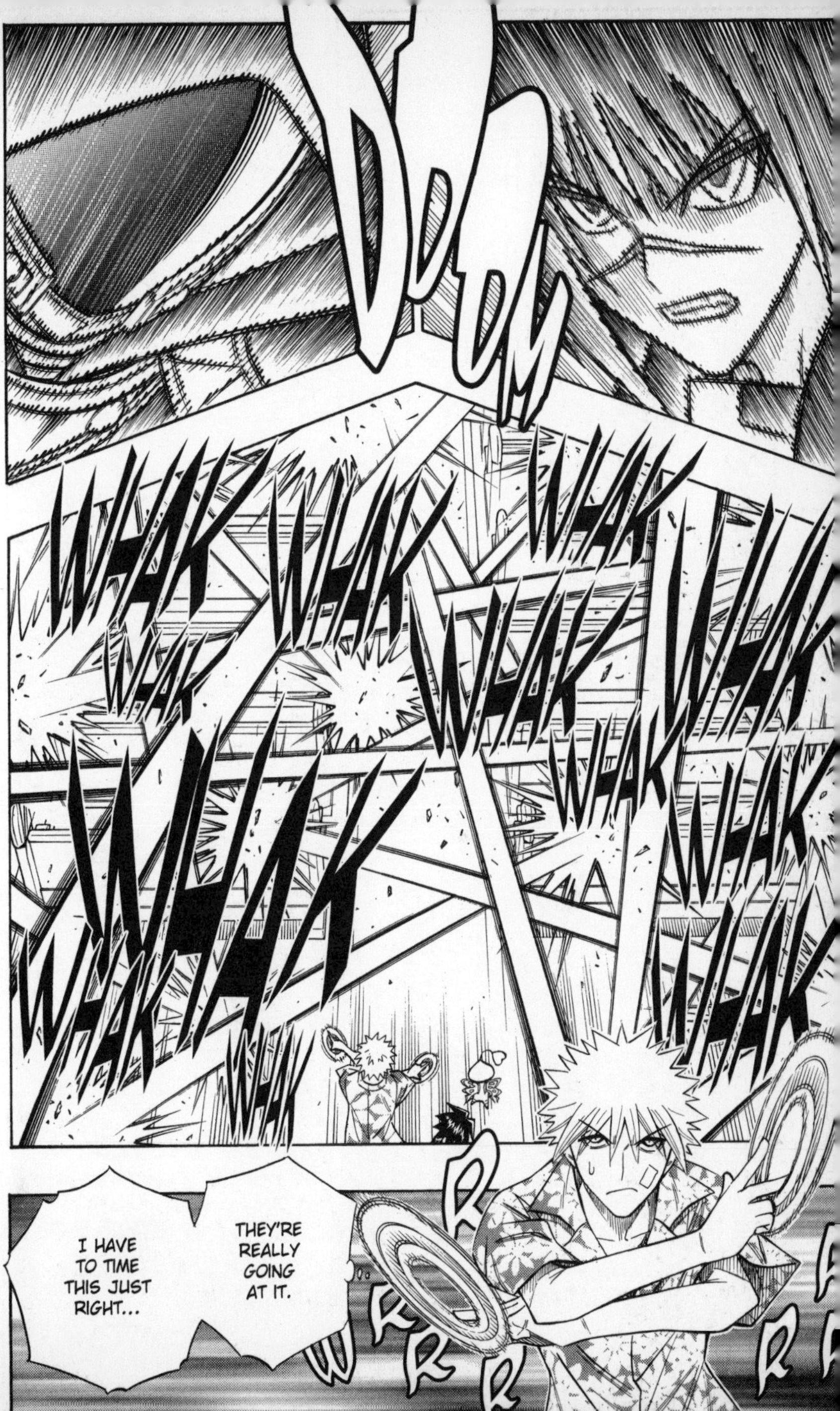
WHAK WHAK WHAK WHAK
WHAK WHAK WHAK WHAK
WHAK WHAK WHAK
THEY'RE REALLY GOING AT IT.
I HAVE TO TIME THIS JUST RIGHT...

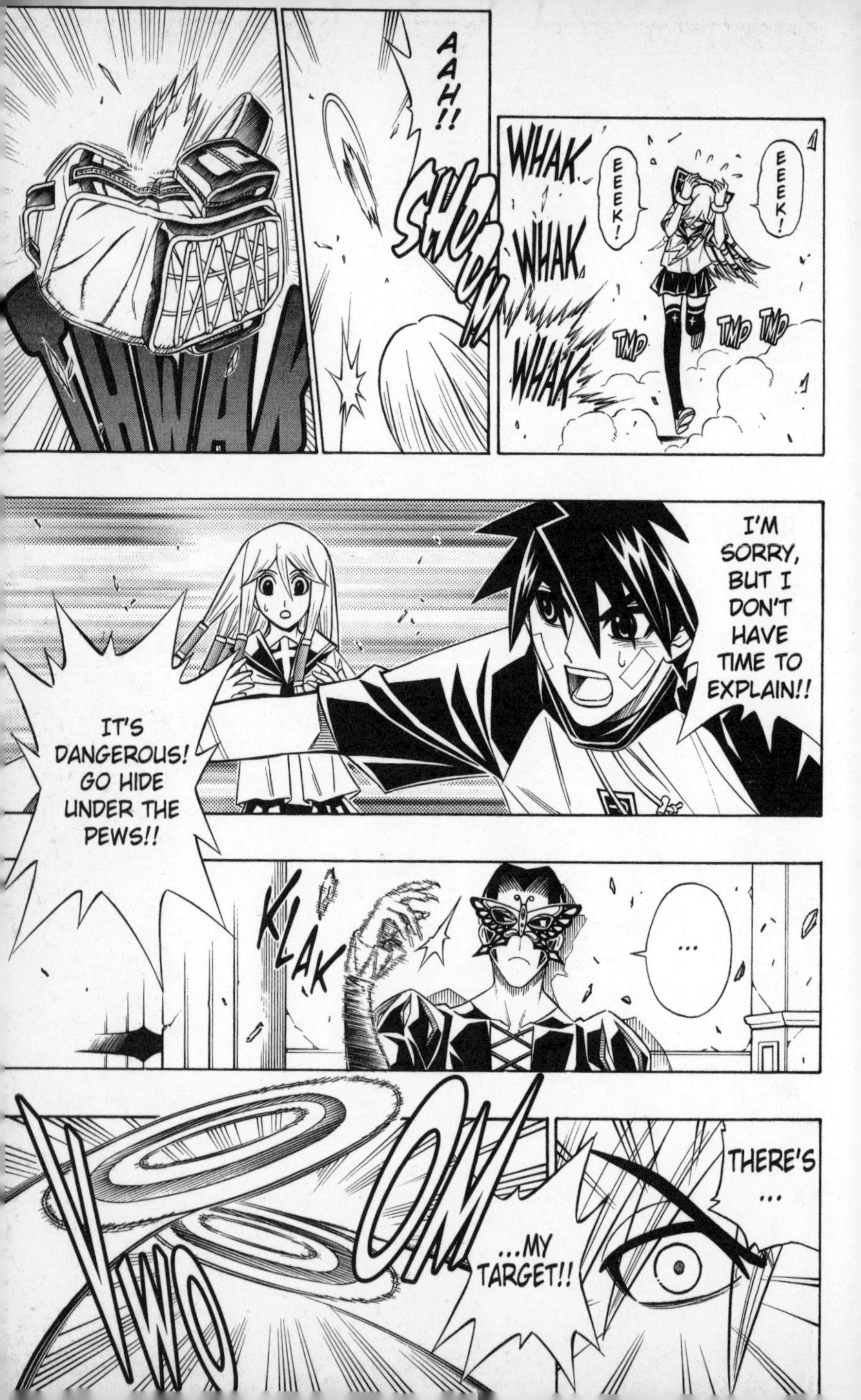
WHAK
WHAK
WHAK
EEEK!
EEEK!
TMP TMP
TMP
AAH!!
THWAK
I'M SORRY, BUT I DON'T HAVE TIME TO EXPLAIN!!
IT'S DANGEROUS! GO HIDE UNDER THE PEWS!!
...
KLAK
THERE'S ...
...MY TARGET!!

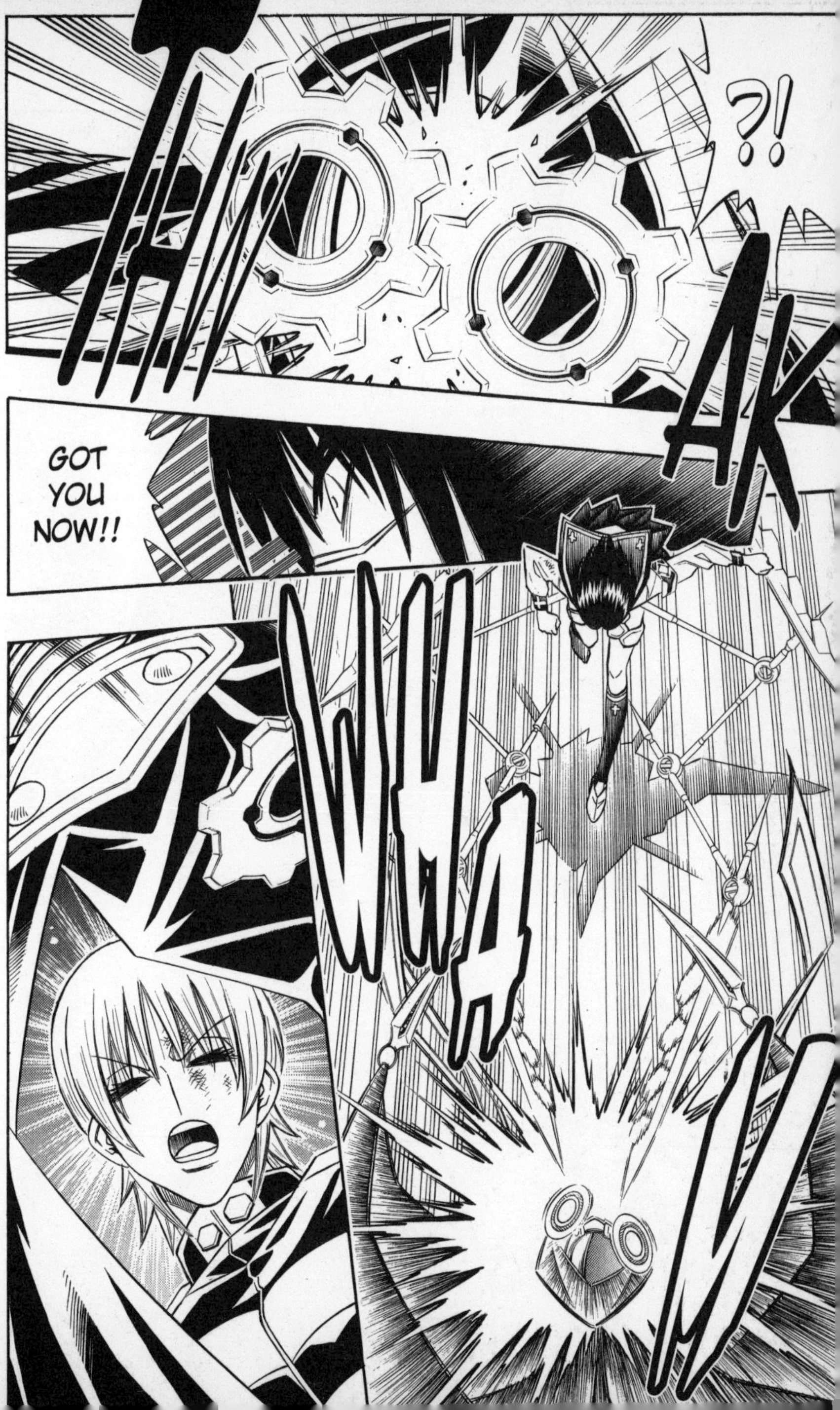
?!
THWOOAK
GOT YOU NOW!!
WHAM

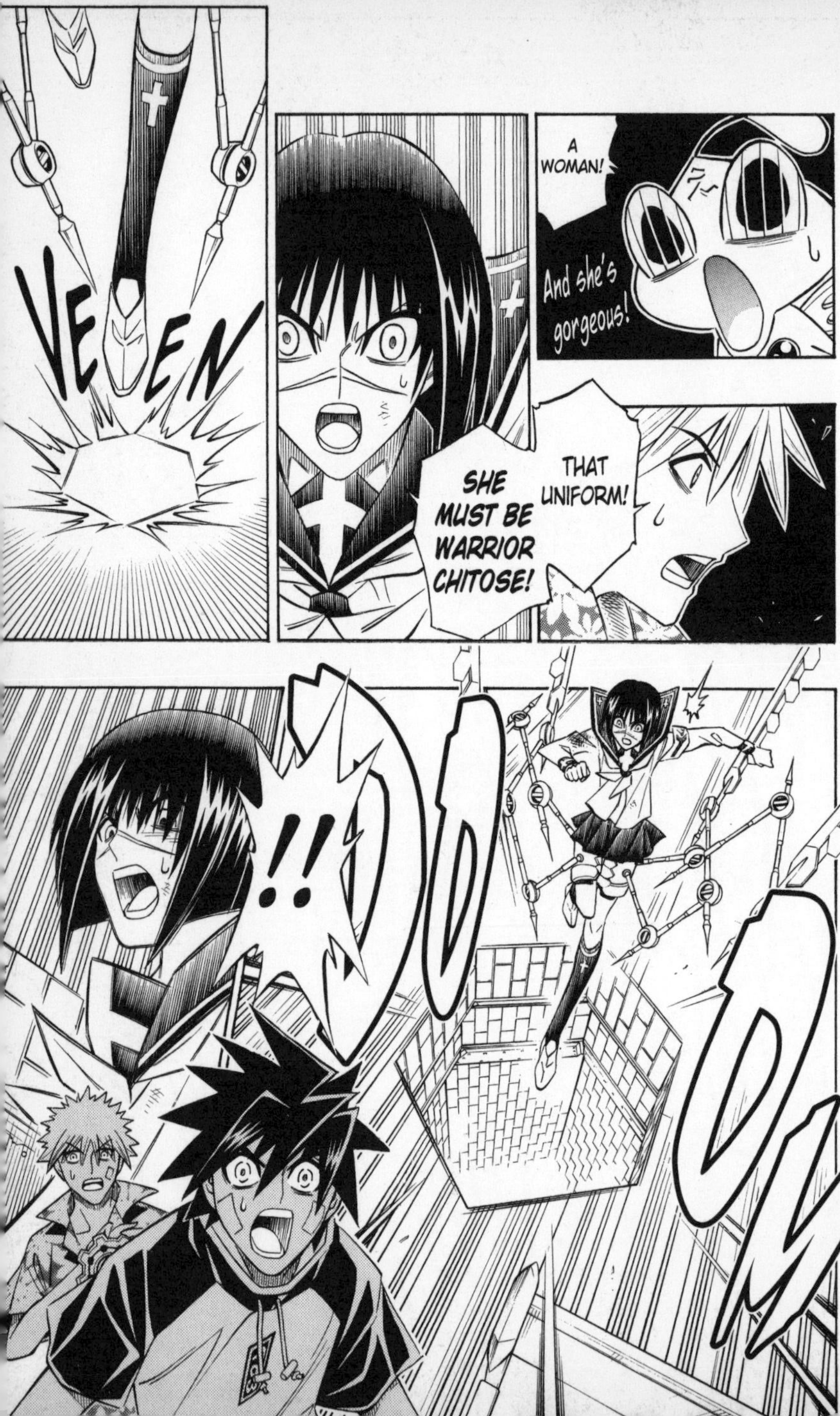
A WOMAN!
And she's gorgeous!
THAT UNIFORM!
SHE MUST BE WARRIOR CHITOSE!
VEEN
!!

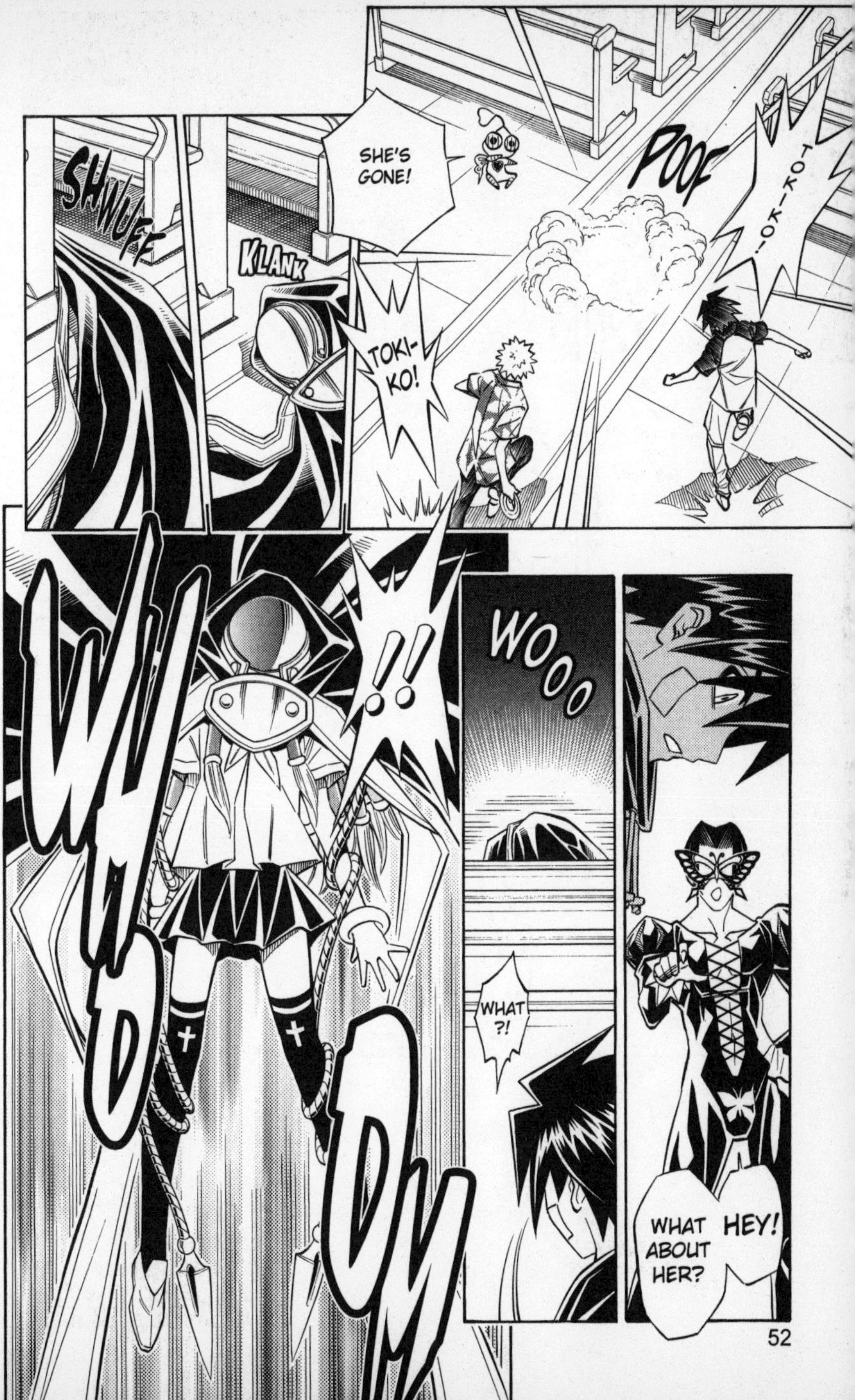
TOKI-KO!
POOF
SHE'S GONE!
TOKI-KO!
KLANK
SHWUFF
HEY!
WHAT ABOUT HER?
WOOO
WHAT?!
!!

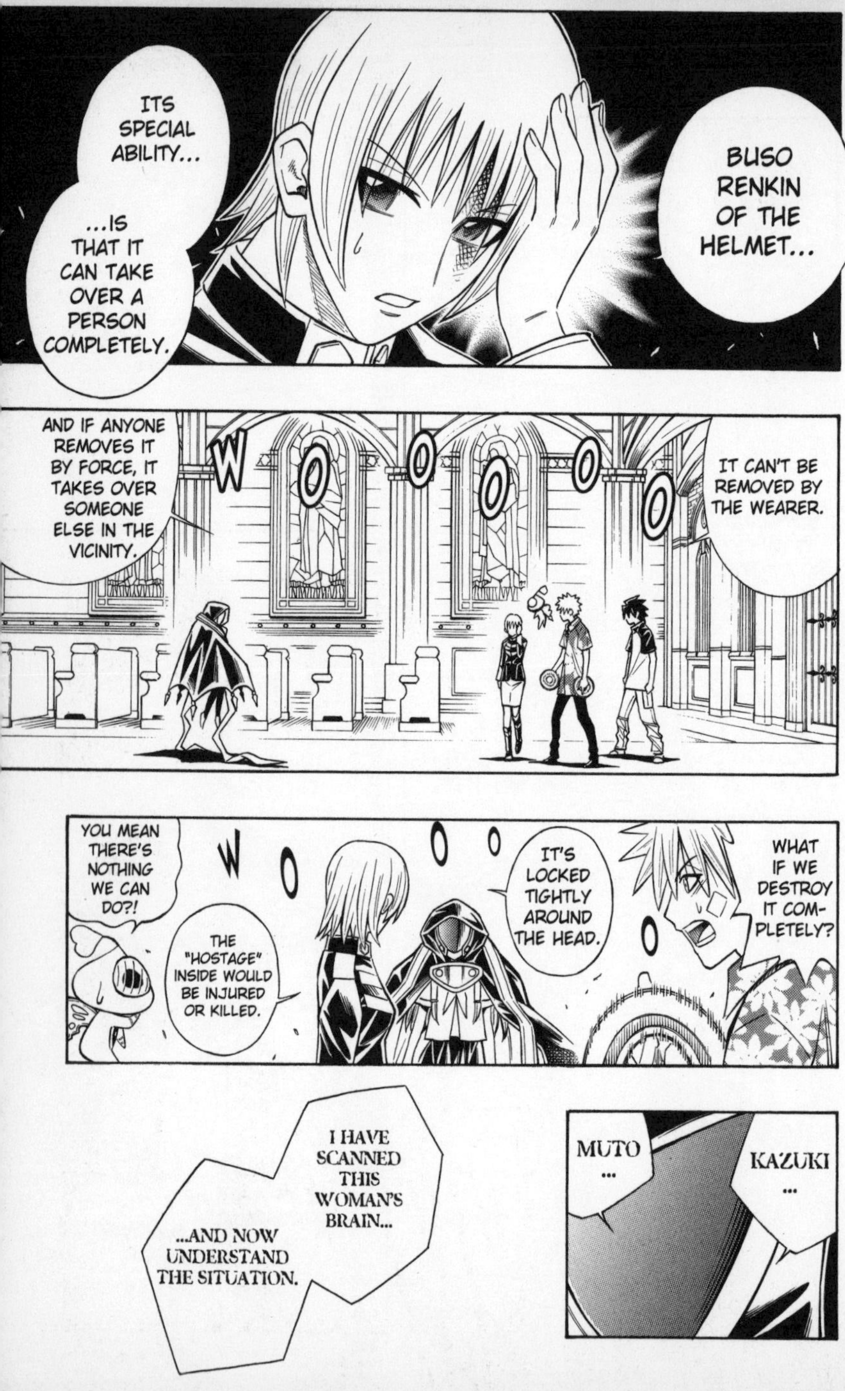
BUSO RENKIN OF THE HELMET...
ITS SPECIAL ABILITY...
...IS THAT IT CAN TAKE OVER A PERSON COMPLETELY.
IT CAN'T BE REMOVED BY THE WEARER.
WOOOOO
AND IF ANYONE REMOVES IT BY FORCE, IT TAKES OVER SOMEONE ELSE IN THE VICINITY.
WHAT IF WE DESTROY IT COMPLETELY?
IT'S LOCKED TIGHTLY AROUND THE HEAD.
WOOOO
THE "HOSTAGE" INSIDE WOULD BE INJURED OR KILLED.
YOU MEAN THERE'S NOTHING WE CAN DO?!
KAZUKI...
MUTO...
I HAVE SCANNED THIS WOMAN'S BRAIN...
...AND NOW UNDERSTAND THE SITUATION.

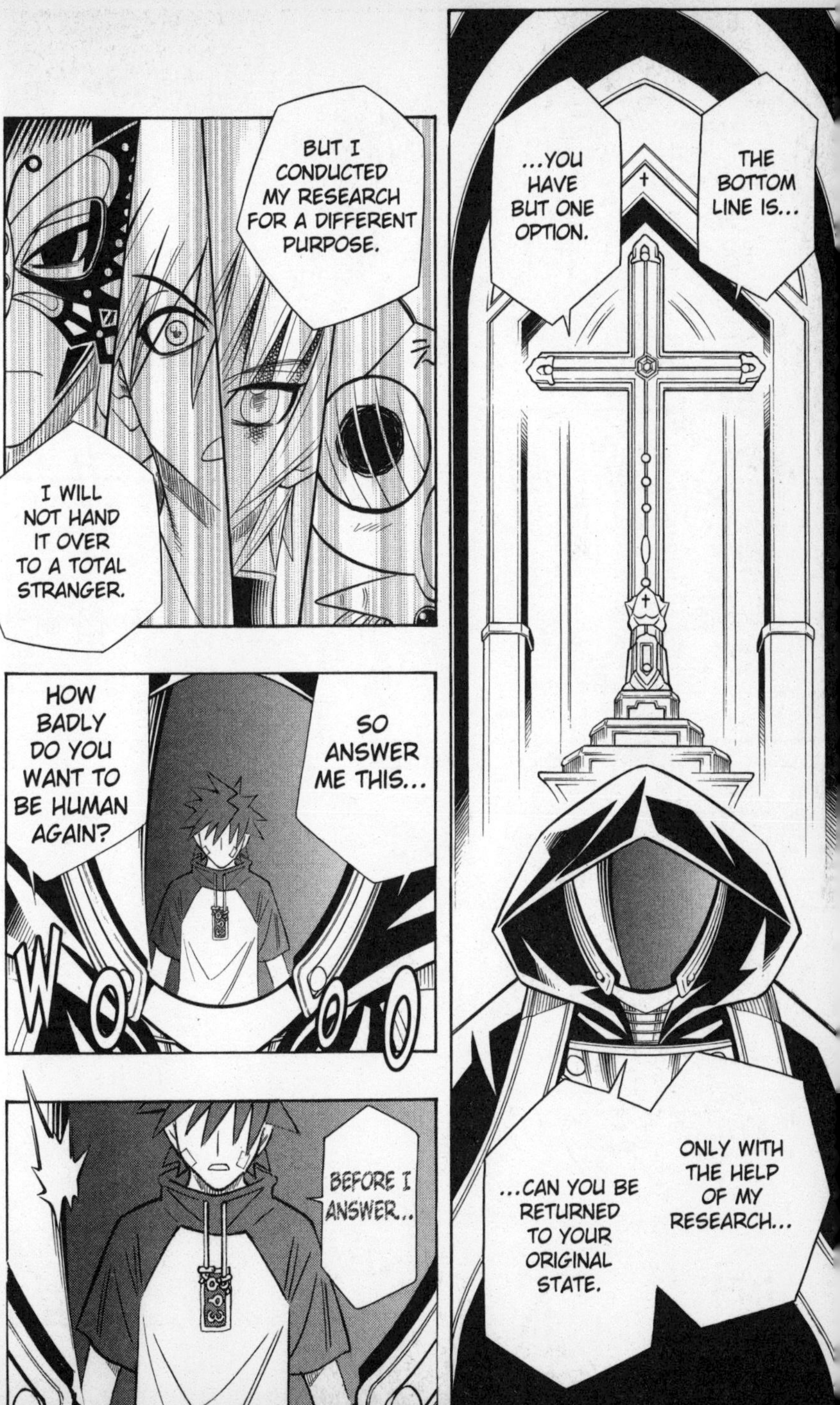
THE BOTTOM LINE IS...
...YOU HAVE BUT ONE OPTION.
ONLY WITH THE HELP OF MY RESEARCH...
...CAN YOU BE RETURNED TO YOUR ORIGINAL STATE.
BUT I CONDUCTED MY RESEARCH FOR A DIFFERENT PURPOSE.
I WILL NOT HAND IT OVER TO A TOTAL STRANGER.
SO ANSWER ME THIS...
HOW BADLY DO YOU WANT TO BE HUMAN AGAIN?
WOOO
BEFORE I ANSWER...

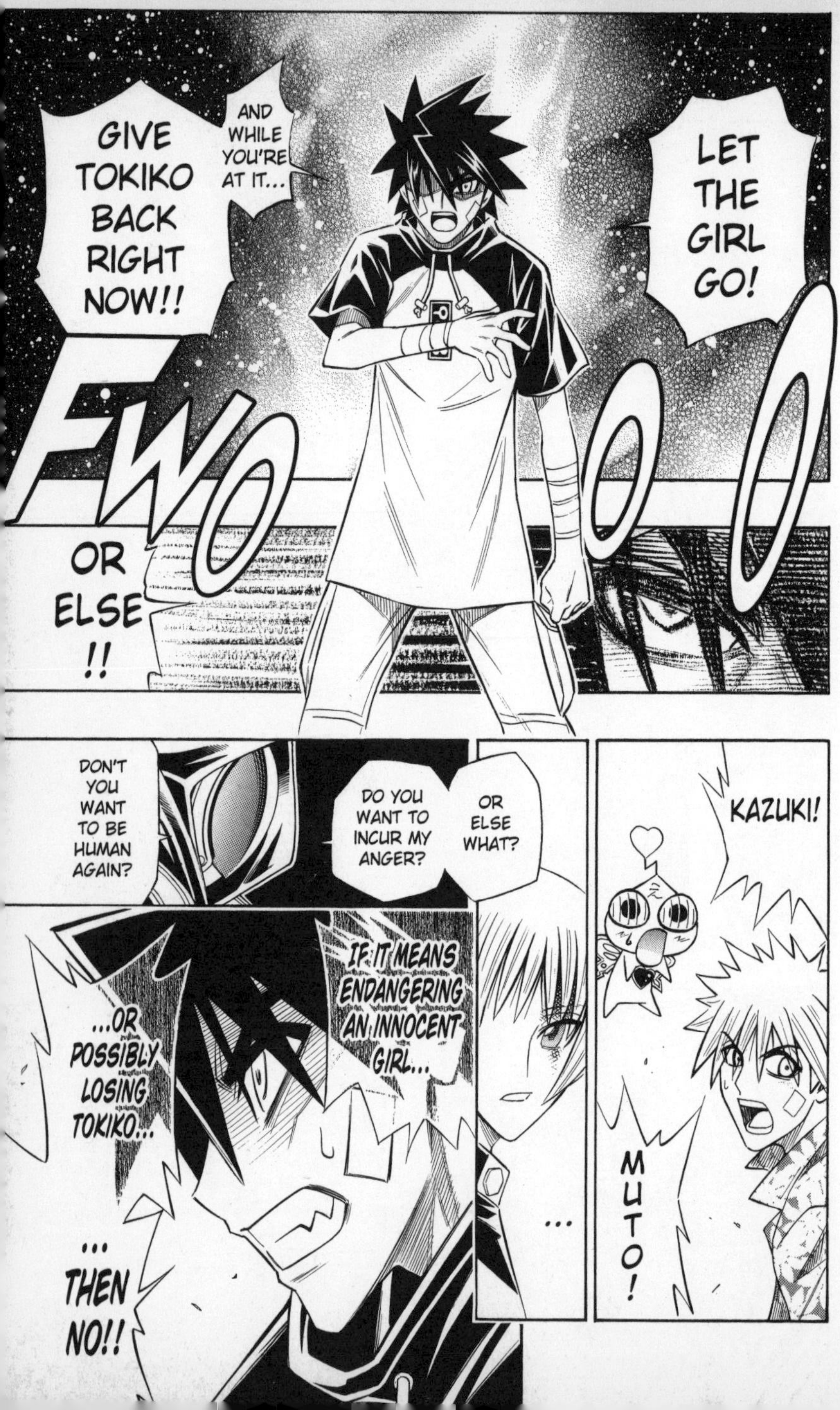
LET THE GIRL GO!
AND WHILE YOU'RE AT IT...
GIVE TOKIKO BACK RIGHT NOW!!
FWOOO
OR ELSE!!
KAZUKI!
MUTO!
...
OR ELSE WHAT?
DO YOU WANT TO INCUR MY ANGER?
DON'T YOU WANT TO BE HUMAN AGAIN?
IF IT MEANS ENDANGERING AN INNOCENT GIRL...
...OR POSSIBLY LOSING TOKIKO...
...THEN NO!!

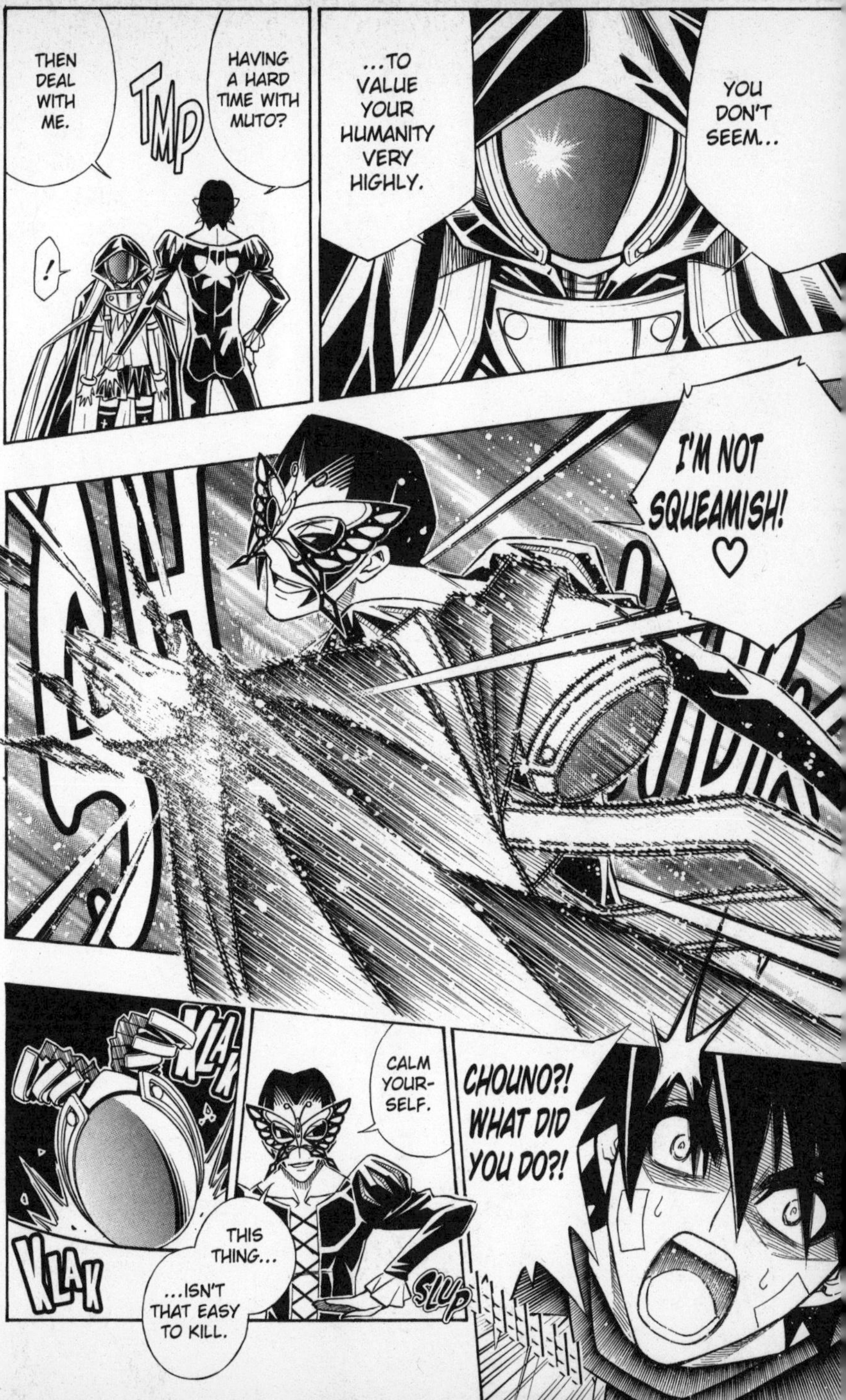
YOU DON'T SEEM...
...TO VALUE YOUR HUMANITY VERY HIGHLY.
HAVING A HARD TIME WITH MUTO?
TMP
THEN DEAL WITH ME.
!
I'M NOT SQUEAMISH! ♡
CHOUNO?! WHAT DID YOU DO?!
CALM YOUR-SELF.
THIS THING...
...ISN'T THAT EASY TO KILL.
SLUP
KLAK
KLAK

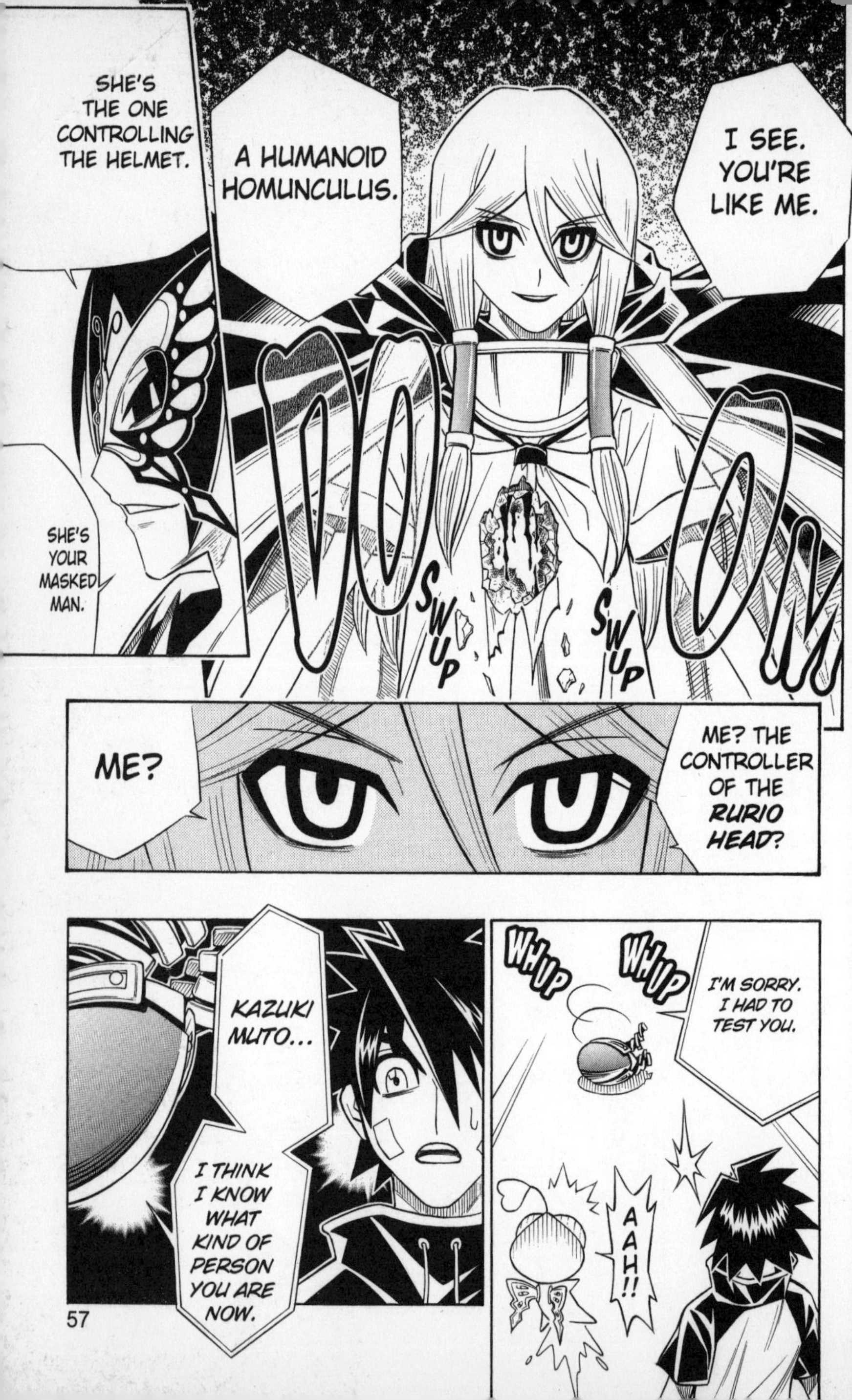
I SEE. YOU'RE LIKE ME.
A HUMANOID HOMUNCULUS.
SHE'S THE ONE CONTROLLING THE HELMET.
SHE'S YOUR MASKED MAN.
DOOM
SWUP
SWUP
ME? THE CONTROLLER OF THE RURIO HEAD?
ME?
WHUP
WHUP
I'M SORRY. I HAD TO TEST YOU.
AAH!!
KAZUKI MUTO...
I THINK I KNOW WHAT KIND OF PERSON YOU ARE NOW.

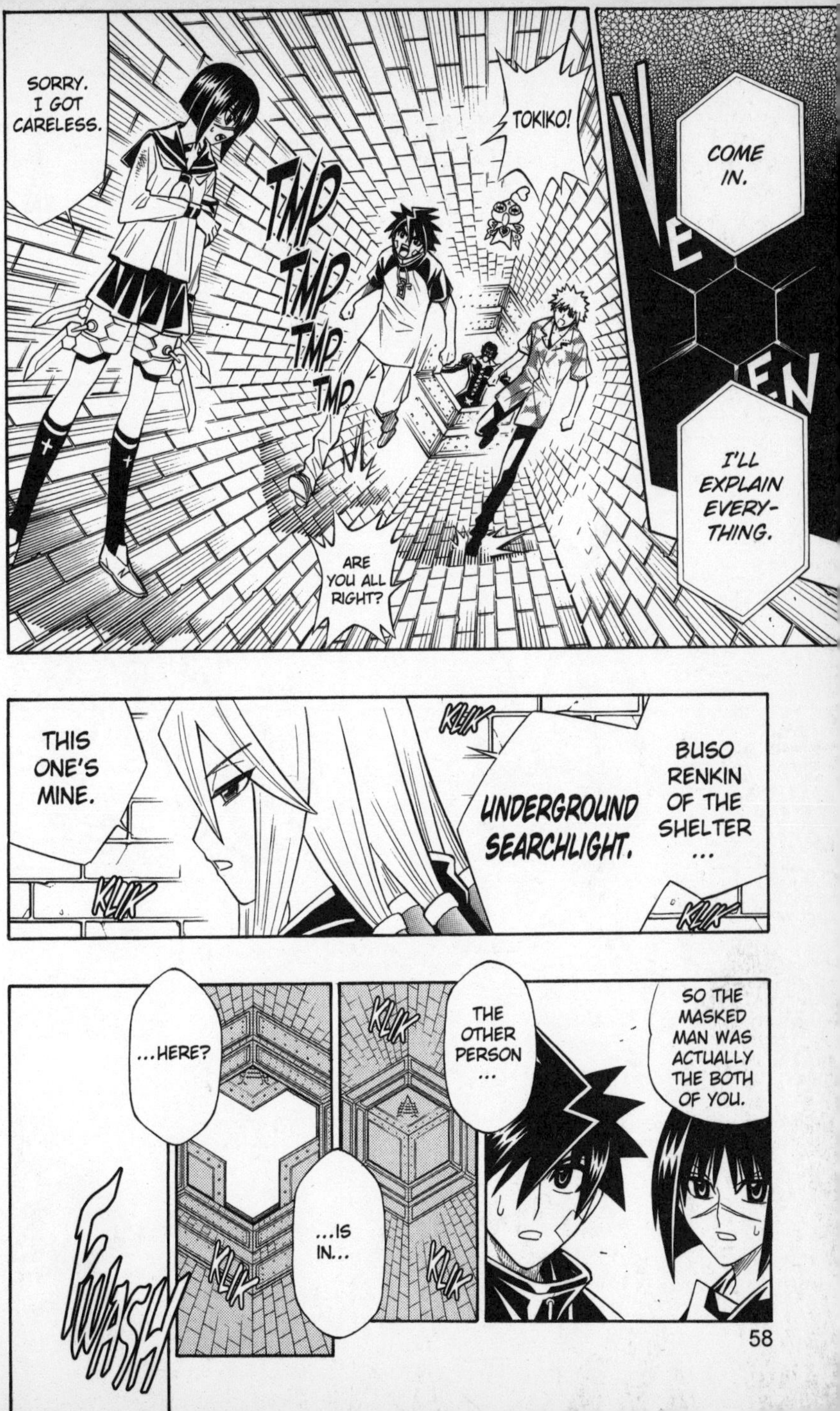

COME IN.
I'LL EXPLAIN EVERY-THING.
TOKIKO!
TMP TMP TMP TMP TMP
ARE YOU ALL RIGHT?
SORRY. I GOT CARELESS.
KLIK
BUSO RENKIN OF THE SHELTER ...
UNDERGROUND SEARCHLIGHT.
KLIK
KLIK
THIS ONE'S MINE.
SO THE MASKED MAN WAS ACTUALLY THE BOTH OF YOU.
THE OTHER PERSON ...
KLIK
KLIK
...IS IN...
KLIK
...HERE?

READ THIS WAY

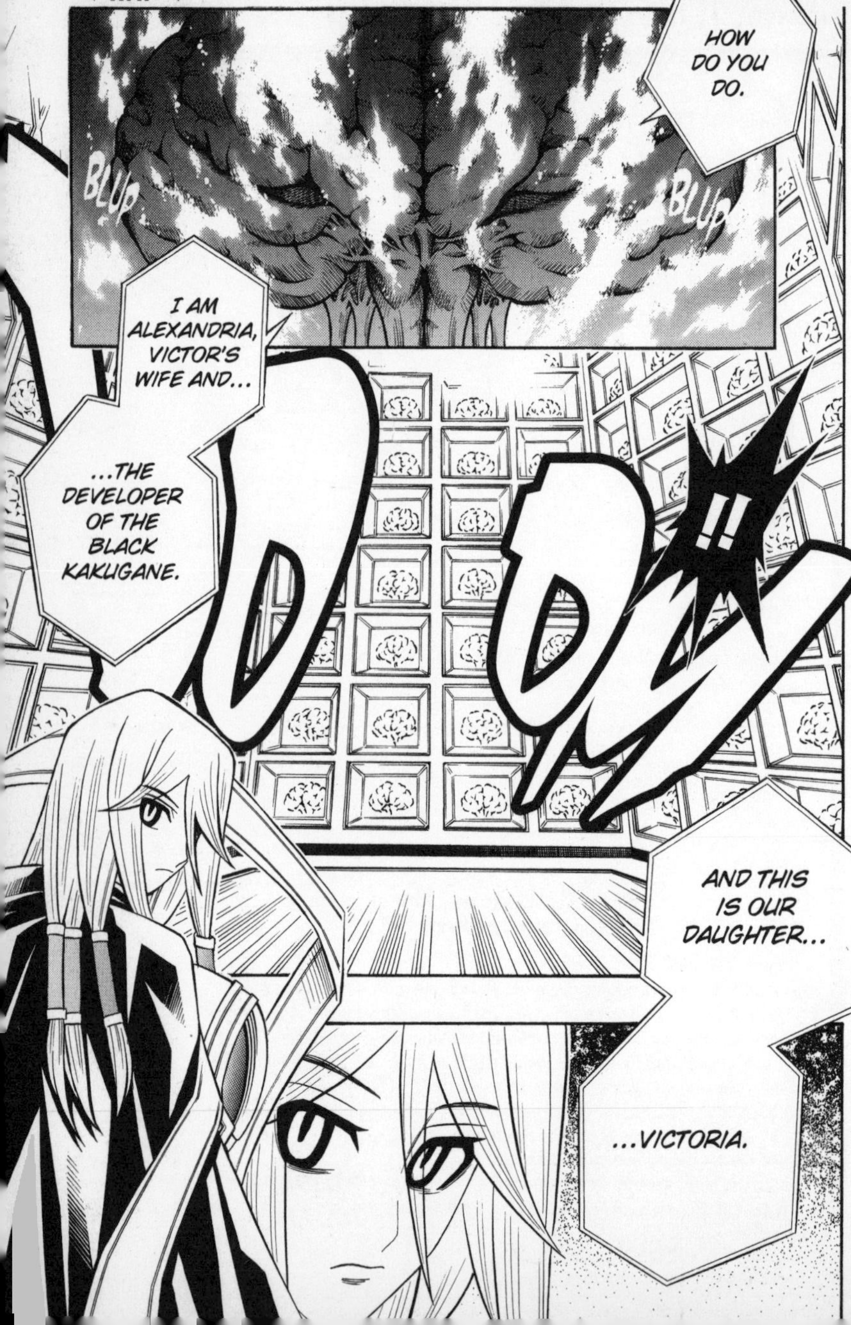
HOW DO YOU DO.
BLUP
BLUP
I AM ALEXANDRIA, VICTOR'S WIFE AND...
...THE DEVELOPER OF THE BLACK KAKUGANE.
AND THIS IS OUR DAUGHTER...
...VICTORIA.

Eat this!
A 5,100-Degree Blaze!!

Buso Renkin File No. 17

ブレイズ オブ グローリー

BLAZE OF GLORY

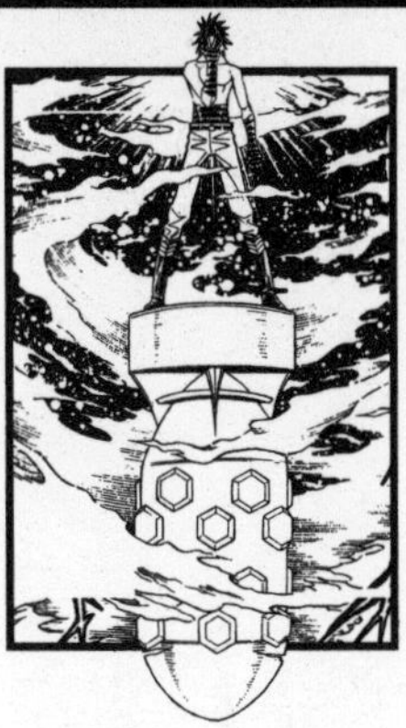

- ○ Kakugane Serial Number: XX (20)
- ○ Creator: Sekima Hiwatari
- ○ Form: Napalm
- ○ Color: Magenta
- ○ Special Abilities: · Cast explosions of napalm fire as well as merge with fire itself.
- ○ Special Traits:
  - · Able to create a blast area of 500 meters in diameter by instantly increasing the air temperature to 5,100 degrees.
  - · Able to convert body into fire, thereby nullifying any physical attack.
  - · By merging with the fire he creates, Hiwatari can control the flames like part of his own body. The more the fire spreads, the more powerful he becomes. (This is the reason he is often called the strongest of the warriors.)
  - · If the fire were extinguished while he was merged with it, Hiwatari would die instantly.

○ Author's Notes:

· I tried to imagine what power would provide the most devastating attack, and the answer I came up with was fire. But pyrokinesis alone would've been too obvious, so I added the ability to merge with fire, which allowed his power to increase with the size of the blaze. Unfortunately, I wasn't able to showcase his powers as much as I'd have liked.

· I based this Buso Renkin on an early napalm bomb and added some details. However, I didn't put too much time into the design because its powers are more important than its looks.

· I got the name for this weapon from the theme song of a Western I saw once. I think there's an American comic book by that title as well.

BLAZE OF GLORY

CHAPTER 77: THE GREAT BATTLE

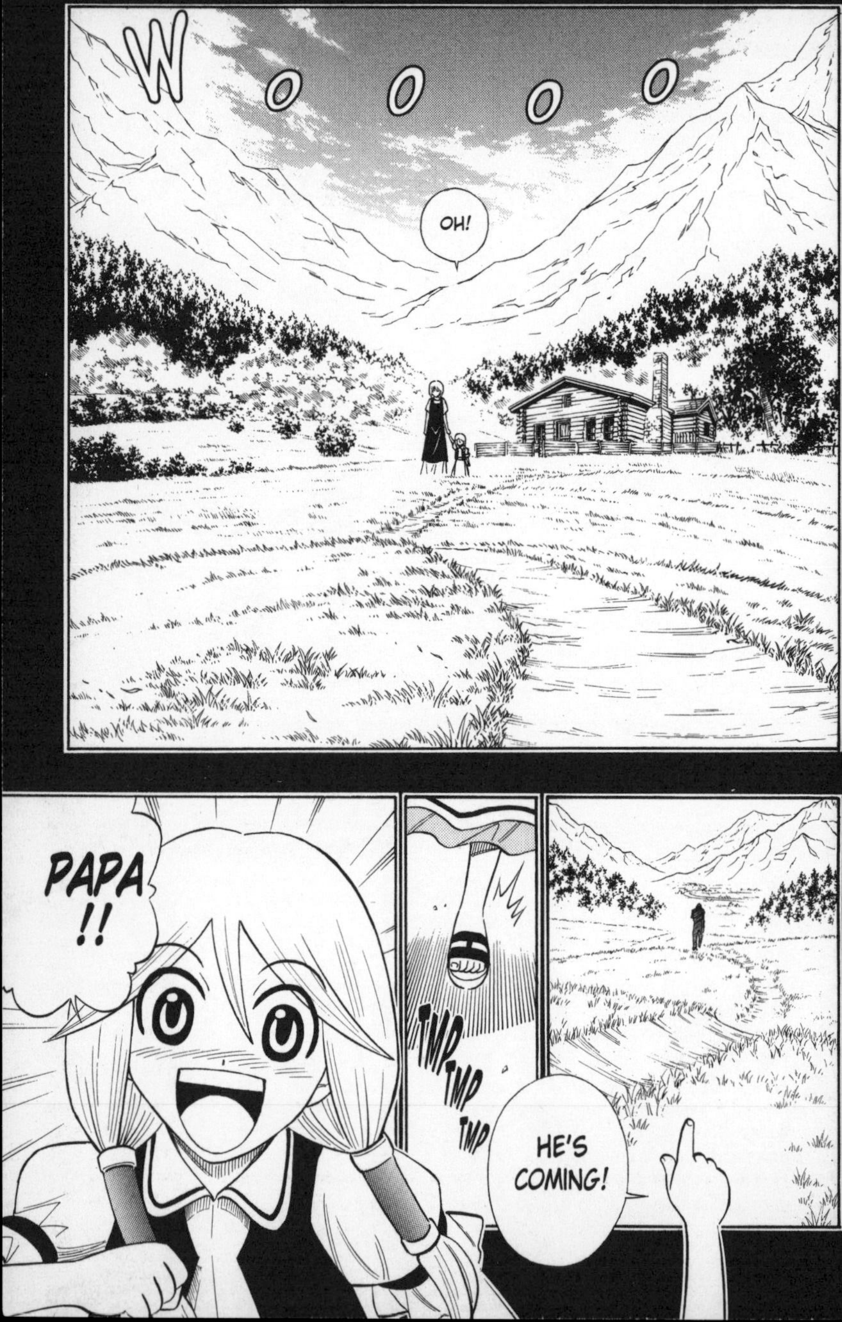
WOOOOO
OH!
TMP TMP TMP
PAPA!!
HE'S COMING!

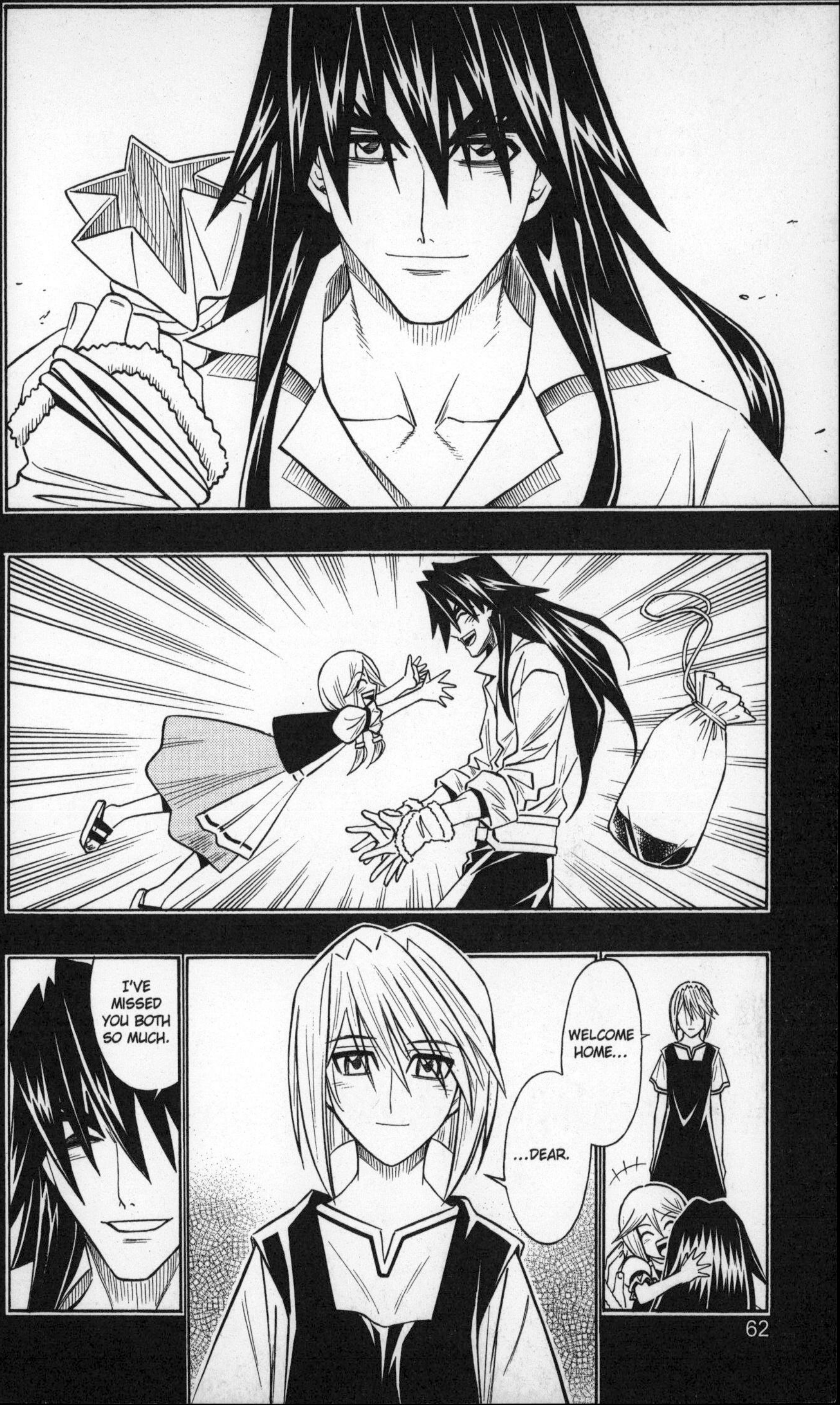
WELCOME HOME...
...DEAR.
I'VE MISSED YOU BOTH SO MUCH.

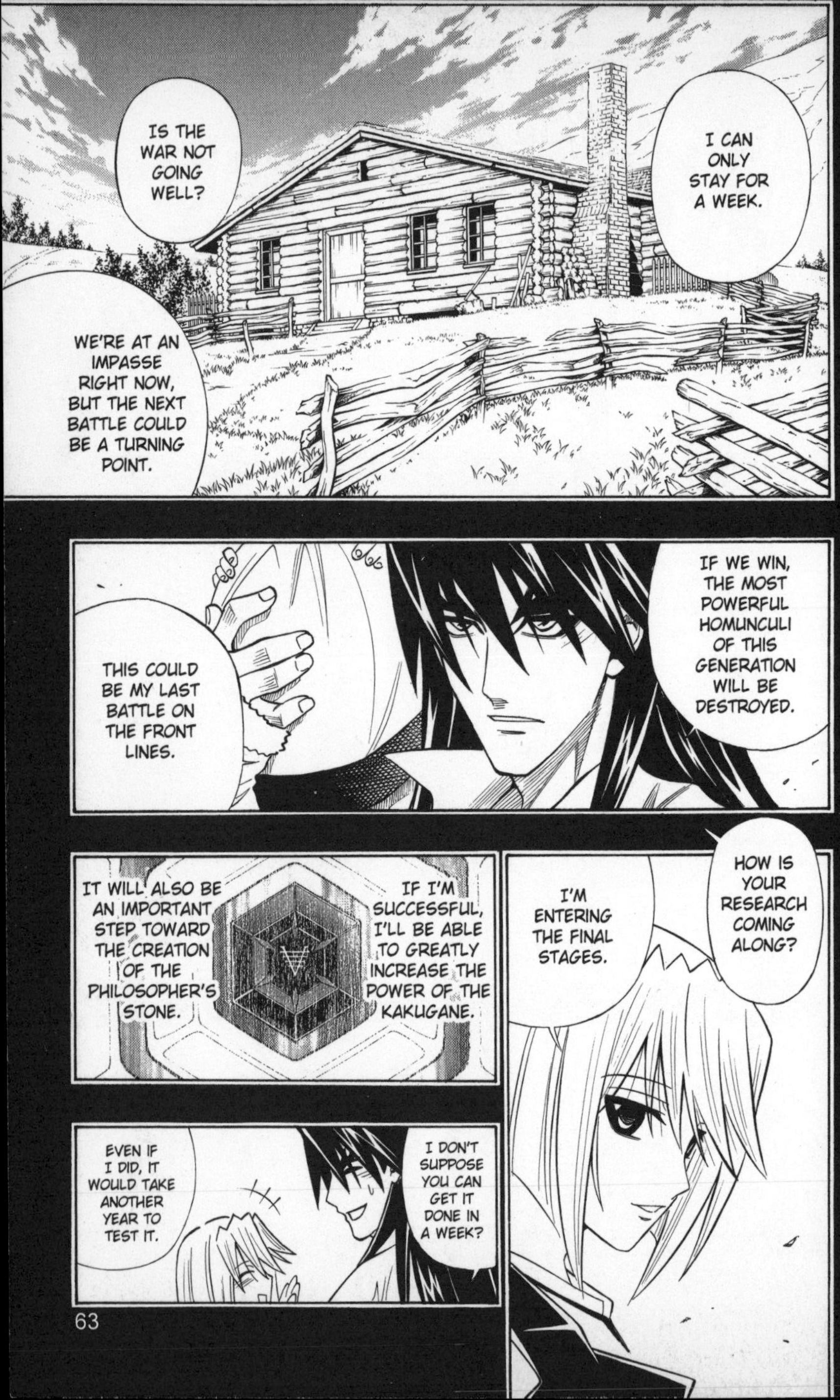
I CAN ONLY STAY FOR A WEEK.
IS THE WAR NOT GOING WELL?
WE'RE AT AN IMPASSE RIGHT NOW, BUT THE NEXT BATTLE COULD BE A TURNING POINT.
IF WE WIN, THE MOST POWERFUL HOMUNCULI OF THIS GENERATION WILL BE DESTROYED.
THIS COULD BE MY LAST BATTLE ON THE FRONT LINES.
HOW IS YOUR RESEARCH COMING ALONG?
I'M ENTERING THE FINAL STAGES.
IF I'M SUCCESSFUL, I'LL BE ABLE TO GREATLY INCREASE THE POWER OF THE KAKUGANE.
IT WILL ALSO BE AN IMPORTANT STEP TOWARD THE CREATION OF THE PHILOSOPHER'S STONE.
I DON'T SUPPOSE YOU CAN GET IT DONE IN A WEEK?
EVEN IF I DID, IT WOULD TAKE ANOTHER YEAR TO TEST IT.

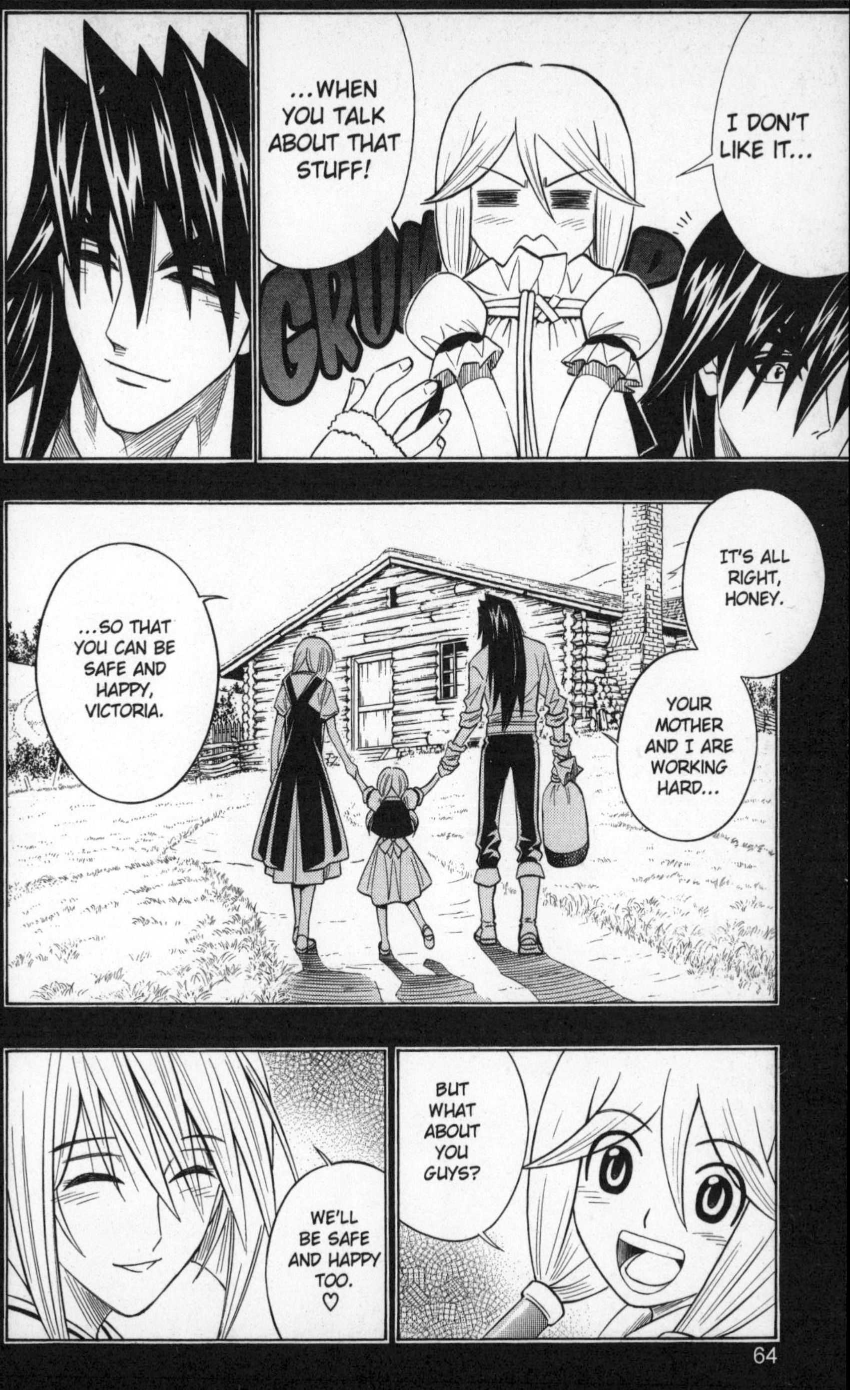
I DON'T LIKE IT...
...WHEN YOU TALK ABOUT THAT STUFF!
IT'S ALL RIGHT, HONEY.
YOUR MOTHER AND I ARE WORKING HARD...
...SO THAT YOU CAN BE SAFE AND HAPPY, VICTORIA.
BUT WHAT ABOUT YOU GUYS?
WE'LL BE SAFE AND HAPPY TOO. ♡

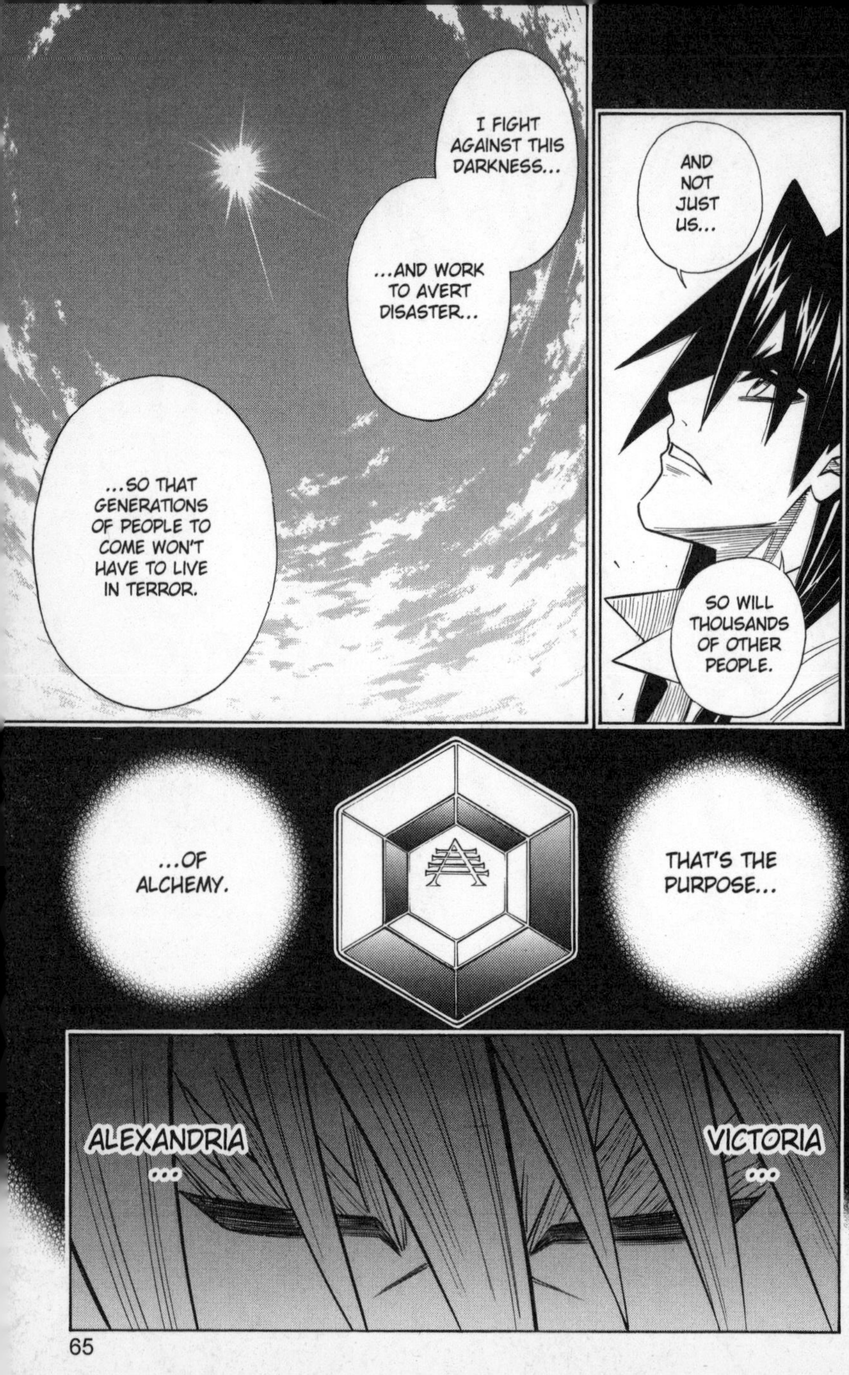
AND NOT JUST US...
SO WILL THOUSANDS OF OTHER PEOPLE.
I FIGHT AGAINST THIS DARKNESS...
...AND WORK TO AVERT DISASTER..
...SO THAT GENERATIONS OF PEOPLE TO COME WON'T HAVE TO LIVE IN TERROR.
THAT'S THE PURPOSE...
...OF ALCHEMY.
VICTORIA...
ALEXANDRIA...

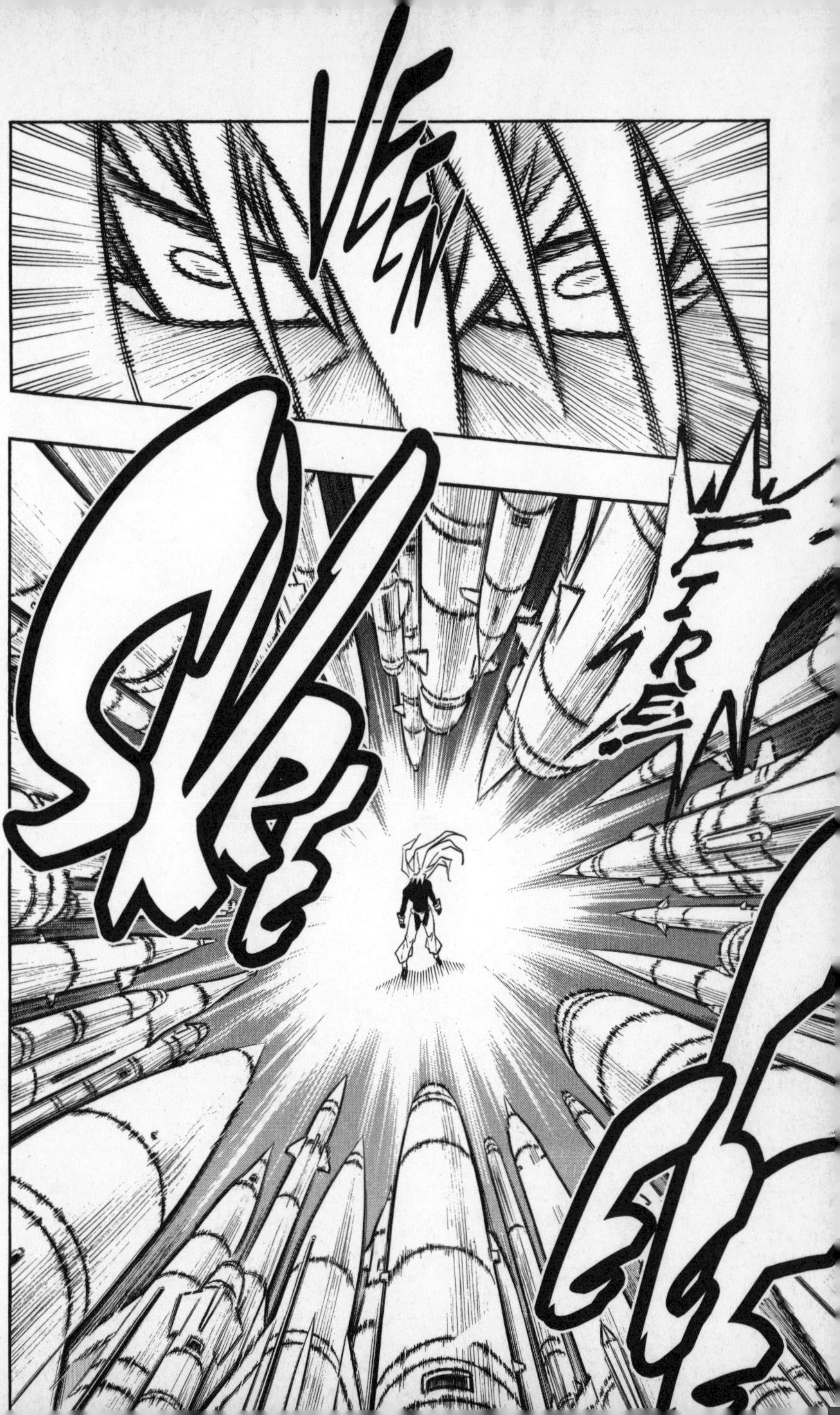
VEEN
WE FIRE...!

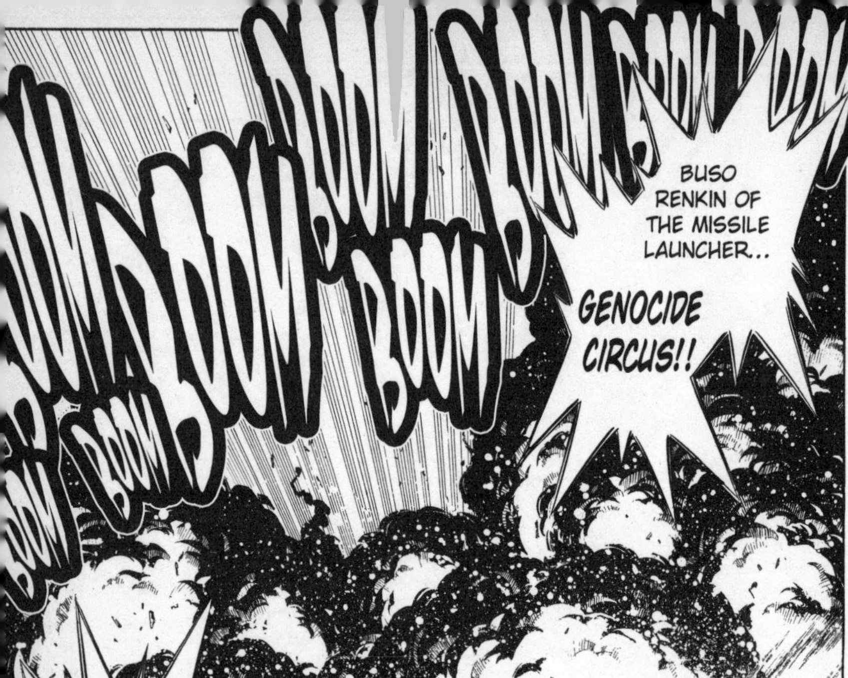
BOOM BOOM BOOM BOOM BOOM BOOM
BUSO RENKIN OF THE MISSILE LAUNCHER...
GENOCIDE CIRCUS!!
ALL THE MISSILES HIT THE TARGET!

CHAPTER 77:

THE GREAT BATTLE

伸宏
和月

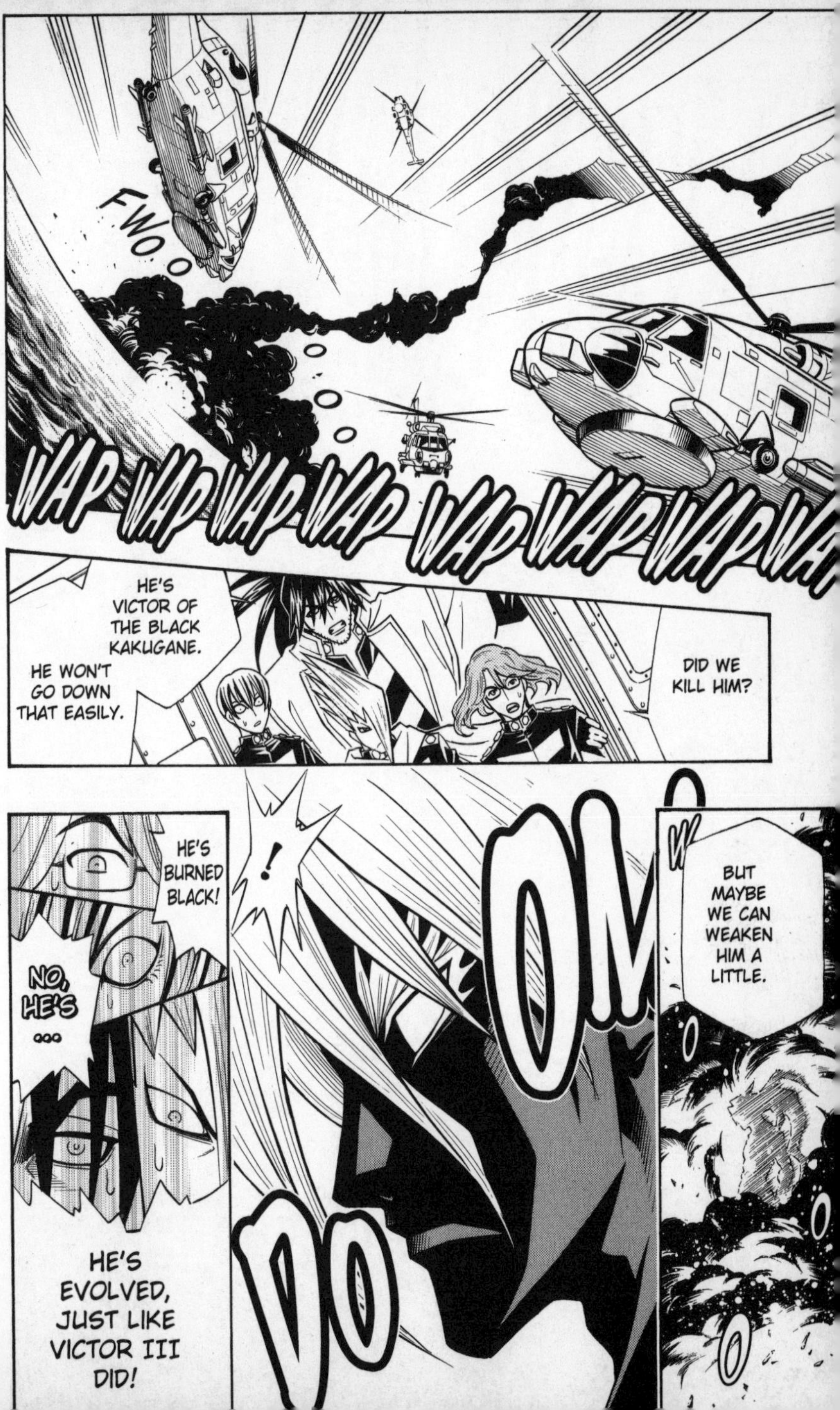
FWOOOO
WAP WAP WAP WAP WAP WAP WAP WAP
DID WE KILL HIM?
HE'S VICTOR OF THE BLACK KAKUGANE.
HE WON'T GO DOWN THAT EASILY.
BUT MAYBE WE CAN WEAKEN HIM A LITTLE.
!
DOOM
HE'S BURNED BLACK!
NO, HE'S...
HE'S EVOLVED, JUST LIKE VICTOR III DID!

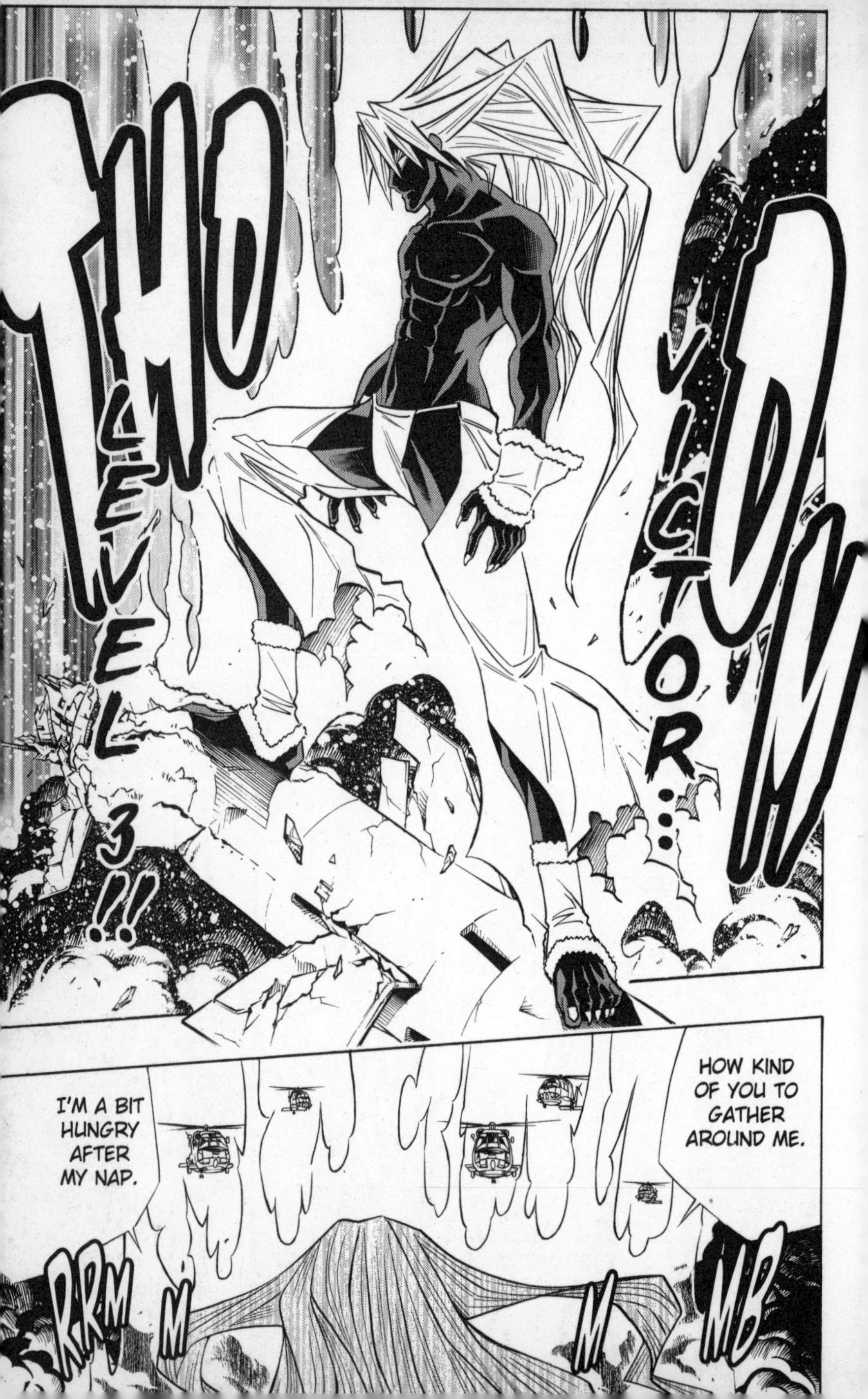
VICTOR...
LEVEL 3!!
HOW KIND OF YOU TO GATHER AROUND ME.
I'M A BIT HUNGRY AFTER MY NAP.

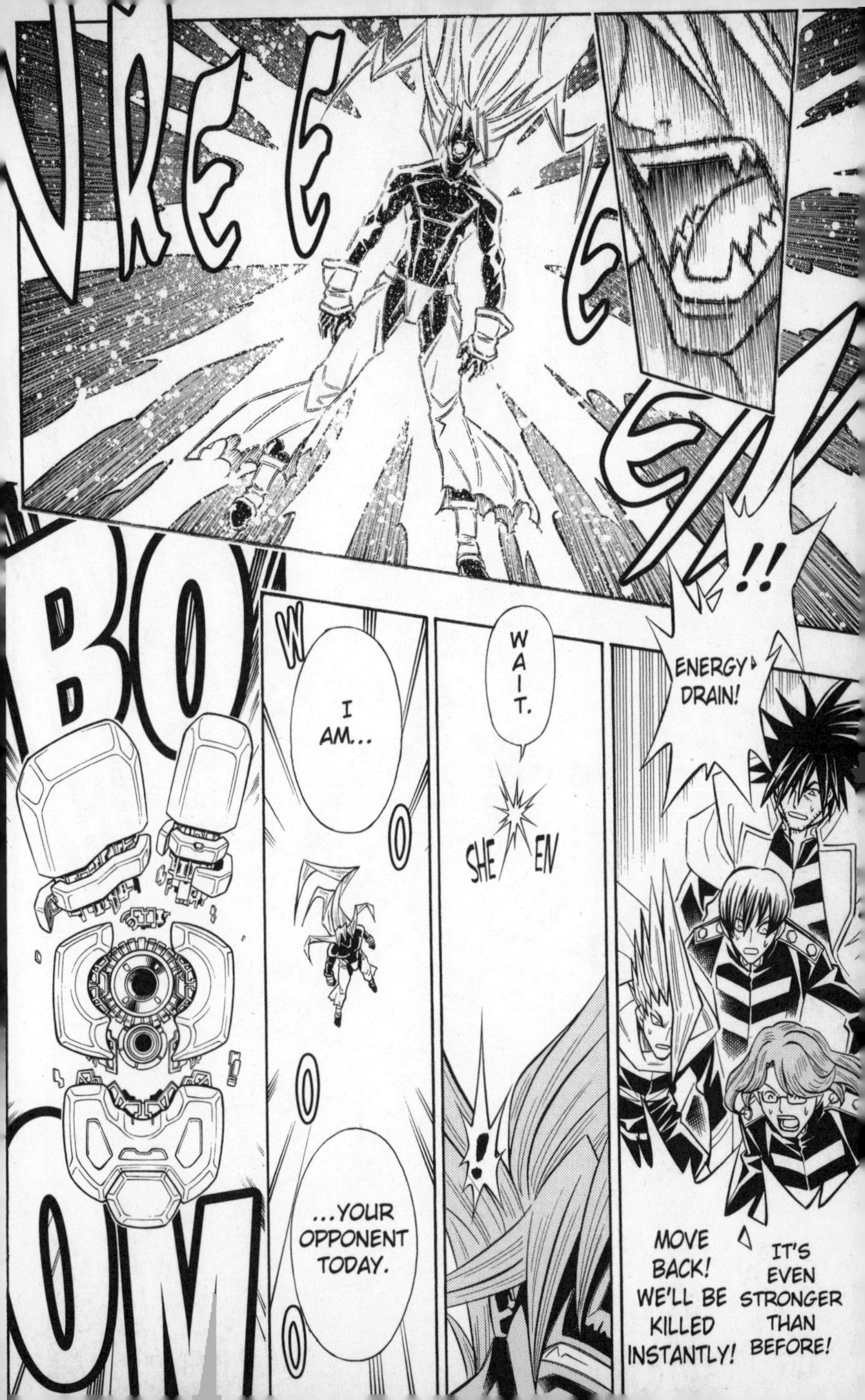
!!
ENERGY DRAIN!
IT'S EVEN STRONGER THAN BEFORE!
MOVE BACK! WE'LL BE KILLED INSTANTLY!
WAIT.
SHEEN
!
I AM...
...YOUR OPPONENT TODAY.
BOOM

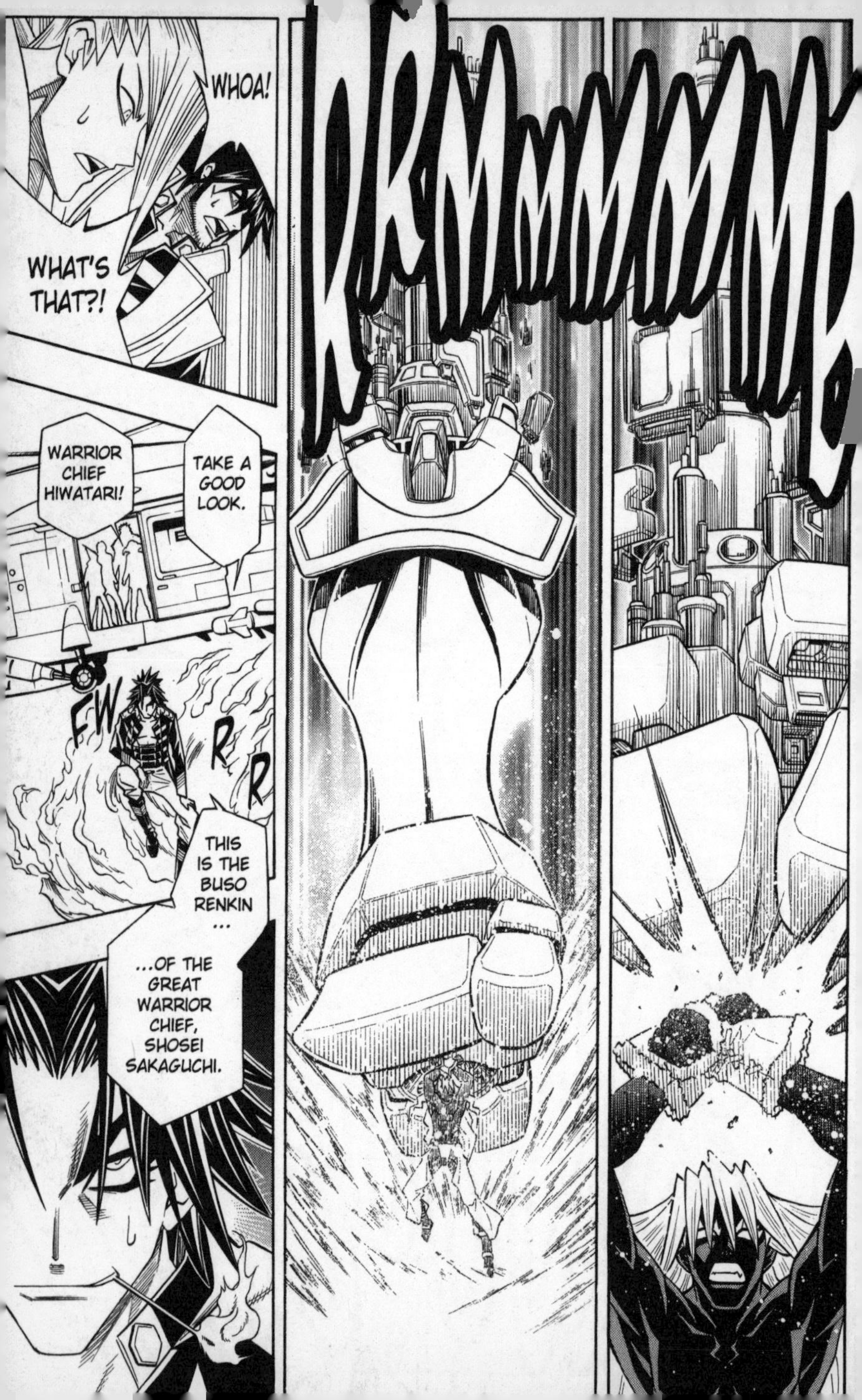
WHOA!
WHAT'S THAT?!
TAKE A GOOD LOOK.
WARRIOR CHIEF HIWATARI!
FWRR
THIS IS THE BUSO RENKIN...
...OF THE GREAT WARRIOR CHIEF, SHOSEI SAKAGUCHI.

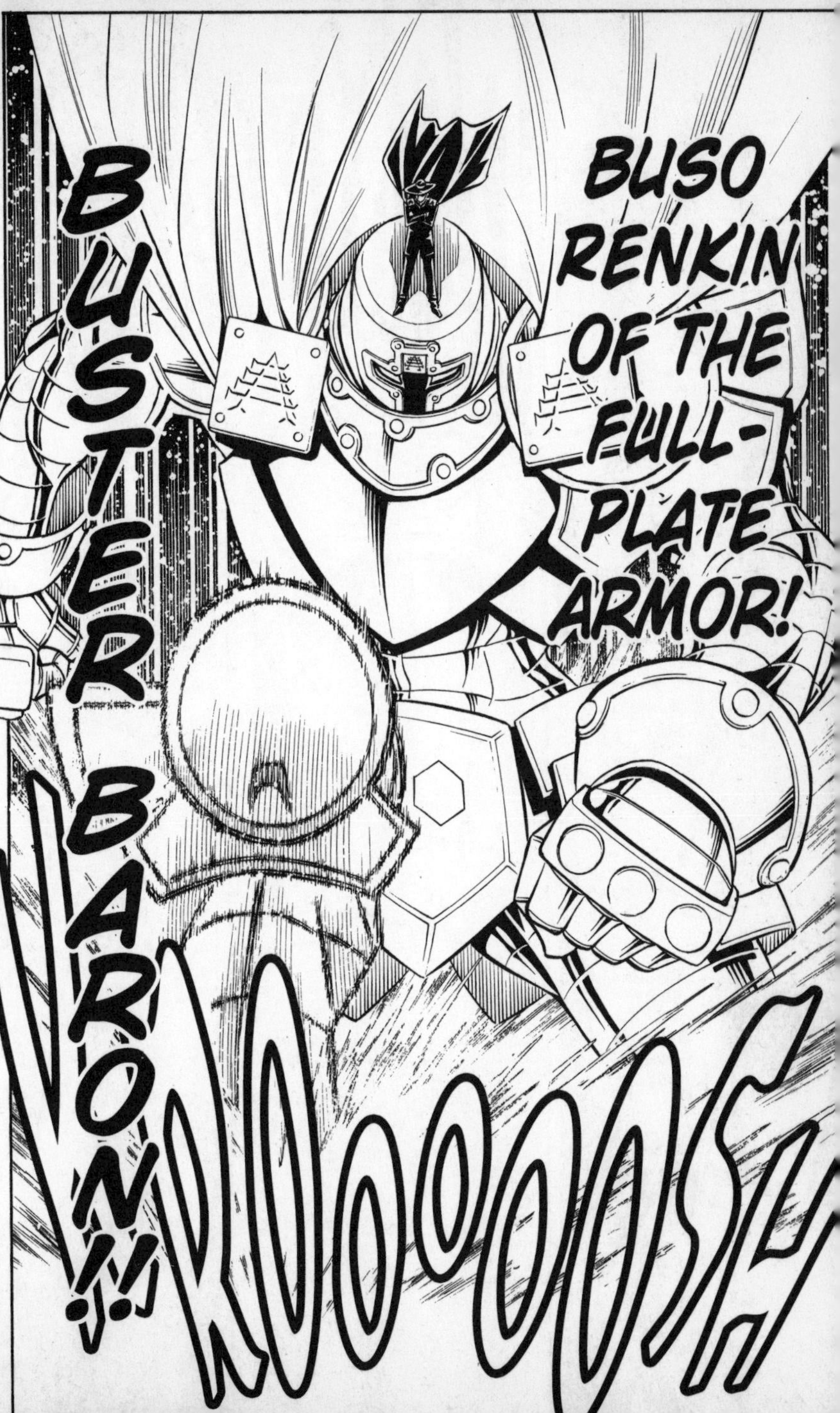
BUSO RENKIN OF THE FULL-PLATE ARMOR!
BUSTER BARON!!
VROOOOOSH

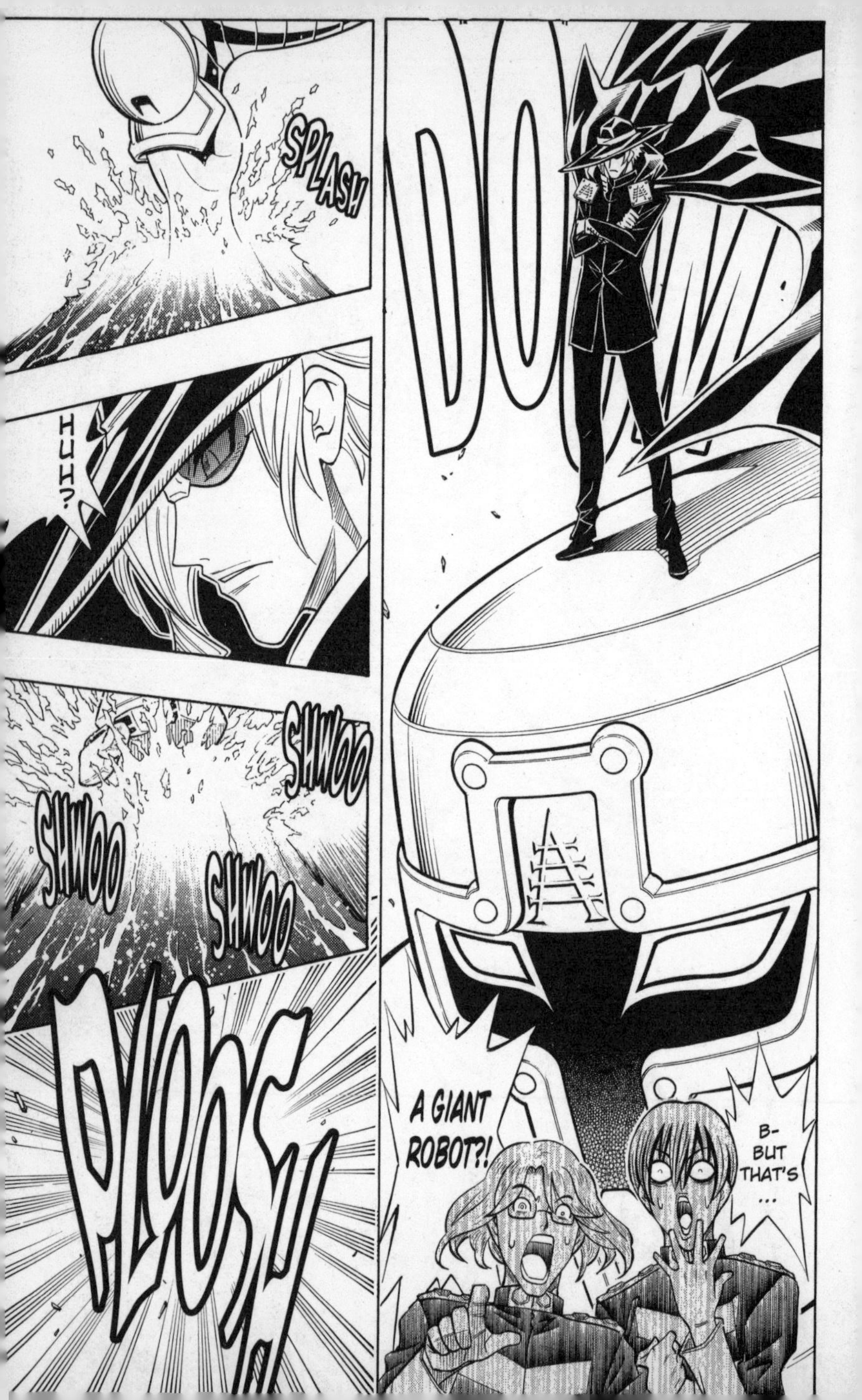
A GIANT ROBOT?!
B-BUT THAT'S...
SPLASH
HUH?
SHWOO
SHWOO
SHWOO

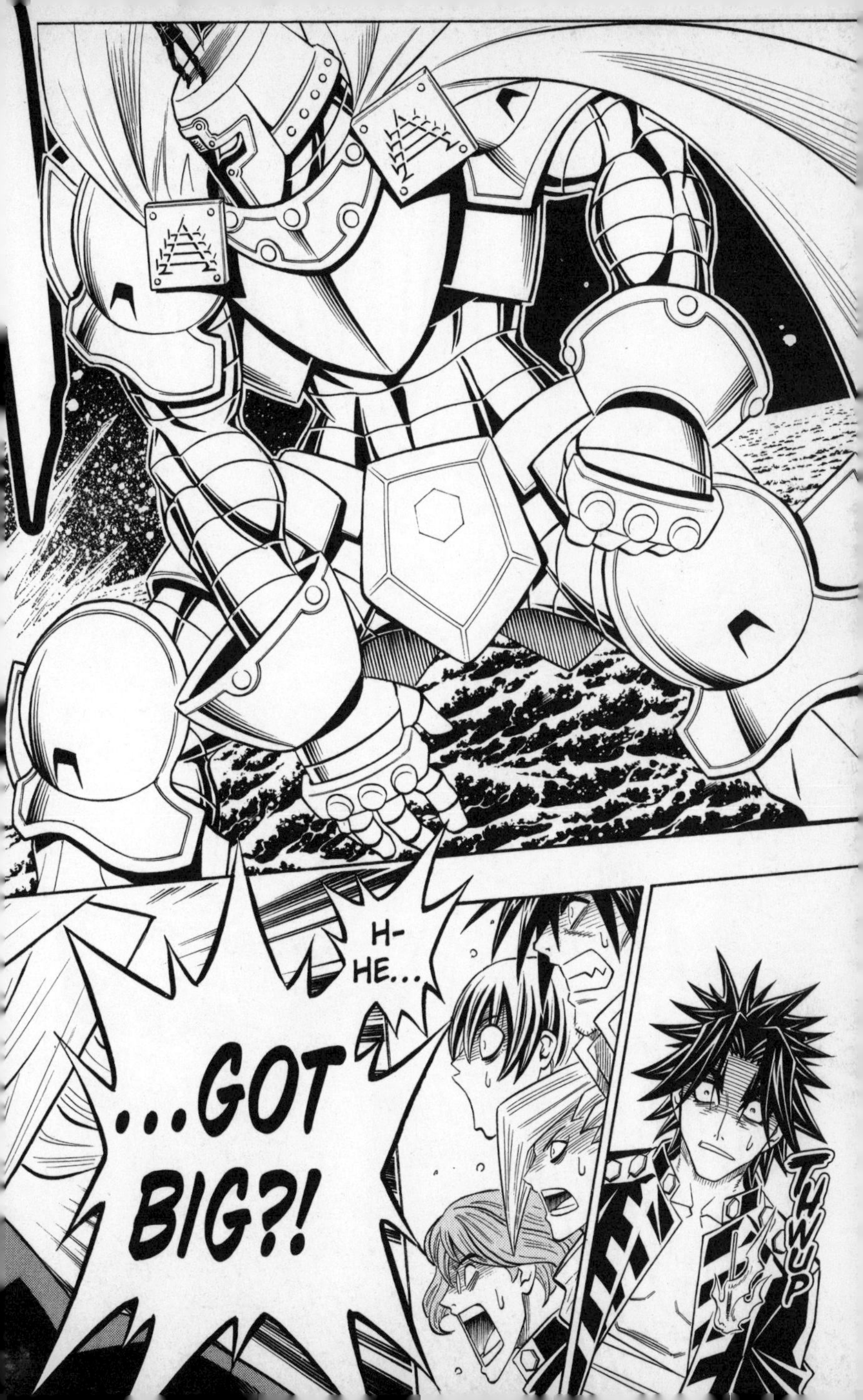
H- HE...
...GOT BIG?!
THWUP

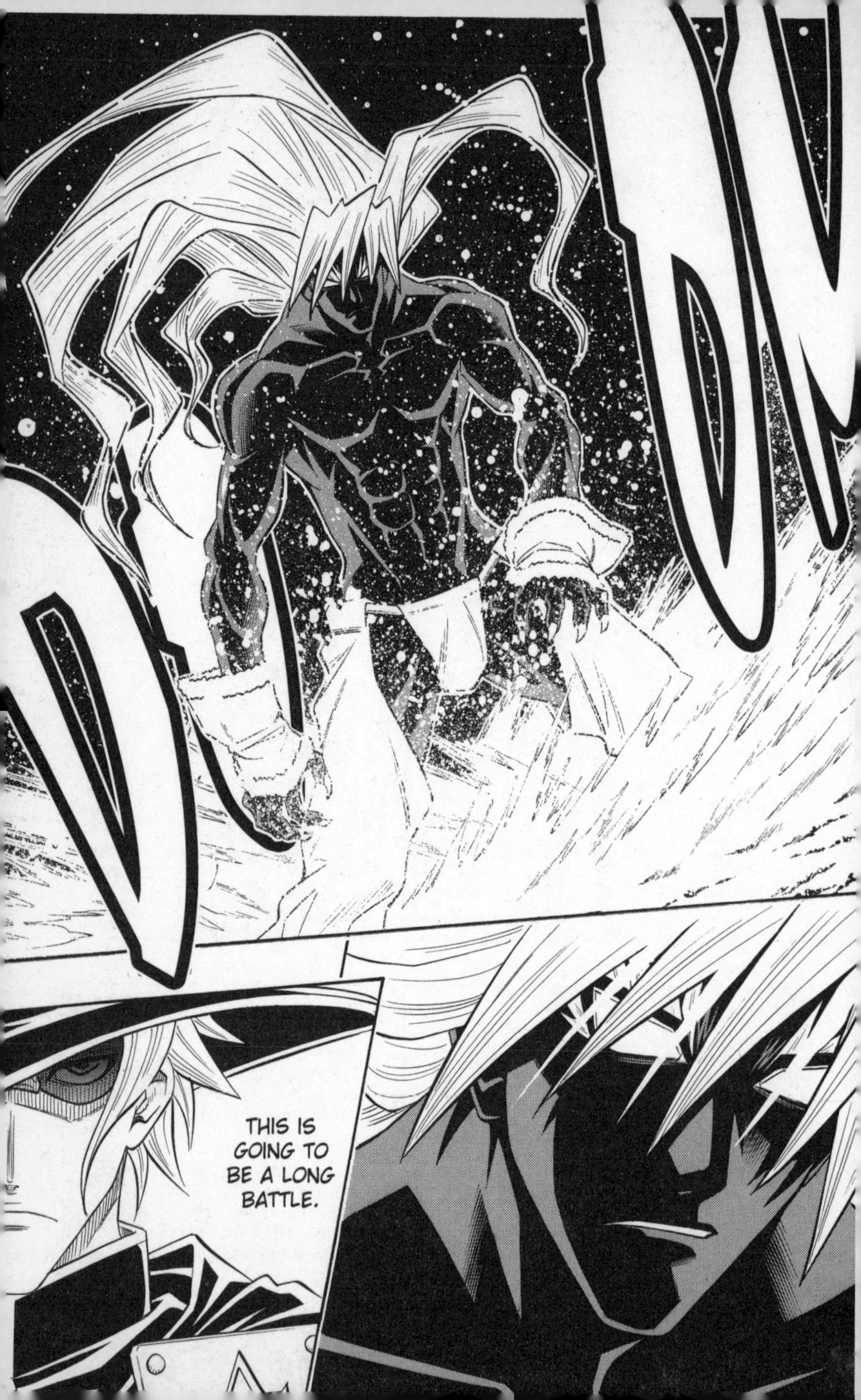
THIS IS GOING TO BE A LONG BATTLE.

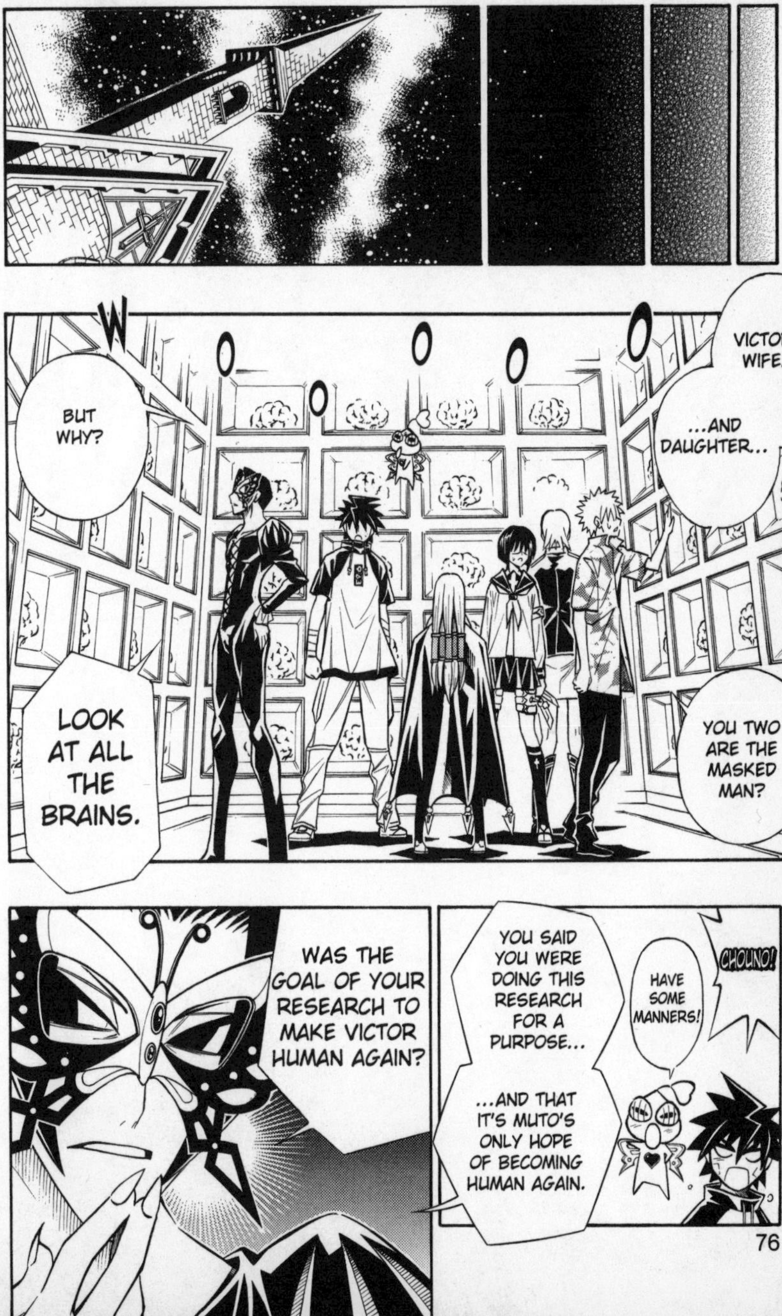
VICTOR'S WIFE...
...AND DAUGHTER...
YOU TWO ARE THE MASKED MAN?
WOOOOOO
BUT WHY?
LOOK AT ALL THE BRAINS.
CHOUNO!
HAVE SOME MANNERS!
YOU SAID YOU WERE DOING THIS RESEARCH FOR A PURPOSE...
...AND THAT IT'S MUTO'S ONLY HOPE OF BECOMING HUMAN AGAIN.
WAS THE GOAL OF YOUR RESEARCH TO MAKE VICTOR HUMAN AGAIN?

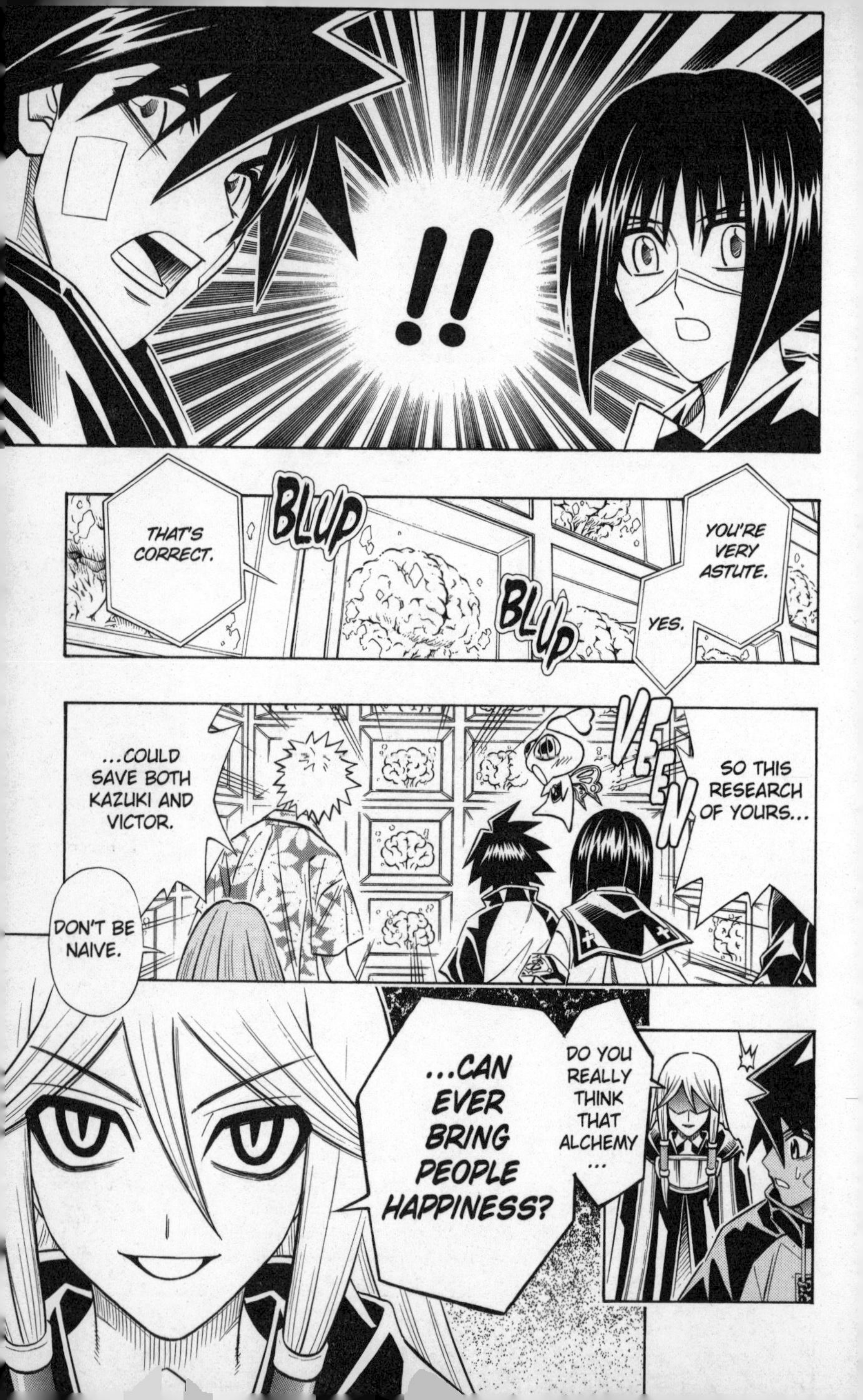
!!
YOU'RE VERY ASTUTE.
YES.
BLUP
BLUP
THAT'S CORRECT.
VEEN
SO THIS RESEARCH OF YOURS...
...COULD SAVE BOTH KAZUKI AND VICTOR.
DON'T BE NAIVE.
DO YOU REALLY THINK THAT ALCHEMY ...
...CAN EVER BRING PEOPLE HAPPINESS?

- Height: 177 cm; Weight: 70 kg
- Born: August 6; Leo; Blood Type: B; Age: 27
- Likes: Cigarettes, BBQ, absurdity
- Dislikes: Hypocrisy, absurdity
- Hobby: Playing with fire
- Special Ability: Able to carry on a casual conversation with a cigarette in his mouth
- Affiliations: Warrior Chief in the Alchemist Army, Re-Extermination Squad Leader

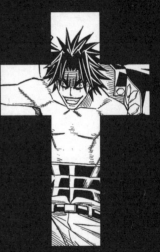

Character File No. 32
SEKIMA HIWATARI

Author's Notes

- I needed to come up with an adversary for Kazuki and Tokiko when they were on the run. He had to be really tough and someone they couldn't reason with. Then I realized that he would probably have to fight Captain Bravo too, so I decided to make Hiwatari Bravo's former teammate. Once I got the dramatic aspects of the story worked out, this is what I ended up with.
- I wanted to focus more on Hiwatari's personality—on why he views the world as absurd while fighting to save it—but the length of the series and my own limitations made it impossible.
- Hiwatari's character became clearer to me as I went along. I think I'll have to explore this personality type in more detail someday.
- I improvised his design. I started with a slightly angled eye, thick eyebrows, a thick outline under the eyes, big pupils, and sharp-fanged teeth to give him the bad guy look. I made his hair look a little like the cropped coifs of a period piece, but I wanted to do something a little different from what I'd done in the past. So this is what I came up with. I'm not sure how I feel about it yet. I think it's a work in progress but I enjoy trying new things.

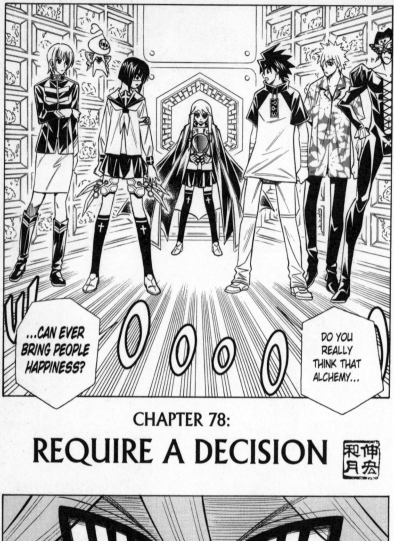

...CAN EVER BRING PEOPLE HAPPINESS?

DO YOU REALLY THINK THAT ALCHEMY...

CHAPTER 78:
REQUIRE A DECISION

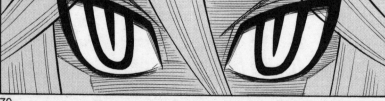

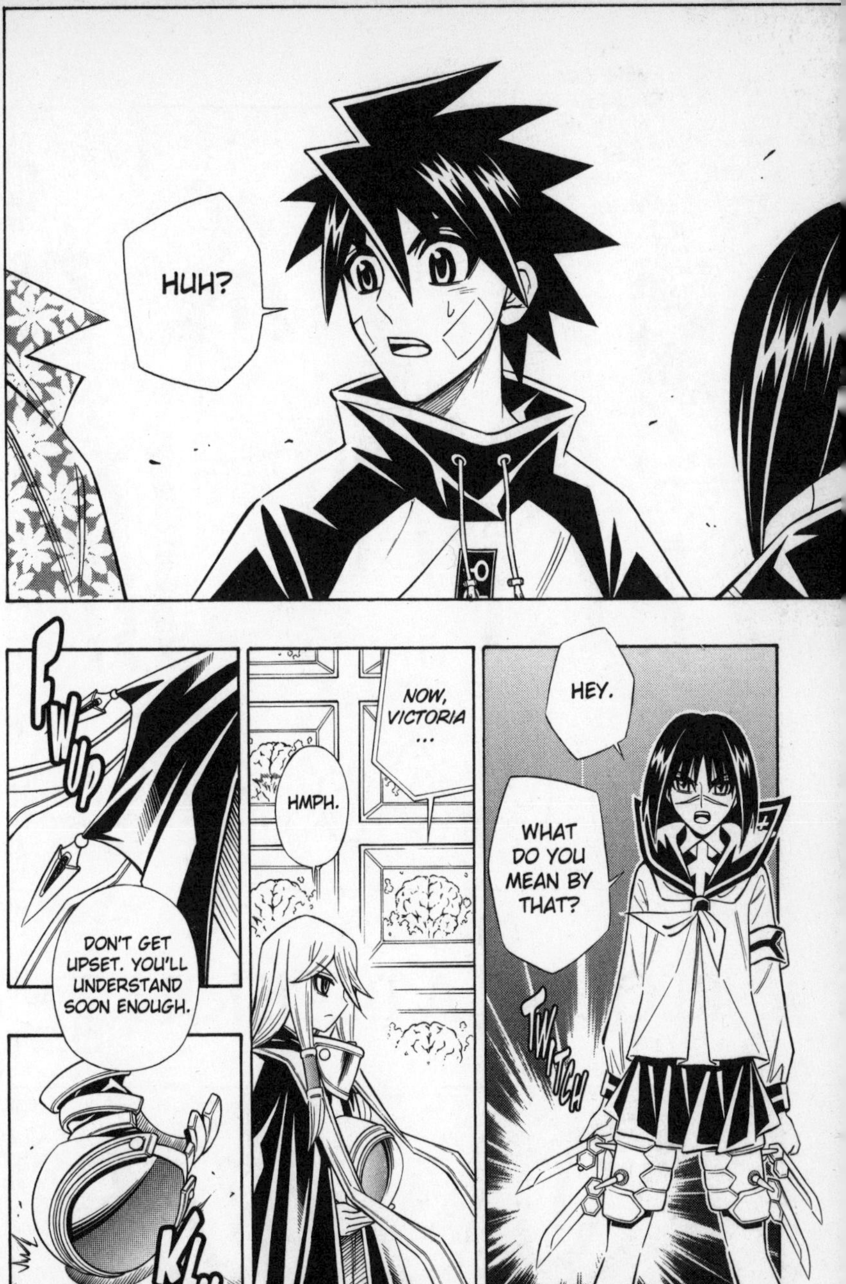
HUH?
HEY.
WHAT DO YOU MEAN BY THAT?
TWITCH
NOW, VICTORIA ...
HMPH.
FWUP
DON'T GET UPSET. YOU'LL UNDERSTAND SOON ENOUGH.
KLUNK

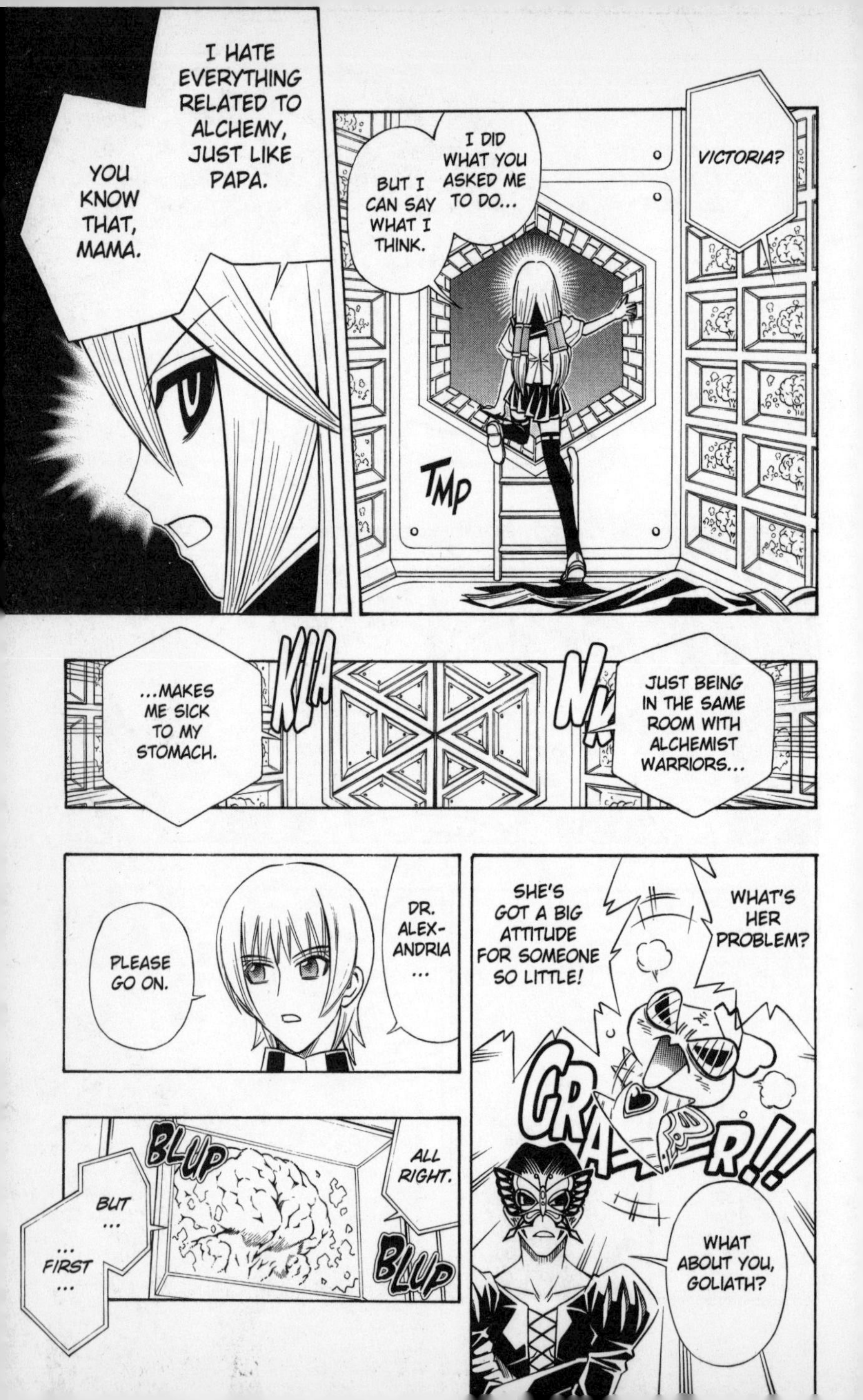
VICTORIA?
I DID WHAT YOU ASKED ME TO DO...
BUT I CAN SAY WHAT I THINK.
TMP
I HATE EVERYTHING RELATED TO ALCHEMY, JUST LIKE PAPA.
YOU KNOW THAT, MAMA.
JUST BEING IN THE SAME ROOM WITH ALCHEMIST WARRIORS...
KIA
...MAKES ME SICK TO MY STOMACH.
WHAT'S HER PROBLEM?
SHE'S GOT A BIG ATTITUDE FOR SOMEONE SO LITTLE!
GRAR!!
WHAT ABOUT YOU, GOLIATH?
DR. ALEX-ANDRIA...
PLEASE GO ON.
ALL RIGHT.
BLUP
BLUP
BUT...
...FIRST...

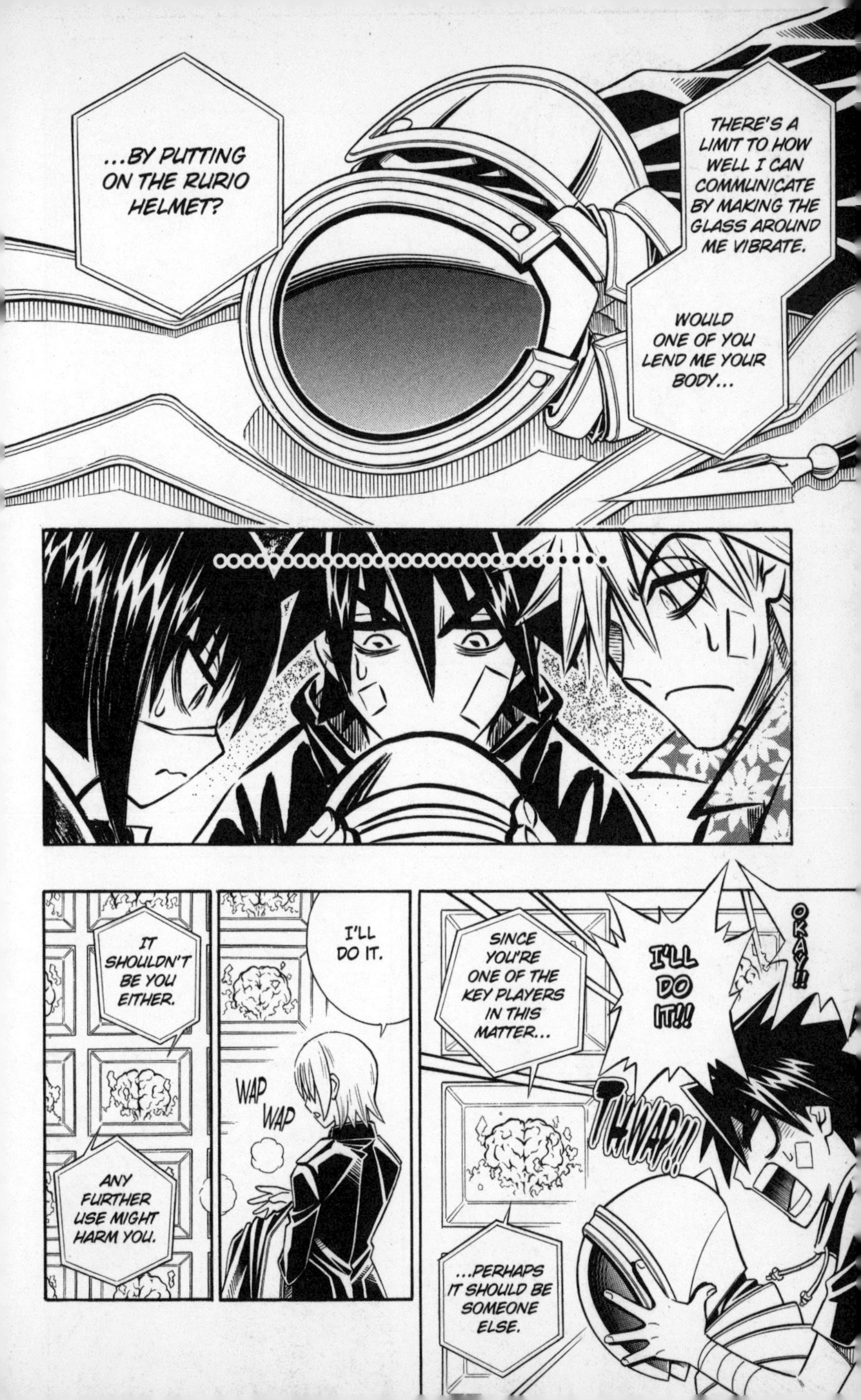
THERE'S A LIMIT TO HOW WELL I CAN COMMUNICATE BY MAKING THE GLASS AROUND ME VIBRATE.
WOULD ONE OF YOU LEND ME YOUR BODY...
...BY PUTTING ON THE RURIO HELMET?
OOOOOOOOOOOOOOOOOOOOOOOOOOOOOOO.....
OKAY!!
I'LL DO IT!!
THWAP!!
SINCE YOU'RE ONE OF THE KEY PLAYERS IN THIS MATTER...
...PERHAPS IT SHOULD BE SOMEONE ELSE.
I'LL DO IT.
WAP
WAP
IT SHOULDN'T BE YOU EITHER.
ANY FURTHER USE MIGHT HARM YOU.

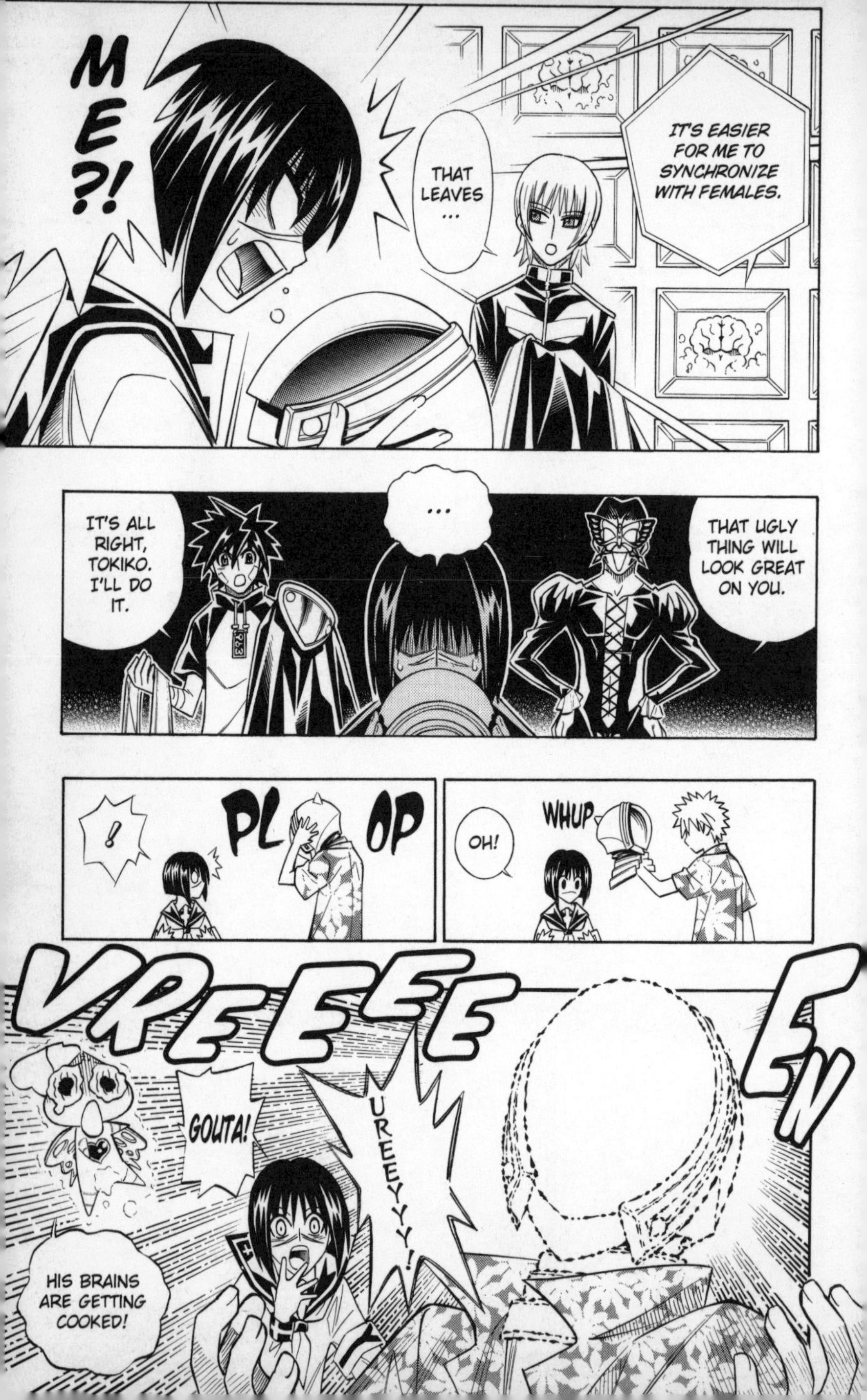
IT'S EASIER FOR ME TO SYNCHRONIZE WITH FEMALES.
THAT LEAVES ...
ME?!
THAT UGLY THING WILL LOOK GREAT ON YOU.
...
IT'S ALL RIGHT, TOKIKO. I'LL DO IT.
WHUP
OH!
PLOP
!
VREEEEEEN
UREEYYY!
GOUTA!
HIS BRAINS ARE GETTING COOKED!

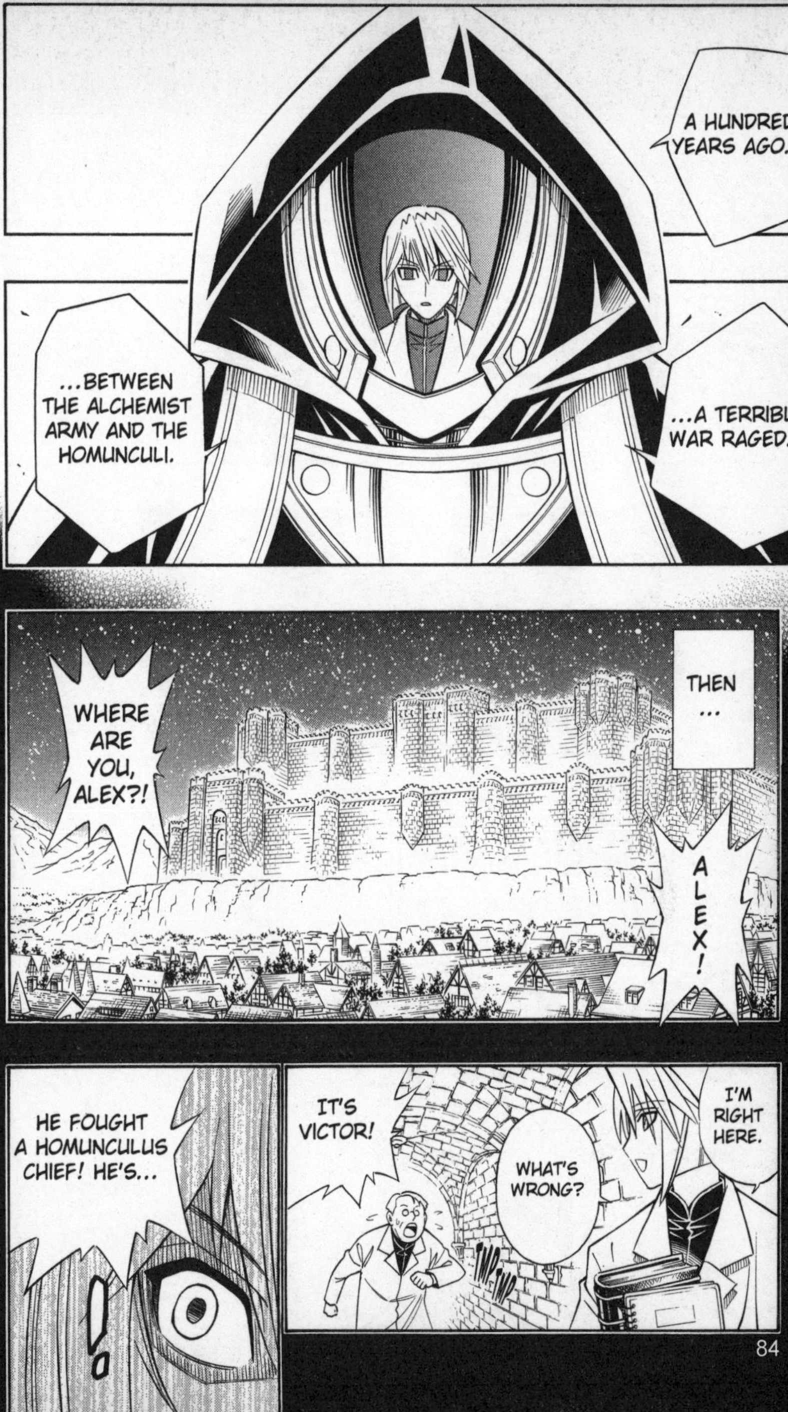
A HUNDRED YEARS AGO...
...A TERRIBLE WAR RAGED...
...BETWEEN THE ALCHEMIST ARMY AND THE HOMUNCULI.
THEN ...
ALEX!
WHERE ARE YOU, ALEX?!
I'M RIGHT HERE.
WHAT'S WRONG?
IT'S VICTOR!
TMP TMP
HE FOUGHT A HOMUNCULUS CHIEF! HE'S...
!

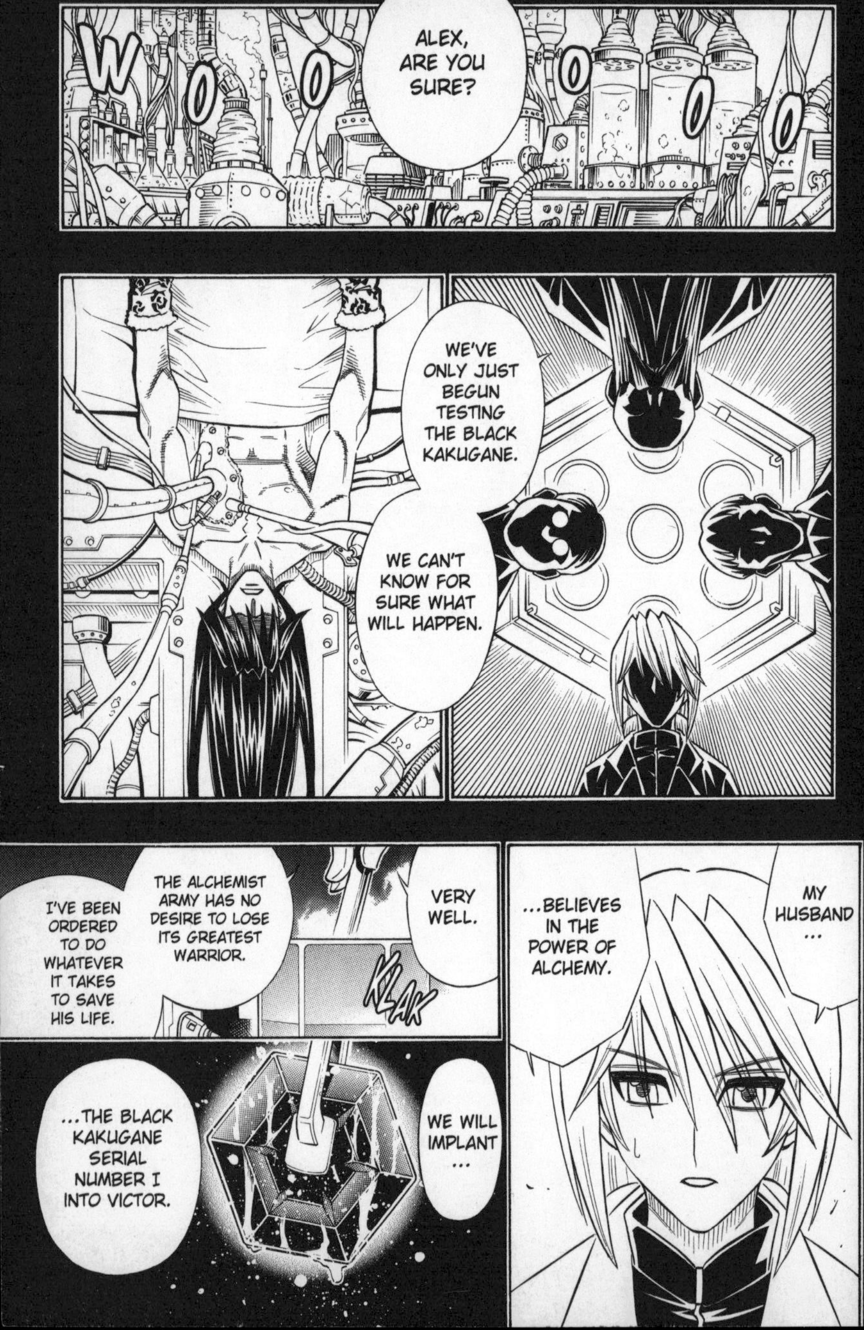

WOOOOOOO
ALEX, ARE YOU SURE?
WE'VE ONLY JUST BEGUN TESTING THE BLACK KAKUGANE.
WE CAN'T KNOW FOR SURE WHAT WILL HAPPEN.
MY HUSBAND ...
...BELIEVES IN THE POWER OF ALCHEMY.
VERY WELL.
THE ALCHEMIST ARMY HAS NO DESIRE TO LOSE ITS GREATEST WARRIOR.
I'VE BEEN ORDERED TO DO WHATEVER IT TAKES TO SAVE HIS LIFE.
KLAK
WE WILL IMPLANT ...
...THE BLACK KAKUGANE SERIAL NUMBER I INTO VICTOR.

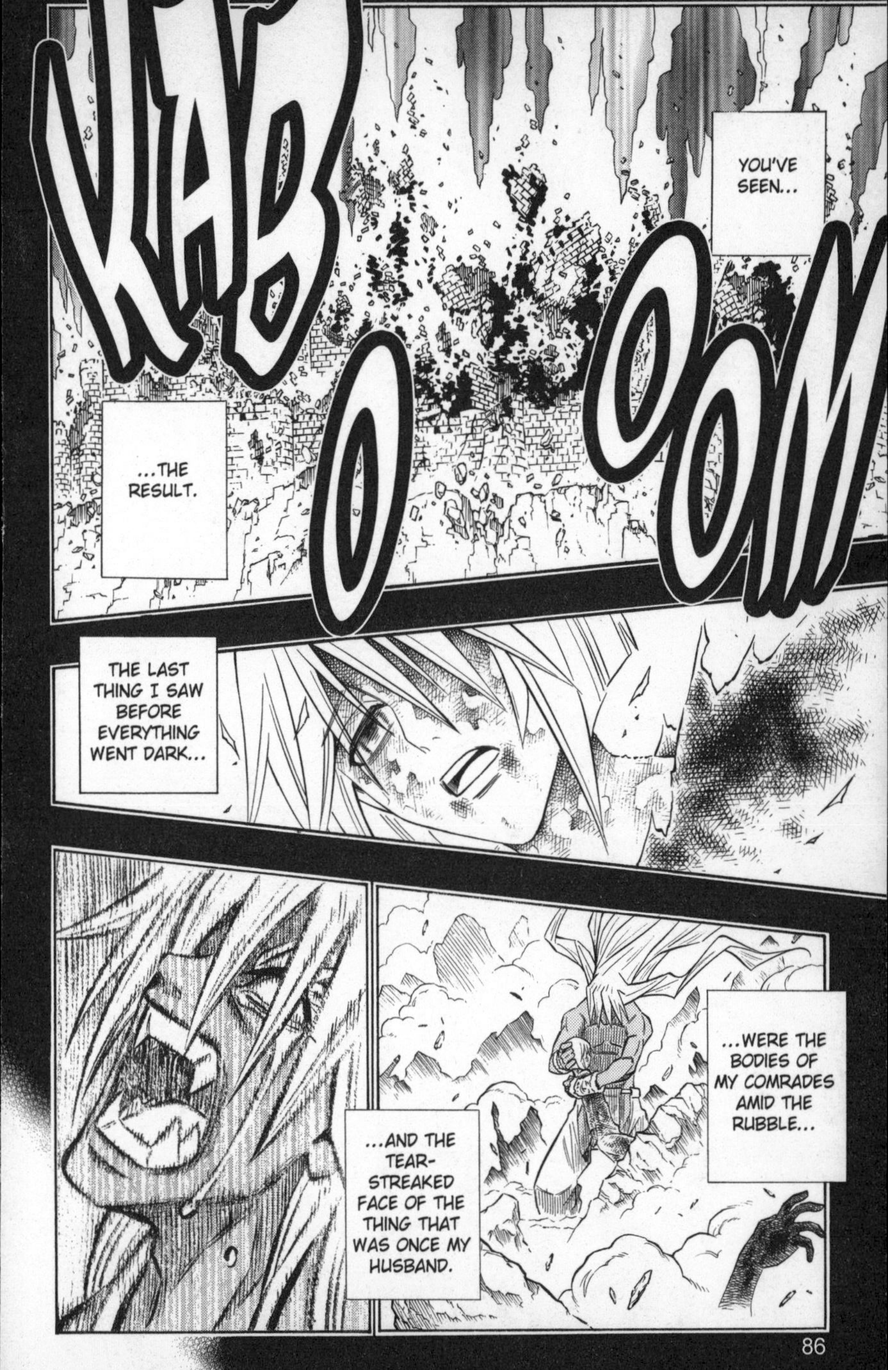
YOU'VE SEEN...
KABOOOM
...THE RESULT.
THE LAST THING I SAW BEFORE EVERYTHING WENT DARK...
...WERE THE BODIES OF MY COMRADES AMID THE RUBBLE...
...AND THE TEAR-STREAKED FACE OF THE THING THAT WAS ONCE MY HUSBAND.

READ THIS WAY

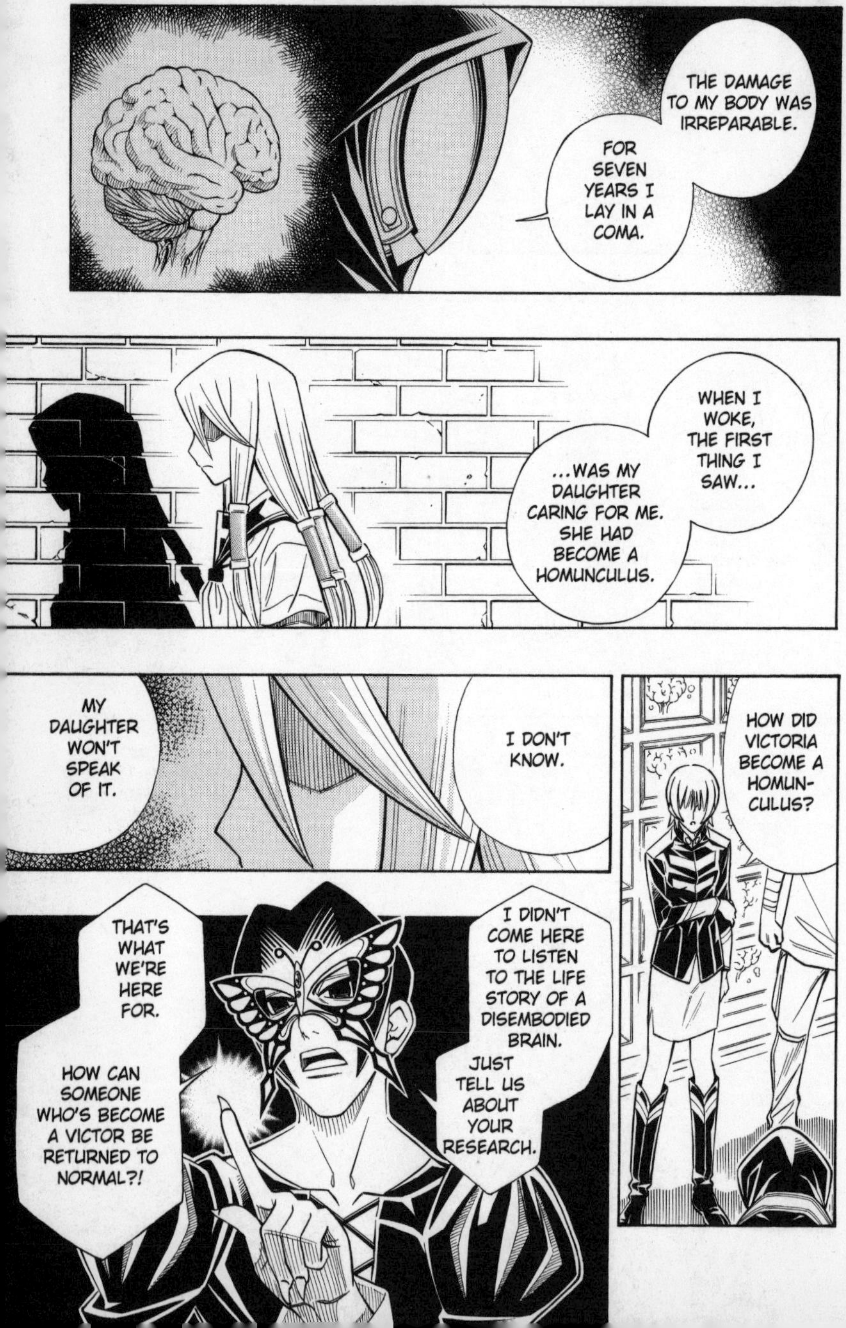
THE DAMAGE TO MY BODY WAS IRREPARABLE.
FOR SEVEN YEARS I LAY IN A COMA.
WHEN I WOKE, THE FIRST THING I SAW...
...WAS MY DAUGHTER CARING FOR ME. SHE HAD BECOME A HOMUNCULUS.
HOW DID VICTORIA BECOME A HOMUN-CULUS?
I DON'T KNOW.
MY DAUGHTER WON'T SPEAK OF IT.
I DIDN'T COME HERE TO LISTEN TO THE LIFE STORY OF A DISEMBODIED BRAIN.
JUST TELL US ABOUT YOUR RESEARCH.
THAT'S WHAT WE'RE HERE FOR.
HOW CAN SOMEONE WHO'S BECOME A VICTOR BE RETURNED TO NORMAL?!

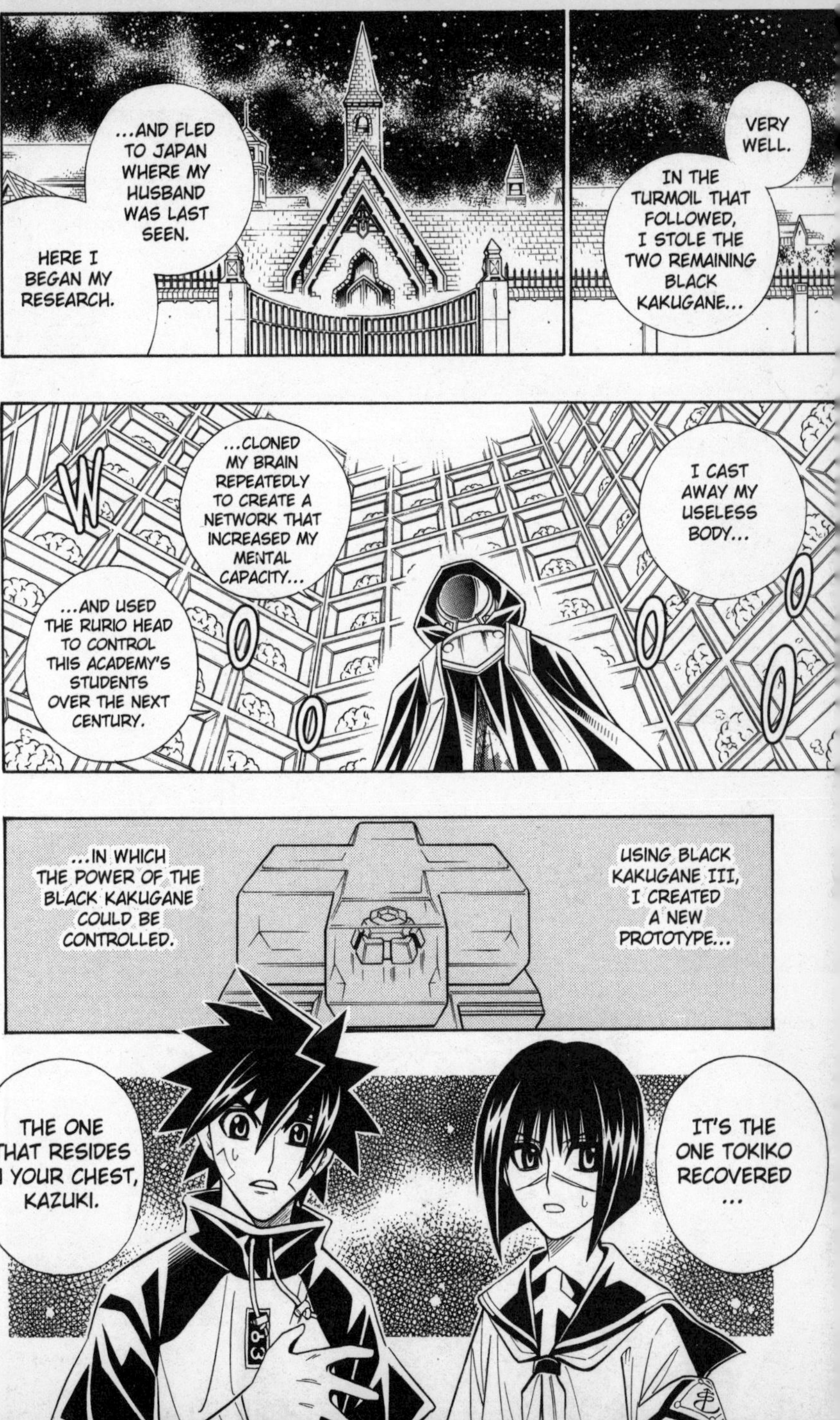
VERY WELL.
IN THE TURMOIL THAT FOLLOWED, I STOLE THE TWO REMAINING BLACK KAKUGANE...
...AND FLED TO JAPAN WHERE MY HUSBAND WAS LAST SEEN.
HERE I BEGAN MY RESEARCH.
I CAST AWAY MY USELESS BODY...
...CLONED MY BRAIN REPEATEDLY TO CREATE A NETWORK THAT INCREASED MY MENTAL CAPACITY...
W
...AND USED THE RURIO HEAD TO CONTROL THIS ACADEMY'S STUDENTS OVER THE NEXT CENTURY.
USING BLACK KAKUGANE III, I CREATED A NEW PROTOTYPE...
...IN WHICH THE POWER OF THE BLACK KAKUGANE COULD BE CONTROLLED.
IT'S THE ONE TOKIKO RECOVERED ...
THE ONE THAT RESIDES IN YOUR CHEST, KAZUKI.

READ THIS WAY

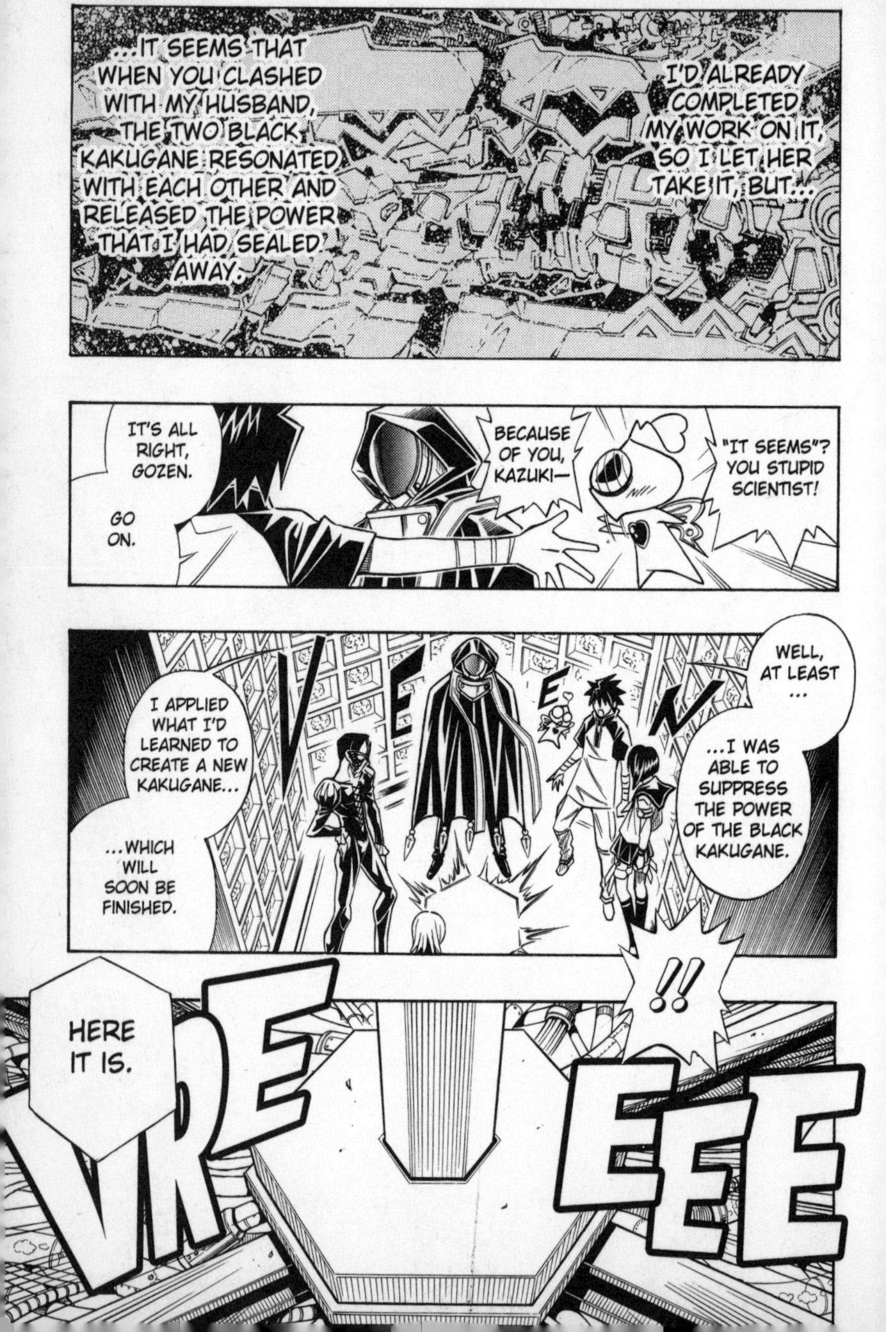
I'D ALREADY COMPLETED MY WORK ON IT, SO I LET HER TAKE IT, BUT...
...IT SEEMS THAT WHEN YOU CLASHED WITH MY HUSBAND, THE TWO BLACK KAKUGANE RESONATED WITH EACH OTHER AND RELEASED THE POWER THAT I HAD SEALED AWAY.
"IT SEEMS"? YOU STUPID SCIENTIST!
BECAUSE OF YOU, KAZUKI—
IT'S ALL RIGHT, GOZEN.
GO ON.
WELL, AT LEAST ...
...I WAS ABLE TO SUPPRESS THE POWER OF THE BLACK KAKUGANE.
VEEN
I APPLIED WHAT I'D LEARNED TO CREATE A NEW KAKUGANE...
...WHICH WILL SOON BE FINISHED.
!!
HERE IT IS.
VREEEE

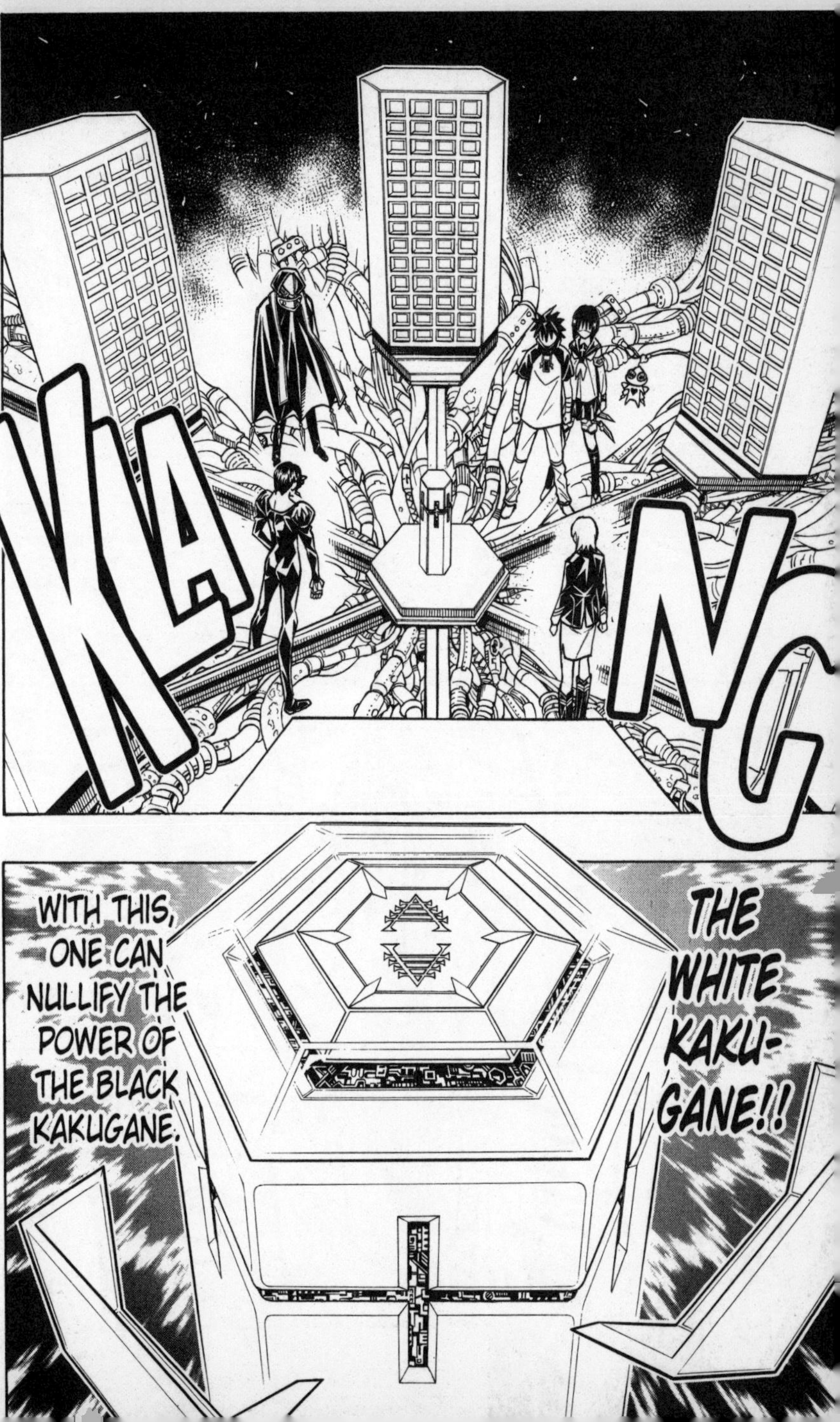
KA
NG
THE WHITE KAKU-GANE!!
WITH THIS, ONE CAN NULLIFY THE POWER OF THE BLACK KAKUGANE.

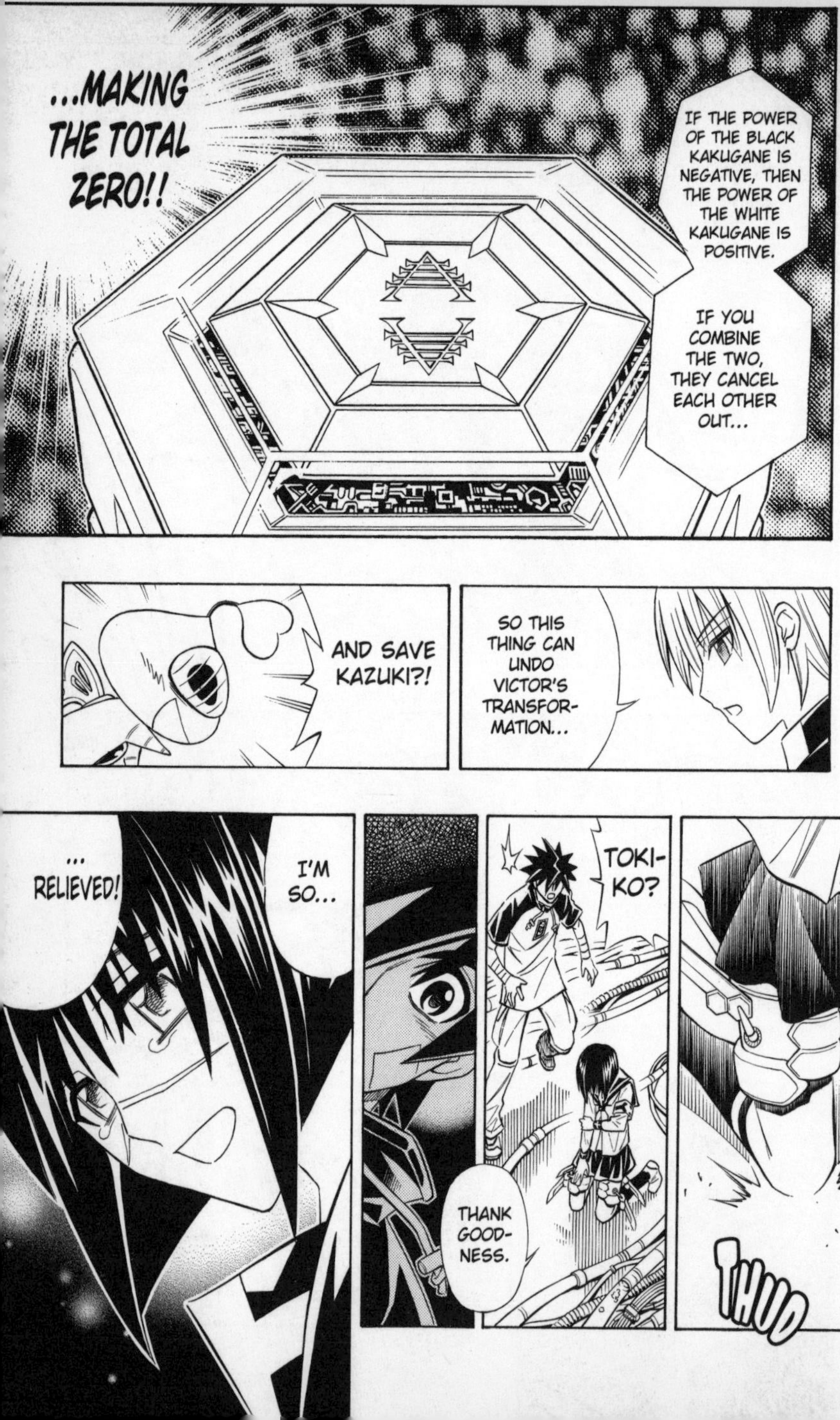
IF THE POWER OF THE BLACK KAKUGANE IS NEGATIVE, THEN THE POWER OF THE WHITE KAKUGANE IS POSITIVE.
IF YOU COMBINE THE TWO, THEY CANCEL EACH OTHER OUT...
...MAKING THE TOTAL ZERO!!
SO THIS THING CAN UNDO VICTOR'S TRANSFOR-MATION...
AND SAVE KAZUKI?!
THUD
TOKI-KO?
THANK GOOD-NESS.
I'M SO...
...RELIEVED!

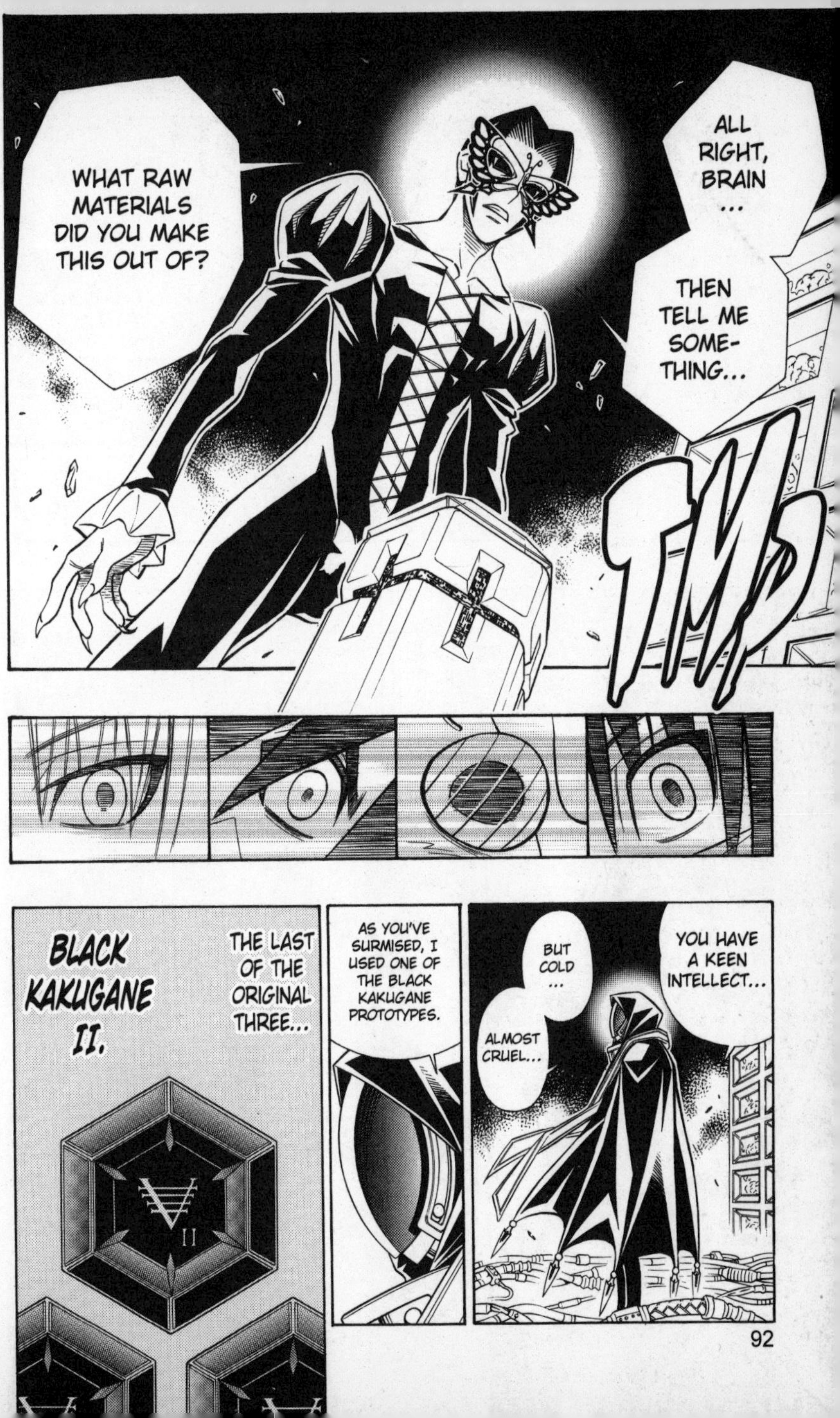

ALL RIGHT, BRAIN ...
THEN TELL ME SOME-THING...
WHAT RAW MATERIALS DID YOU MAKE THIS OUT OF?
TMP
YOU HAVE A KEEN INTELLECT...
BUT COLD ...
ALMOST CRUEL...
AS YOU'VE SURMISED, I USED ONE OF THE BLACK KAKUGANE PROTOTYPES.
THE LAST OF THE ORIGINAL THREE...
BLACK KAKUGANE II.

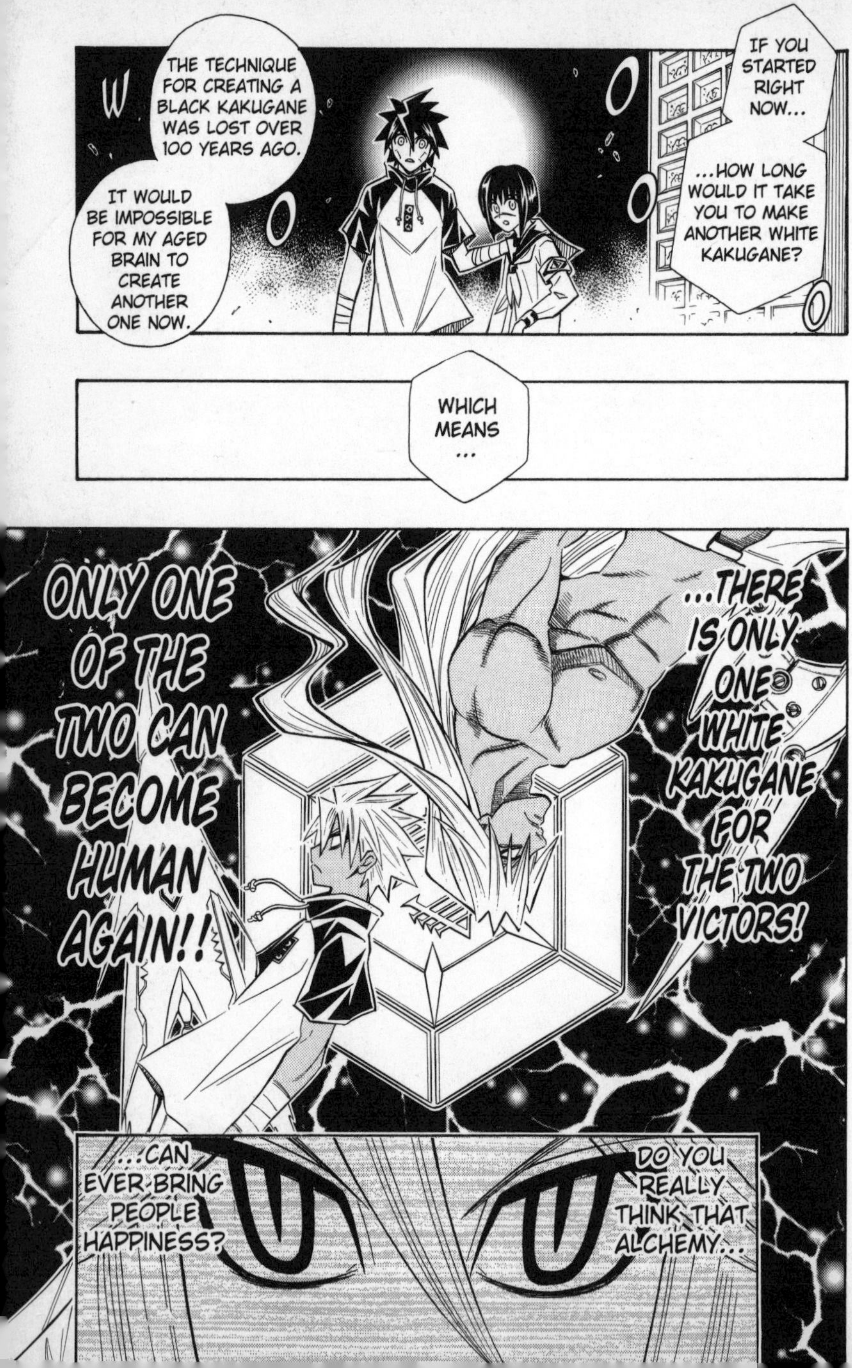
IF YOU STARTED RIGHT NOW...
...HOW LONG WOULD IT TAKE YOU TO MAKE ANOTHER WHITE KAKUGANE?
THE TECHNIQUE FOR CREATING A BLACK KAKUGANE WAS LOST OVER 100 YEARS AGO.
IT WOULD BE IMPOSSIBLE FOR MY AGED BRAIN TO CREATE ANOTHER ONE NOW.
WHICH MEANS ...
...THERE IS ONLY ONE WHITE KAKUGANE FOR THE TWO VICTORS!
ONLY ONE OF THE TWO CAN BECOME HUMAN AGAIN!!
DO YOU REALLY THINK THAT ALCHEMY...
...CAN EVER BRING PEOPLE HAPPINESS?

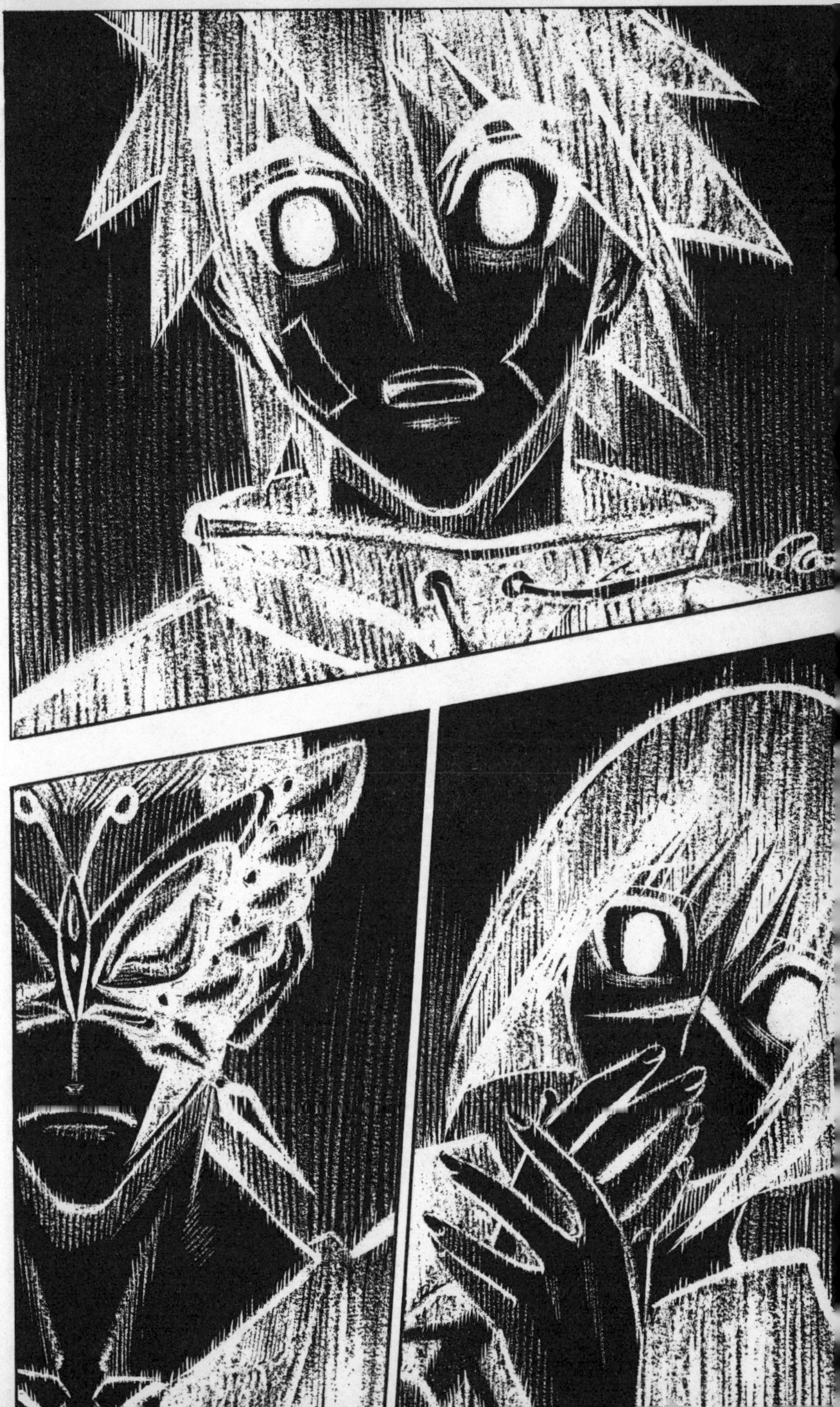

READ THIS WAY

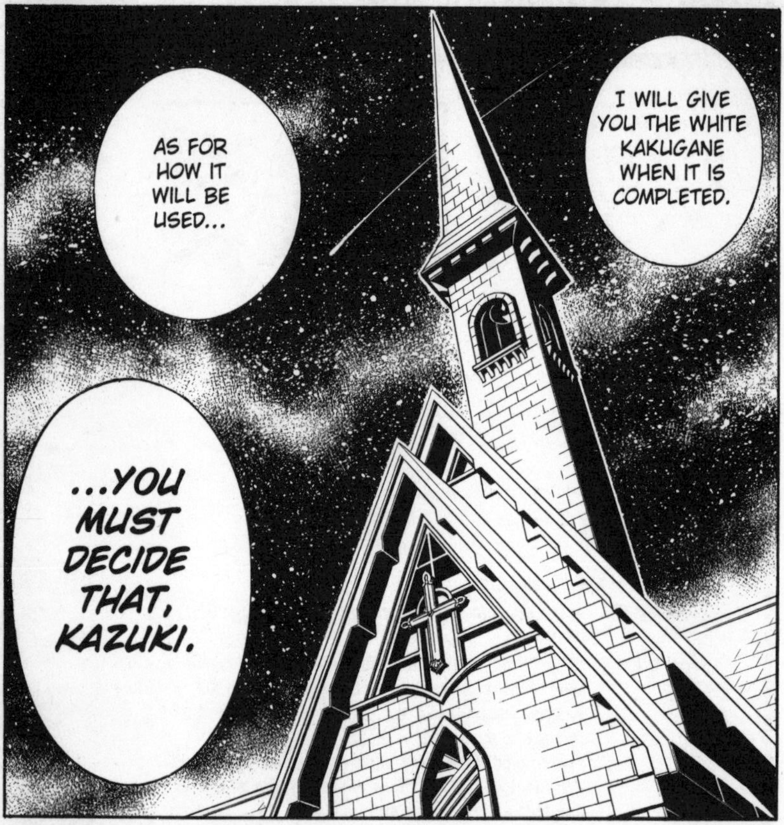
I WILL GIVE YOU THE WHITE KAKUGANE WHEN IT IS COMPLETED.
AS FOR HOW IT WILL BE USED...
...YOU MUST DECIDE THAT, KAZUKI.

ESTIMATED TIME UNTIL KAZUKI MUTO PERMANENTLY TRANSFORMS INTO A VICTOR:

— 25 DAYS —

BUT THE DECISION MUST BE MADE.

The Phantom of the Academy!

Buso Renkin File No. 18

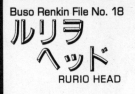

RURIO HEAD

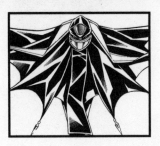

- Kakugane Serial Number: L (50)
- Creator: Alexandria Powered
- Form: Helmet
- Colors: Orange and Metallic Black
- Special Abilities: · Able to take over and control anyone who puts the helmet on.
- Special Traits: · The effectiveness of the control is determined by the level of synchronization with the wearer. When the synchronization is low, the target moves stiffly and the damage to the wearer is greater.
  - · Able to read its wearer's brainwave patterns, thoughts and memories. (But if the victim resists, not all of their thoughts and memories can be read.)
  - · The sharp points on the cape are the primary offensive weapons.
  - · Able to communicate for brief periods by creating vibrations in the glass faceplate.

- Author's Notes:
- · This Buso Renkin was the product of necessity (Alexandria's current disembodied form, the need for Kazuki to hear her story, which the readers know already from a different perspective, etc.)
- · The design came from a movie about alchemy that I really liked called *Vidocq*.
- · The name comes from the title of a song, "Fuusha Otoko Rurio" (Windmill Man Rurio) by the band Kinniku Shojo Tai. I really like this song.

LAST CHAPTER: BOY MEETS BATTLE GIRL

TWO VICTORS, AND ONLY ONE WHITE KAKUGANE!

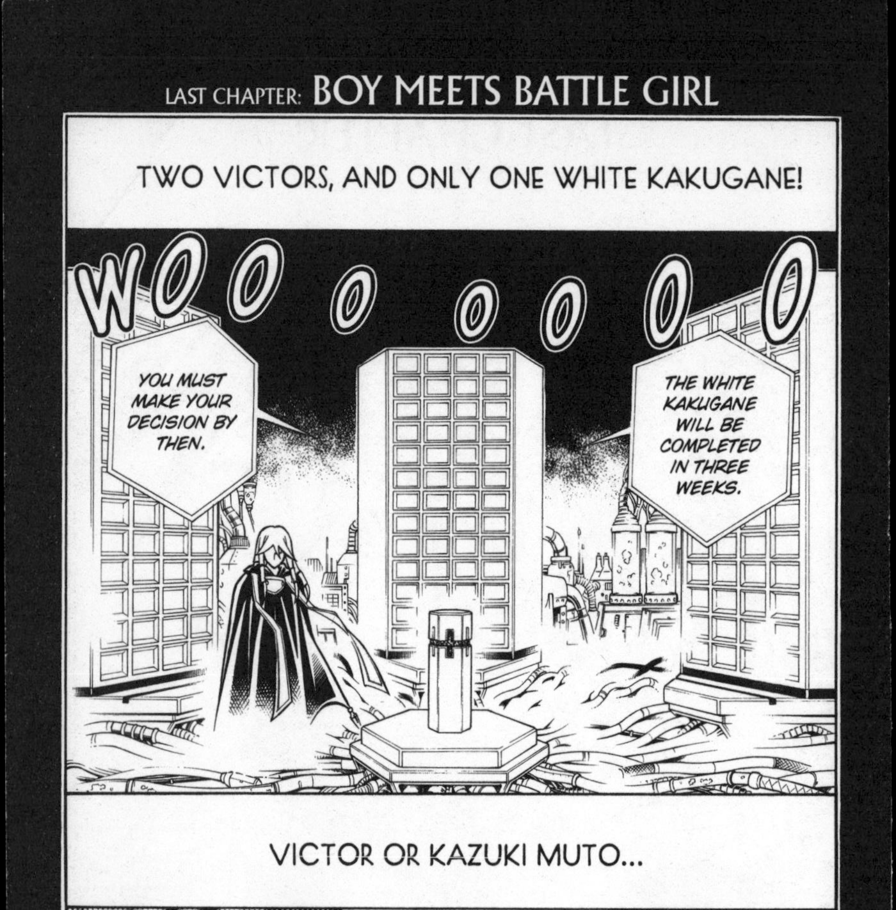
WOOOOOOOO
THE WHITE KAKUGANE WILL BE COMPLETED IN THREE WEEKS.
YOU MUST MAKE YOUR DECISION BY THEN.

VICTOR OR KAZUKI MUTO...

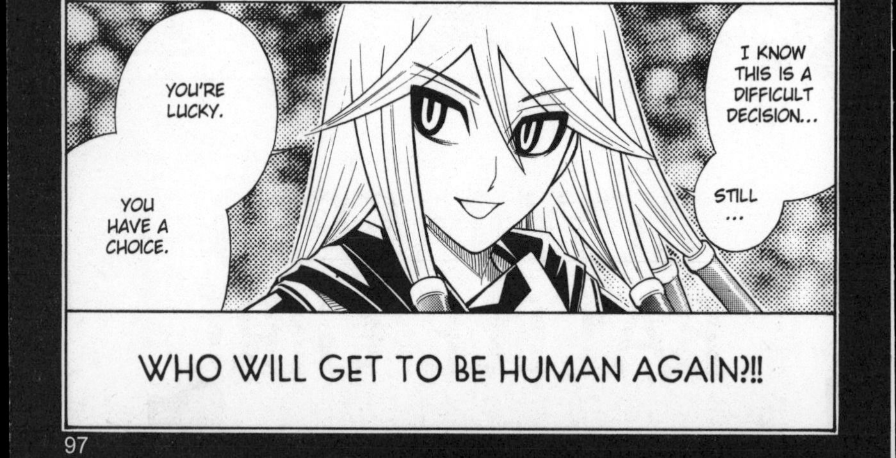
I KNOW THIS IS A DIFFICULT DECISION...
STILL...
YOU'RE LUCKY.
YOU HAVE A CHOICE.

WHO WILL GET TO BE HUMAN AGAIN?!!

LAST CHAPTER:

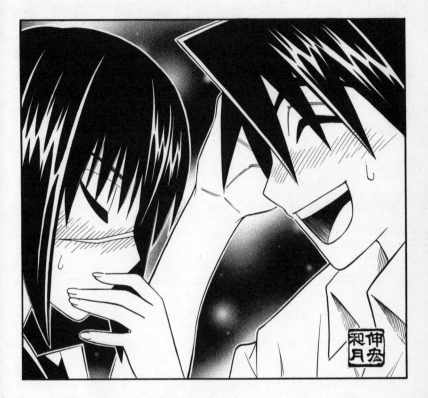

BOY MEETS BATTLE GIRL

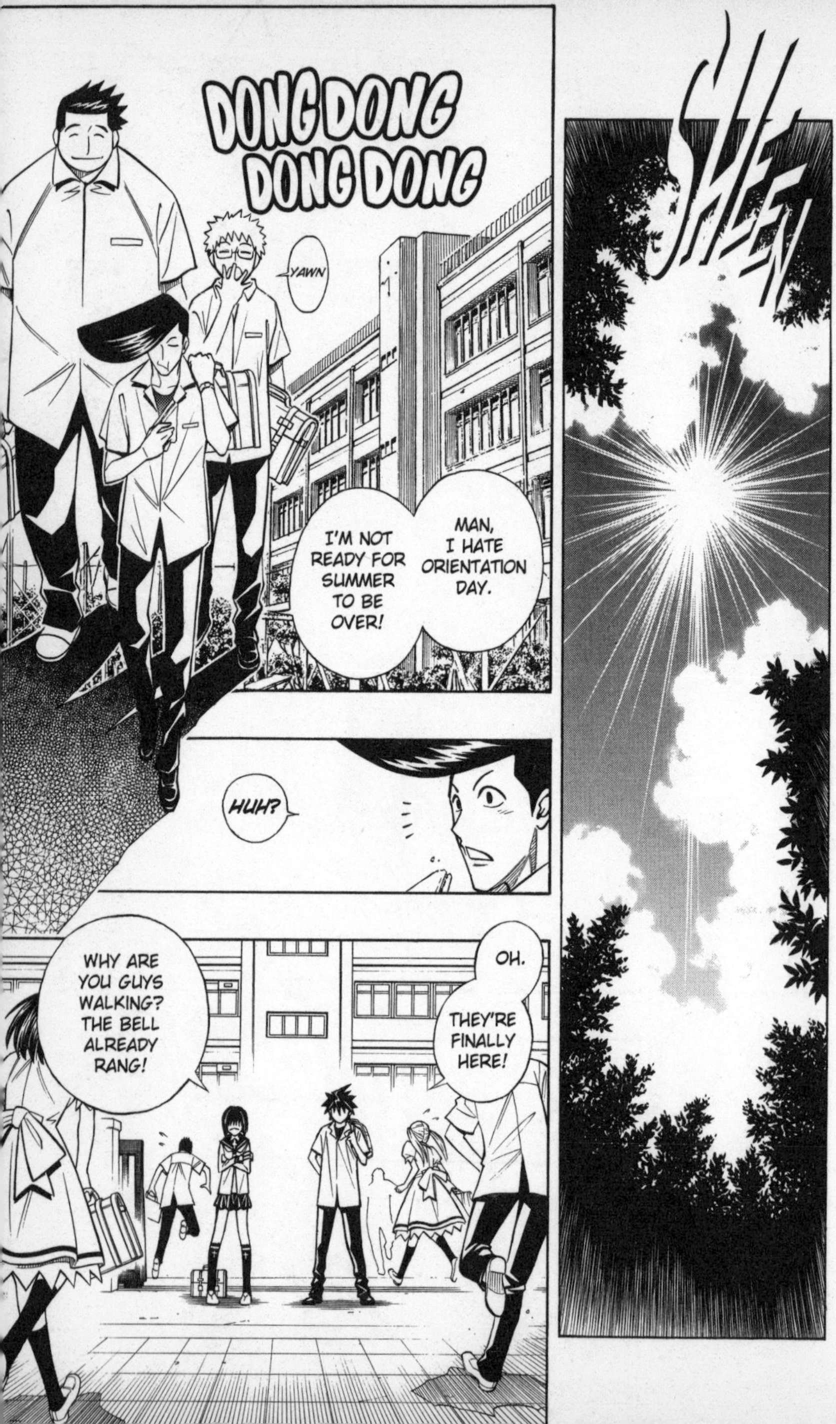
SHEEN
DONG DONG DONG DONG
YAWN
MAN, I HATE ORIENTATION DAY.
I'M NOT READY FOR SUMMER TO BE OVER!
HUH?
OH.
THEY'RE FINALLY HERE!
WHY ARE YOU GUYS WALKING? THE BELL ALREADY RANG!

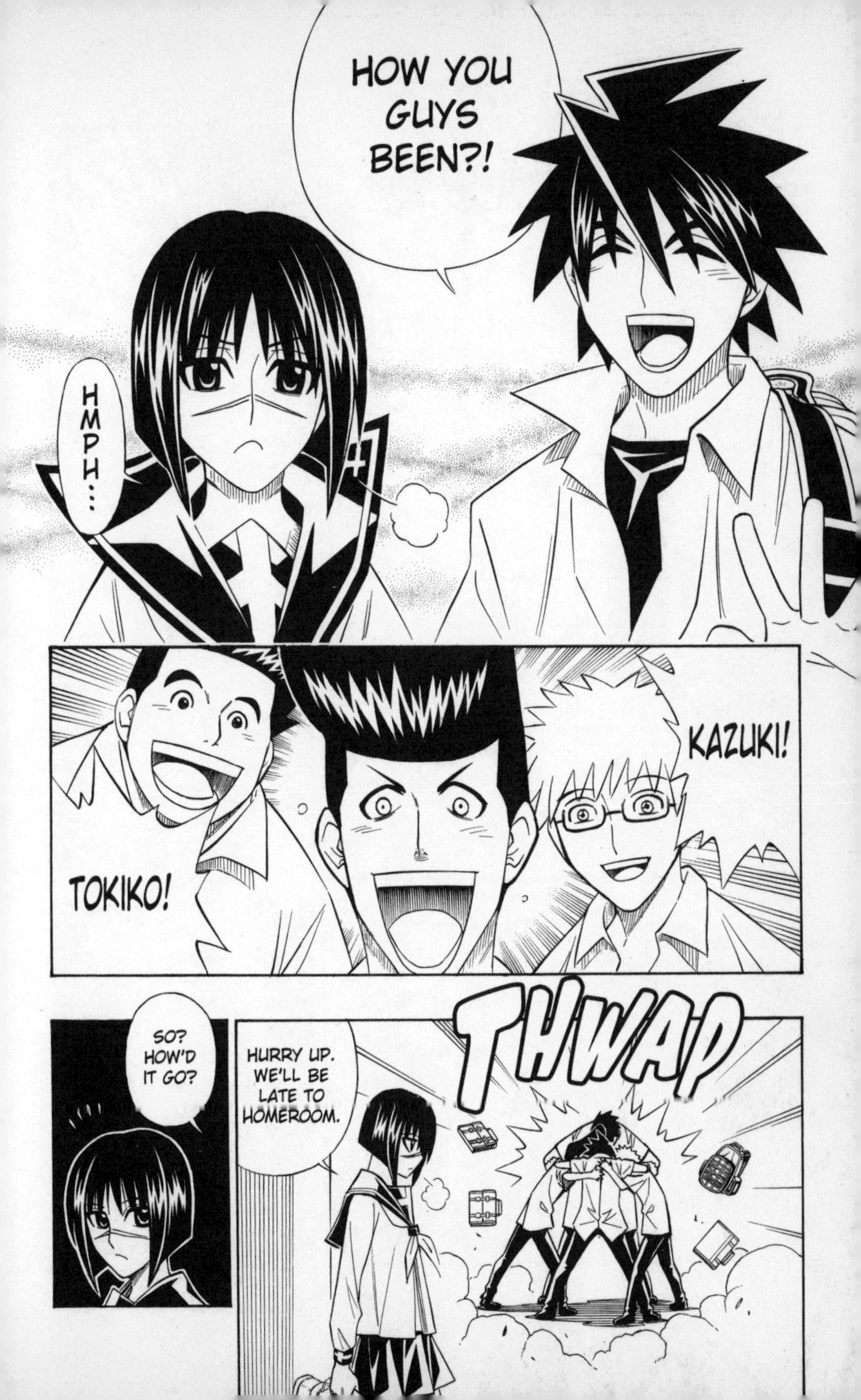
HOW YOU GUYS BEEN?!
HMPH...
KAZUKI!
TOKIKO!
THWAP
HURRY UP. WE'LL BE LATE TO HOMEROOM.
SO? HOW'D IT GO?

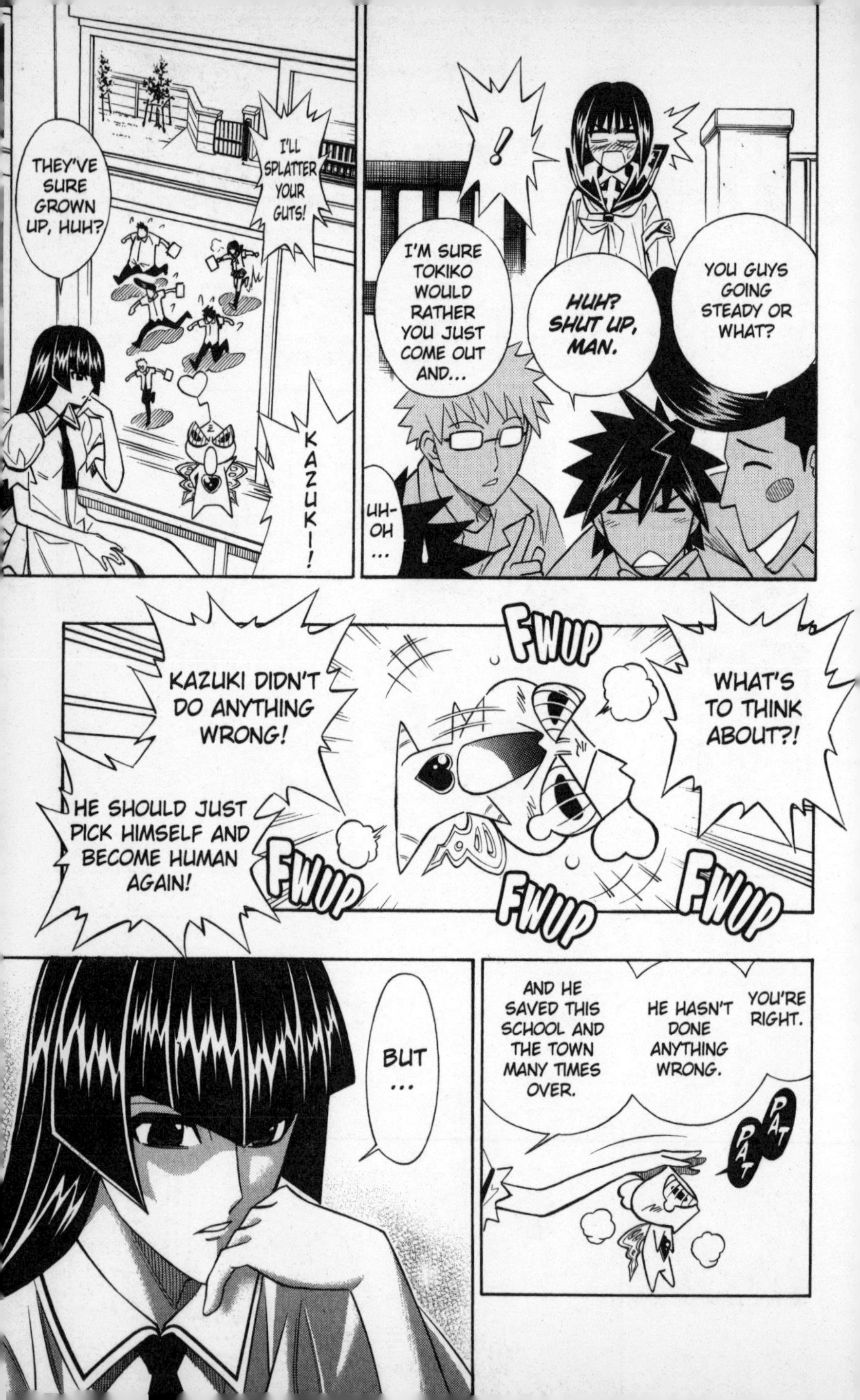
!
YOU GUYS GOING STEADY OR WHAT?
HUH? SHUT UP, MAN.
I'M SURE TOKIKO WOULD RATHER YOU JUST COME OUT AND...
UH-OH...
I'LL SPLATTER YOUR GUTS!
THEY'VE SURE GROWN UP, HUH?
KAZUKI!
WHAT'S TO THINK ABOUT?!
FWUP
FWUP
KAZUKI DIDN'T DO ANYTHING WRONG!
HE SHOULD JUST PICK HIMSELF AND BECOME HUMAN AGAIN!
FWUP
FWUP
YOU'RE RIGHT.
HE HASN'T DONE ANYTHING WRONG.
AND HE SAVED THIS SCHOOL AND THE TOWN MANY TIMES OVER.
PAT PAT
BUT...

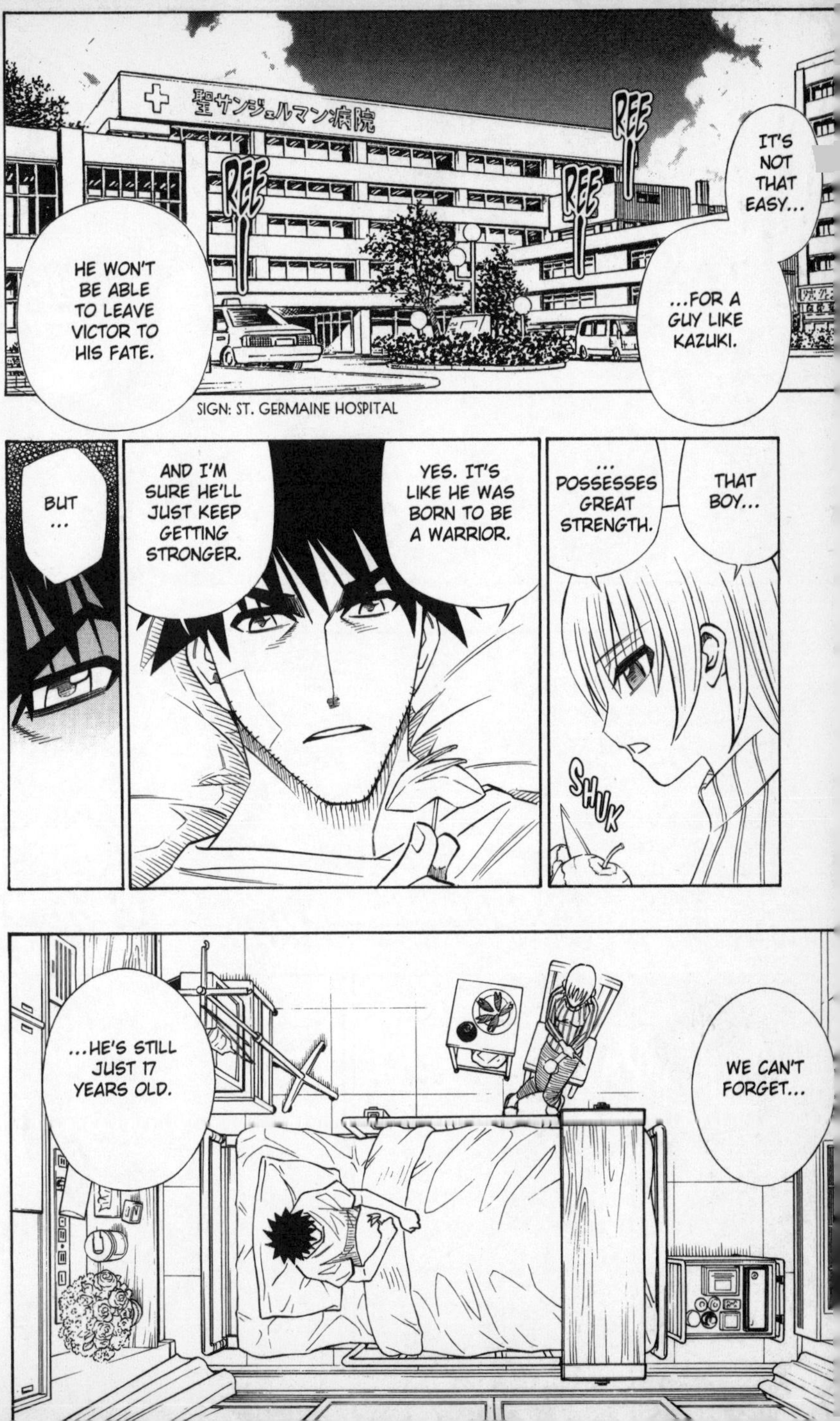
IT'S NOT THAT EASY...
...FOR A GUY LIKE KAZUKI.
REE
REE
REE
聖サンジェルマン病院
HE WON'T BE ABLE TO LEAVE VICTOR TO HIS FATE.
SIGN: ST. GERMAINE HOSPITAL
THAT BOY...
...POSSESSES GREAT STRENGTH.
SHUK
YES. IT'S LIKE HE WAS BORN TO BE A WARRIOR.
AND I'M SURE HE'LL JUST KEEP GETTING STRONGER.
BUT ...
WE CAN'T FORGET...
...HE'S STILL JUST 17 YEARS OLD.

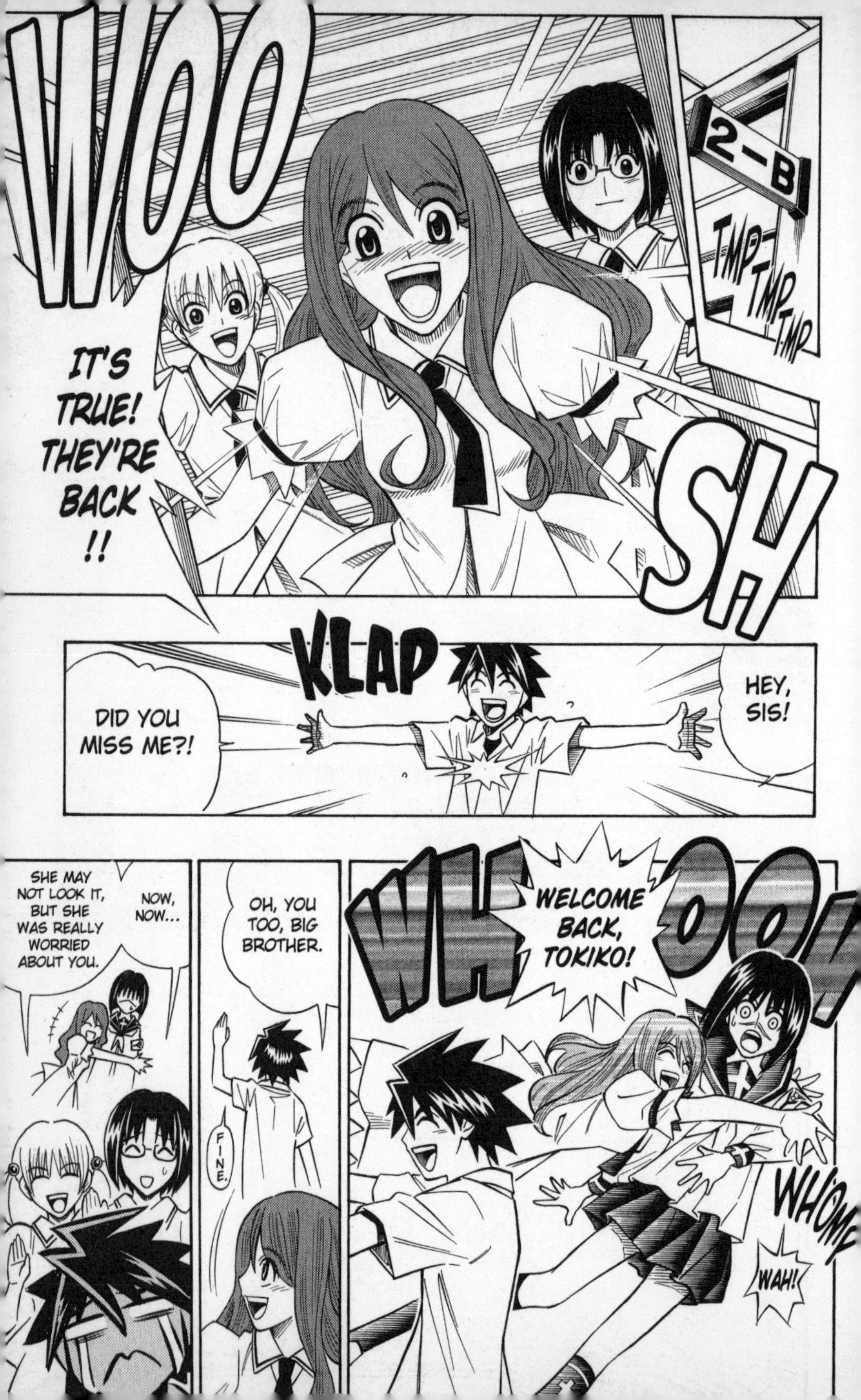
2-B
TMP-TMP-TMP-TMP
WOO
SH
IT'S TRUE! THEY'RE BACK!!
HEY, SIS!
KLAP
DID YOU MISS ME?!
WELCOME BACK, TOKIKO!
WAH!
OH, YOU TOO, BIG BROTHER.
FINE.
NOW, NOW...
SHE MAY NOT LOOK IT, BUT SHE WAS REALLY WORRIED ABOUT YOU.

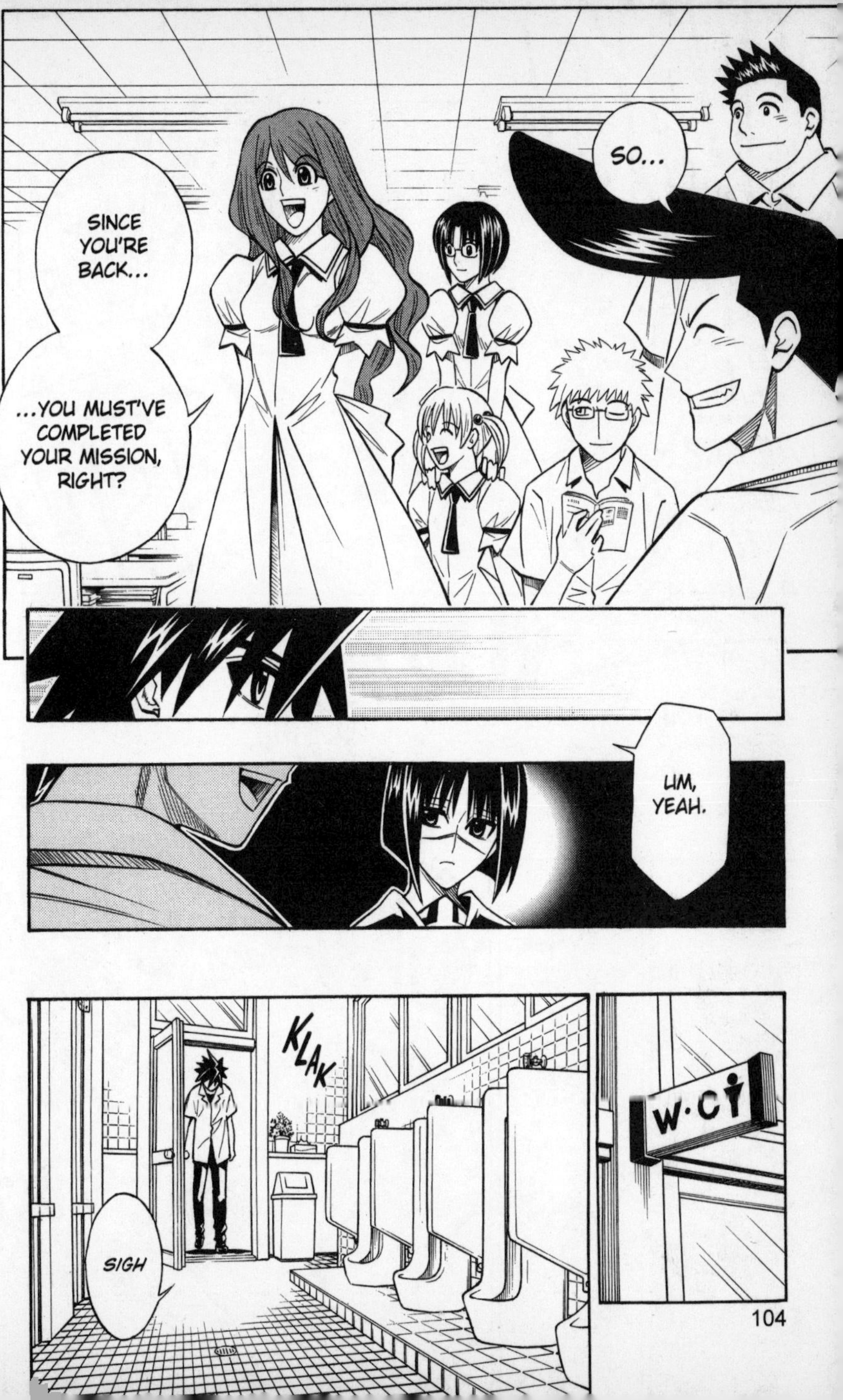
SO...
SINCE YOU'RE BACK...
...YOU MUST'VE COMPLETED YOUR MISSION, RIGHT?
UM, YEAH.
W·C
KLAK
SIGH

READ THIS WAY

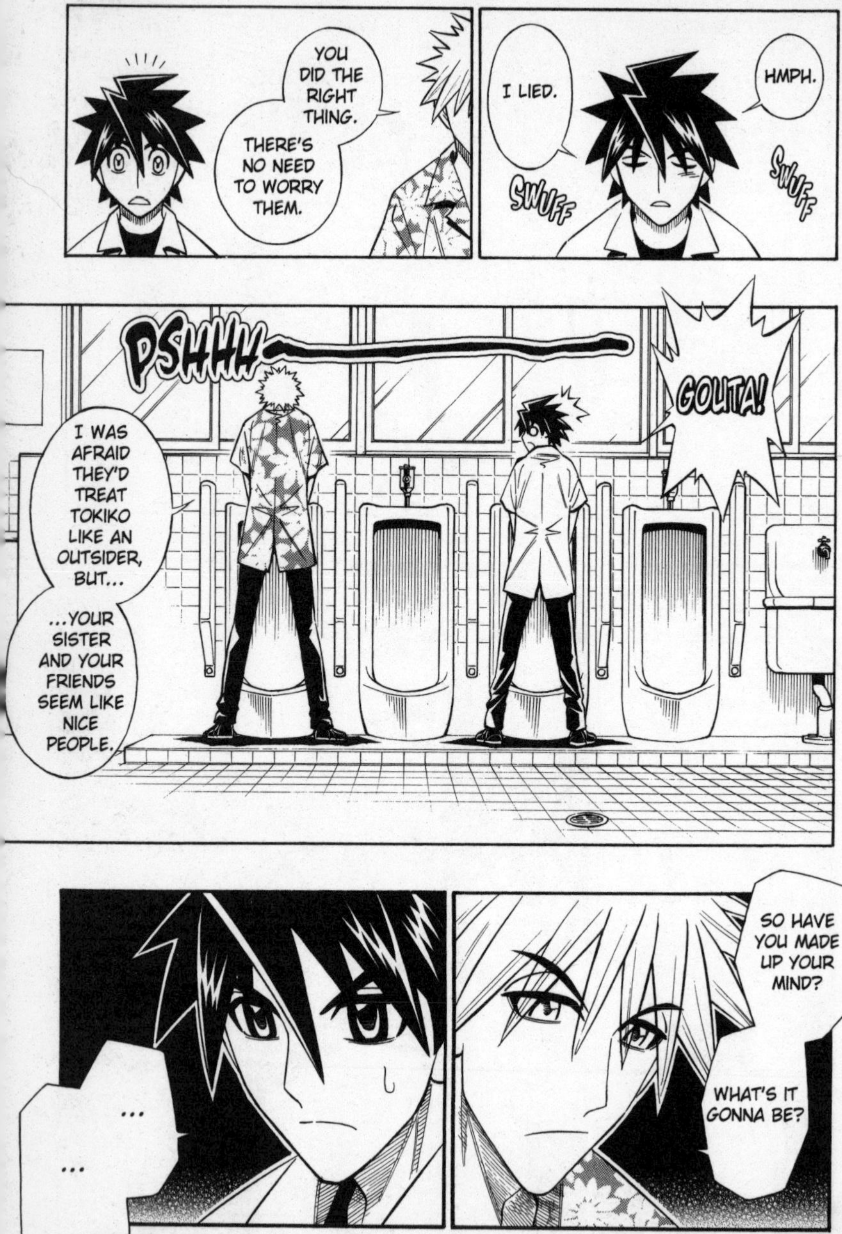
HMPH.
SWUFF
I LIED.
SWUFF
YOU DID THE RIGHT THING.
THERE'S NO NEED TO WORRY THEM.
GOUTA!
PSHHH
I WAS AFRAID THEY'D TREAT TOKIKO LIKE AN OUTSIDER, BUT...
...YOUR SISTER AND YOUR FRIENDS SEEM LIKE NICE PEOPLE.
SO HAVE YOU MADE UP YOUR MIND?
WHAT'S IT GONNA BE?
... ...

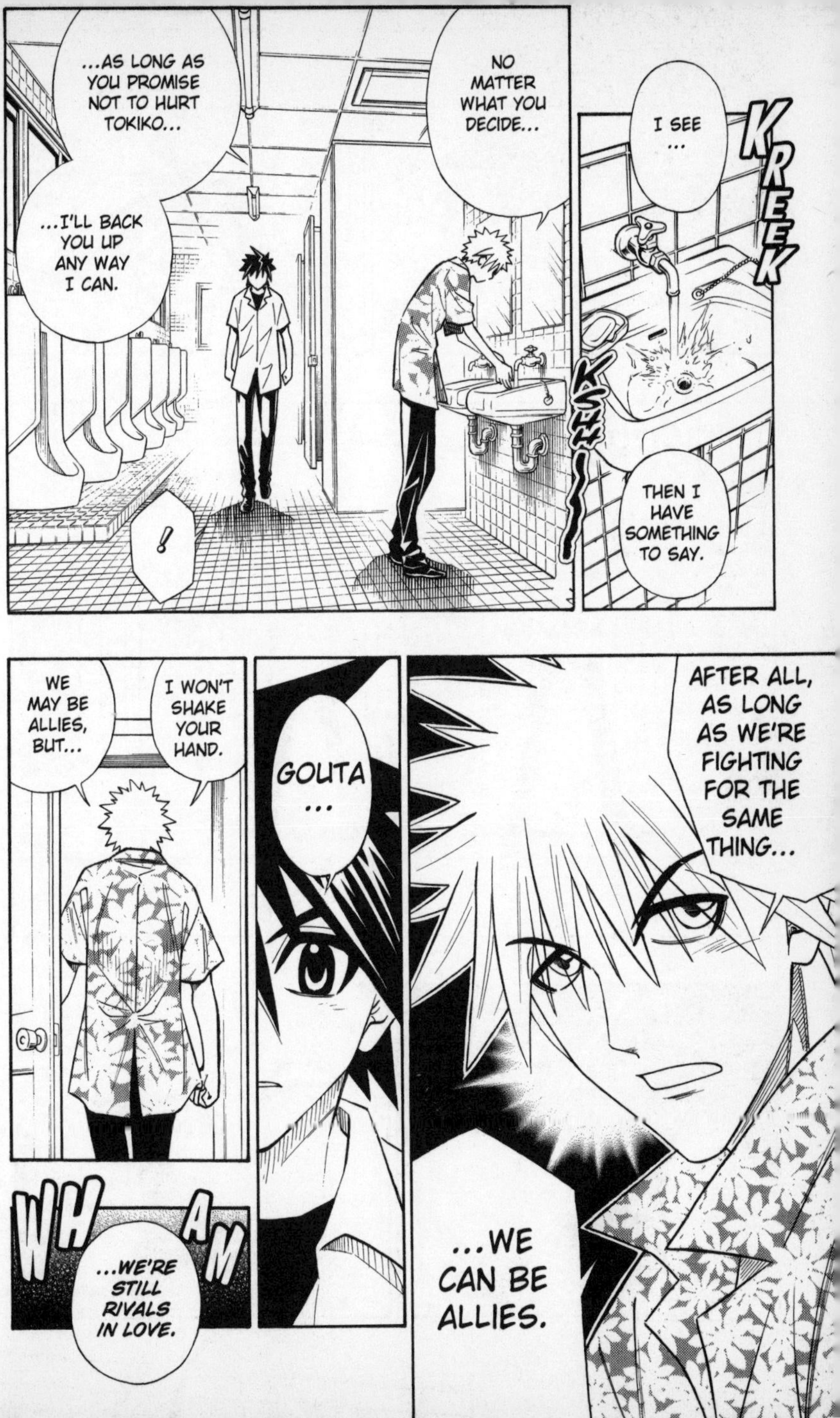
I SEE ...
KREEK
KSHHH
THEN I HAVE SOMETHING TO SAY.
NO MATTER WHAT YOU DECIDE...
...AS LONG AS YOU PROMISE NOT TO HURT TOKIKO...
...I'LL BACK YOU UP ANY WAY I CAN.
!
AFTER ALL, AS LONG AS WE'RE FIGHTING FOR THE SAME THING...
...WE CAN BE ALLIES.
GOUTA ...
WE MAY BE ALLIES, BUT...
I WON'T SHAKE YOUR HAND.
WHAM
...WE'RE STILL RIVALS IN LOVE.

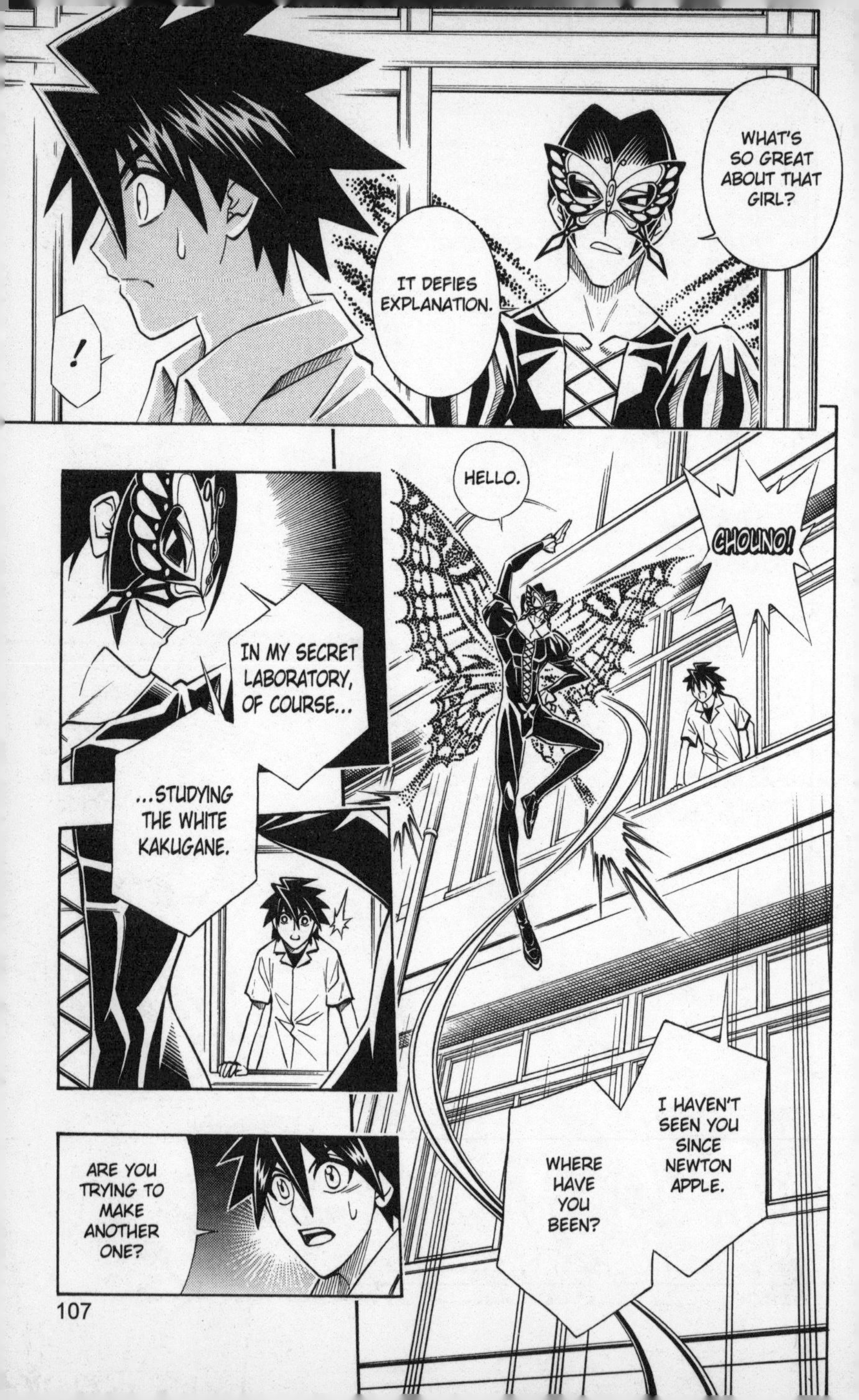
WHAT'S SO GREAT ABOUT THAT GIRL?
IT DEFIES EXPLANATION.
!
HELLO.
CHOUNO!
I HAVEN'T SEEN YOU SINCE NEWTON APPLE.
WHERE HAVE YOU BEEN?
IN MY SECRET LABORATORY, OF COURSE...
...STUDYING THE WHITE KAKUGANE.
ARE YOU TRYING TO MAKE ANOTHER ONE?

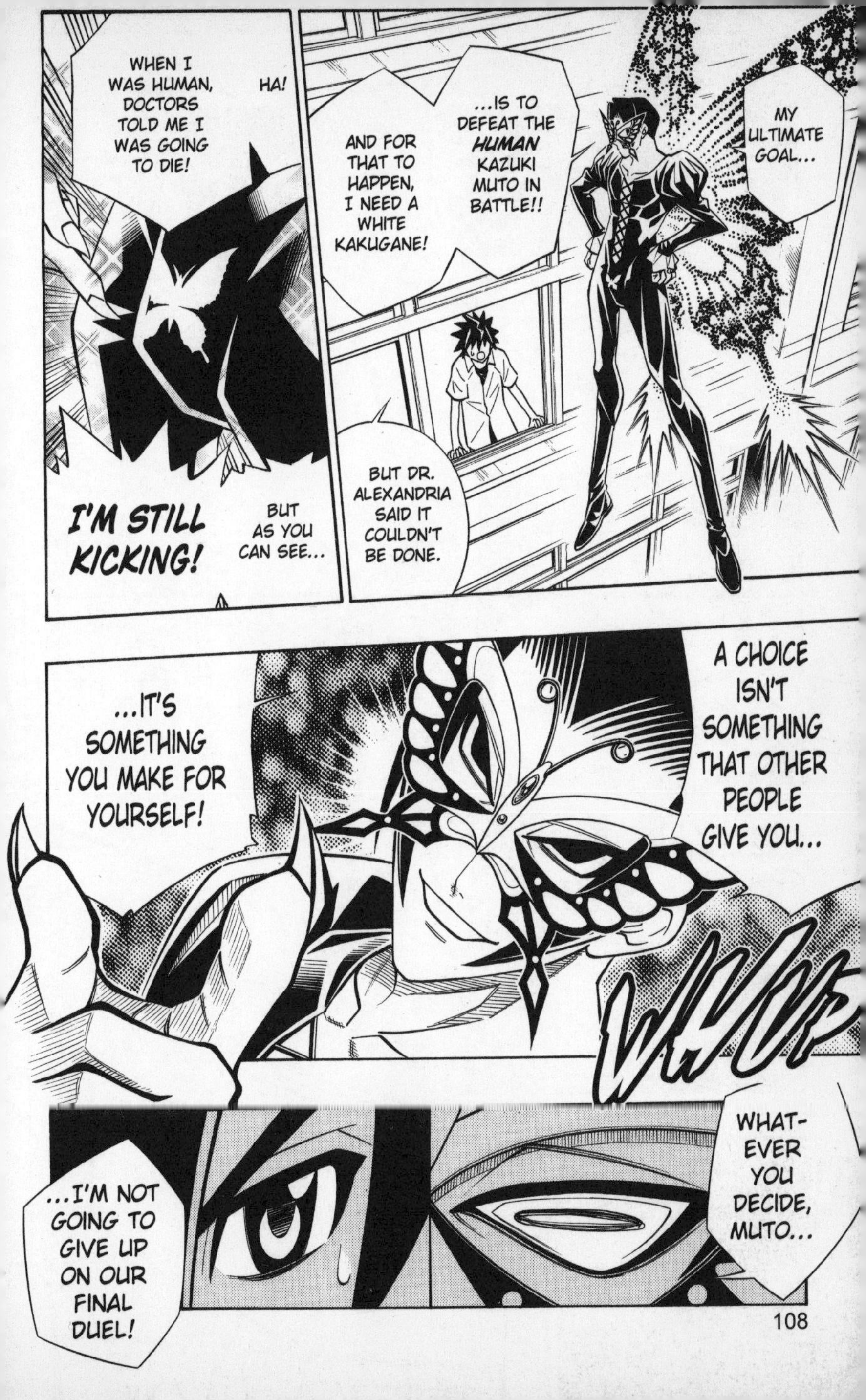
MY ULTIMATE GOAL...
...IS TO DEFEAT THE *HUMAN* KAZUKI MUTO IN BATTLE!!
AND FOR THAT TO HAPPEN, I NEED A WHITE KAKUGANE!
BUT DR. ALEXANDRIA SAID IT COULDN'T BE DONE.
HA!
WHEN I WAS HUMAN, DOCTORS TOLD ME I WAS GOING TO DIE!
BUT AS YOU CAN SEE...
I'M STILL KICKING!
A CHOICE ISN'T SOMETHING THAT OTHER PEOPLE GIVE YOU...
...IT'S SOMETHING YOU MAKE FOR YOURSELF!
WHAT-EVER YOU DECIDE, MUTO...
...I'M NOT GOING TO GIVE UP ON OUR FINAL DUEL!

READ THIS WAY

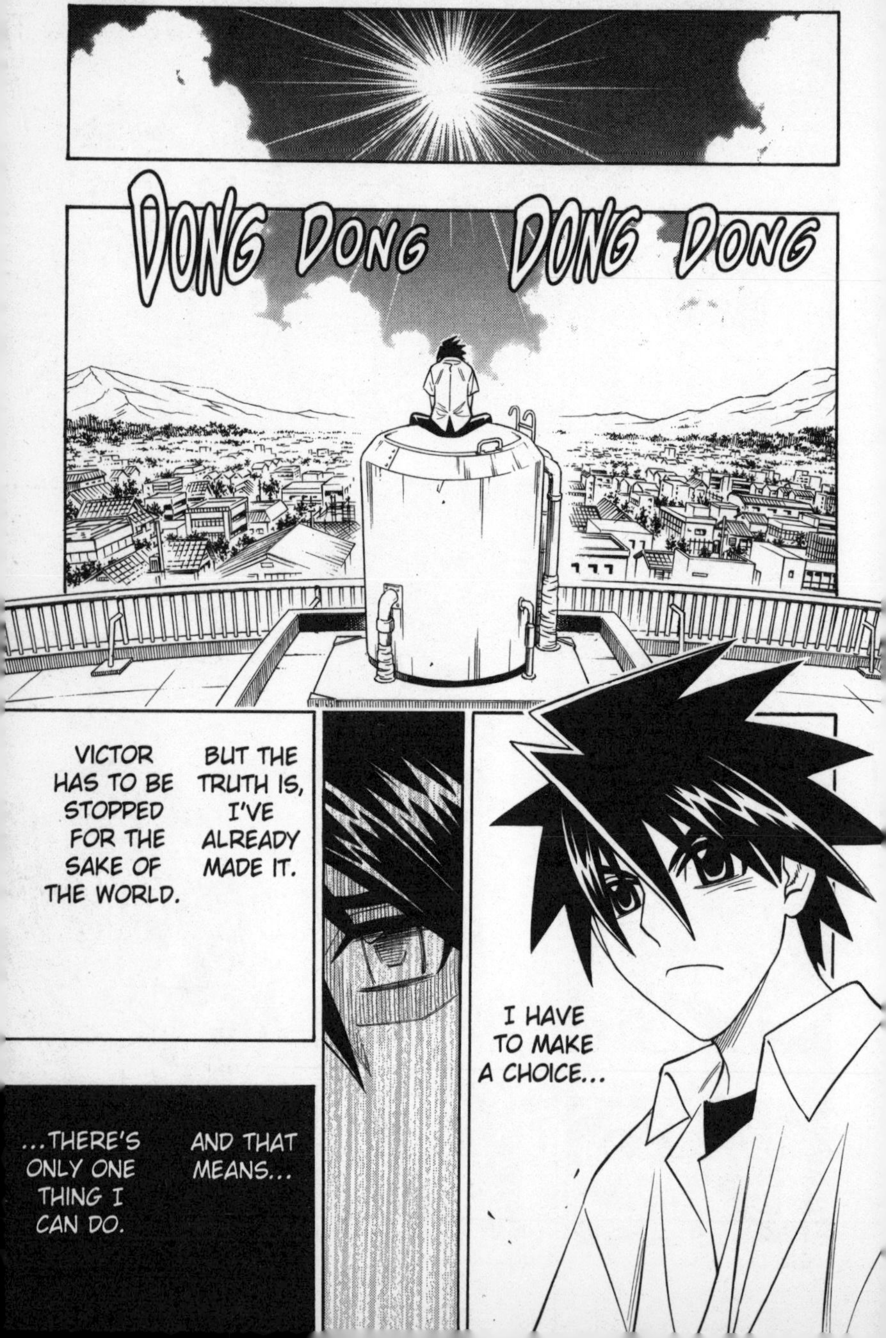
DONG DONG DONG DONG
I HAVE TO MAKE A CHOICE...
BUT THE TRUTH IS, I'VE ALREADY MADE IT.
VICTOR HAS TO BE STOPPED FOR THE SAKE OF THE WORLD.
AND THAT MEANS...
...THERE'S ONLY ONE THING I CAN DO.

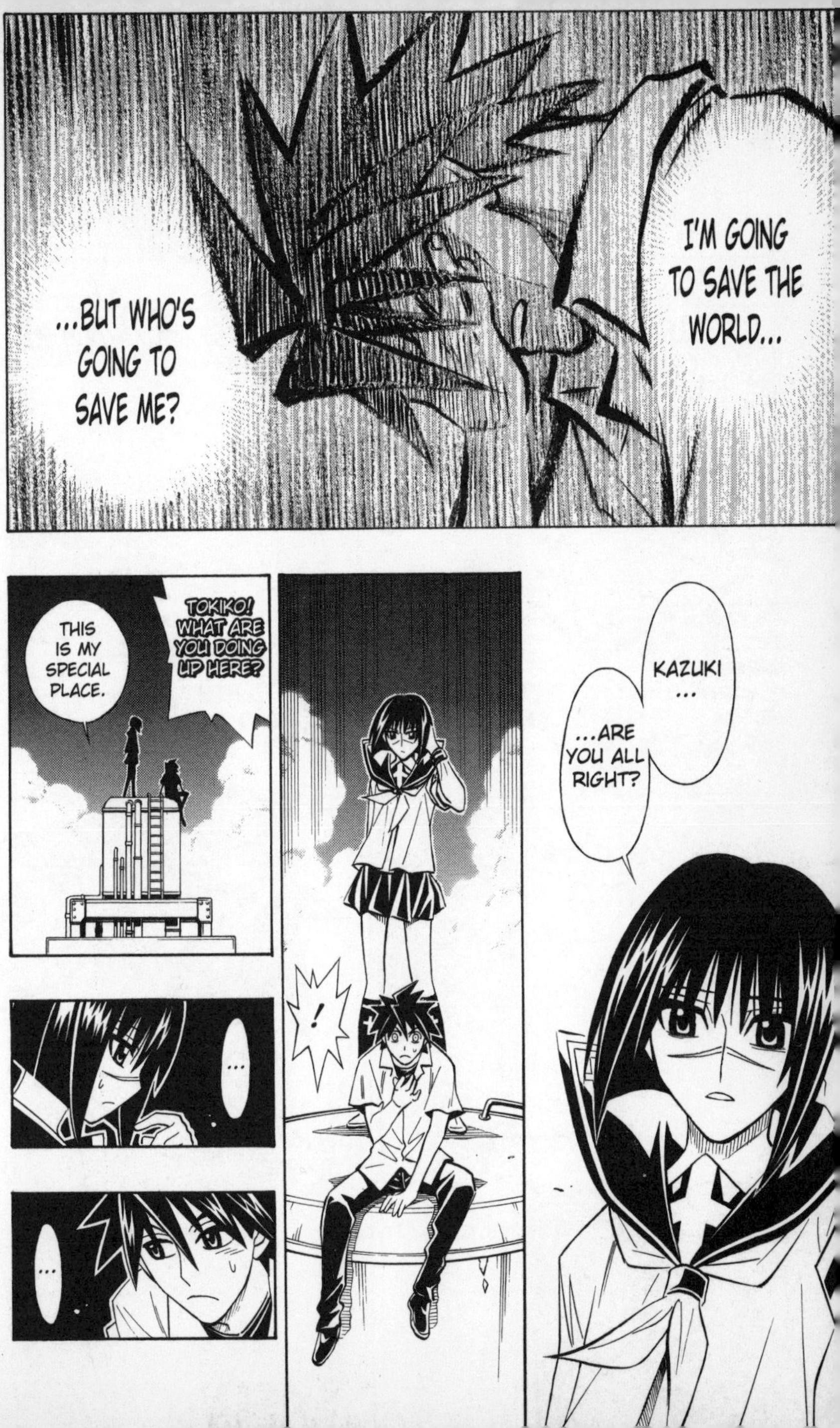
I'M GOING TO SAVE THE WORLD...
...BUT WHO'S GOING TO SAVE ME?
KAZUKI ...
...ARE YOU ALL RIGHT?
!
TOKIKO! WHAT ARE YOU DOING UP HERE?
THIS IS MY SPECIAL PLACE.
...
...

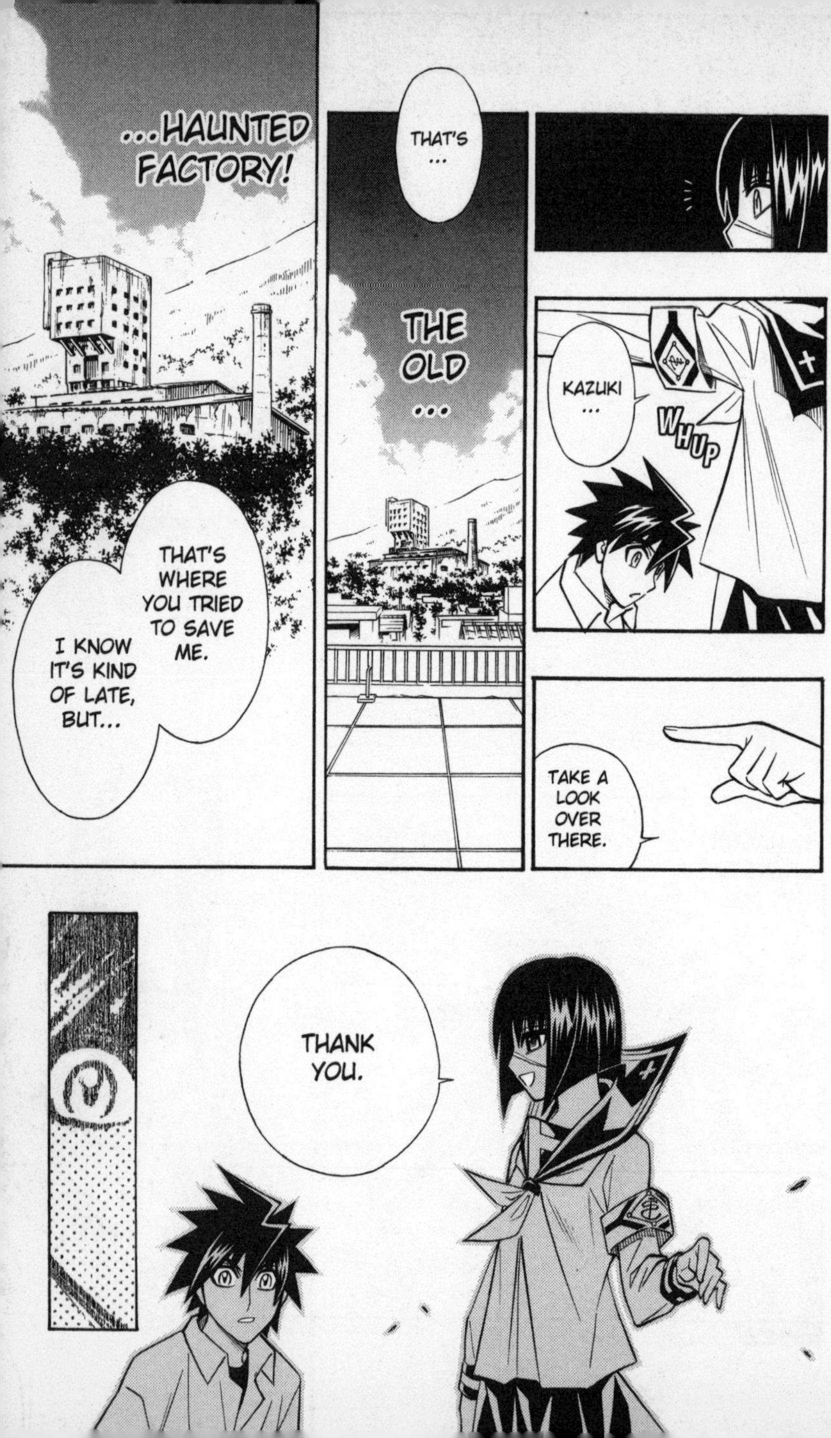
KAZUKI ...
WHUP
TAKE A LOOK OVER THERE.
THAT'S ...
THE OLD ...
...HAUNTED FACTORY!
THAT'S WHERE YOU TRIED TO SAVE ME.
I KNOW IT'S KIND OF LATE, BUT...
THANK YOU.

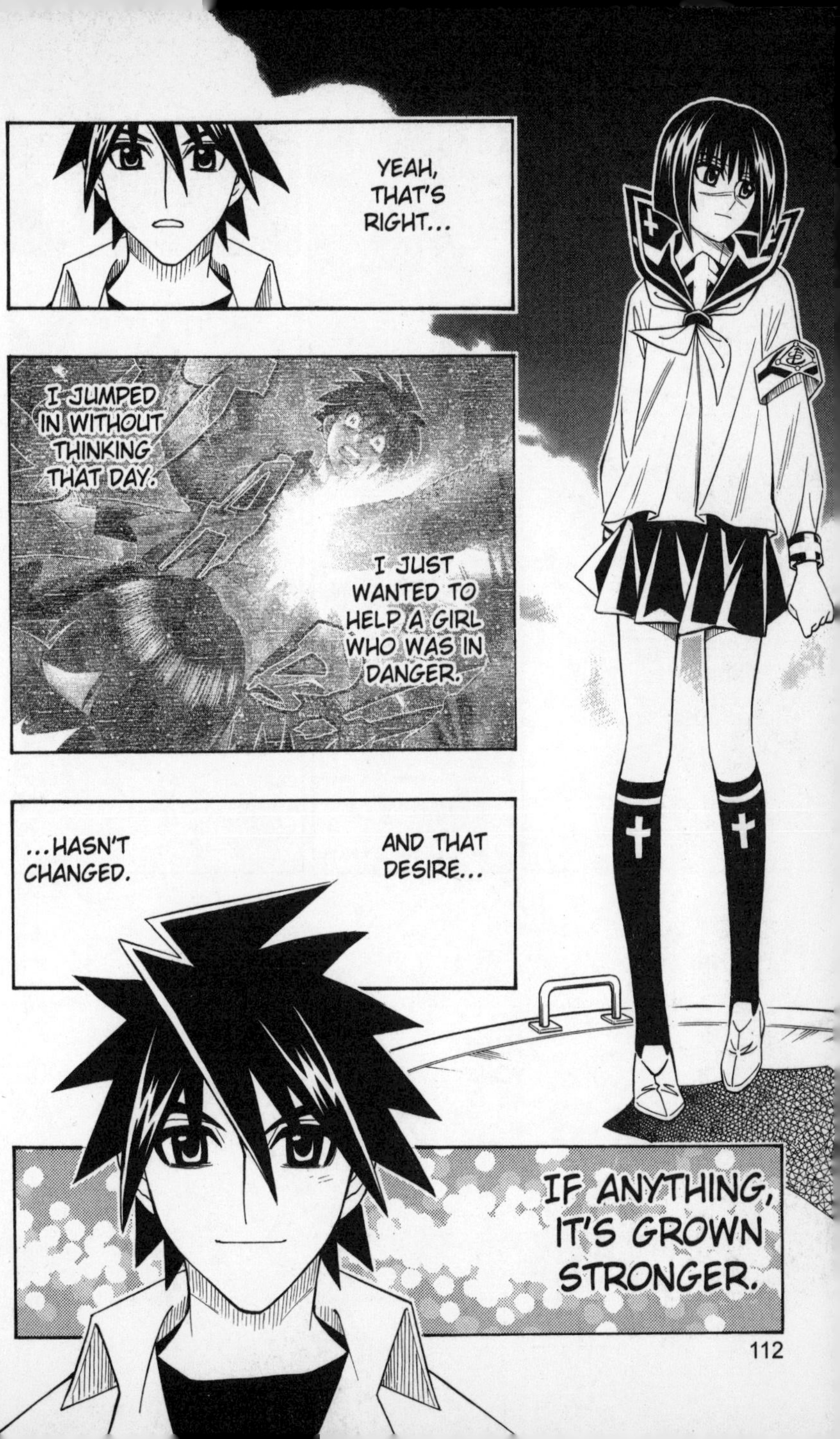
YEAH, THAT'S RIGHT...
I JUMPED IN WITHOUT THINKING THAT DAY.
I JUST WANTED TO HELP A GIRL WHO WAS IN DANGER.
AND THAT DESIRE...
...HASN'T CHANGED.
IF ANYTHING, IT'S GROWN STRONGER.

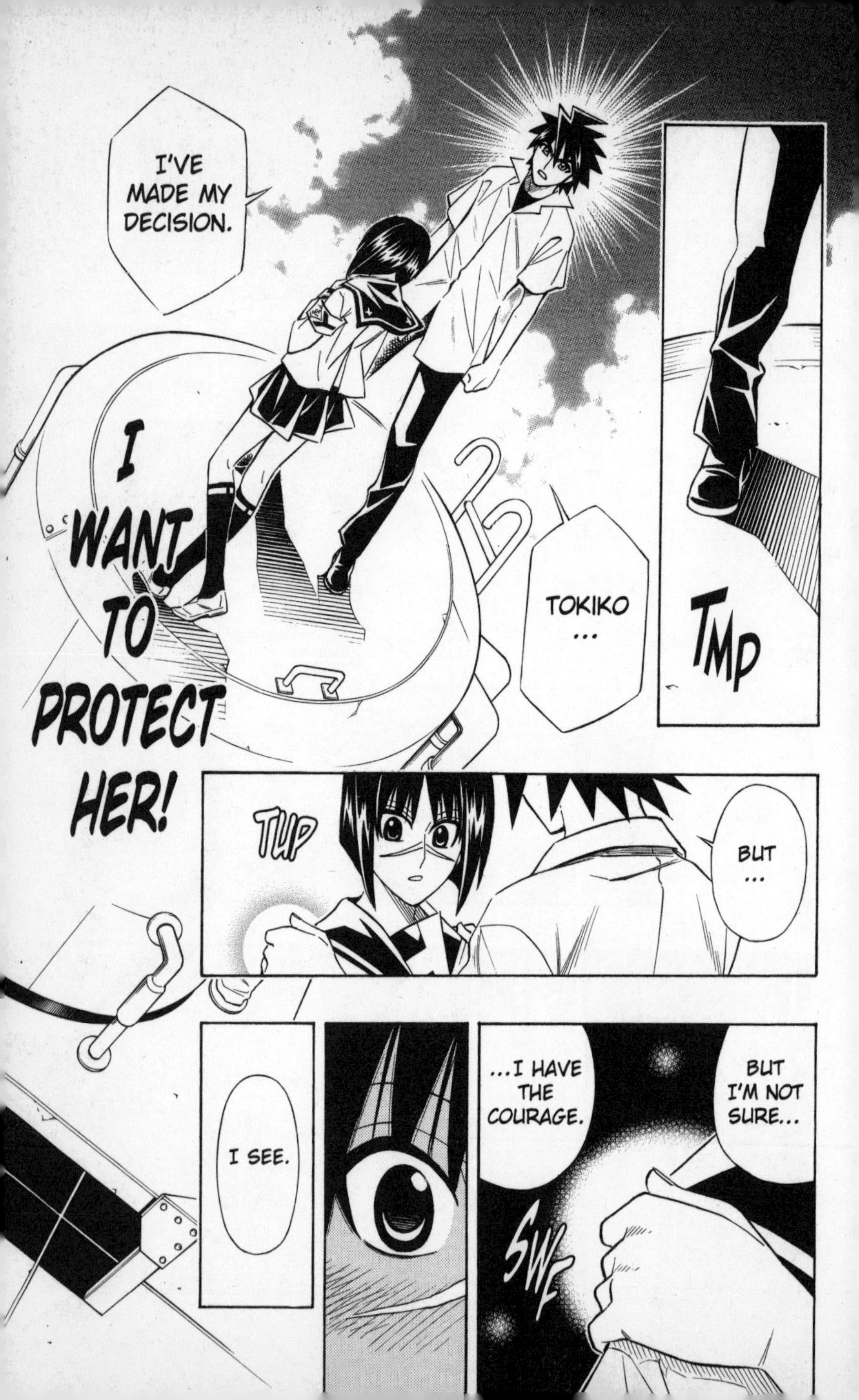
TMP
TOKIKO ...
I'VE MADE MY DECISION.
I WANT TO PROTECT HER!
BUT ...
TUP
BUT I'M NOT SURE...
...I HAVE THE COURAGE.
SWF
I SEE.

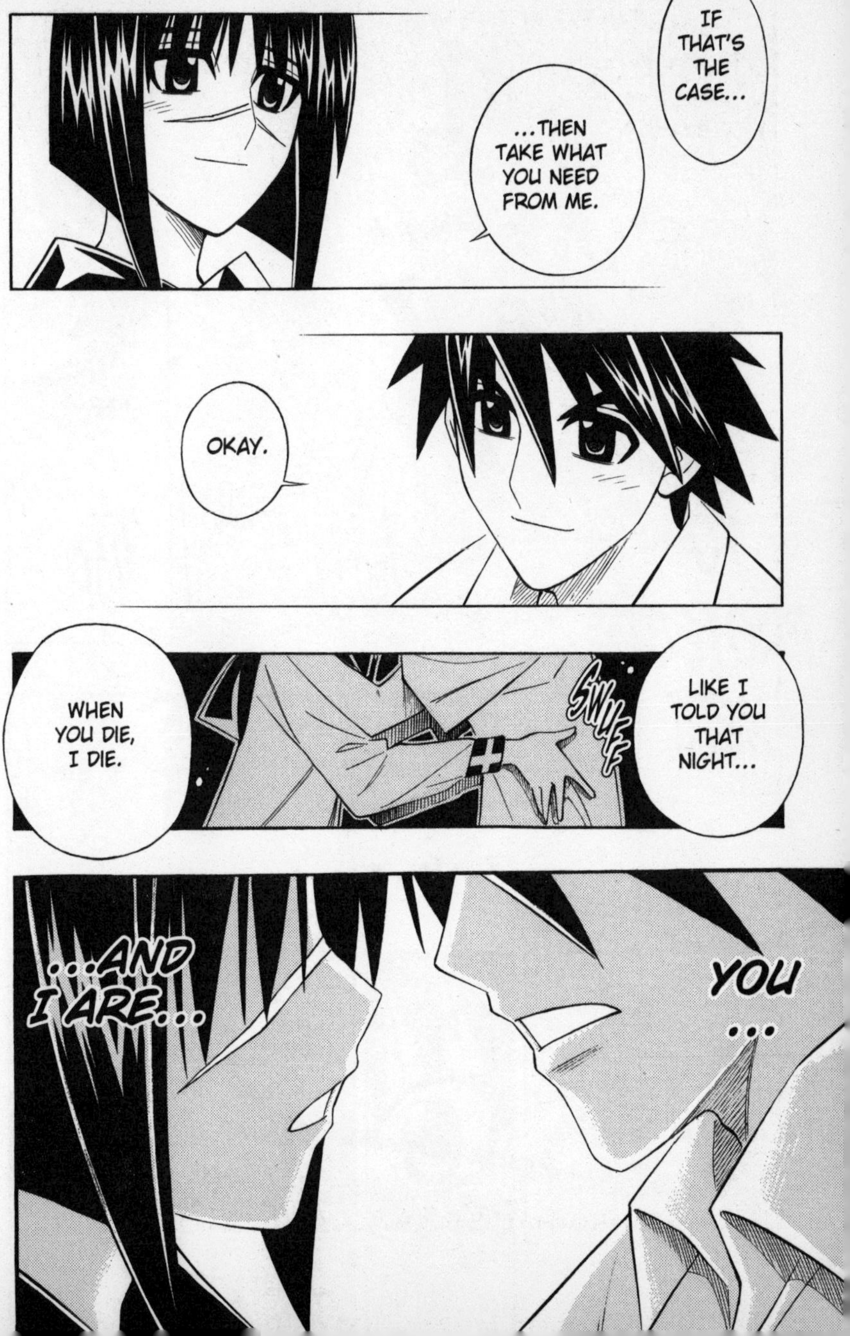
IF THAT'S THE CASE...
...THEN TAKE WHAT YOU NEED FROM ME.
OKAY.
LIKE I TOLD YOU THAT NIGHT...
SWUFF
WHEN YOU DIE, I DIE.
YOU...
...AND I ARE...

READ THIS WAY

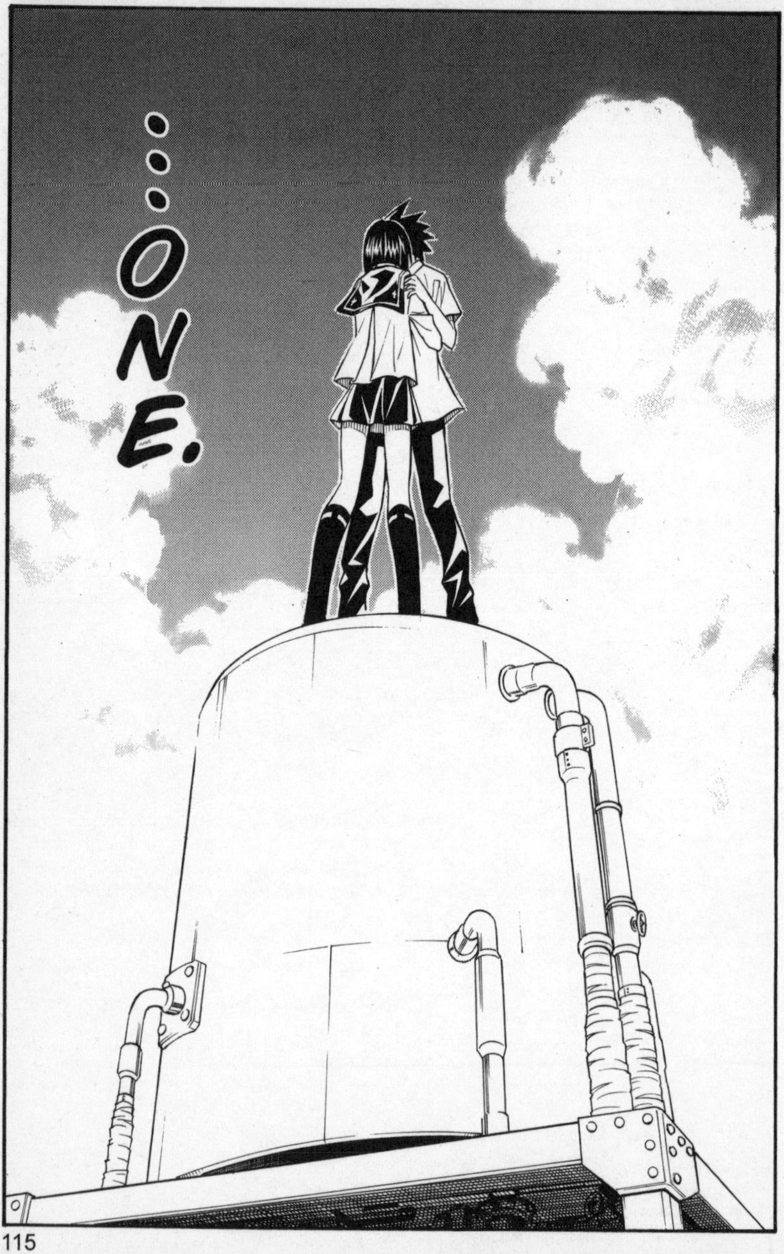
...ONE.

- · Height: 172 cm; Weight: 58 kg
- · Born: February 2; Aquarius; Blood Type: O; Age: 27
  (The above data was taken before she lost her body.)
- · Likes: Husband, daughter, and alchemy
- · Dislikes: Herself
- · Hobby: Making meat pies
- · Special Ability: Able to be like a mother to anyone
- · Affiliations: Former member of the Alchemist Army,
                  Assistant Section Chief of Philosopher's Stone
                  Research

Character File No. 16
ALEXANDRIA POWERED

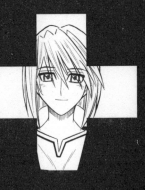

Author's Notes

- · She is one of the perpetrators of a great tragedy, though she had no ill intent when she created the black kakugane. She has suffered a great deal because of her creation and has worked tirelessly to repair the wrong she did, but she is unable to do it on her own. She's a well thought-out and balanced character.
- · This is one of the few times I've had the opportunity to do a maternal character. (I think there was one in *Rurouni Kenshin*...) I wish she could have had more of a chance to be motherly toward Kazuki and the others.
- · She's basically a bunch of disembodied brains. I thought this would have special appeal for people of my generation who remember Dr. Mamo, the villain from the first *Lupin III* movie. Originally, she was going to be one big brain, but that was such a cliché. So instead, I made her a cluster of cloned brains shaped like a mass of salmon roe. But something so grotesque might not have gotten past the censors, so I went with an array of brains in glass tanks. I still wish I could've done the salmon egg thing though.
- · I came up with Alexandria's human form on the spot. Since Victor was designed to be a counterpart for Kazuki, I designed her as a counterpart for Tokiko. I tinkered with her hairstyle a little and that was it. I think she turned out pretty well for a design I threw together on the spot.

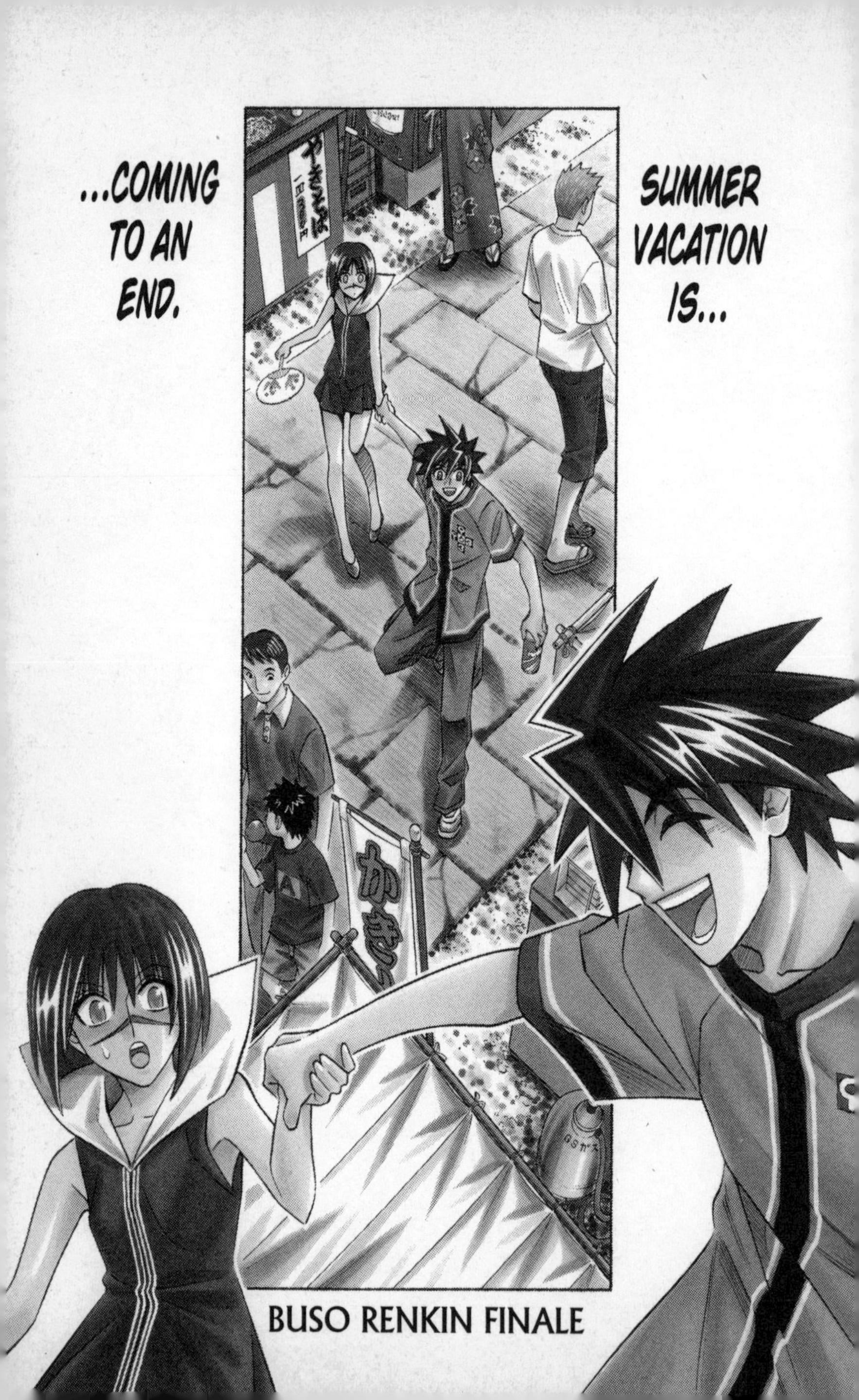
SUMMER VACATION IS...
...COMING TO AN END.
BUSO RENKIN FINALE

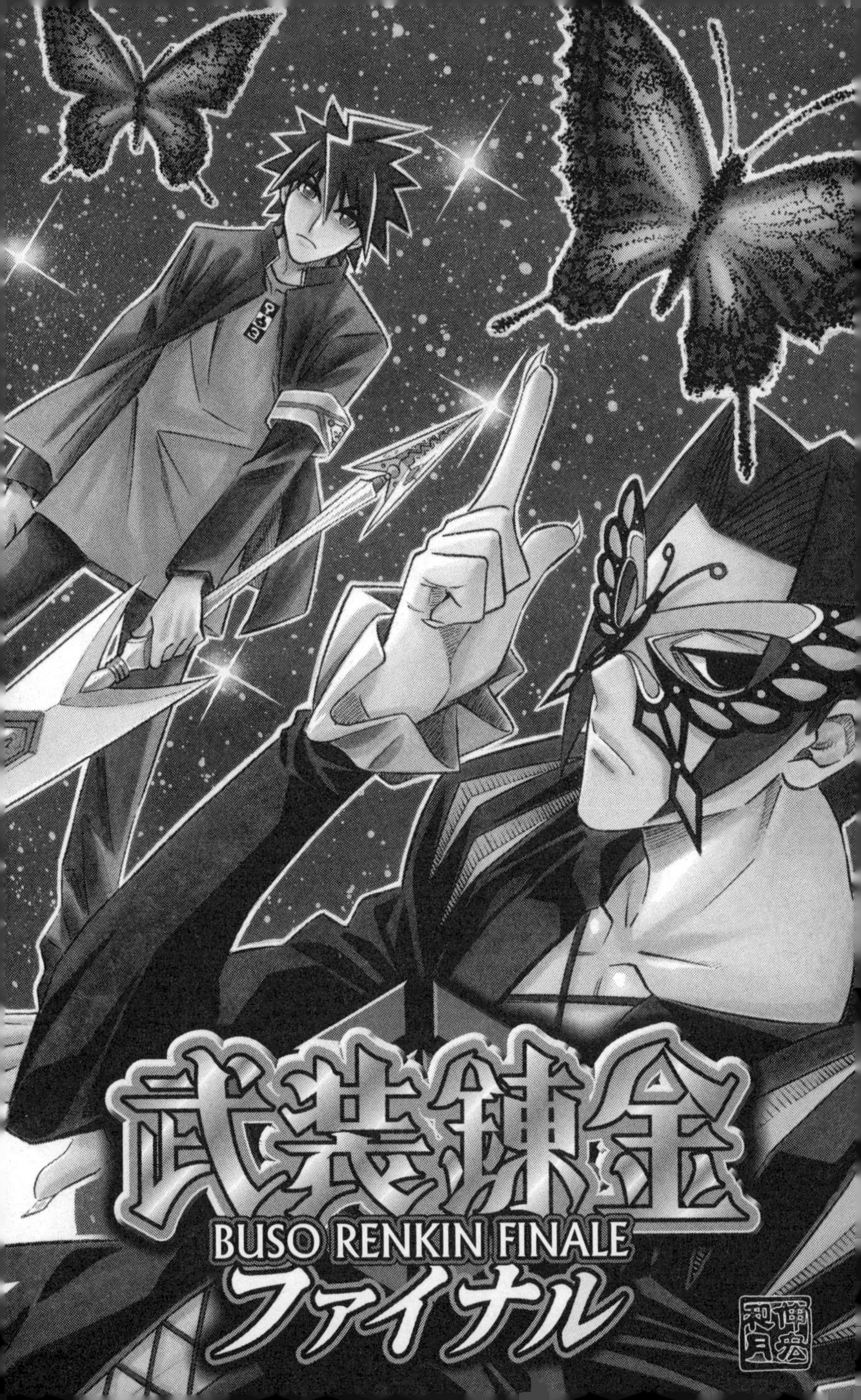
武装錬金
BUSO RENKIN FINALE
ファイナル

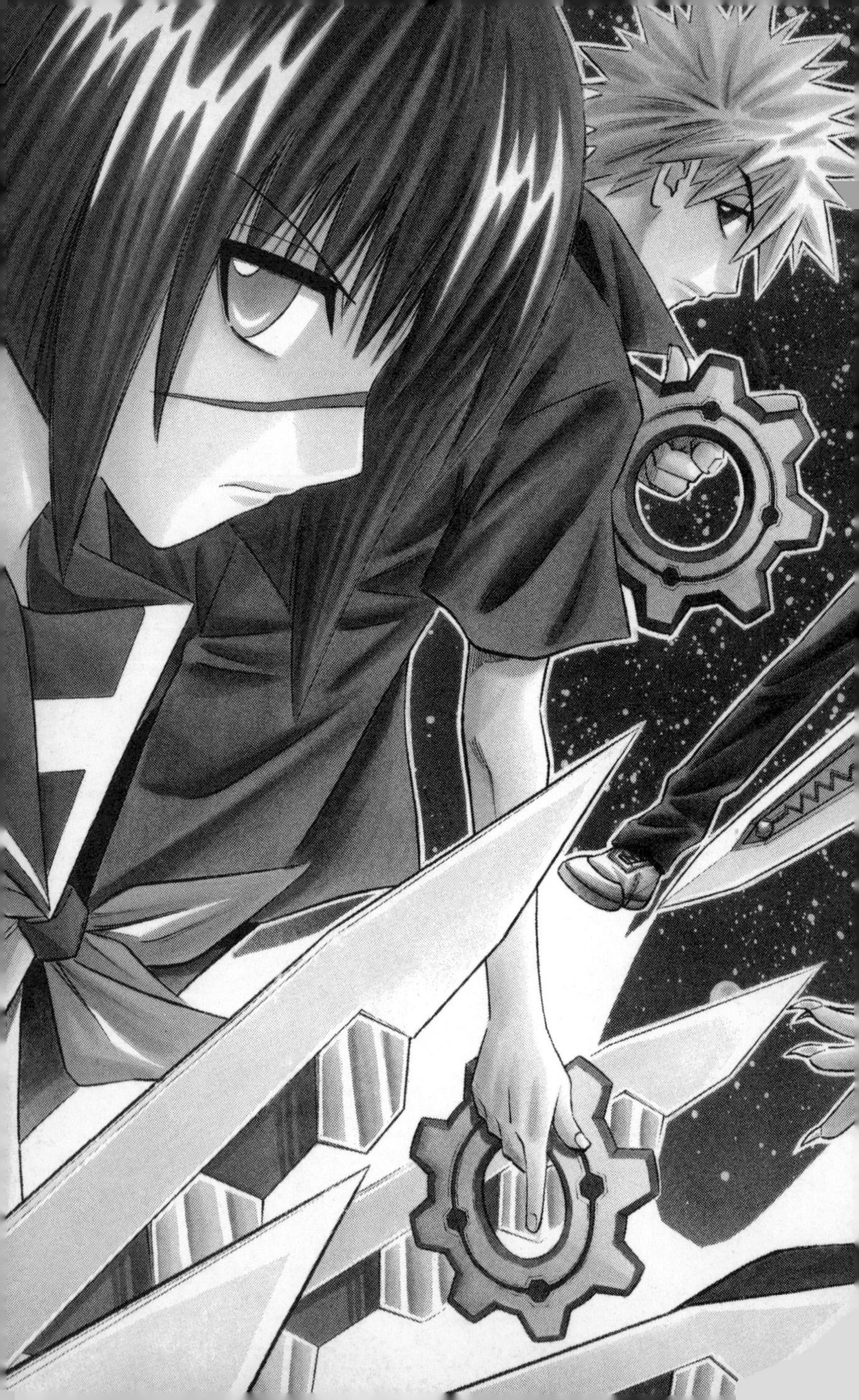

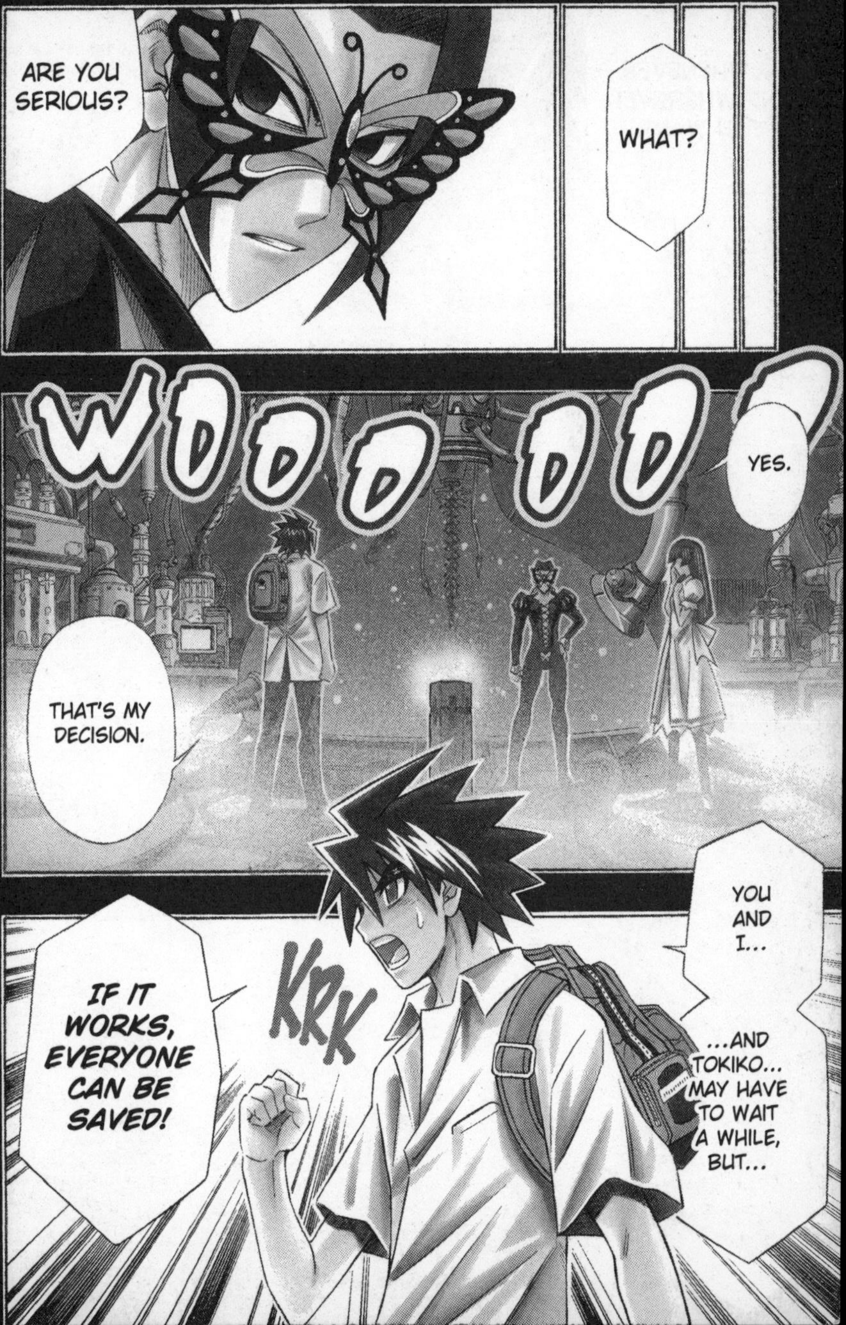
WHAT?
ARE YOU SERIOUS?
WOOOOO
YES.
THAT'S MY DECISION.
YOU AND I...
...AND TOKIKO... MAY HAVE TO WAIT A WHILE, BUT...
KRK
IF IT WORKS, EVERYONE CAN BE SAVED!

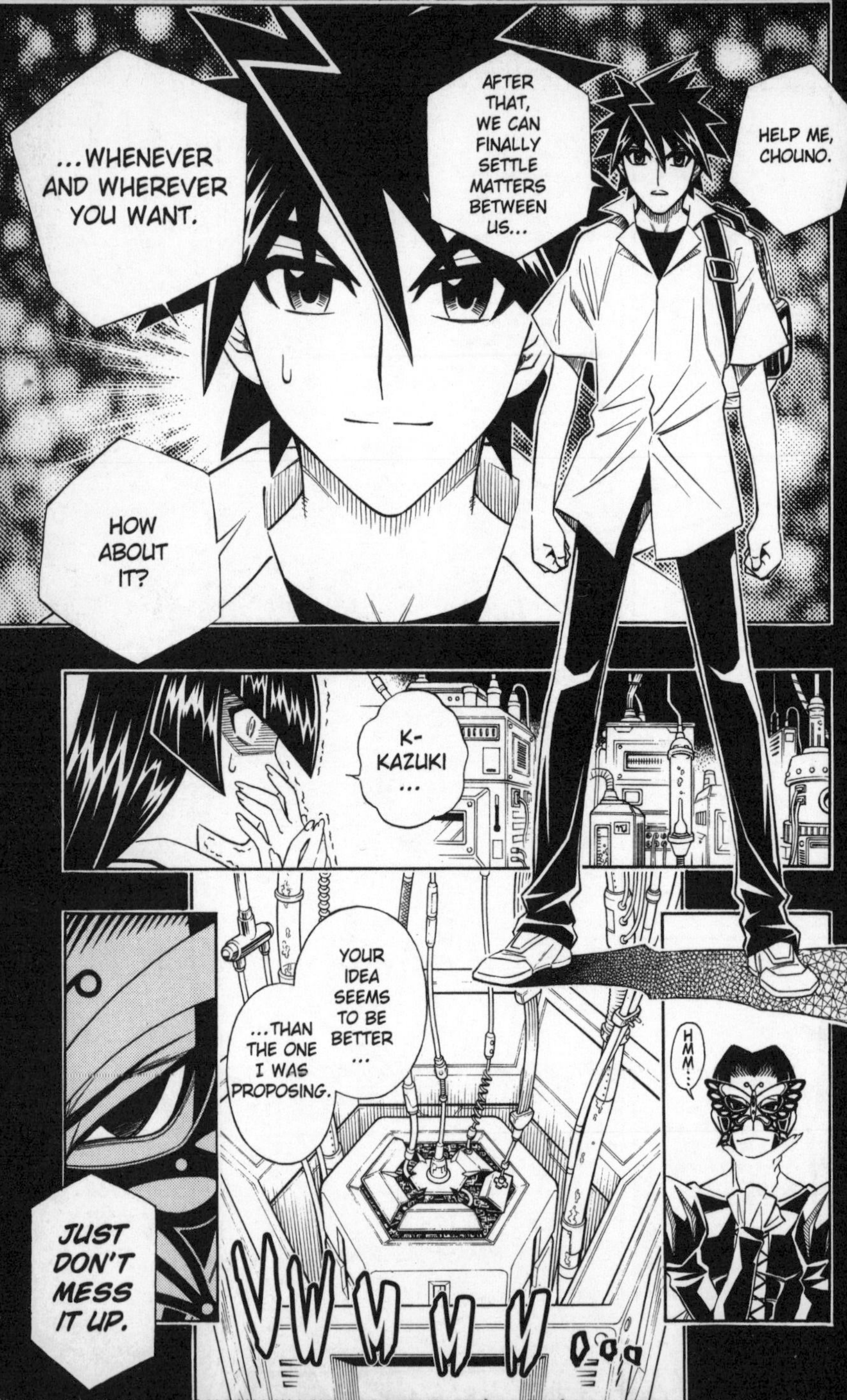
HELP ME, CHOUNO.
AFTER THAT, WE CAN FINALLY SETTLE MATTERS BETWEEN US...
...WHENEVER AND WHEREVER YOU WANT.
HOW ABOUT IT?
K-KAZUKI...
HMM...
YOUR IDEA SEEMS TO BE BETTER...
...THAN THE ONE I WAS PROPOSING.
JUST DON'T MESS IT UP.
VWMMM

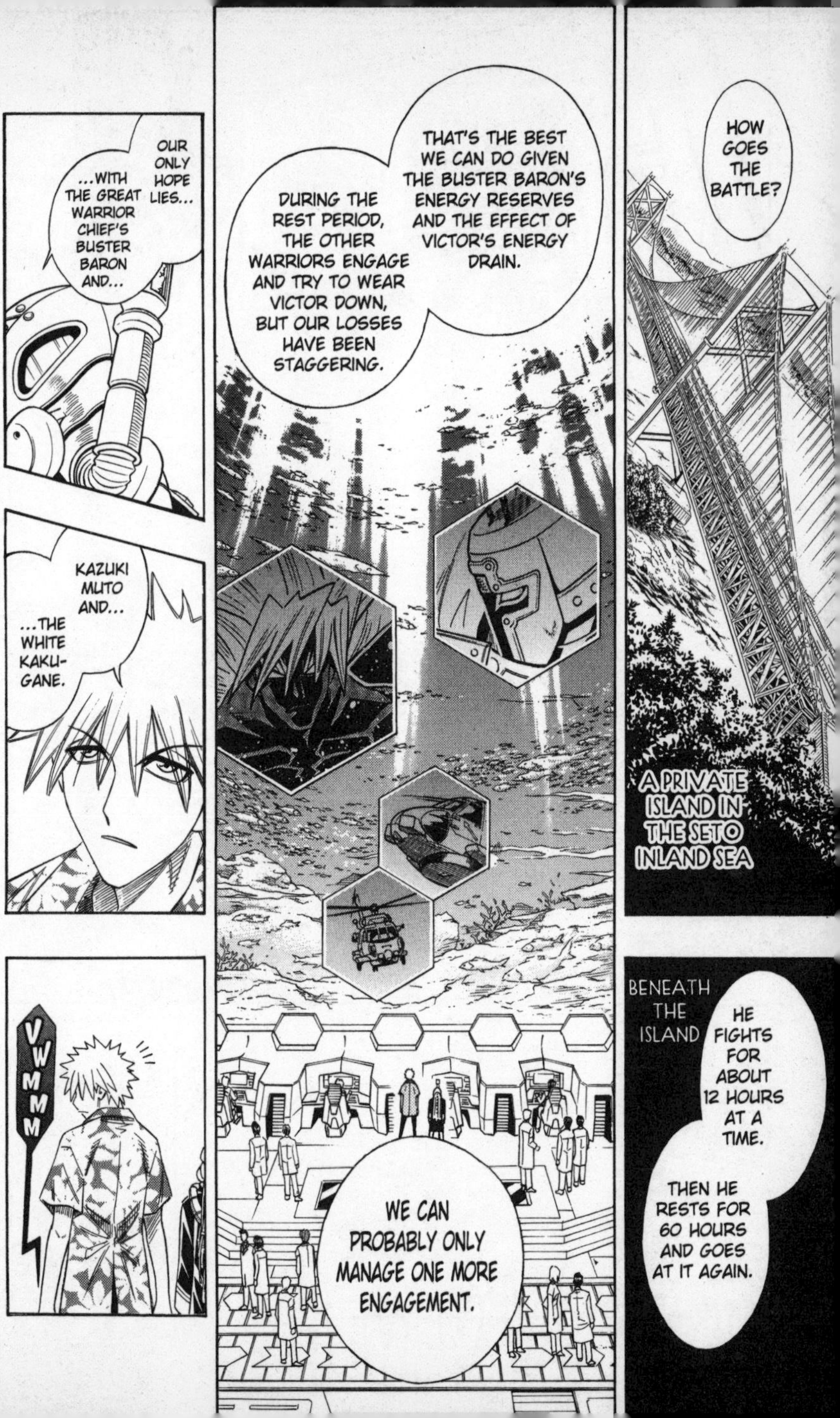
HOW GOES THE BATTLE?
A PRIVATE ISLAND IN THE SETO INLAND SEA
BENEATH THE ISLAND
HE FIGHTS FOR ABOUT 12 HOURS AT A TIME.
THEN HE RESTS FOR 60 HOURS AND GOES AT IT AGAIN.
THAT'S THE BEST WE CAN DO GIVEN THE BUSTER BARON'S ENERGY RESERVES AND THE EFFECT OF VICTOR'S ENERGY DRAIN.
DURING THE REST PERIOD, THE OTHER WARRIORS ENGAGE AND TRY TO WEAR VICTOR DOWN, BUT OUR LOSSES HAVE BEEN STAGGERING.
WE CAN PROBABLY ONLY MANAGE ONE MORE ENGAGEMENT.
OUR ONLY HOPE LIES...
...WITH THE GREAT WARRIOR CHIEF'S BUSTER BARON AND...
KAZUKI MUTO AND...
...THE WHITE KAKU-GANE.
VWMMM

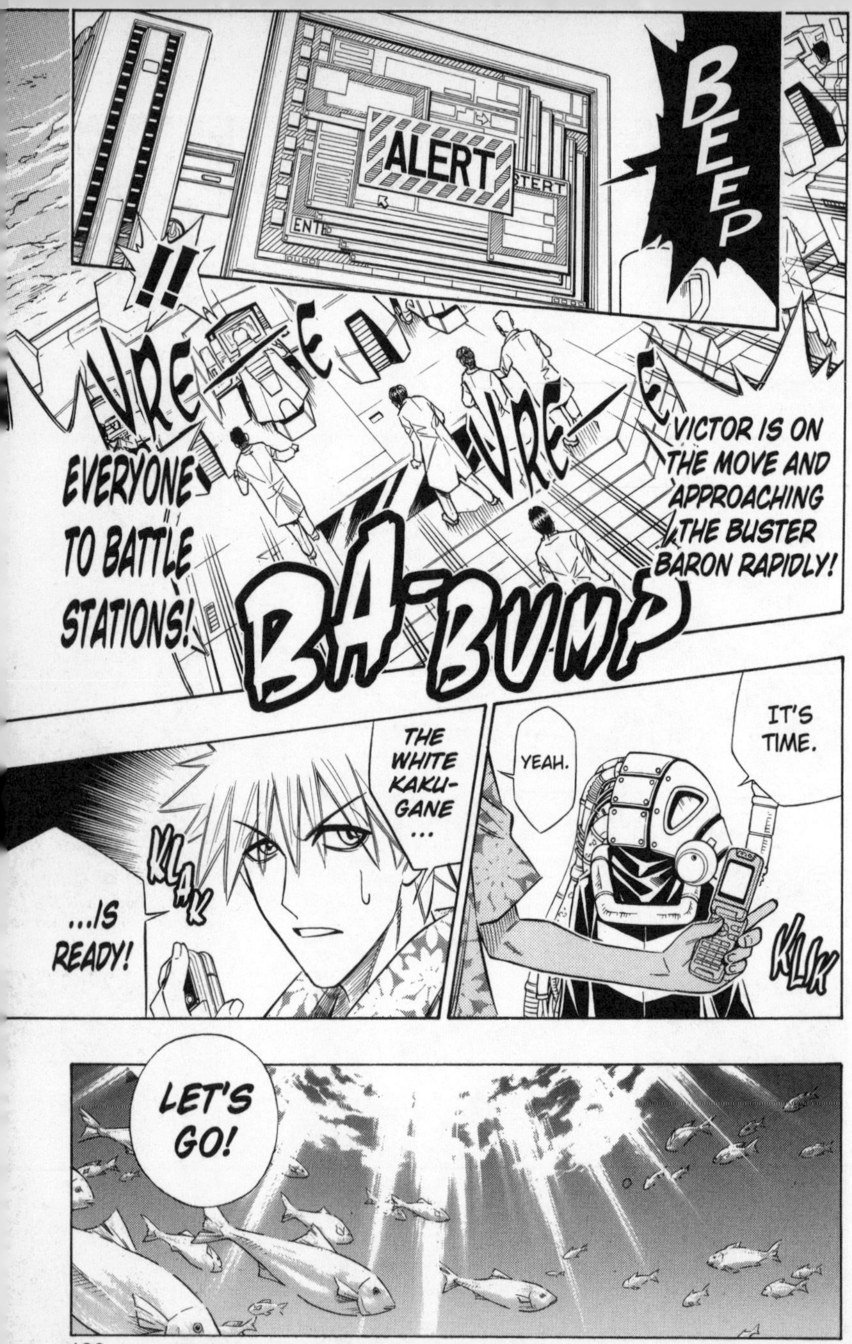
BEEP
ALERT
!!
VICTOR IS ON THE MOVE AND APPROACHING THE BUSTER BARON RAPIDLY!
VRE
EVERYONE TO BATTLE STATIONS!
BA-BUMP
IT'S TIME.
YEAH.
KLIK
THE WHITE KAKUGANE...
KLAK
...IS READY!
LET'S GO!

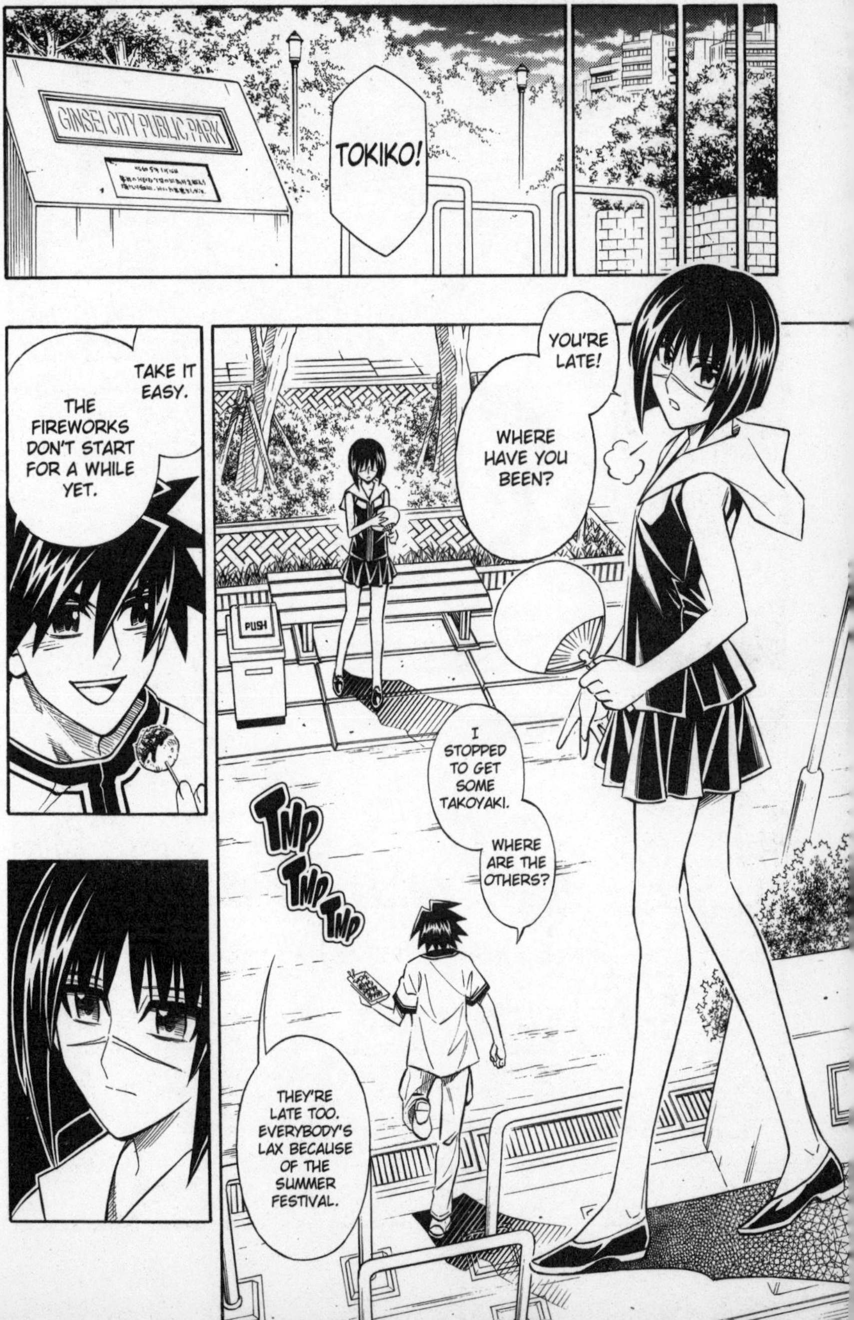
TOKIKO!
GINSEI CITY PUBLIC PARK
YOU'RE LATE!
WHERE HAVE YOU BEEN?
I STOPPED TO GET SOME TAKOYAKI.
WHERE ARE THE OTHERS?
PUSH
TMP TMP TMP TMP
THEY'RE LATE TOO. EVERYBODY'S LAX BECAUSE OF THE SUMMER FESTIVAL.
TAKE IT EASY.
THE FIREWORKS DON'T START FOR A WHILE YET.

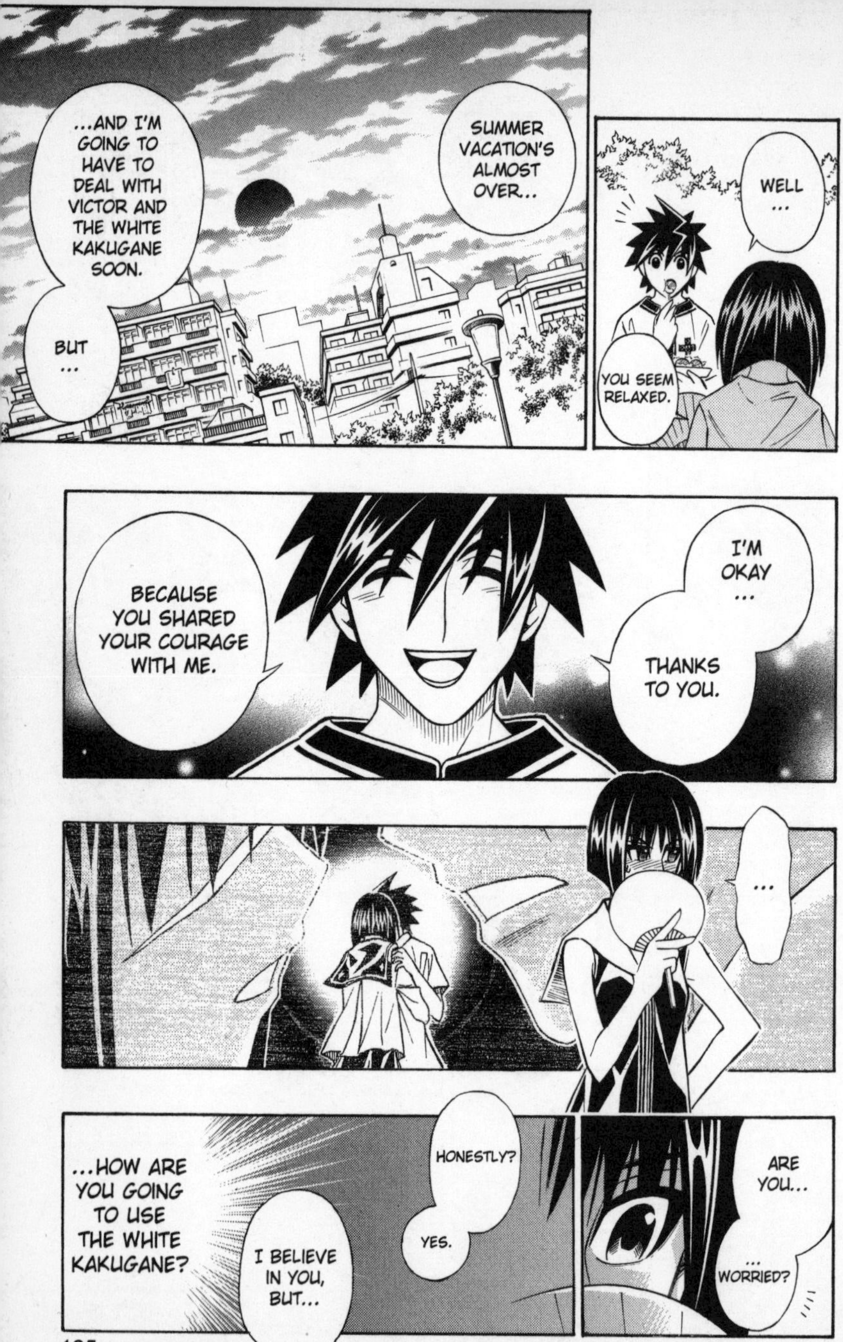
WELL...
YOU SEEM RELAXED.
SUMMER VACATION'S ALMOST OVER...
...AND I'M GOING TO HAVE TO DEAL WITH VICTOR AND THE WHITE KAKUGANE SOON.
BUT...
I'M OKAY...
THANKS TO YOU.
BECAUSE YOU SHARED YOUR COURAGE WITH ME.
...
ARE YOU...
...WORRIED?
HONESTLY?
YES.
I BELIEVE IN YOU, BUT...
...HOW ARE YOU GOING TO USE THE WHITE KAKUGANE?

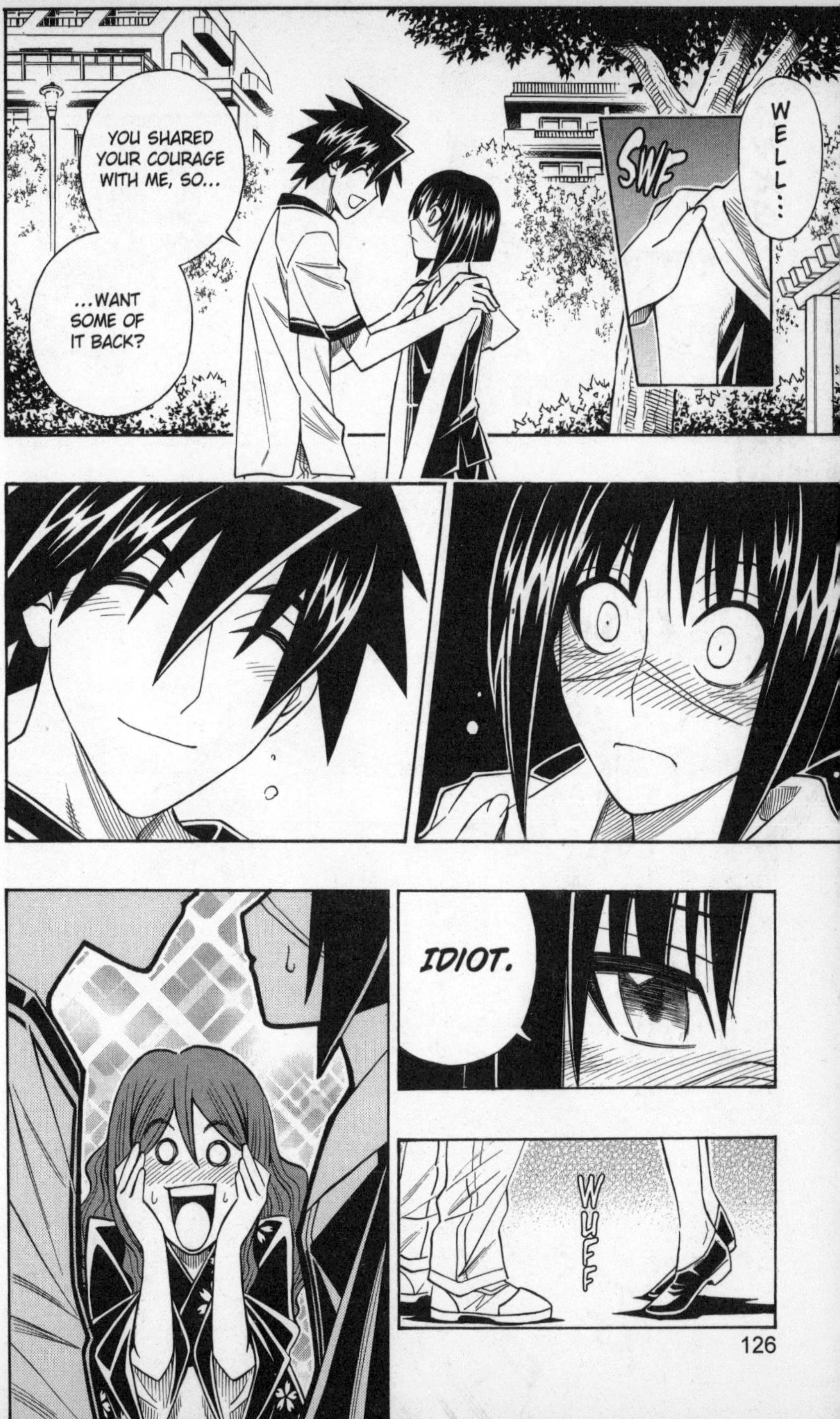
WELL...
SWF
YOU SHARED YOUR COURAGE WITH ME, SO...
...WANT SOME OF IT BACK?
IDIOT.
WUFF

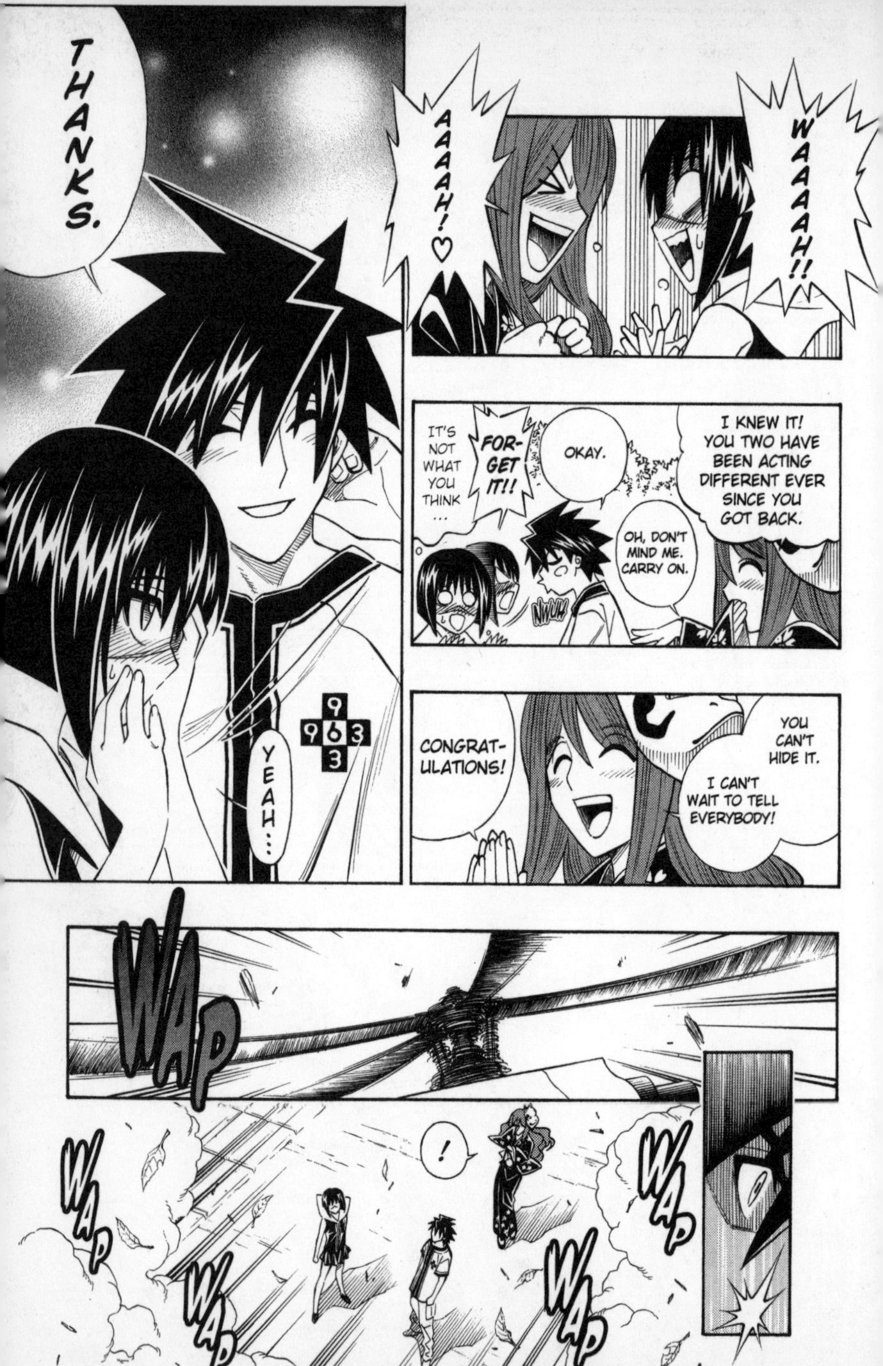
WAAAAAH!!
AAAAAH!♥
I KNEW IT! YOU TWO HAVE BEEN ACTING DIFFERENT EVER SINCE YOU GOT BACK.
OKAY.
FOR-GET IT!!
IT'S NOT WHAT YOU THINK…
OH, DON'T MIND ME. CARRY ON.
NWUH
YOU CAN'T HIDE IT.
I CAN'T WAIT TO TELL EVERYBODY!
CONGRAT-ULATIONS!
THANKS.
YEAH…
WAP
WAP
!
WAP
WAP
WAP

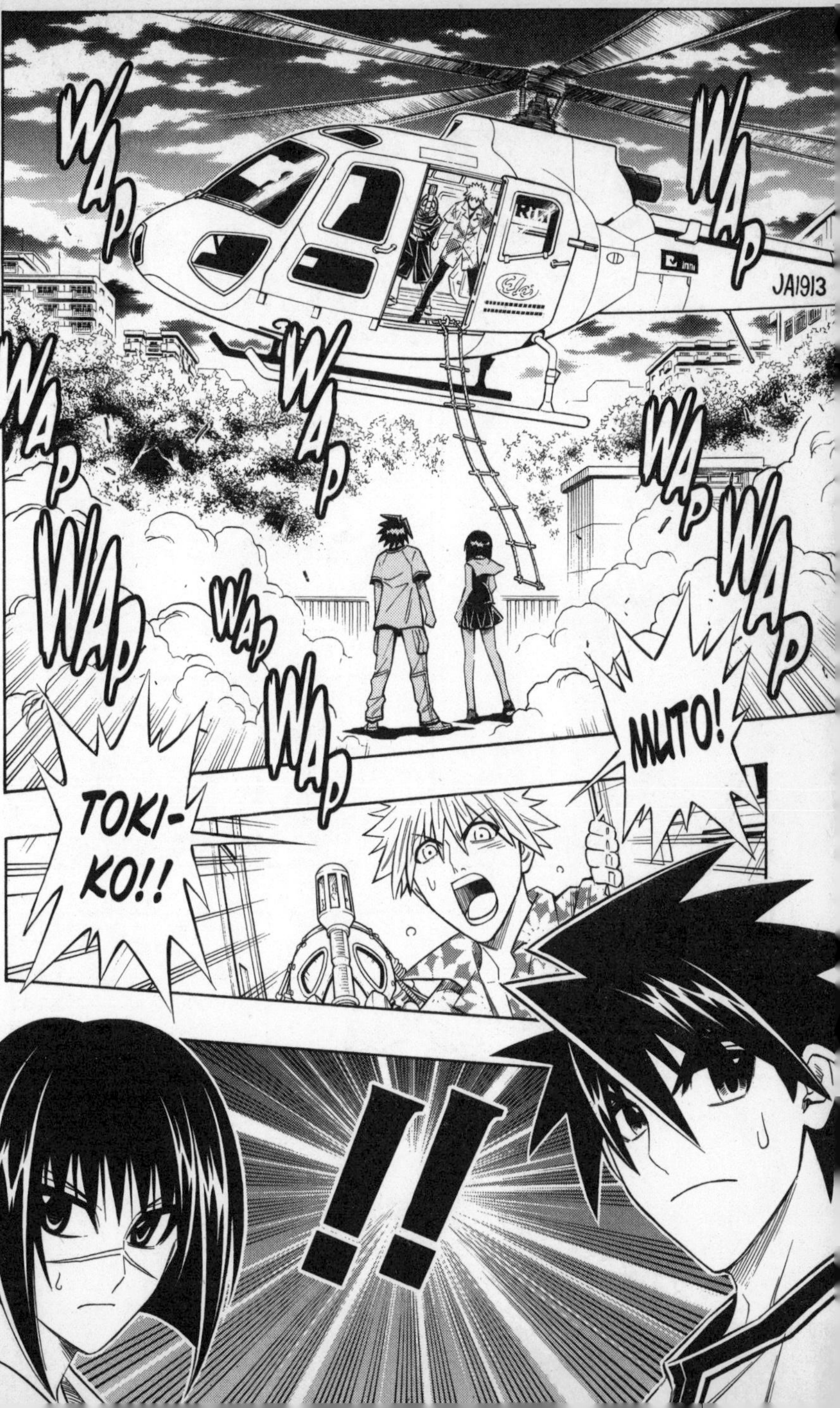

WAP
WAP
JA1913
WAP
WAP
WAP
WAP
WAP
WAP
WAP
WAP
MUTO!
TOKI-KO!!
!!

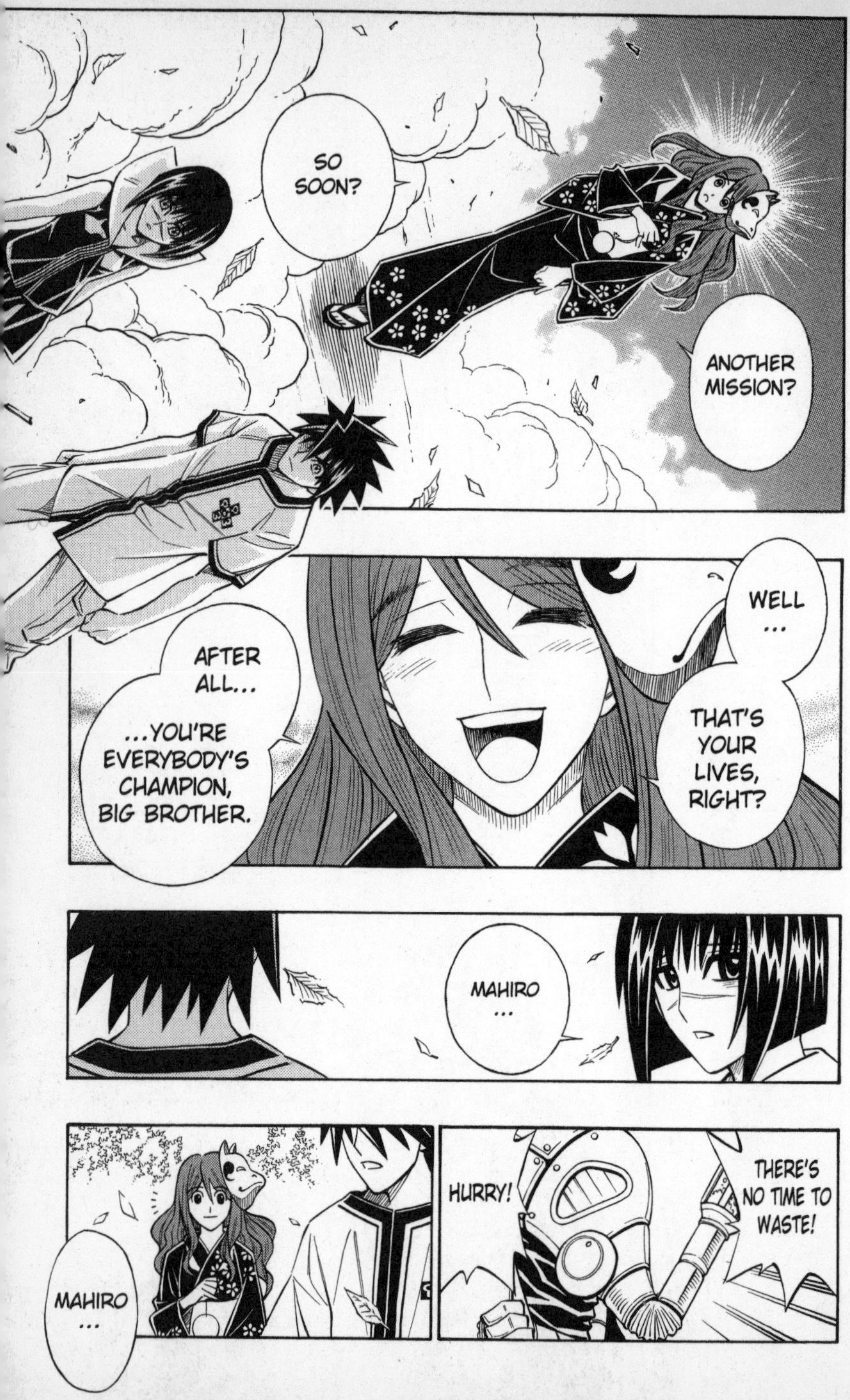
ANOTHER MISSION?
SO SOON?
WELL...
THAT'S YOUR LIVES, RIGHT?
AFTER ALL...
...YOU'RE EVERYBODY'S CHAMPION, BIG BROTHER.
MAHIRO...
THERE'S NO TIME TO WASTE!
HURRY!
MAHIRO...

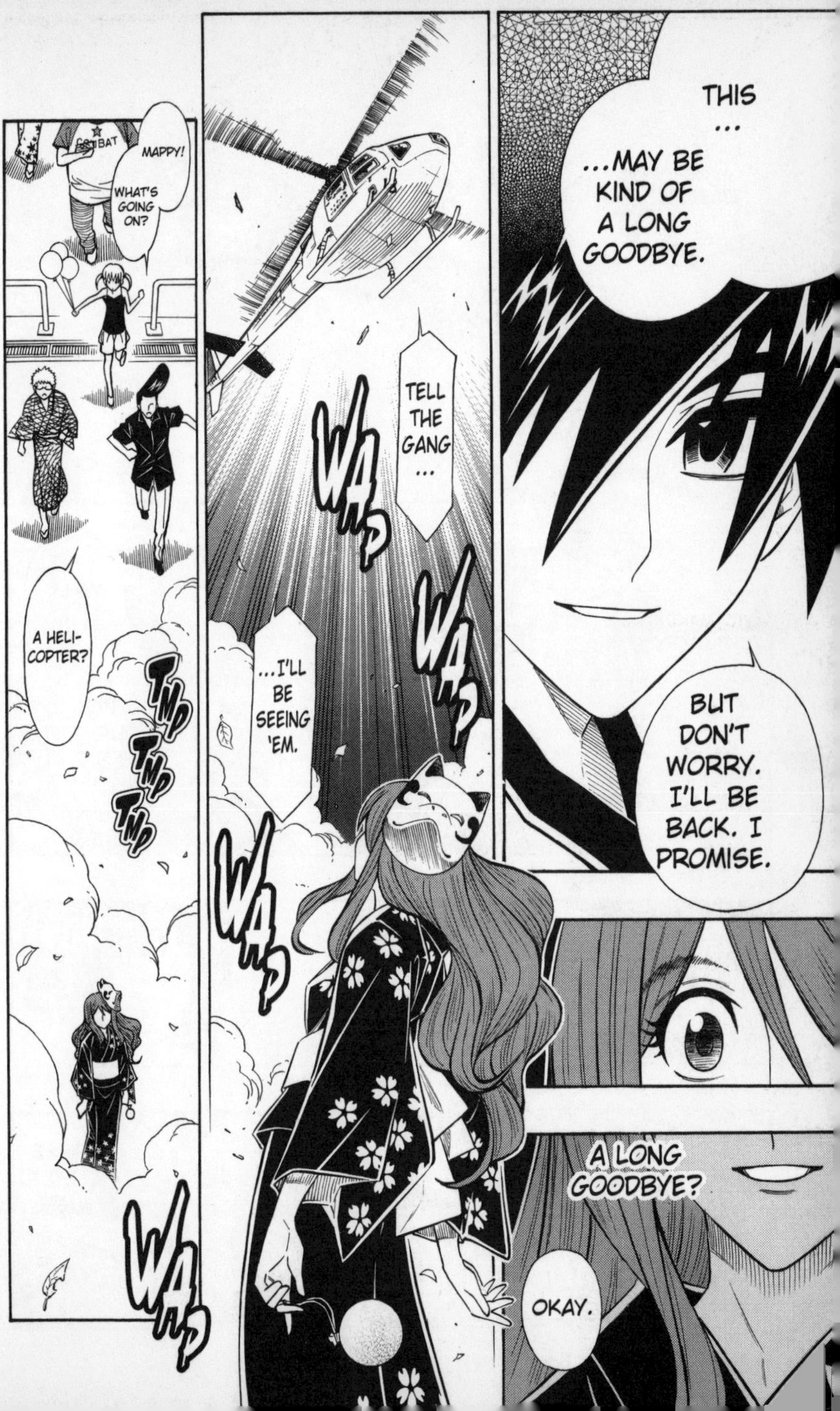
THIS ...
...MAY BE KIND OF A LONG GOODBYE.
BUT DON'T WORRY. I'LL BE BACK. I PROMISE.
A LONG GOODBYE?
OKAY.
TELL THE GANG ...
...I'LL BE SEEING 'EM.
WAP WAP WAP WAP
MAPPY!
WHAT'S GOING ON?
A HELI-COPTER?
TMP TMP TMP

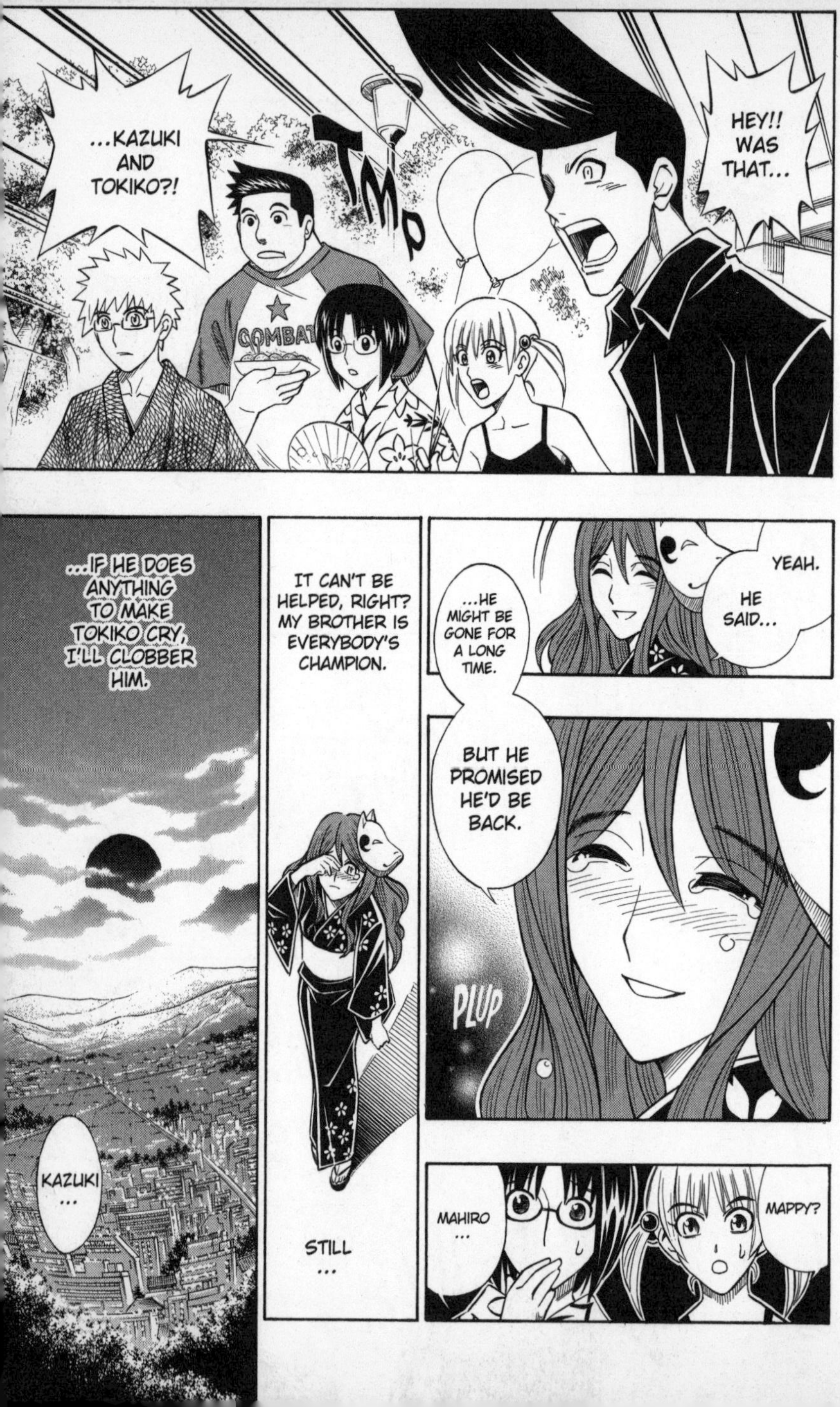
HEY!! WAS THAT...
TMP
...KAZUKI AND TOKIKO?!
YEAH.
HE SAID...
...HE MIGHT BE GONE FOR A LONG TIME.
BUT HE PROMISED HE'D BE BACK.
PLUP
MAPPY?
MAHIRO ...
IT CAN'T BE HELPED, RIGHT? MY BROTHER IS EVERYBODY'S CHAMPION.
STILL ...
...IF HE DOES ANYTHING TO MAKE TOKIKO CRY, I'LL CLOBBER HIM.
KAZUKI ...

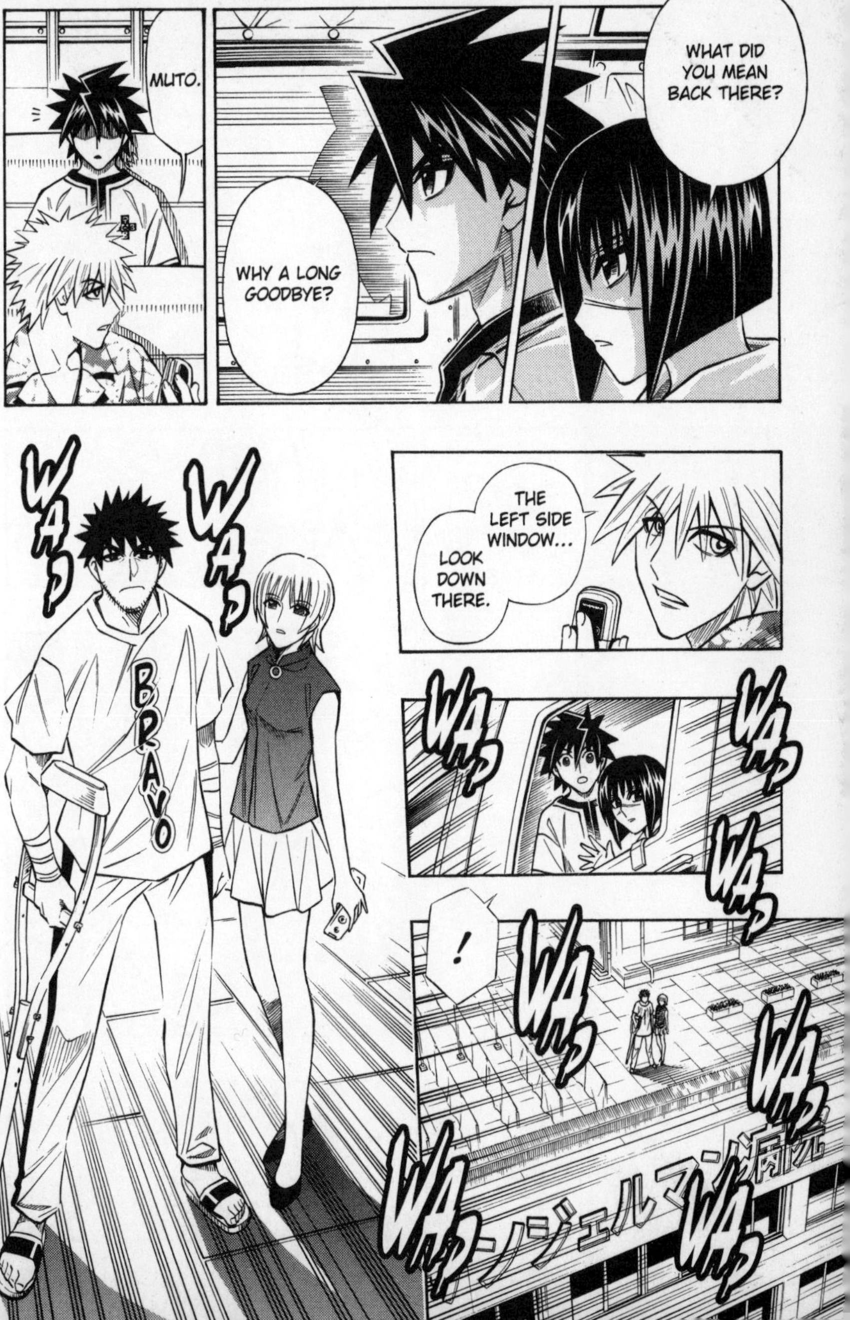
WHAT DID YOU MEAN BACK THERE?
WHY A LONG GOODBYE?
MUTO.
THE LEFT SIDE WINDOW...
LOOK DOWN THERE.
WAP
WAP
WAP
!
WAP
WAP
WAP
WAP
WAP
WAP
BRAVO

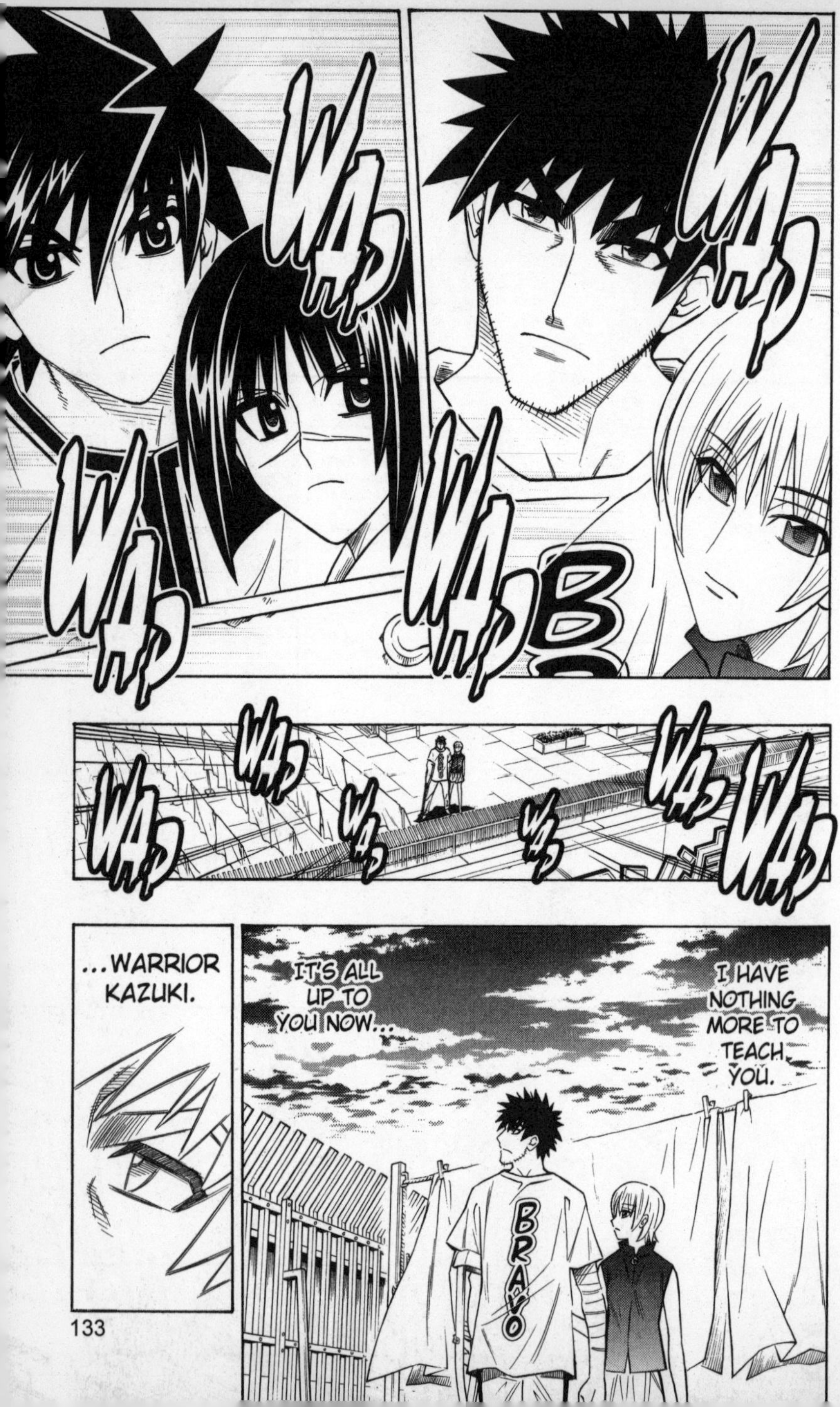
WA WA
WA WA
WA WA
WA WA
WA WA WA WA
I HAVE NOTHING MORE TO TEACH YOU.
IT'S ALL UP TO YOU NOW...
...WARRIOR KAZUKI.
BRAVO

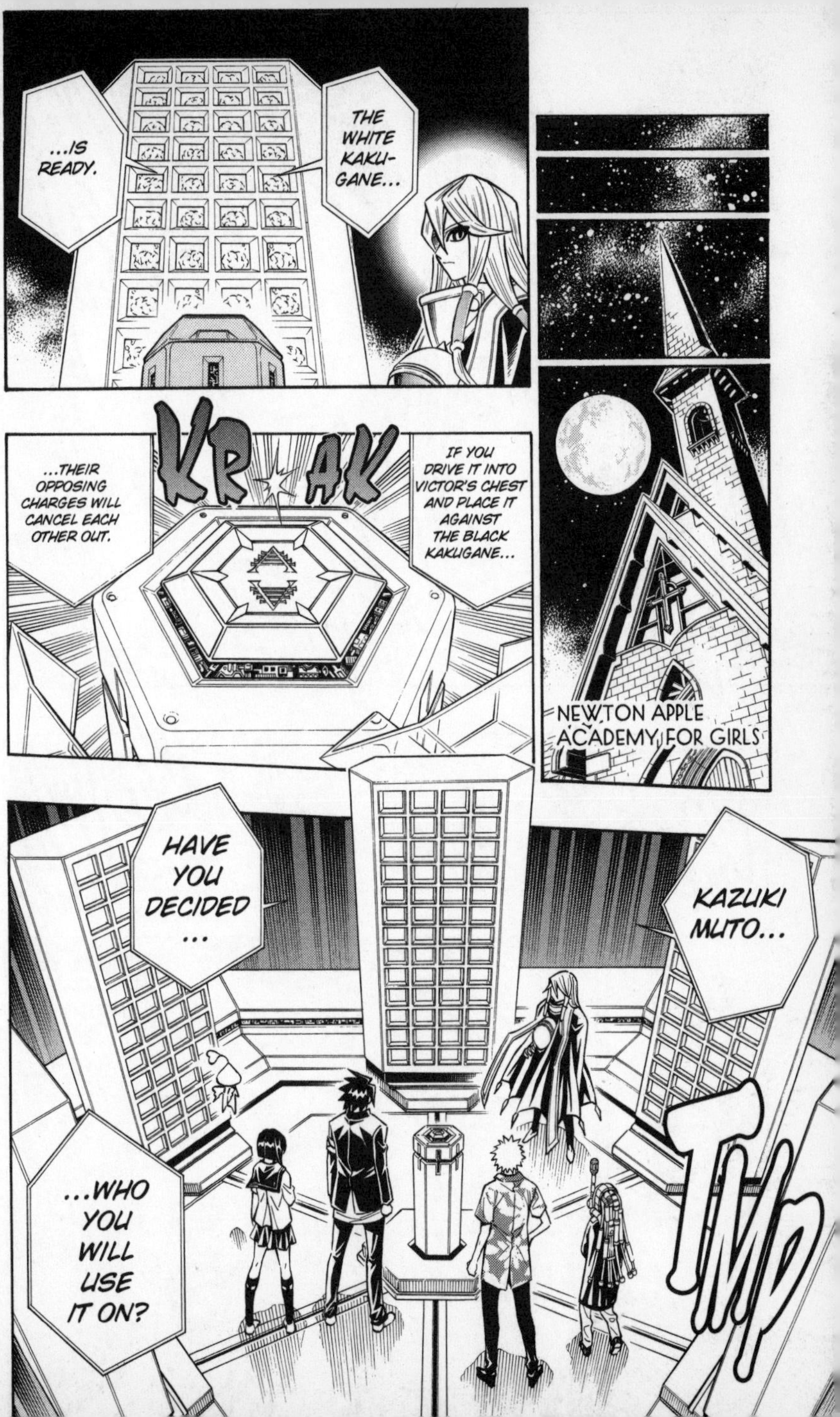
NEWTON APPLE ACADEMY FOR GIRLS
THE WHITE KAKUGANE...
...IS READY.
IF YOU DRIVE IT INTO VICTOR'S CHEST AND PLACE IT AGAINST THE BLACK KAKUGANE...
KRAK
...THEIR OPPOSING CHARGES WILL CANCEL EACH OTHER OUT.
KAZUKI MUTO...
HAVE YOU DECIDED...
THMP
...WHO YOU WILL USE IT ON?

READ THIS WAY

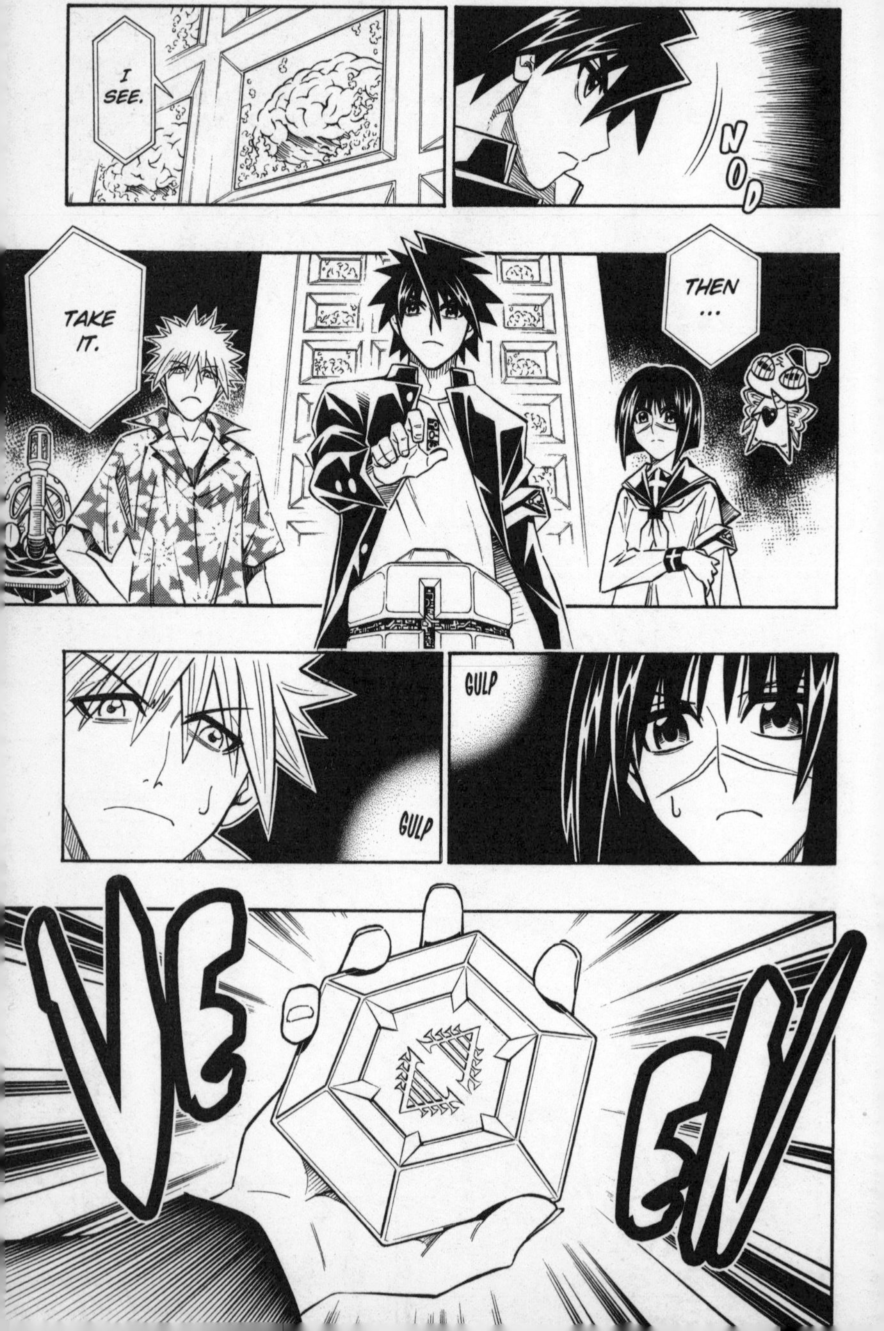
NOD
I SEE.
THEN...
TAKE IT.
GULP
GULP

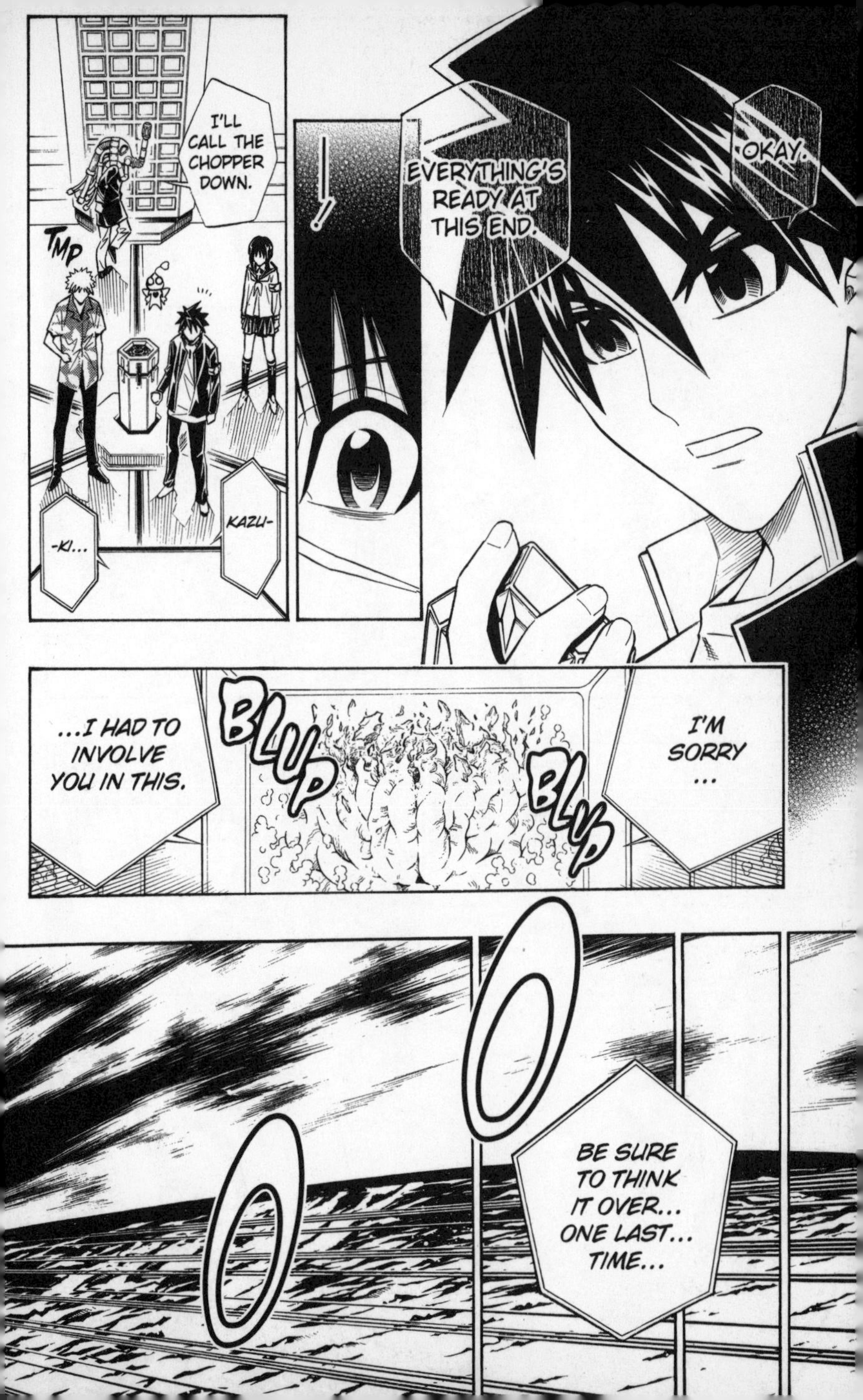
OKAY.
EVERYTHING'S READY AT THIS END.
!
I'LL CALL THE CHOPPER DOWN.
TMP
KAZU-
-KI...
I'M SORRY ...
BLUP
BLUP
...I HAD TO INVOLVE YOU IN THIS.
BE SURE TO THINK IT OVER... ONE LAST... TIME...

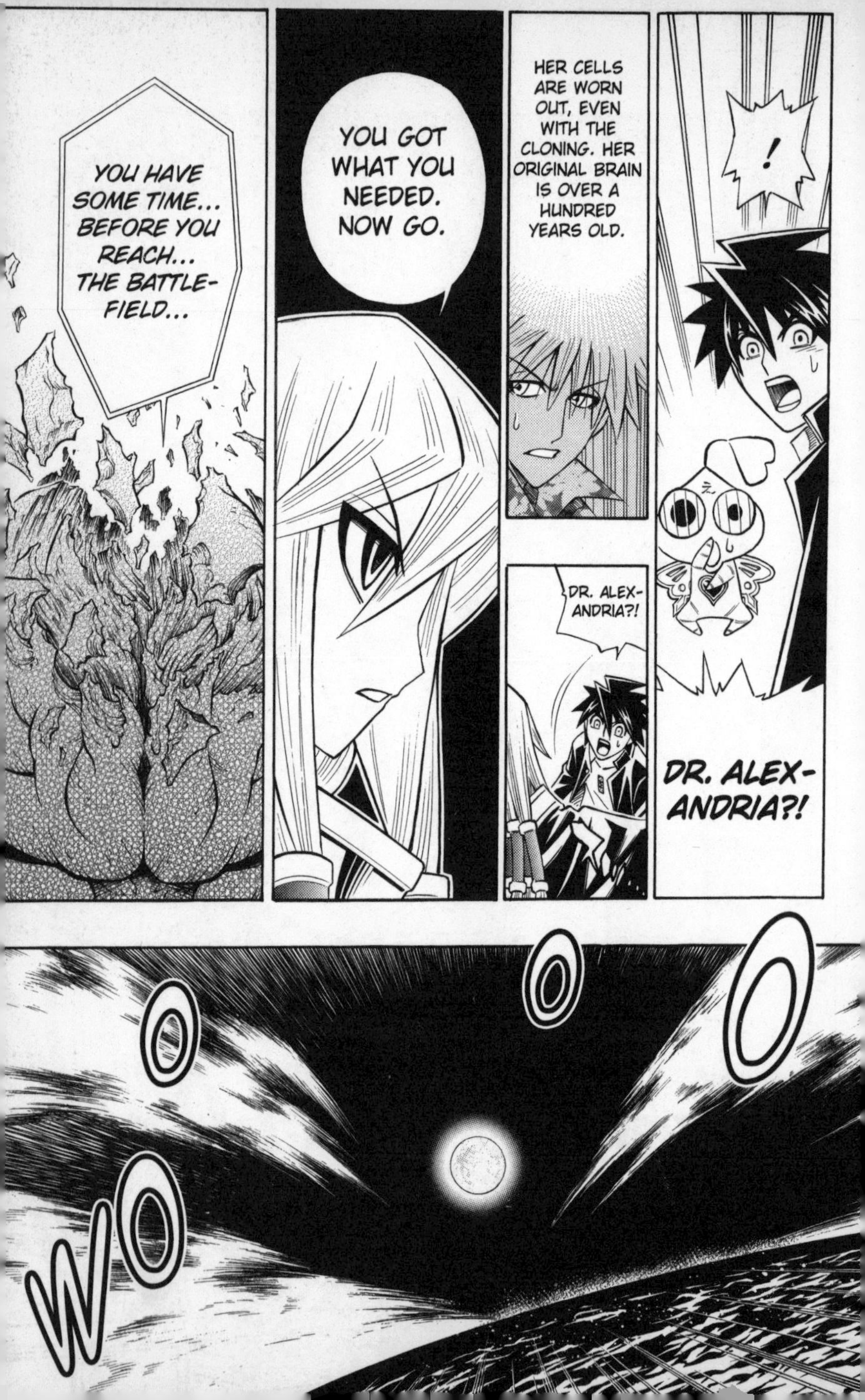
!
DR. ALEX-ANDRIA?!
HER CELLS ARE WORN OUT, EVEN WITH THE CLONING. HER ORIGINAL BRAIN IS OVER A HUNDRED YEARS OLD.
DR. ALEX-ANDRIA?!
YOU GOT WHAT YOU NEEDED. NOW GO.
YOU HAVE SOME TIME... BEFORE YOU REACH... THE BATTLE-FIELD...
WOOOO

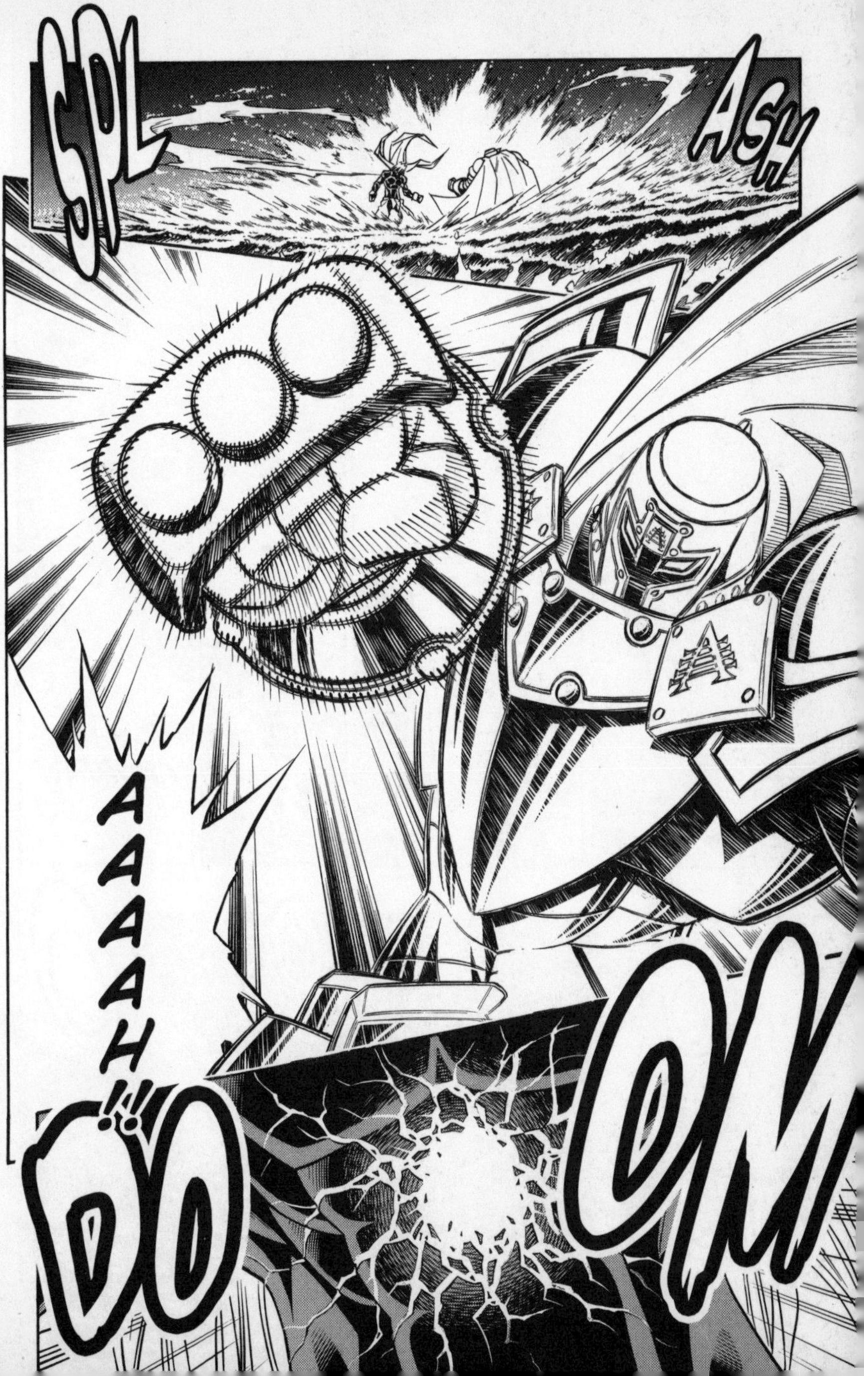
SPL
ASH
AAAAAH!!
DO
OM

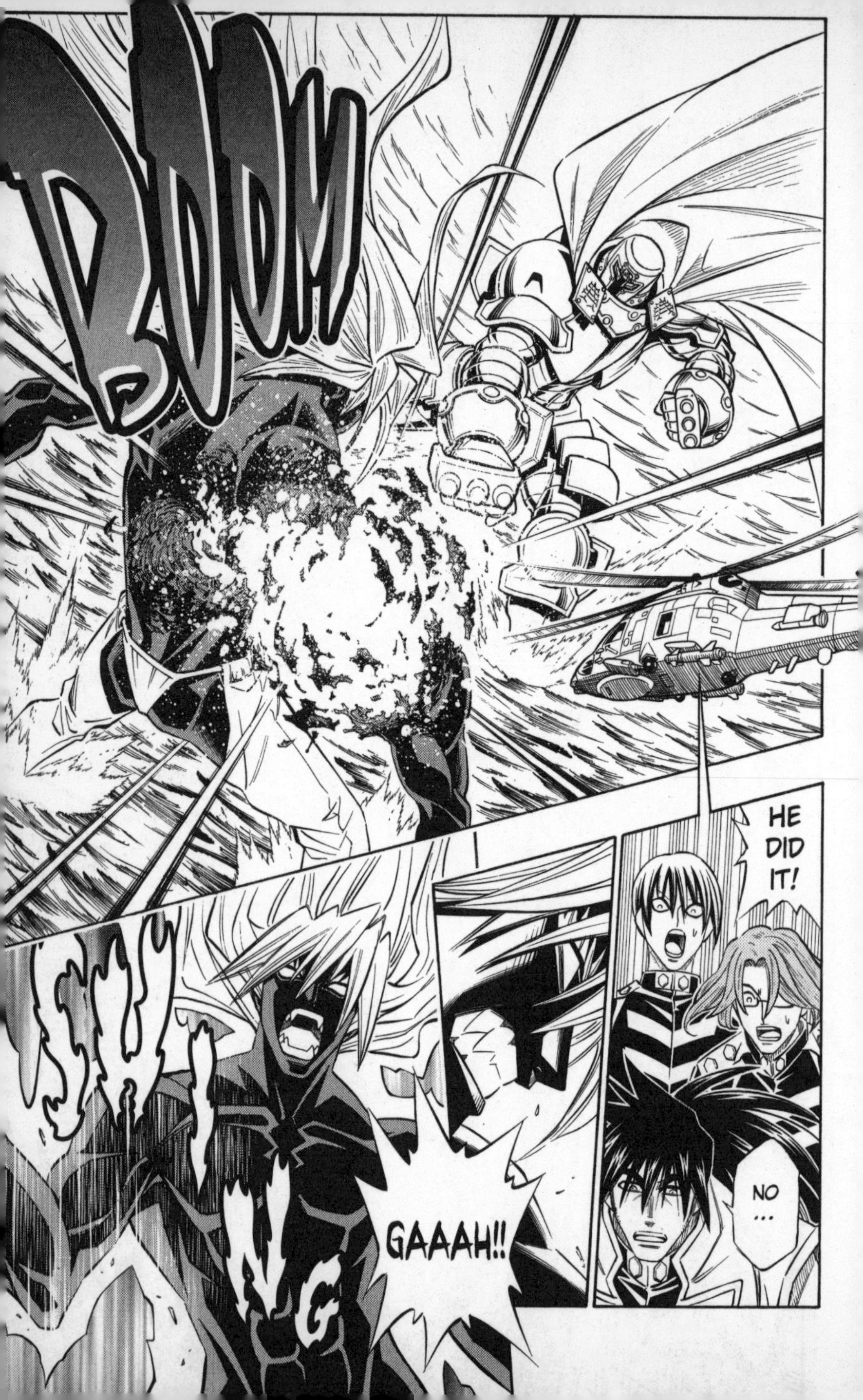
DOOOM
HE DID IT!
NO...
GAAAH!!

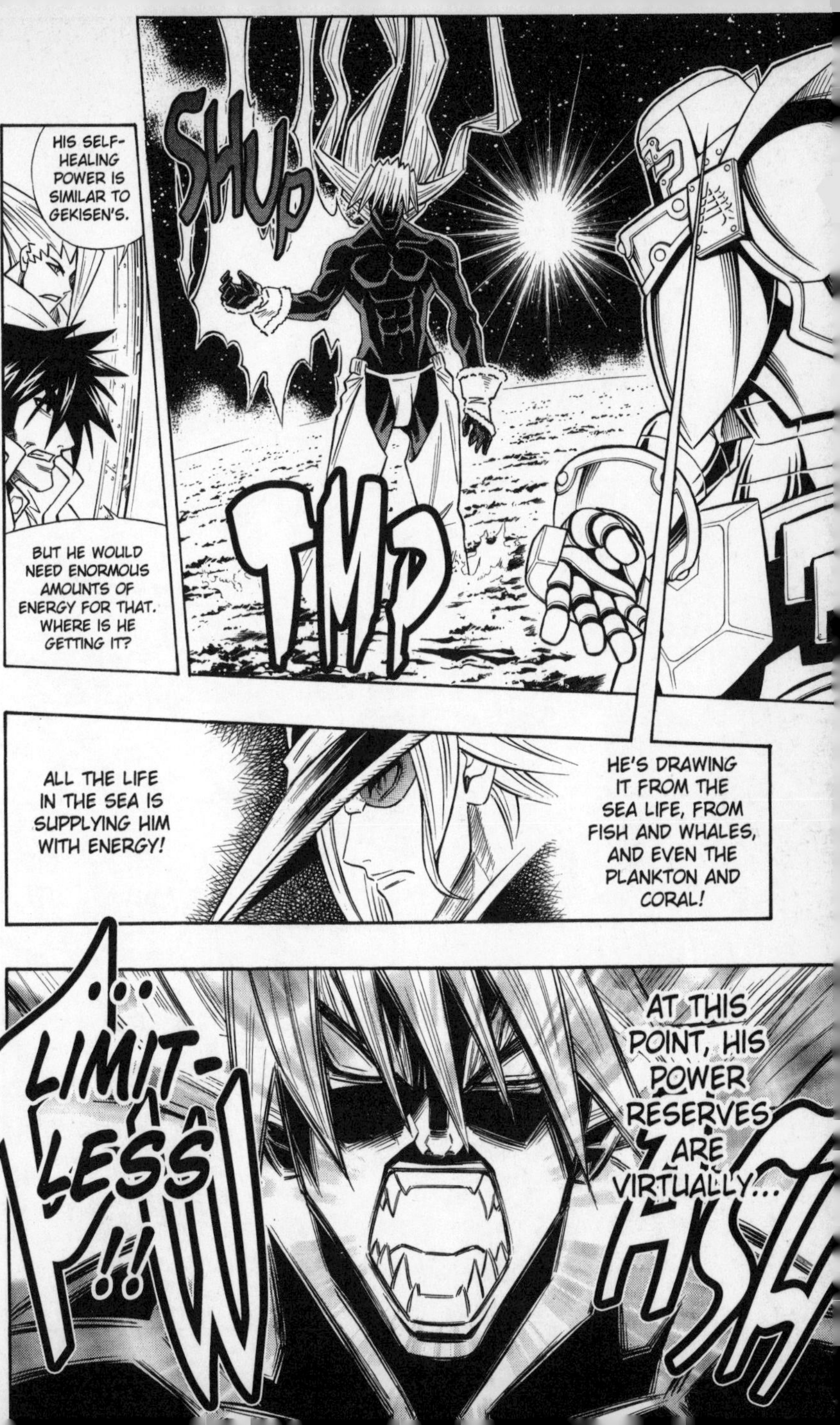
SHUP
TMP
HIS SELF-HEALING POWER IS SIMILAR TO GEKISEN'S.
BUT HE WOULD NEED ENORMOUS AMOUNTS OF ENERGY FOR THAT. WHERE IS HE GETTING IT?
HE'S DRAWING IT FROM THE SEA LIFE, FROM FISH AND WHALES, AND EVEN THE PLANKTON AND CORAL!
ALL THE LIFE IN THE SEA IS SUPPLYING HIM WITH ENERGY!
AT THIS POINT, HIS POWER RESERVES ARE VIRTUALLY...
...LIMIT-LESS!!

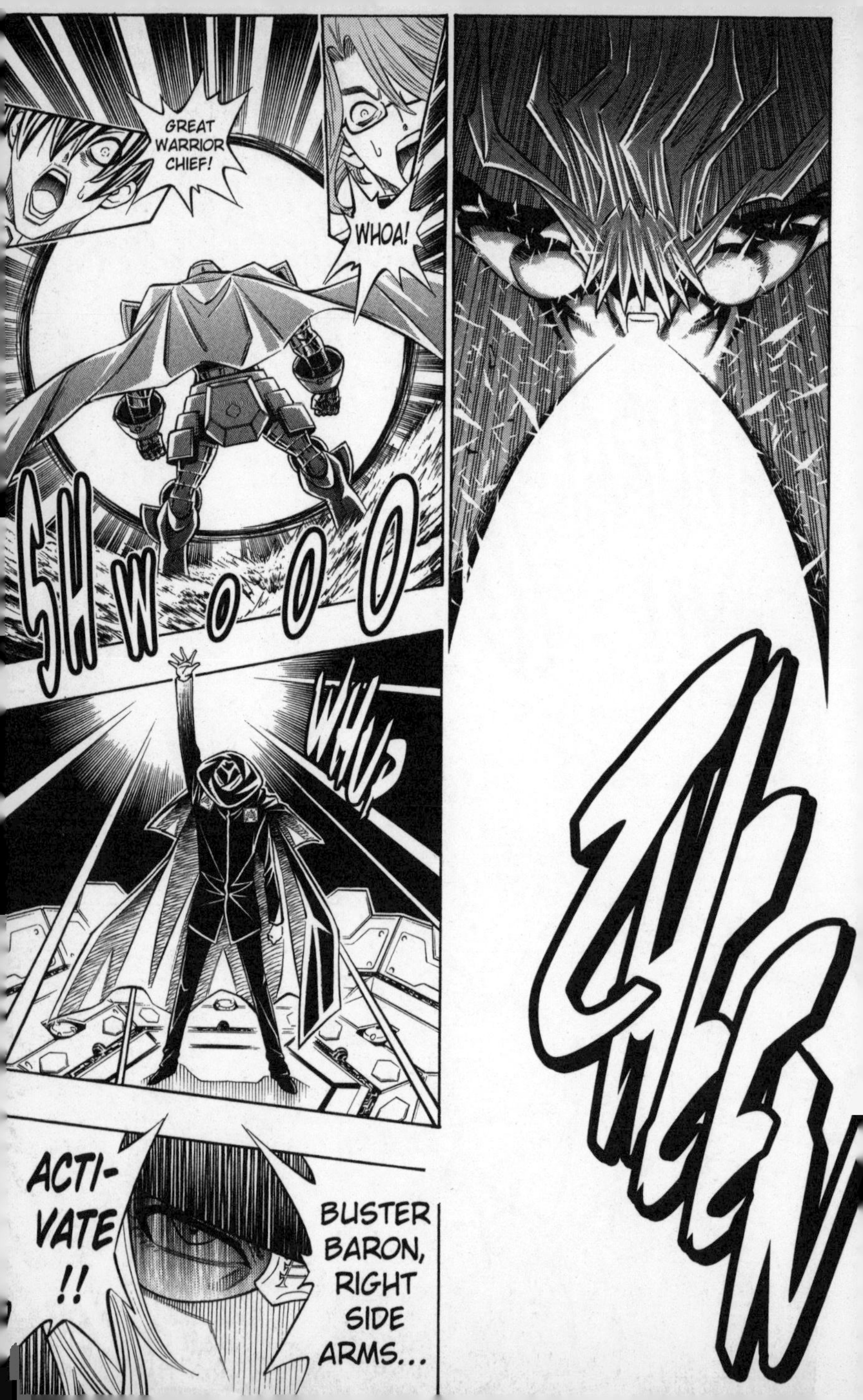
WHOA!
GREAT WARRIOR CHIEF!
SHWOOO
WHUP
BUSTER BARON, RIGHT SIDE ARMS...
ACTI-VATE!!

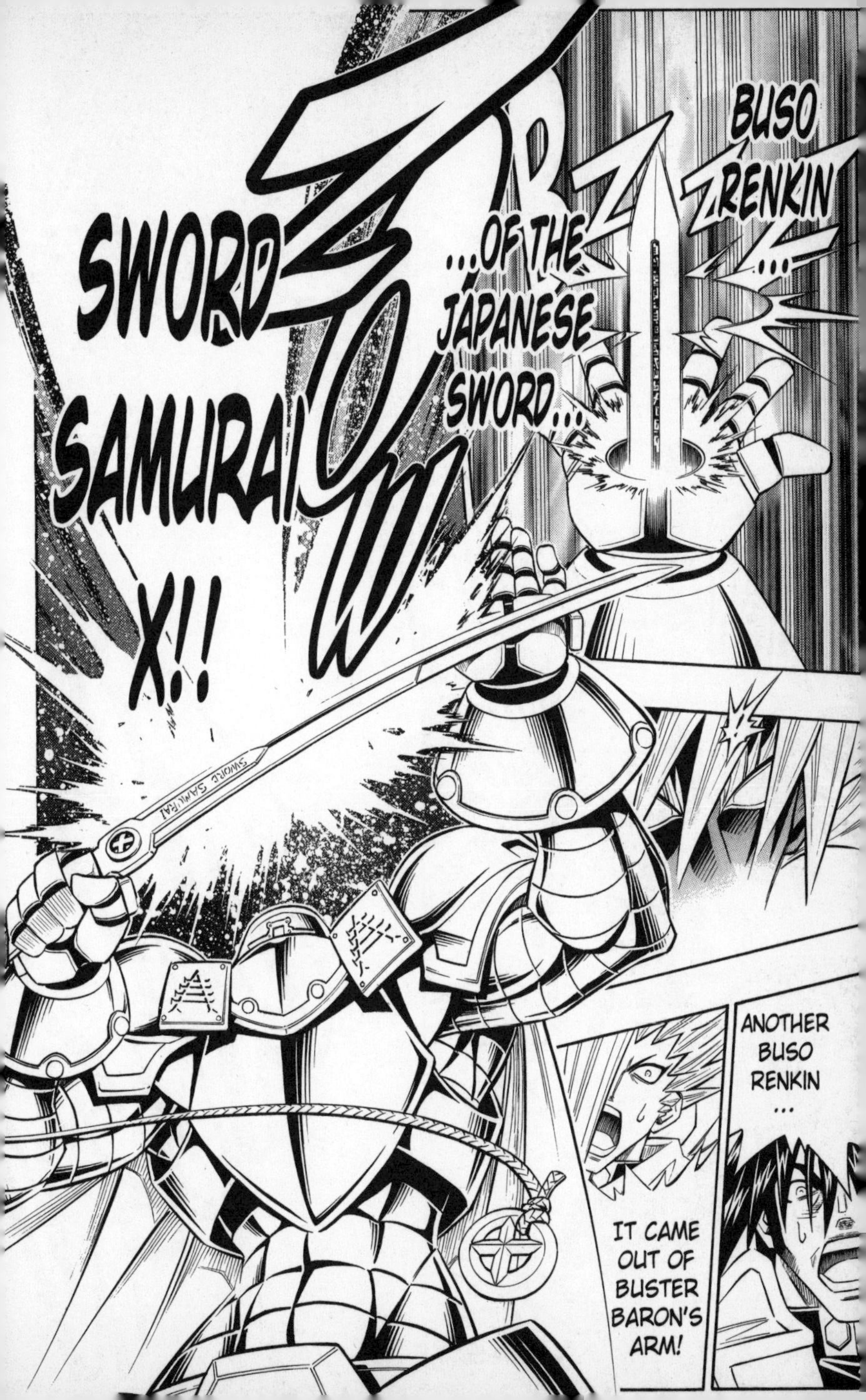
BUSO RENKIN...
...OF THE JAPANESE SWORD...
SWORD SAMURAI X!!
ANOTHER BUSO RENKIN ...
IT CAME OUT OF BUSTER BARON'S ARM!

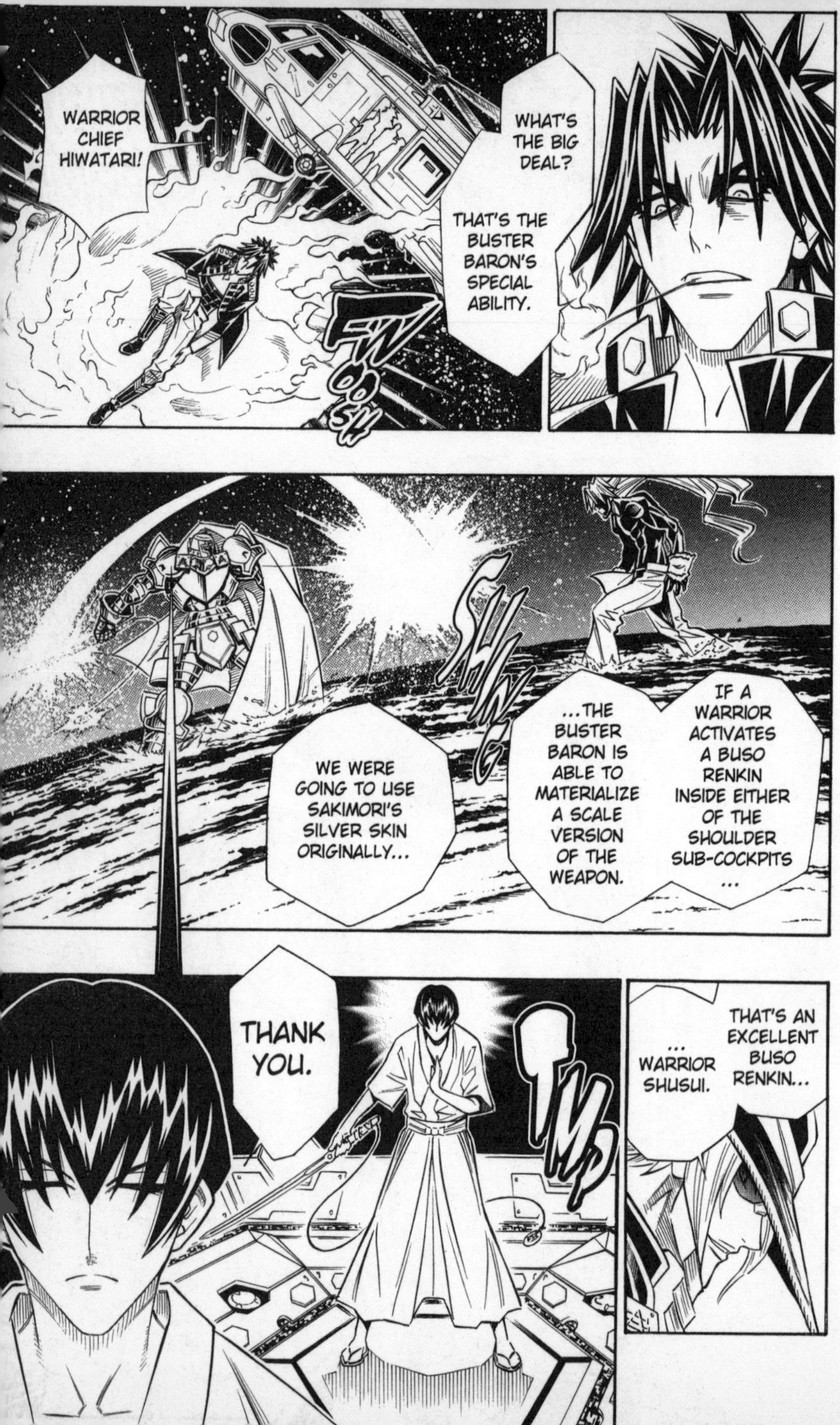
WHAT'S THE BIG DEAL?
THAT'S THE BUSTER BARON'S SPECIAL ABILITY.
WARRIOR CHIEF HIWATARI!
FWOOSH
IF A WARRIOR ACTIVATES A BUSO RENKIN INSIDE EITHER OF THE SHOULDER SUB-COCKPITS...
...THE BUSTER BARON IS ABLE TO MATERIALIZE A SCALE VERSION OF THE WEAPON.
WE WERE GOING TO USE SAKIMORI'S SILVER SKIN ORIGINALLY...
SHING
THAT'S AN EXCELLENT BUSO RENKIN...
...WARRIOR SHUSUI.
TMP
THANK YOU.

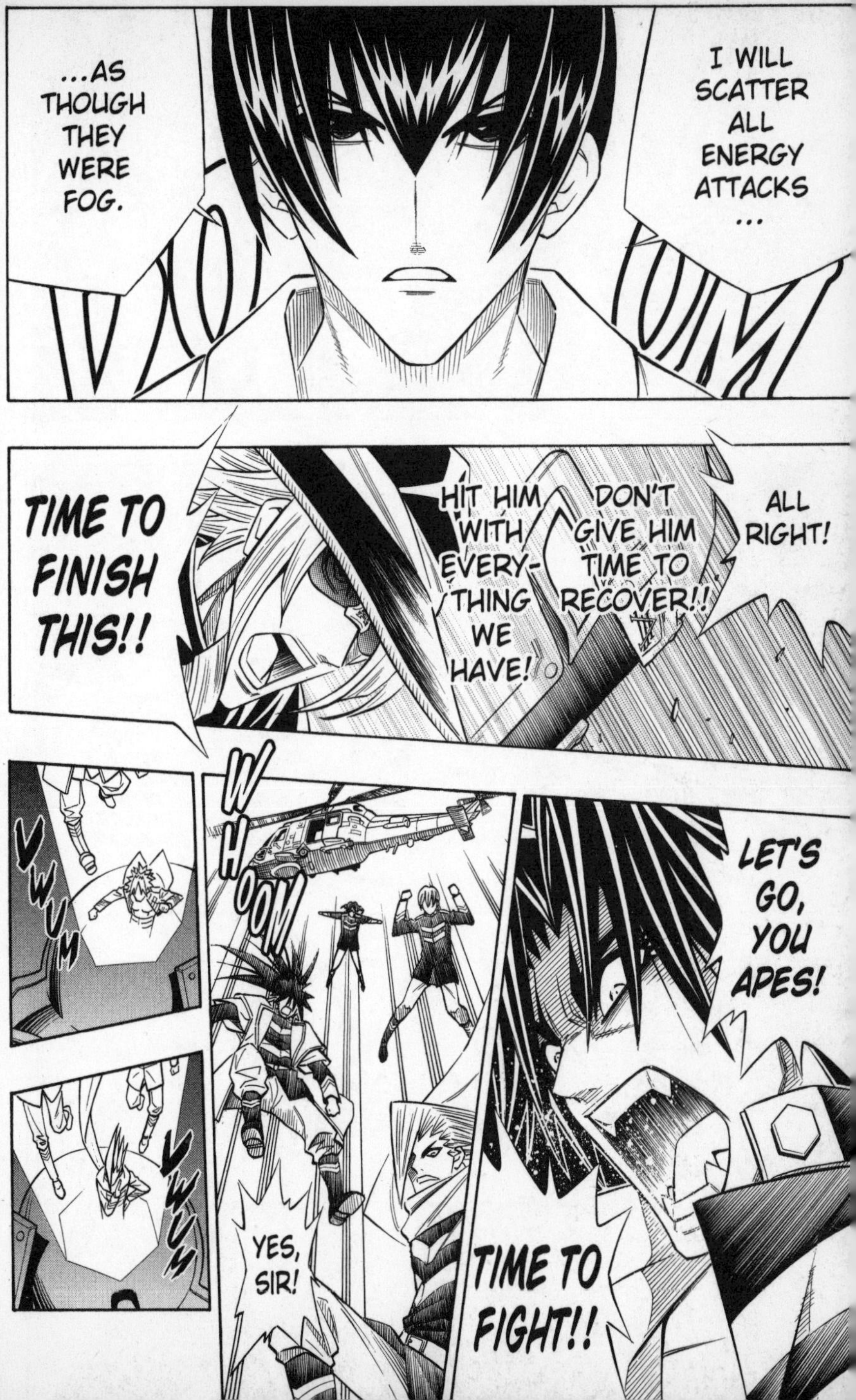
I WILL SCATTER ALL ENERGY ATTACKS...
...AS THOUGH THEY WERE FOG.
ALL RIGHT!
DON'T GIVE HIM TIME TO RECOVER!!
HIT HIM WITH EVERY-THING WE HAVE!
TIME TO FINISH THIS!!
LET'S GO, YOU APES!
TIME TO FIGHT!!
WHOOM
YES, SIR!
VWUM
VWUM

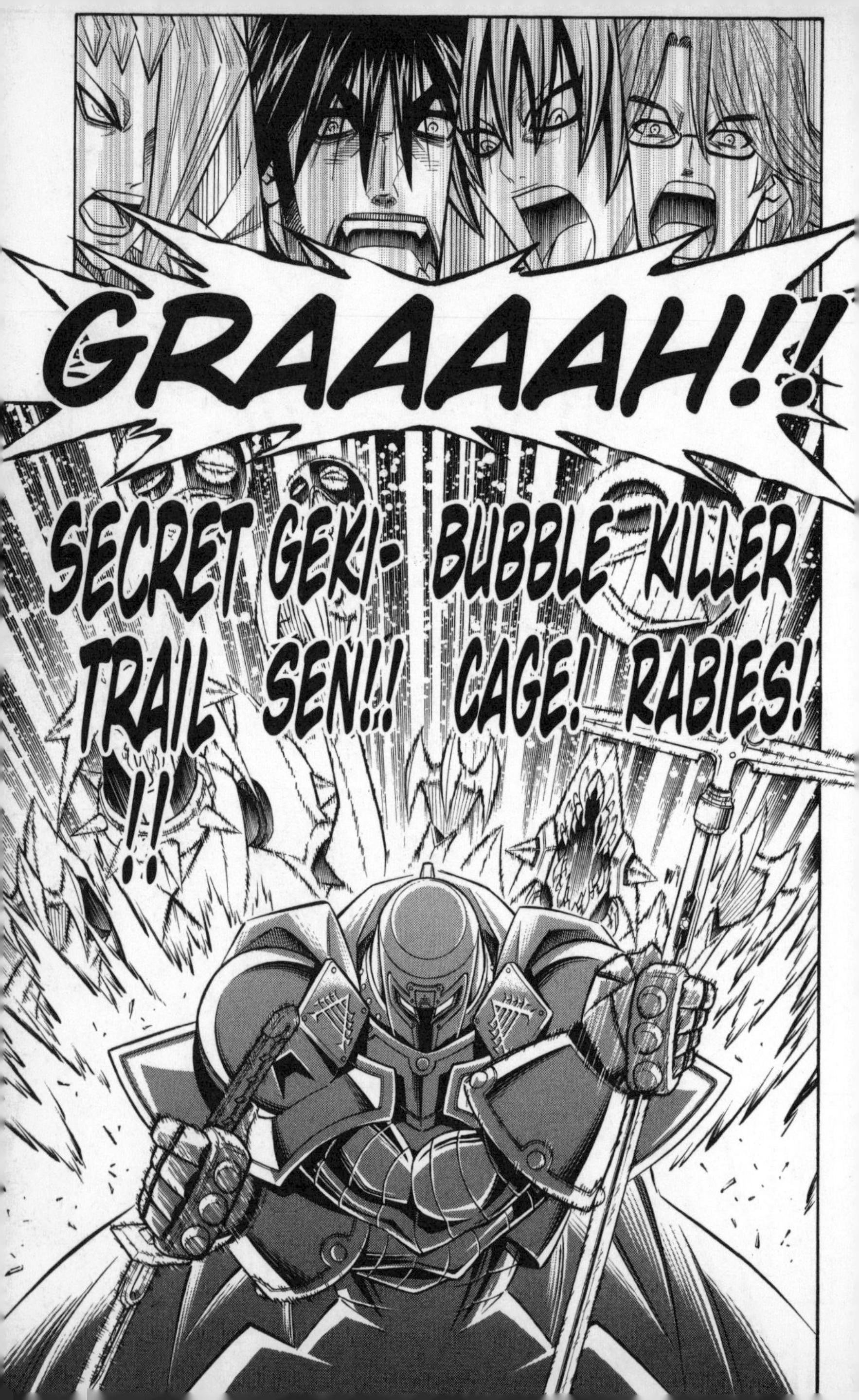
GRAAAAH!!
KILLER RABIES!
BUBBLE CAGE!
GEKI-SEN!!
SECRET TRAIL!!

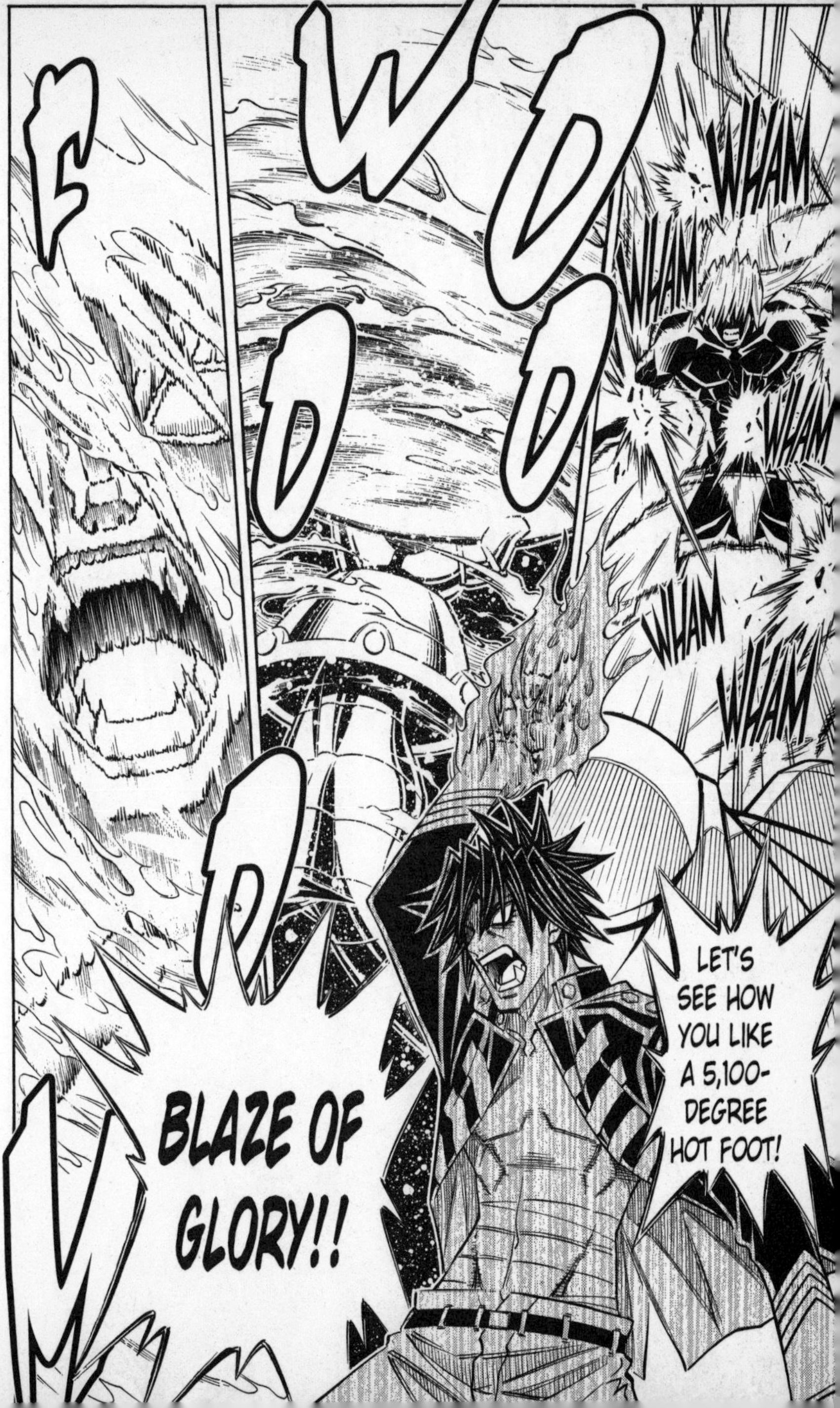
WHAM
WHAM
WHAM
WHAM
WHAM
LET'S SEE HOW YOU LIKE A 5,100-DEGREE HOT FOOT!
BLAZE OF GLORY!!
FWOOOOM

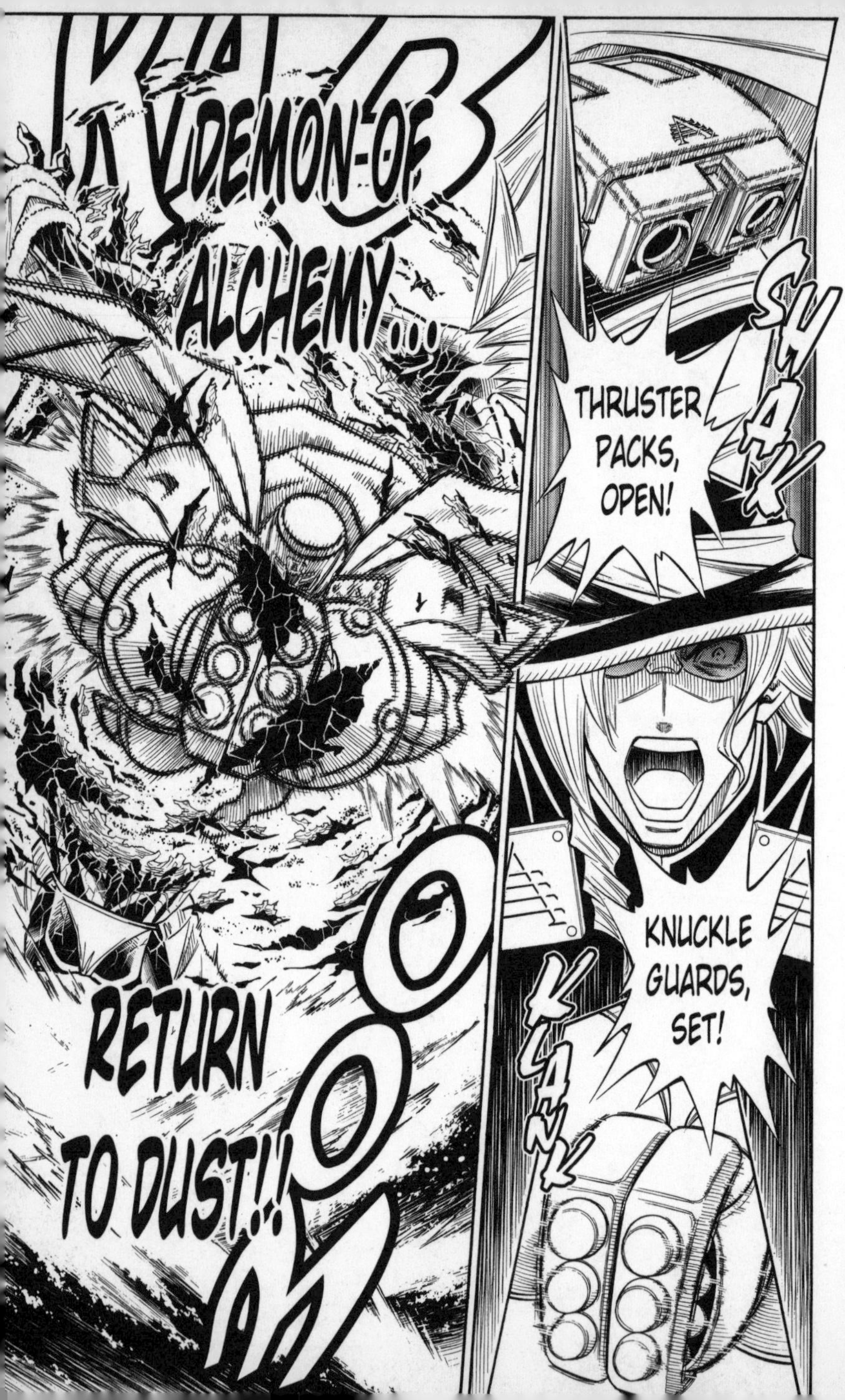
SHAK
THRUSTER PACKS, OPEN!
KLANK
KNUCKLE GUARDS, SET!
A DEMON OF ALCHEMY...
RETURN TO DUST!!

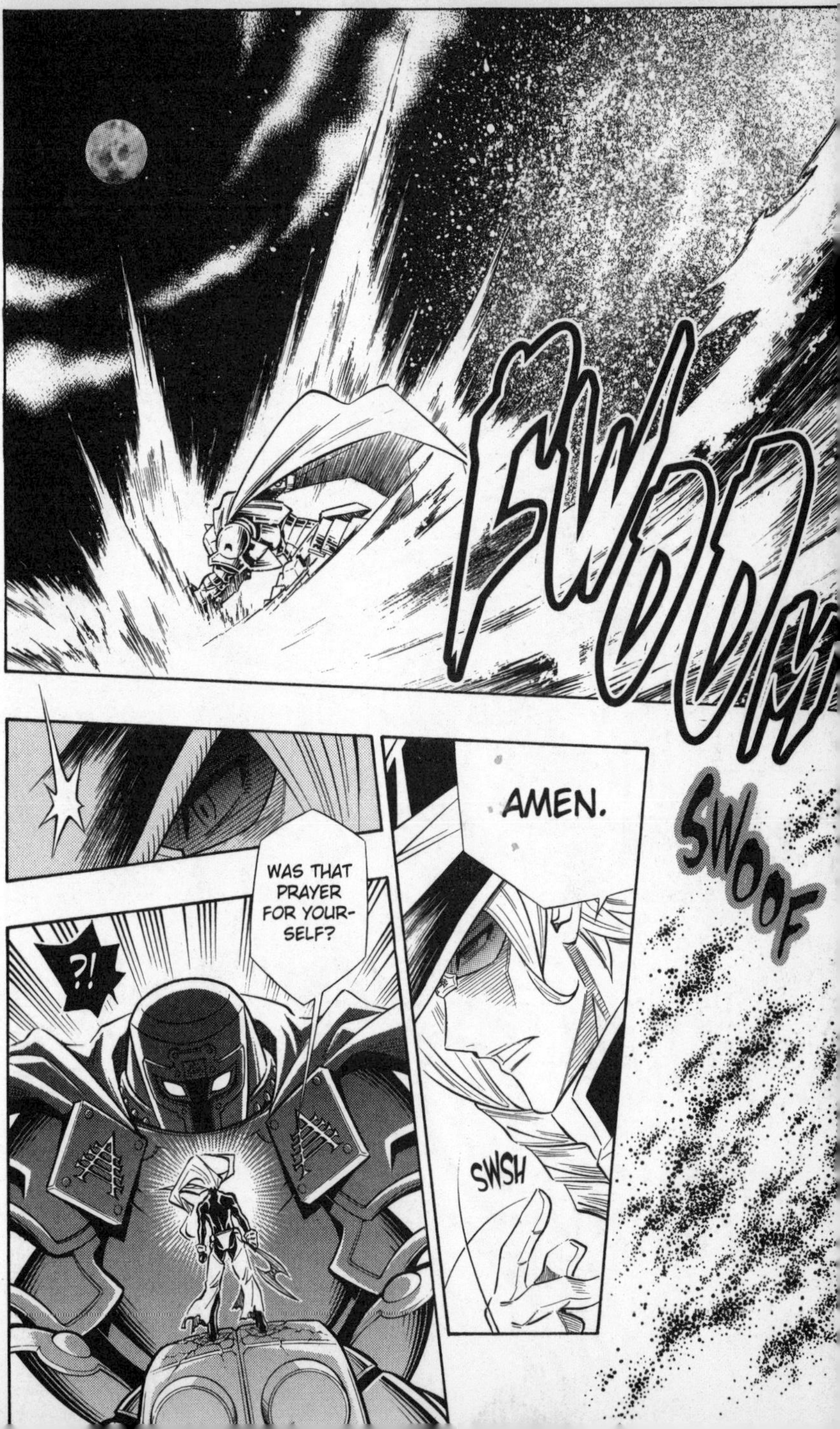
FWOOOM
AMEN.
SWOOF
SWSH
WAS THAT PRAYER FOR YOUR-SELF?
?!

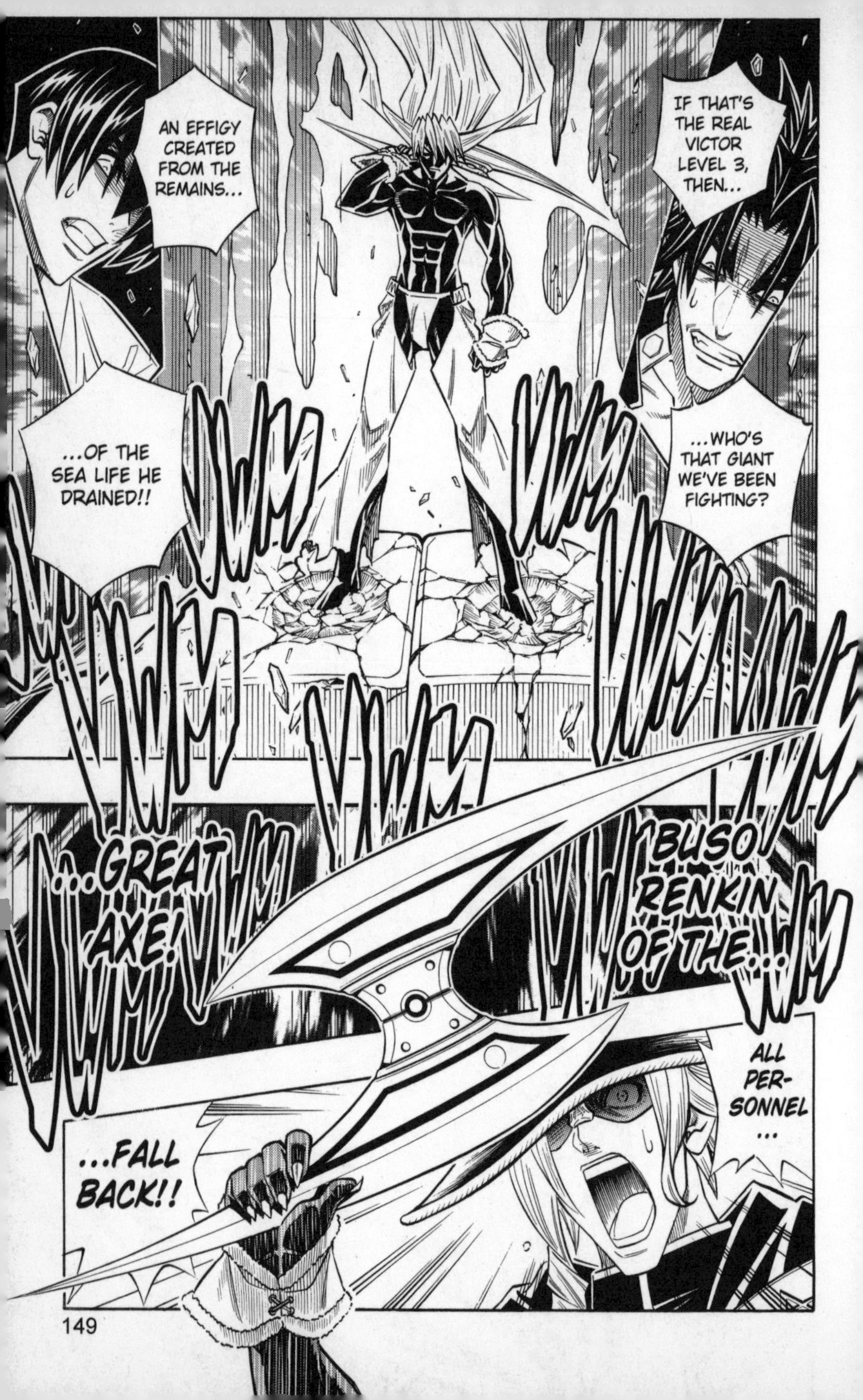
IF THAT'S THE REAL VICTOR LEVEL 3, THEN...
...WHO'S THAT GIANT WE'VE BEEN FIGHTING?
AN EFFIGY CREATED FROM THE REMAINS...
...OF THE SEA LIFE HE DRAINED!!
BUSO RENKIN OF THE...
...GREAT AXE!
ALL PER-SONNEL...
...FALL BACK!!

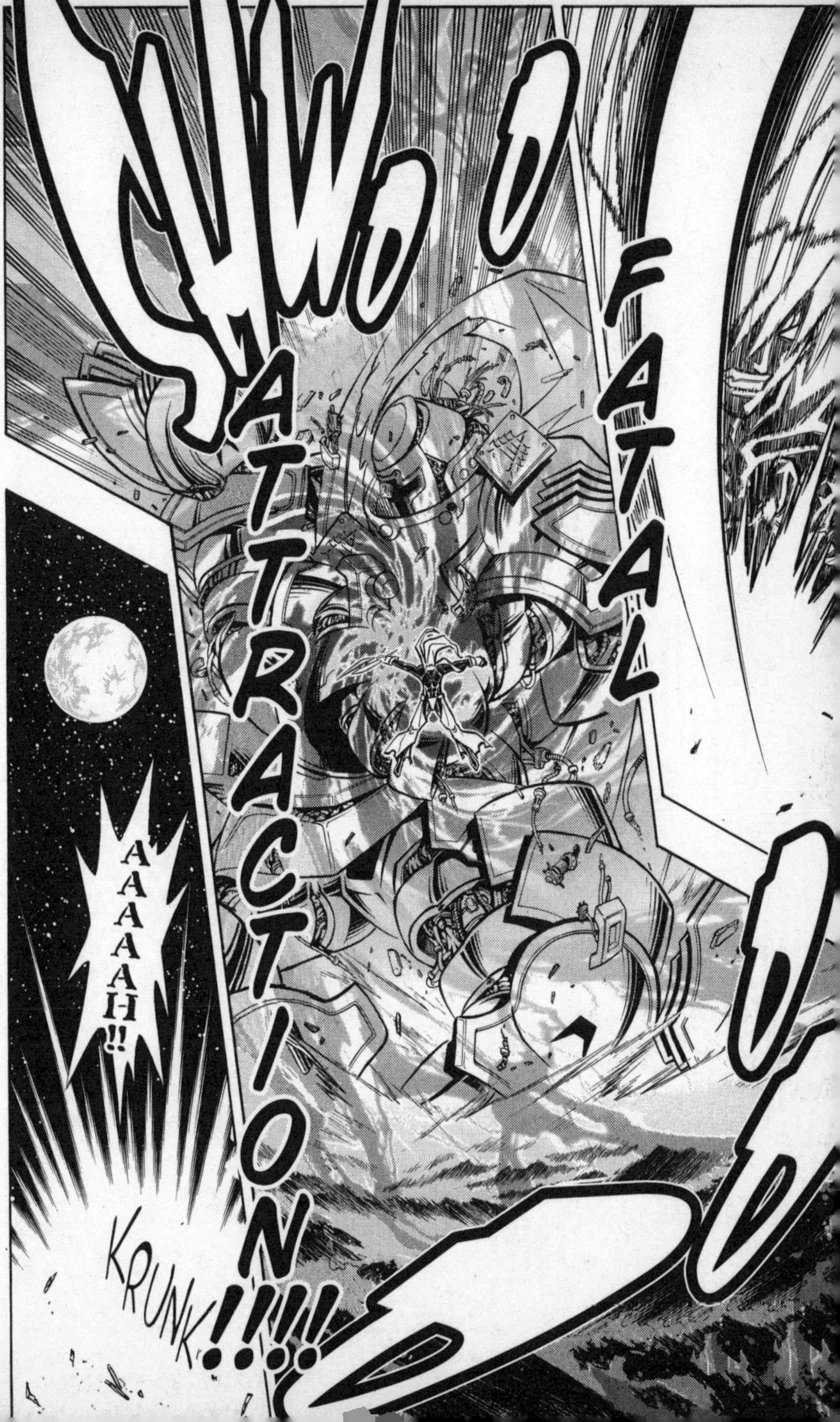
FATAL ATTRACTION!!!!!
AAAAAH!!
KRUNK

READ THIS WAY

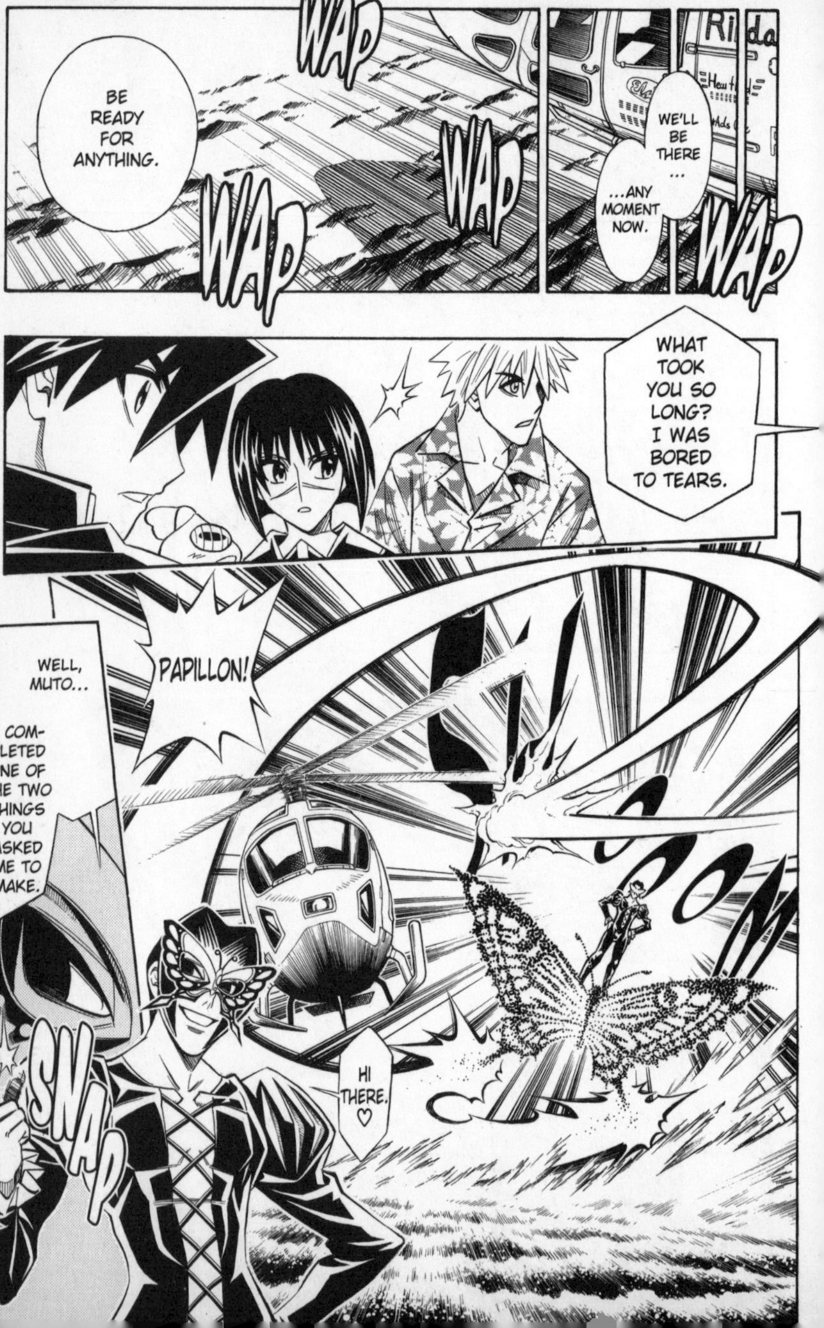
WE'LL BE THERE...
...ANY MOMENT NOW.
WAP
WAP
WAP
BE READY FOR ANYTHING.
WAP
WHAT TOOK YOU SO LONG? I WAS BORED TO TEARS.
PAPILLON!
BOOM
WELL, MUTO...
I COMPLETED ONE OF THE TWO THINGS YOU ASKED ME TO MAKE.
HI THERE. ♡
SNAP

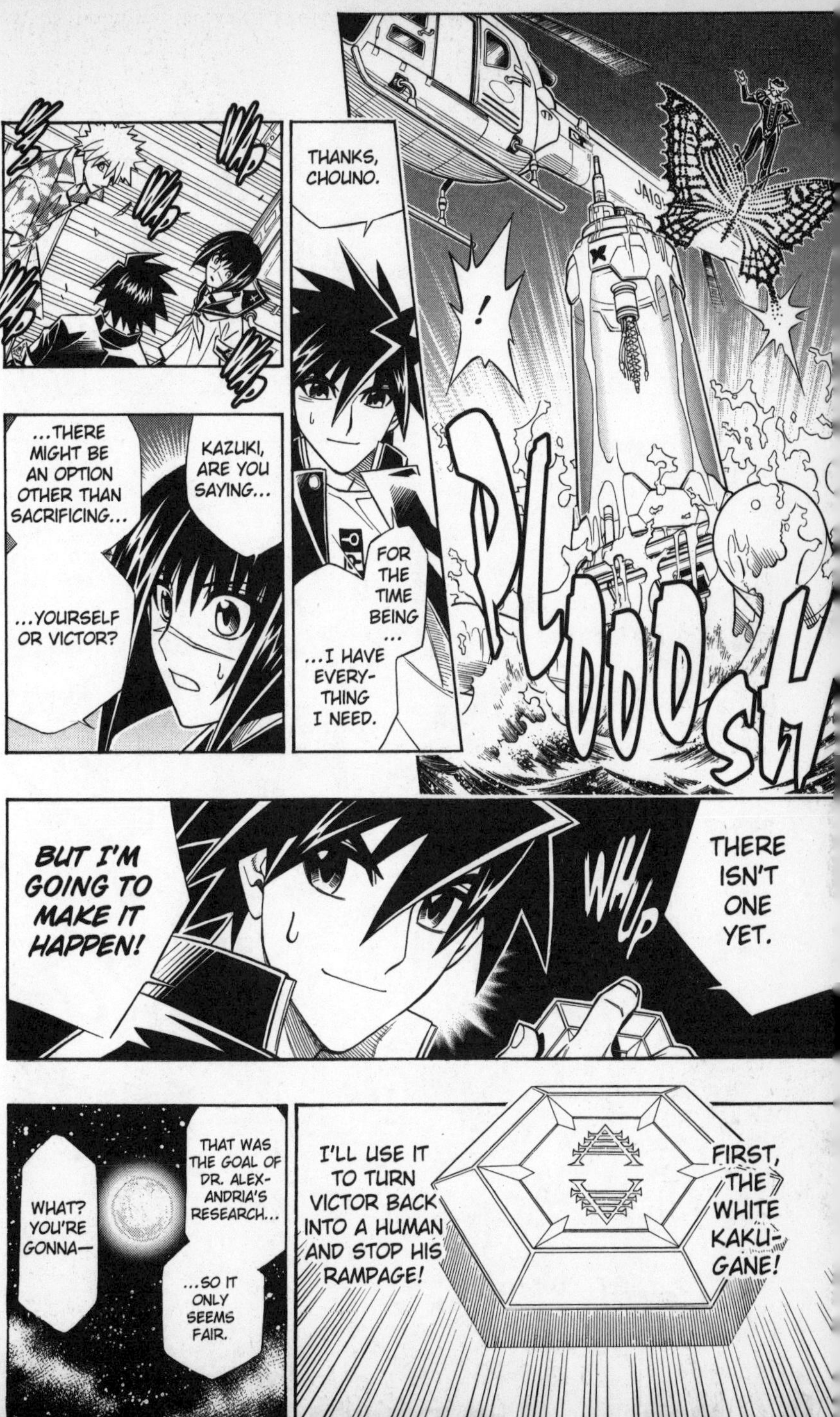
!
PLOOOSH
THANKS, CHOUNO.
FOR THE TIME BEING...
...I HAVE EVERYTHING I NEED.
WAP
WAP
WAP
WAP
WAP
KAZUKI, ARE YOU SAYING...
...THERE MIGHT BE AN OPTION OTHER THAN SACRIFICING...
...YOURSELF OR VICTOR?
THERE ISN'T ONE YET.
WHUP
BUT I'M GOING TO MAKE IT HAPPEN!
FIRST, THE WHITE KAKU-GANE!
I'LL USE IT TO TURN VICTOR BACK INTO A HUMAN AND STOP HIS RAMPAGE!
THAT WAS THE GOAL OF DR. ALEX-ANDRIA'S RESEARCH...
WHAT? YOU'RE GONNA—
...SO IT ONLY SEEMS FAIR.

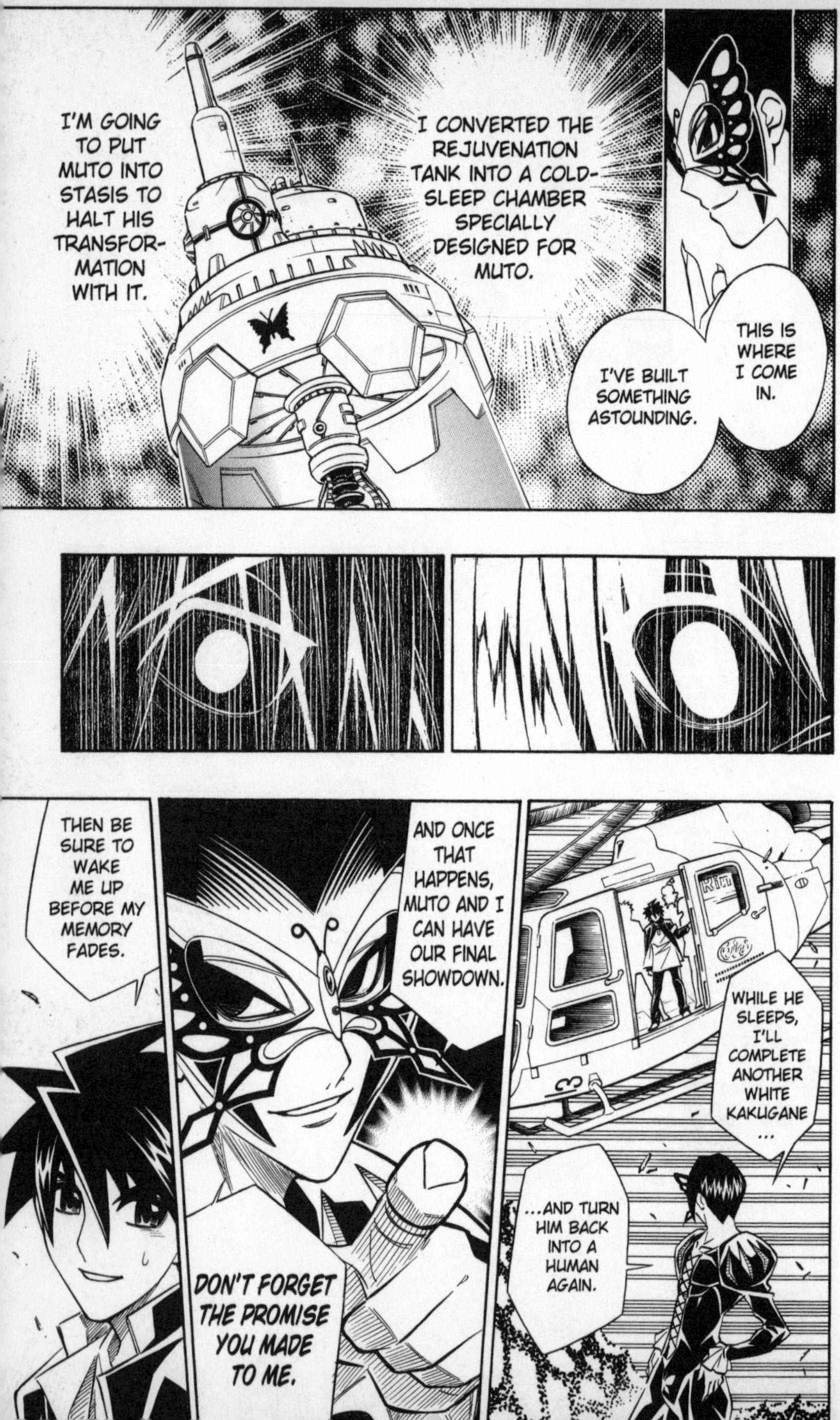
THIS IS WHERE I COME IN.
I'VE BUILT SOMETHING ASTOUNDING.
I CONVERTED THE REJUVENATION TANK INTO A COLD-SLEEP CHAMBER SPECIALLY DESIGNED FOR MUTO.
I'M GOING TO PUT MUTO INTO STASIS TO HALT HIS TRANSFORMATION WITH IT.
WHILE HE SLEEPS, I'LL COMPLETE ANOTHER WHITE KAKUGANE ...
...AND TURN HIM BACK INTO A HUMAN AGAIN.
AND ONCE THAT HAPPENS, MUTO AND I CAN HAVE OUR FINAL SHOWDOWN.
DON'T FORGET THE PROMISE YOU MADE TO ME.
THEN BE SURE TO WAKE ME UP BEFORE MY MEMORY FADES.

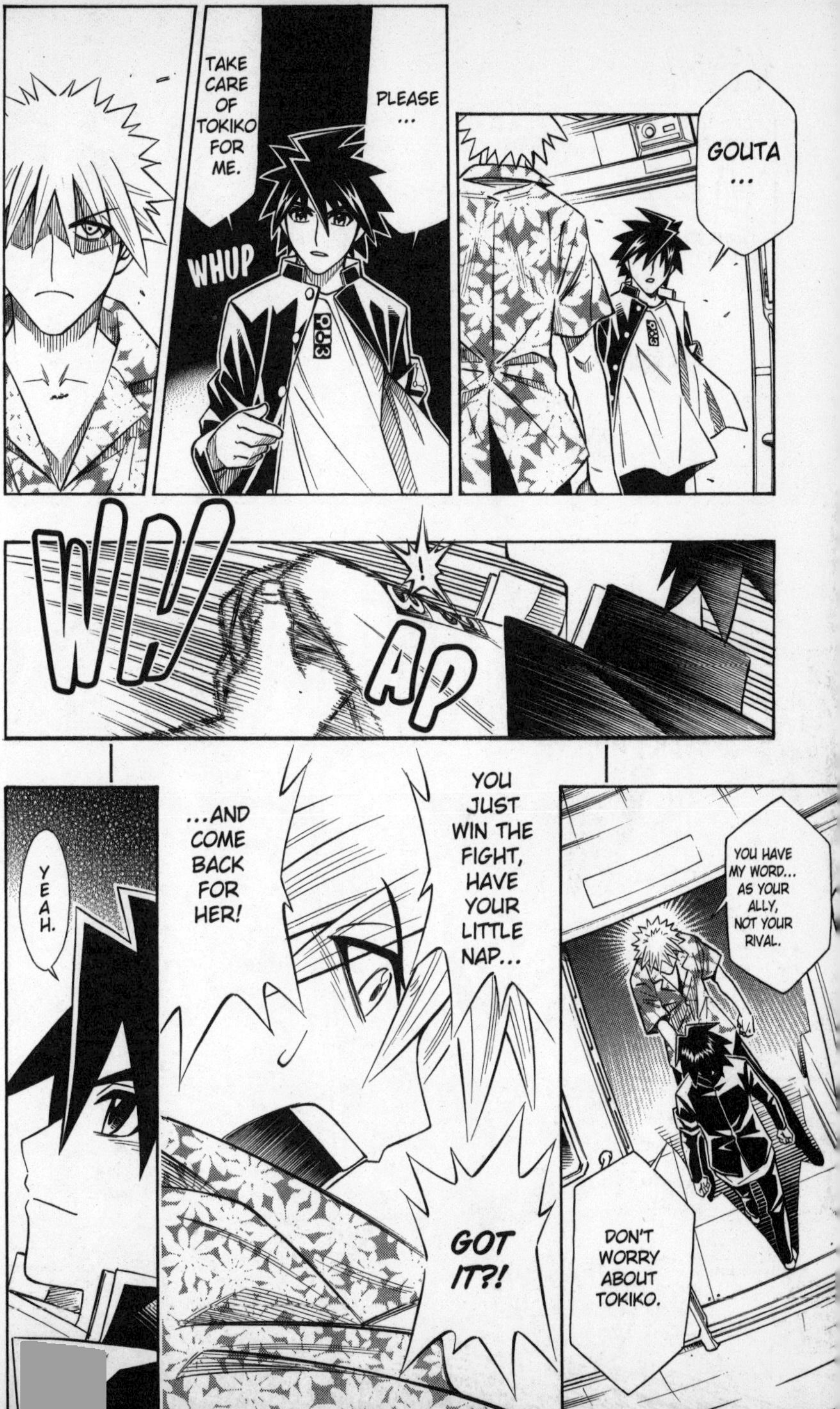
GOUTA...
TAKE CARE OF TOKIKO FOR ME.
PLEASE...
WHUP
WHAP
YOU HAVE MY WORD... AS YOUR ALLY, NOT YOUR RIVAL.
DON'T WORRY ABOUT TOKIKO.
YOU JUST WIN THE FIGHT, HAVE YOUR LITTLE NAP...
...AND COME BACK FOR HER!
GOT IT?!
YEAH.

READ THIS WAY

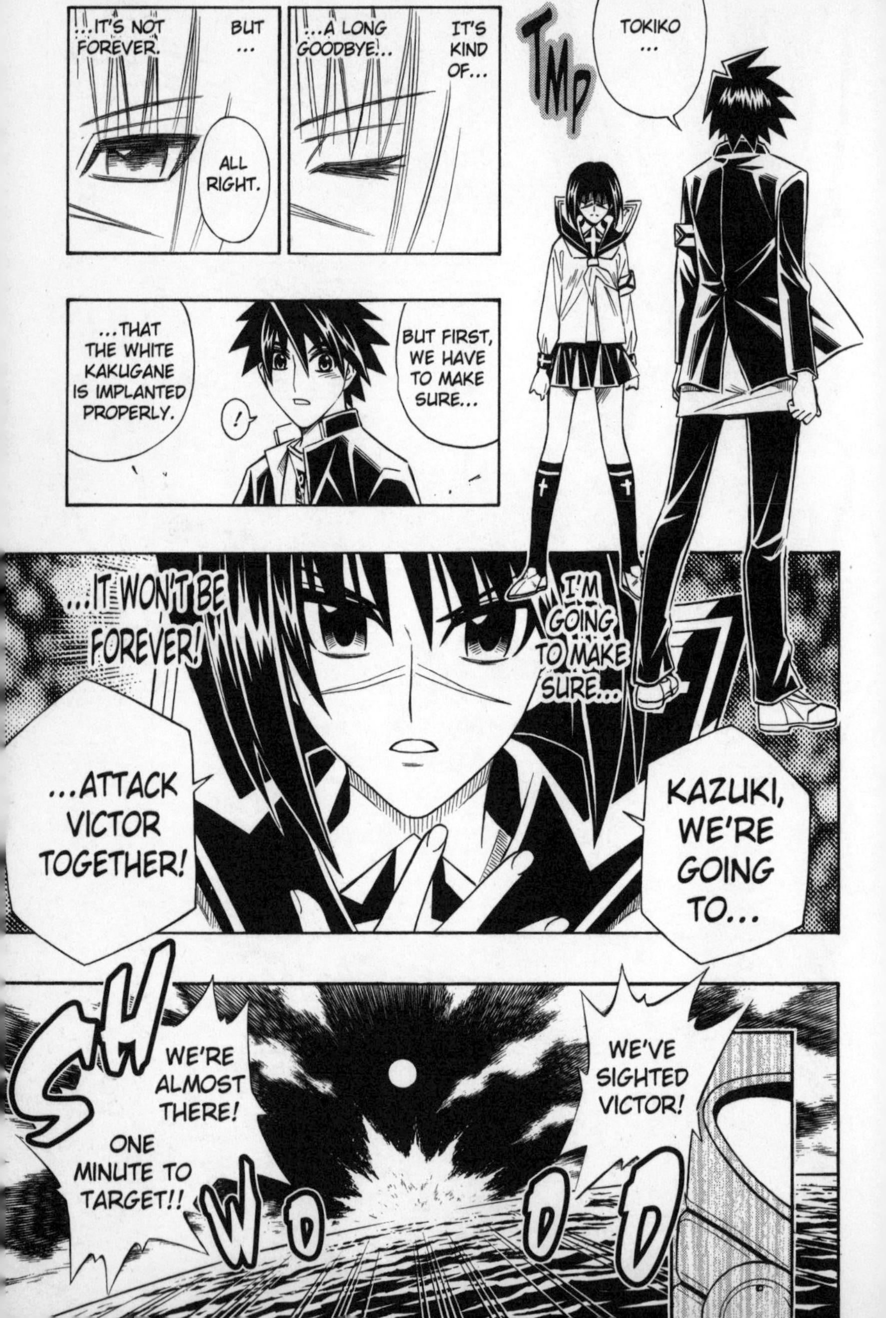
TMP
TOKIKO ...
IT'S KIND OF...
...A LONG GOODBYE...
BUT ...
...IT'S NOT FOREVER.
ALL RIGHT.
BUT FIRST, WE HAVE TO MAKE SURE...
...THAT THE WHITE KAKUGANE IS IMPLANTED PROPERLY.
!
I'M GOING TO MAKE SURE...
...IT WON'T BE FOREVER!
KAZUKI, WE'RE GOING TO...
...ATTACK VICTOR TOGETHER!
WE'VE SIGHTED VICTOR!
WE'RE ALMOST THERE!
ONE MINUTE TO TARGET!!
SHWOOO

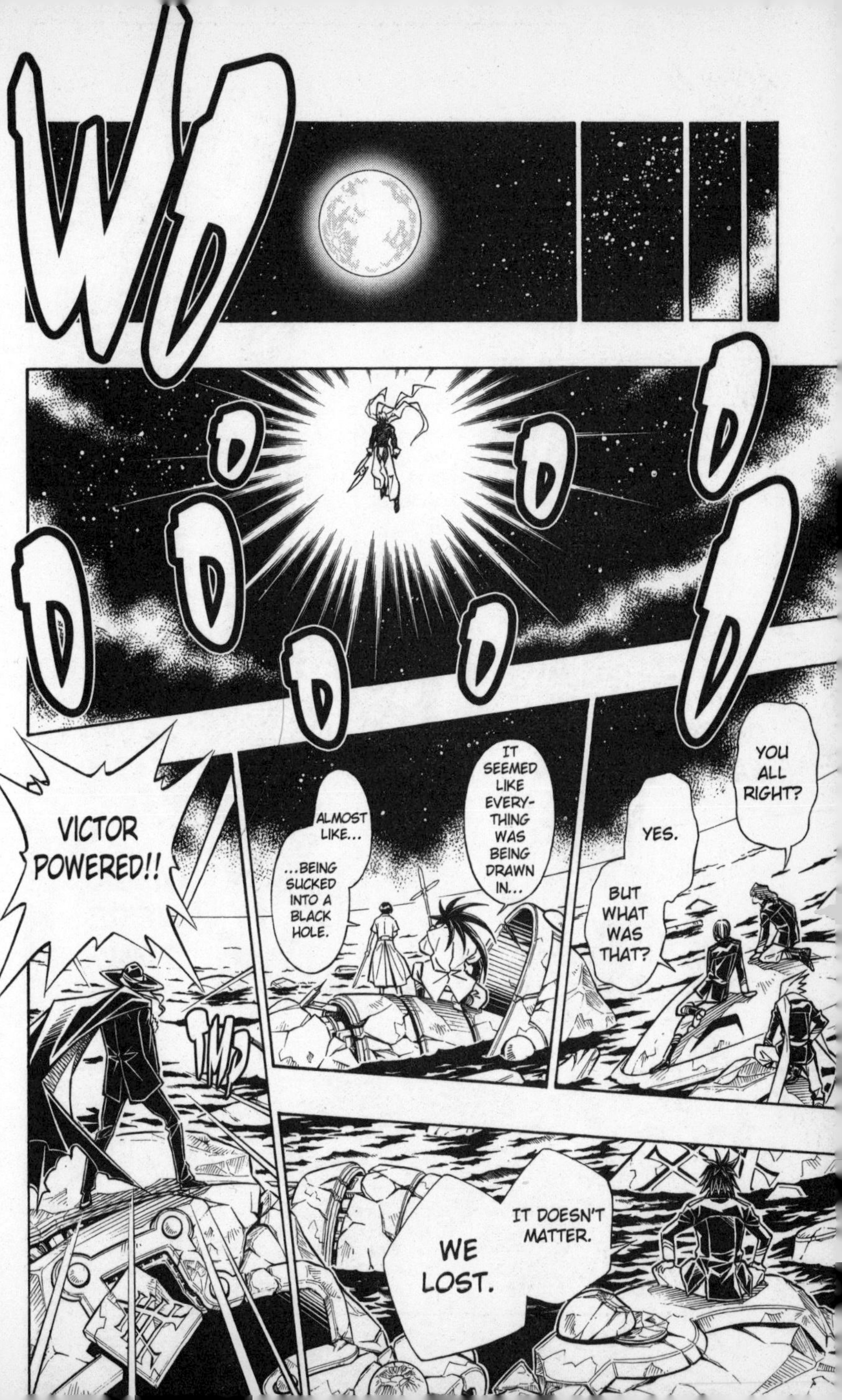
YOU ALL RIGHT?
YES.
BUT WHAT WAS THAT?
IT SEEMED LIKE EVERYTHING WAS BEING DRAWN IN...
ALMOST LIKE...
...BEING SUCKED INTO A BLACK HOLE.
IT DOESN'T MATTER.
WE LOST.
VICTOR POWERED!!

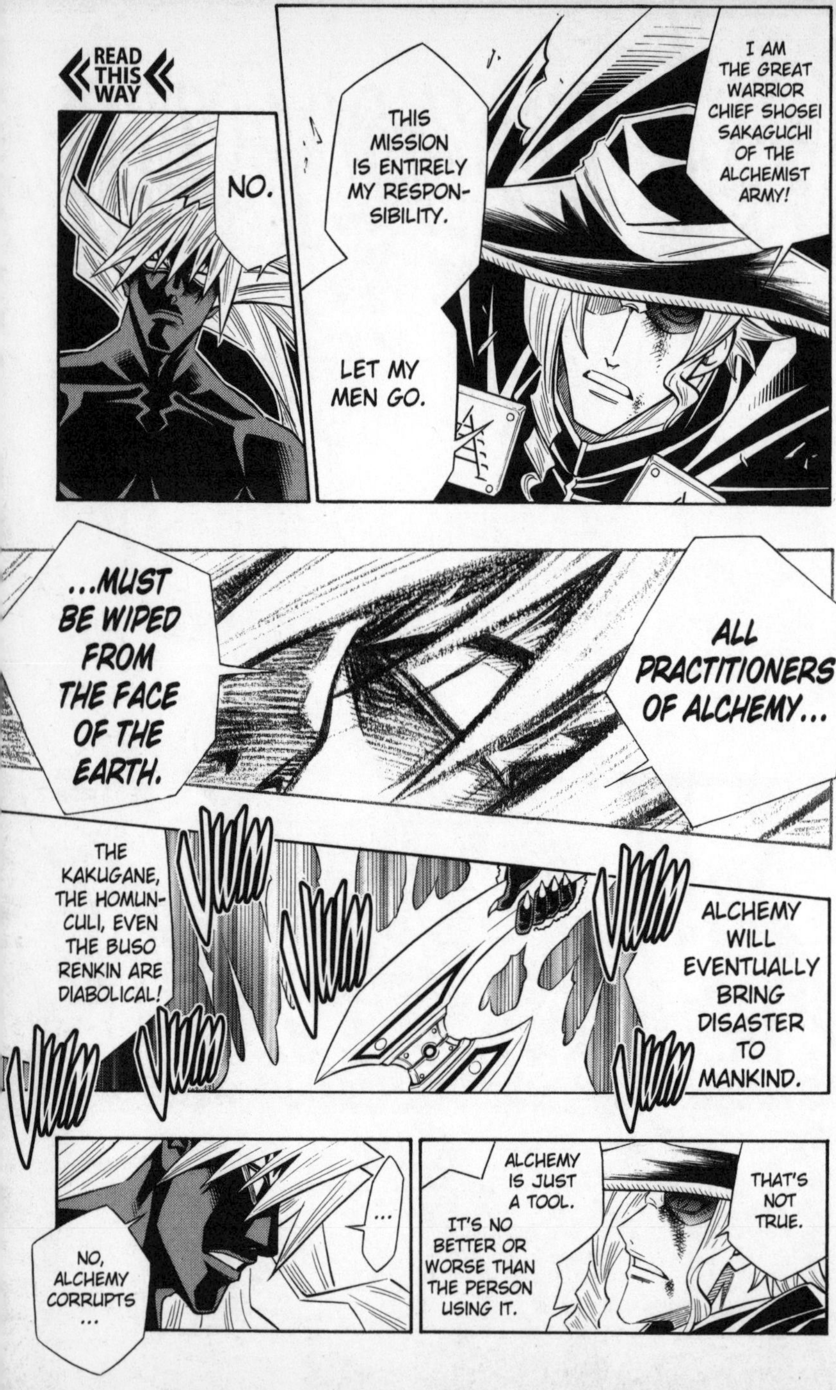
READ THIS WAY
I AM THE GREAT WARRIOR CHIEF SHOSEI SAKAGUCHI OF THE ALCHEMIST ARMY!
THIS MISSION IS ENTIRELY MY RESPON-SIBILITY.
LET MY MEN GO.
NO.
ALL PRACTITIONERS OF ALCHEMY...
...MUST BE WIPED FROM THE FACE OF THE EARTH.
ALCHEMY WILL EVENTUALLY BRING DISASTER TO MANKIND.
THE KAKUGANE, THE HOMUN-CULI, EVEN THE BUSO RENKIN ARE DIABOLICAL!
THAT'S NOT TRUE.
ALCHEMY IS JUST A TOOL.
IT'S NO BETTER OR WORSE THAN THE PERSON USING IT.
...
NO, ALCHEMY CORRUPTS ...

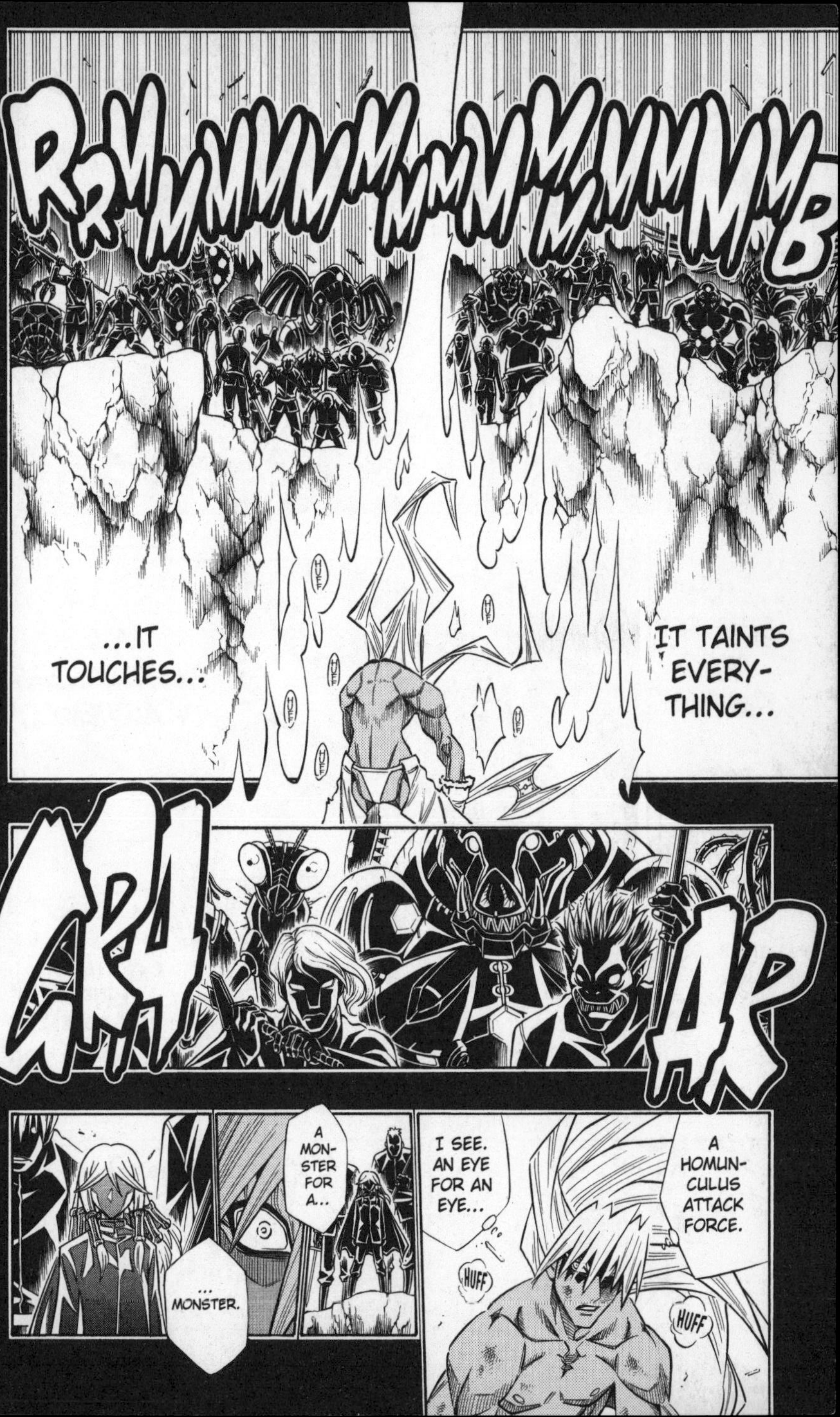
IT TAINTS EVERY-THING...
...IT TOUCHES...
HUFF
HUFF
HUFF
A HOMUN-CULUS ATTACK FORCE.
I SEE. AN EYE FOR AN EYE...
HUFF
HUFF
A MON-STER FOR A...
... MONSTER.

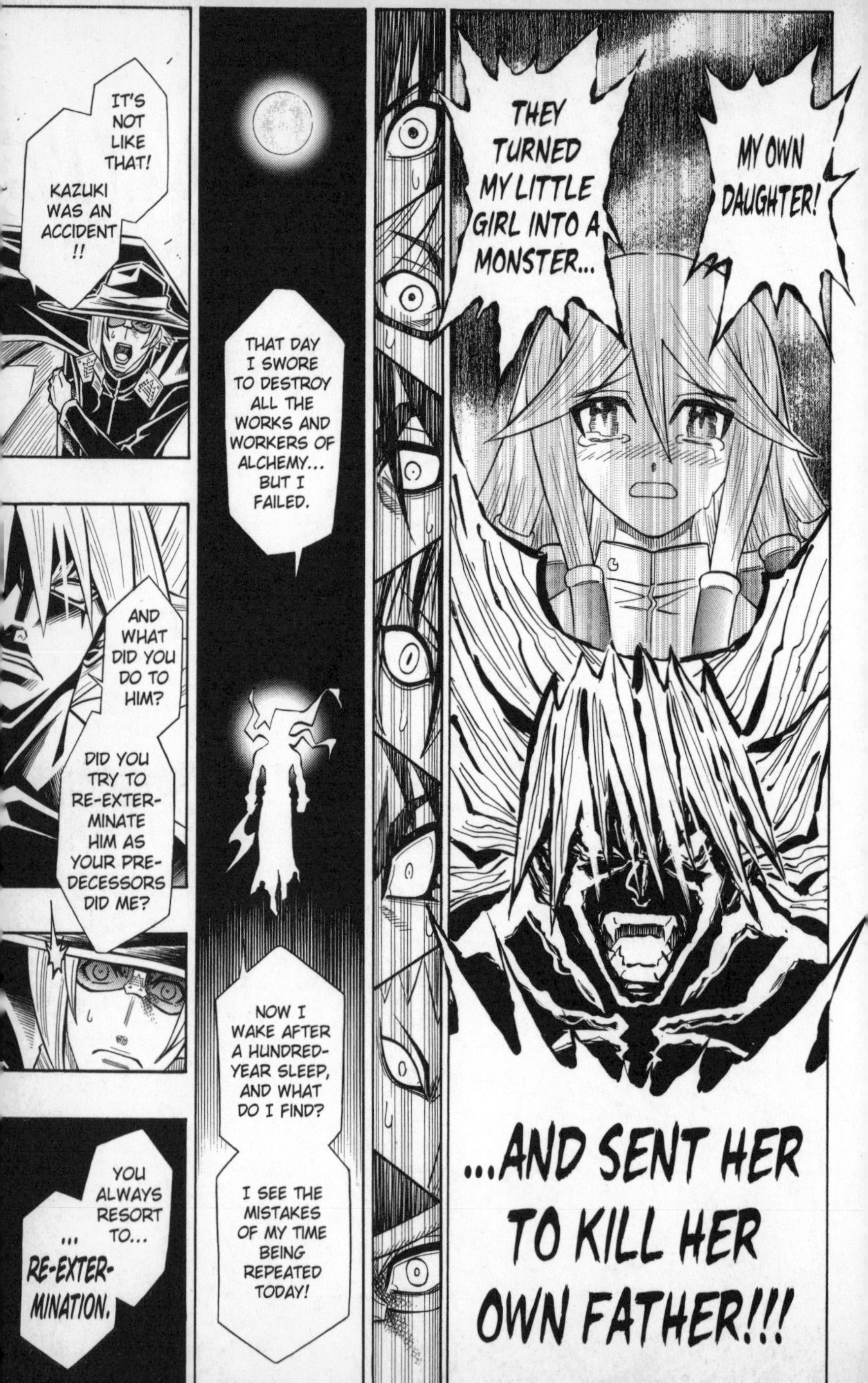
THEY TURNED MY LITTLE GIRL INTO A MONSTER...
MY OWN DAUGHTER!
...AND SENT HER TO KILL HER OWN FATHER!!!
THAT DAY I SWORE TO DESTROY ALL THE WORKS AND WORKERS OF ALCHEMY... BUT I FAILED.
NOW I WAKE AFTER A HUNDRED-YEAR SLEEP, AND WHAT DO I FIND?
I SEE THE MISTAKES OF MY TIME BEING REPEATED TODAY!
IT'S NOT LIKE THAT! KAZUKI WAS AN ACCIDENT!!
AND WHAT DID YOU DO TO HIM?
DID YOU TRY TO RE-EXTERMINATE HIM AS YOUR PREDECESSORS DID ME?
YOU ALWAYS RESORT TO...
... RE-EXTERMINATION.

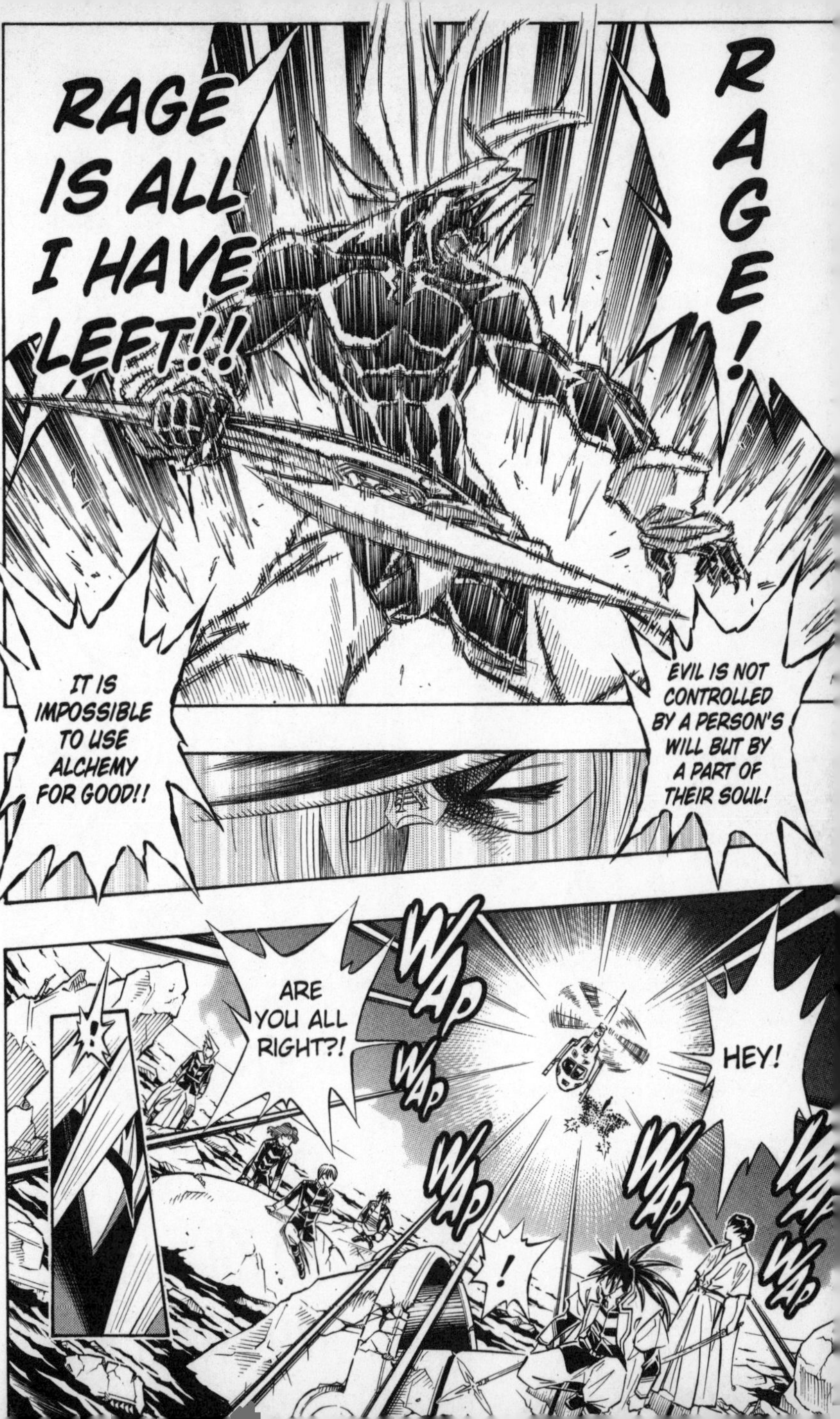
RAGE!
RAGE IS ALL I HAVE LEFT!!
EVIL IS NOT CONTROLLED BY A PERSON'S WILL BUT BY A PART OF THEIR SOUL!
IT IS IMPOSSIBLE TO USE ALCHEMY FOR GOOD!!
HEY!
WAP WAP
WAP
ARE YOU ALL RIGHT?!
WAP WAP
WAP
!
!

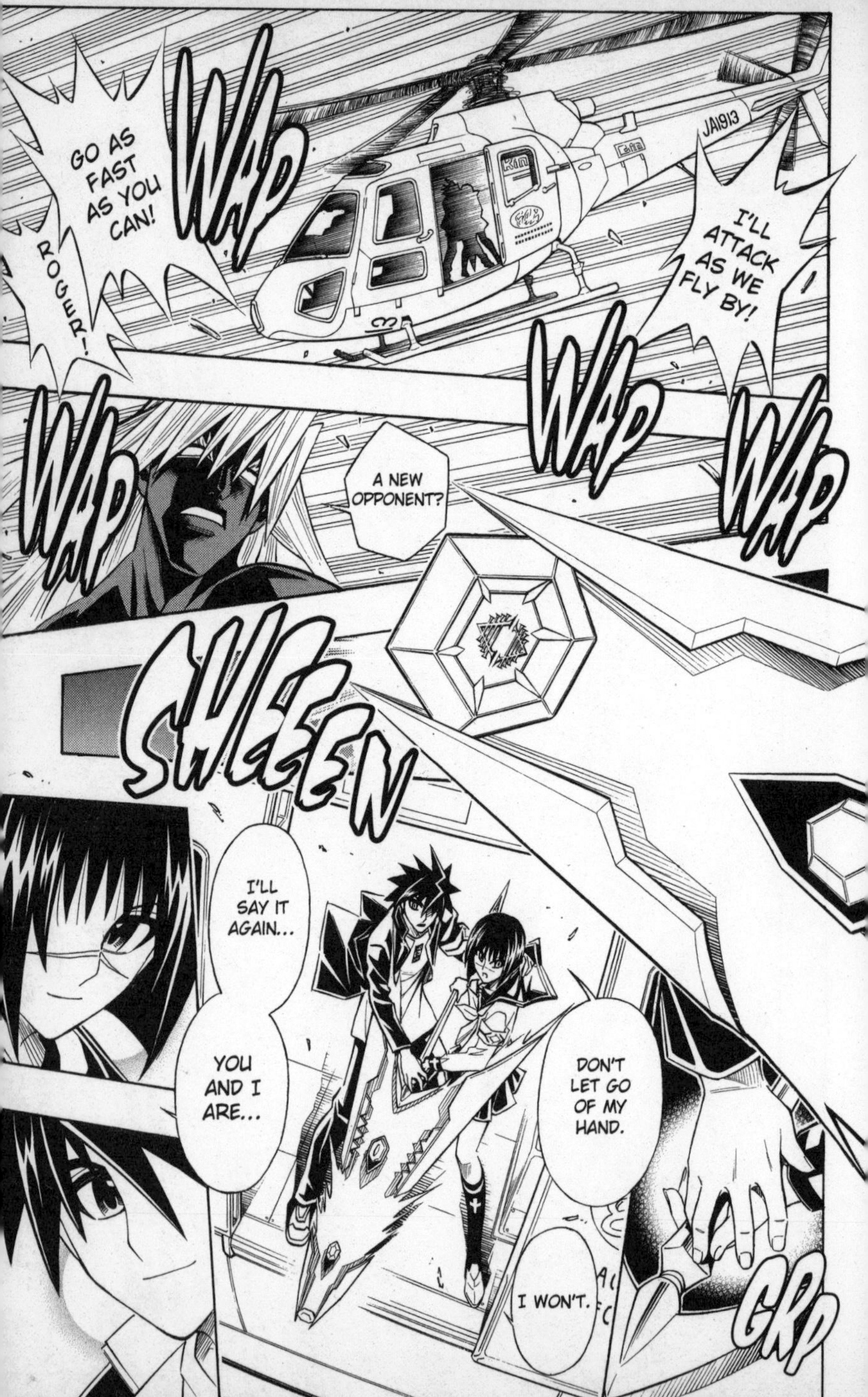
JA1913
I'LL ATTACK AS WE FLY BY!
WHAP
GO AS FAST AS YOU CAN!
ROGER!
WHAP WHAP
WHAP
A NEW OPPONENT?
WHAP
SHEEN
DON'T LET GO OF MY HAND.
I WON'T.
GRIP
I'LL SAY IT AGAIN...
YOU AND I ARE...

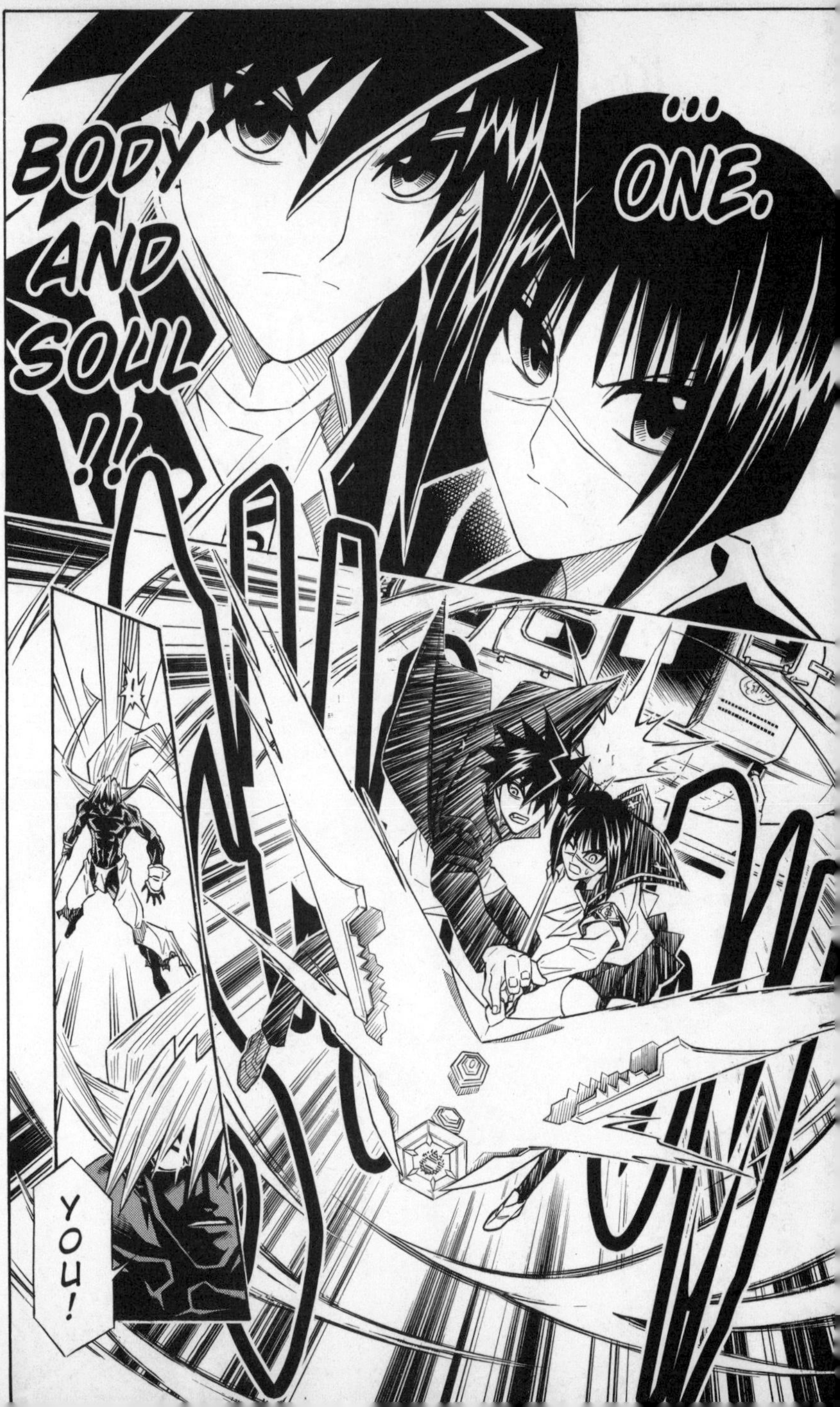
...ONE.
BODY AND SOUL!!
YOU!

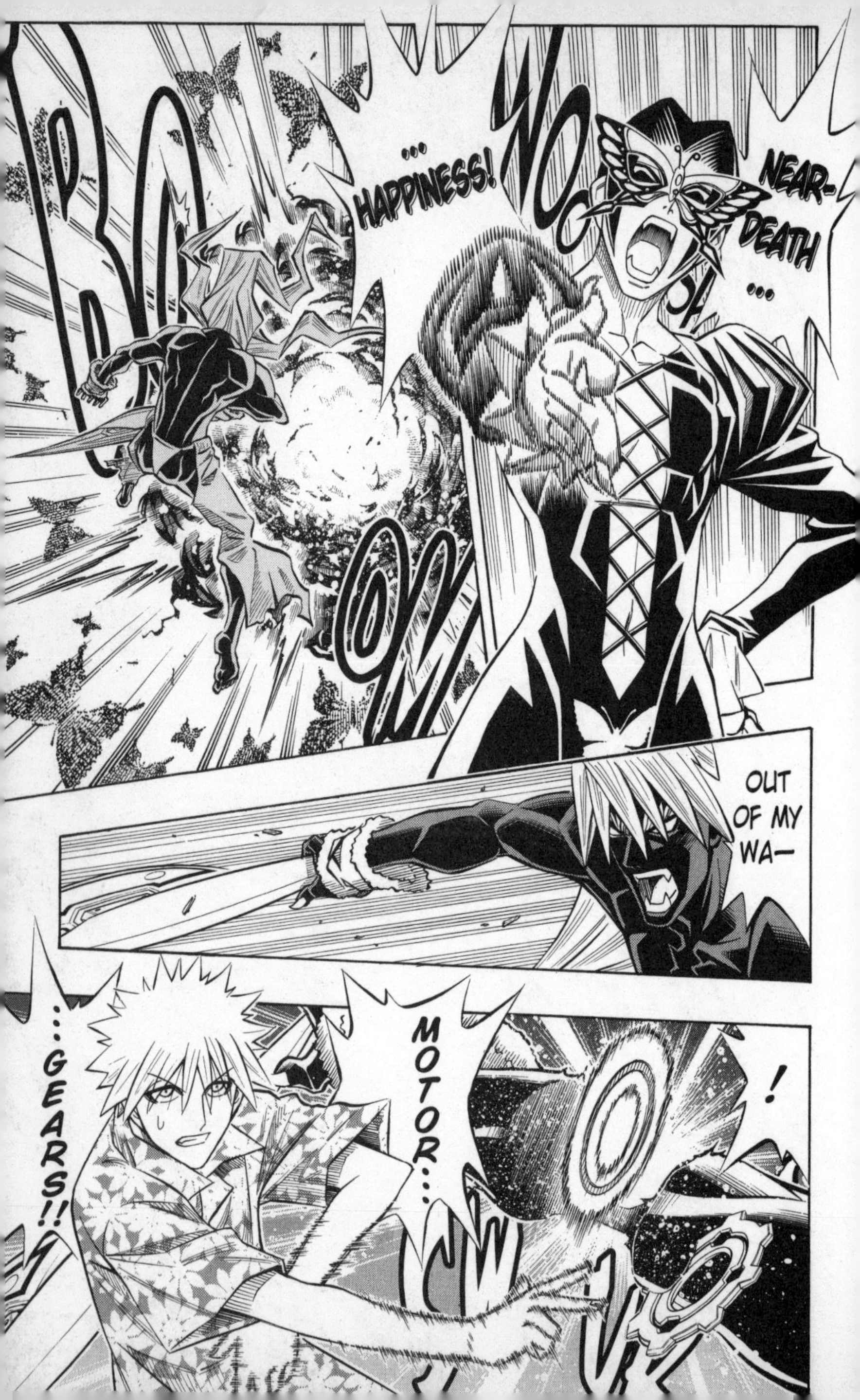
NEAR-DEATH...
...HAPPINESS!
OUT OF MY WA—
!
MOTOR...
...GEARS!!

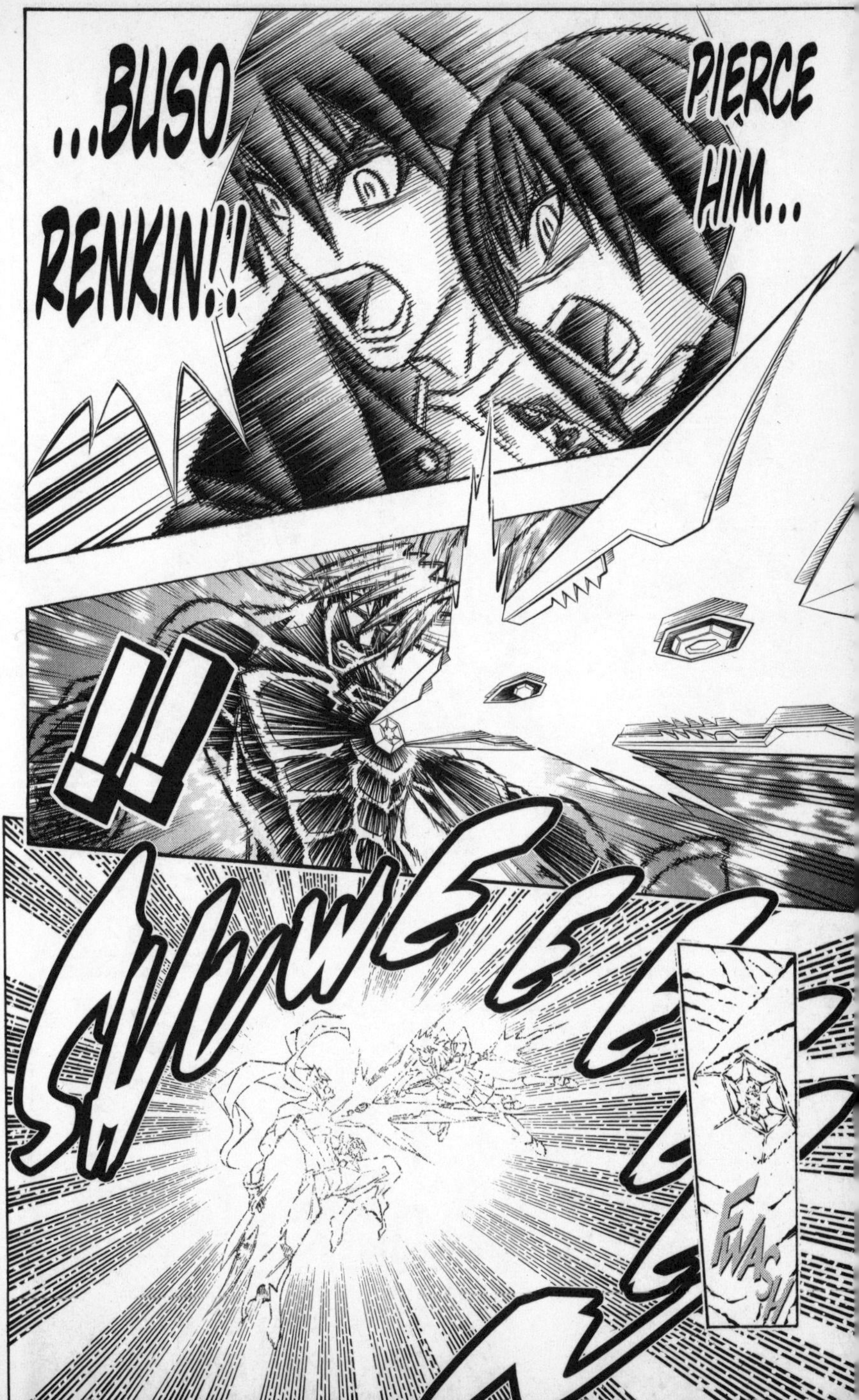
PIERCE HIM...
...BUSO RENKIN!!
!!
FWASH

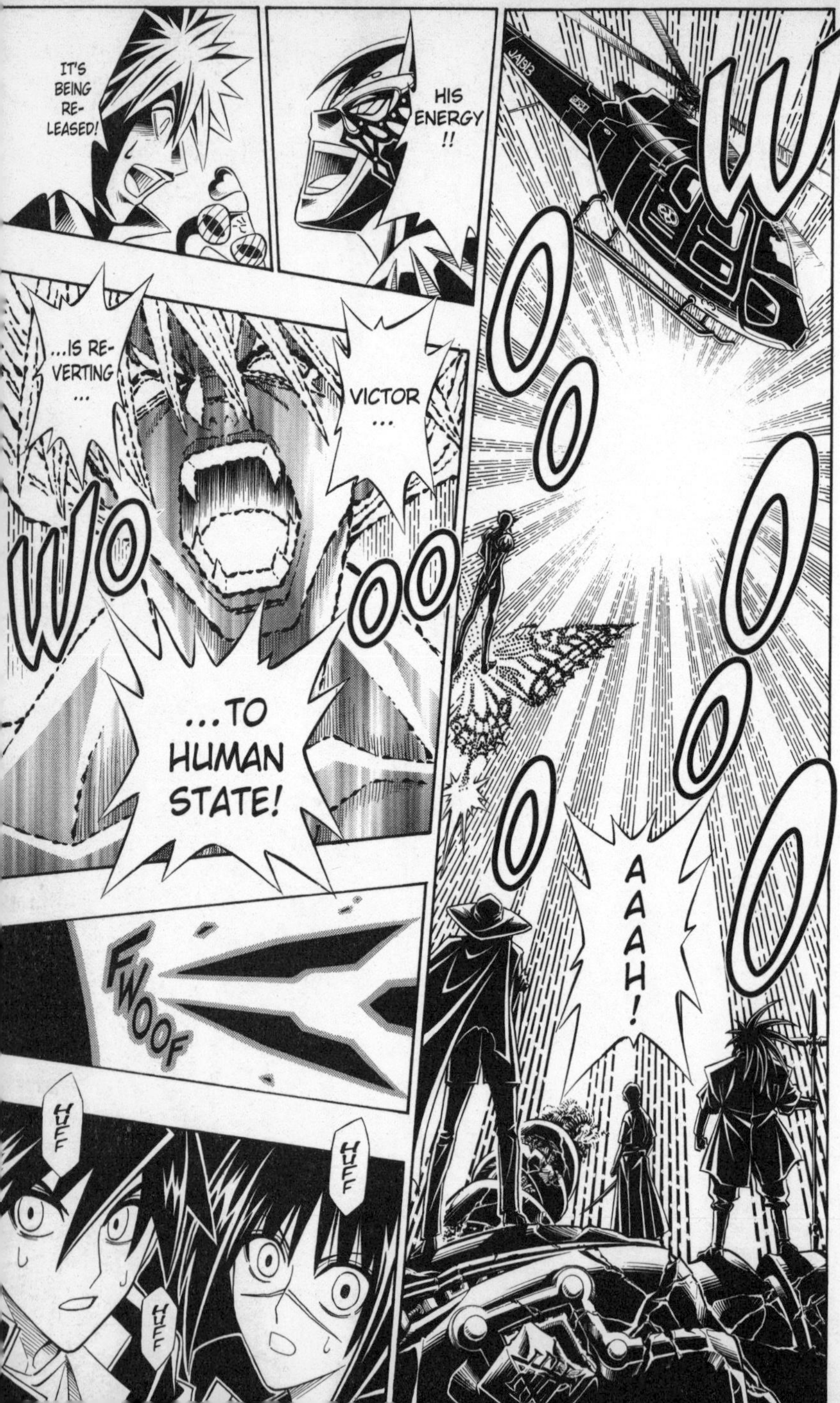
WOOOOOOO
AAAH!
HIS ENERGY!!
IT'S BEING RE-LEASED!
VICTOR...
...IS RE-VERTING...
WOOOO
...TO HUMAN STATE!
FWOOF
HUFF
HUFF
HUFF

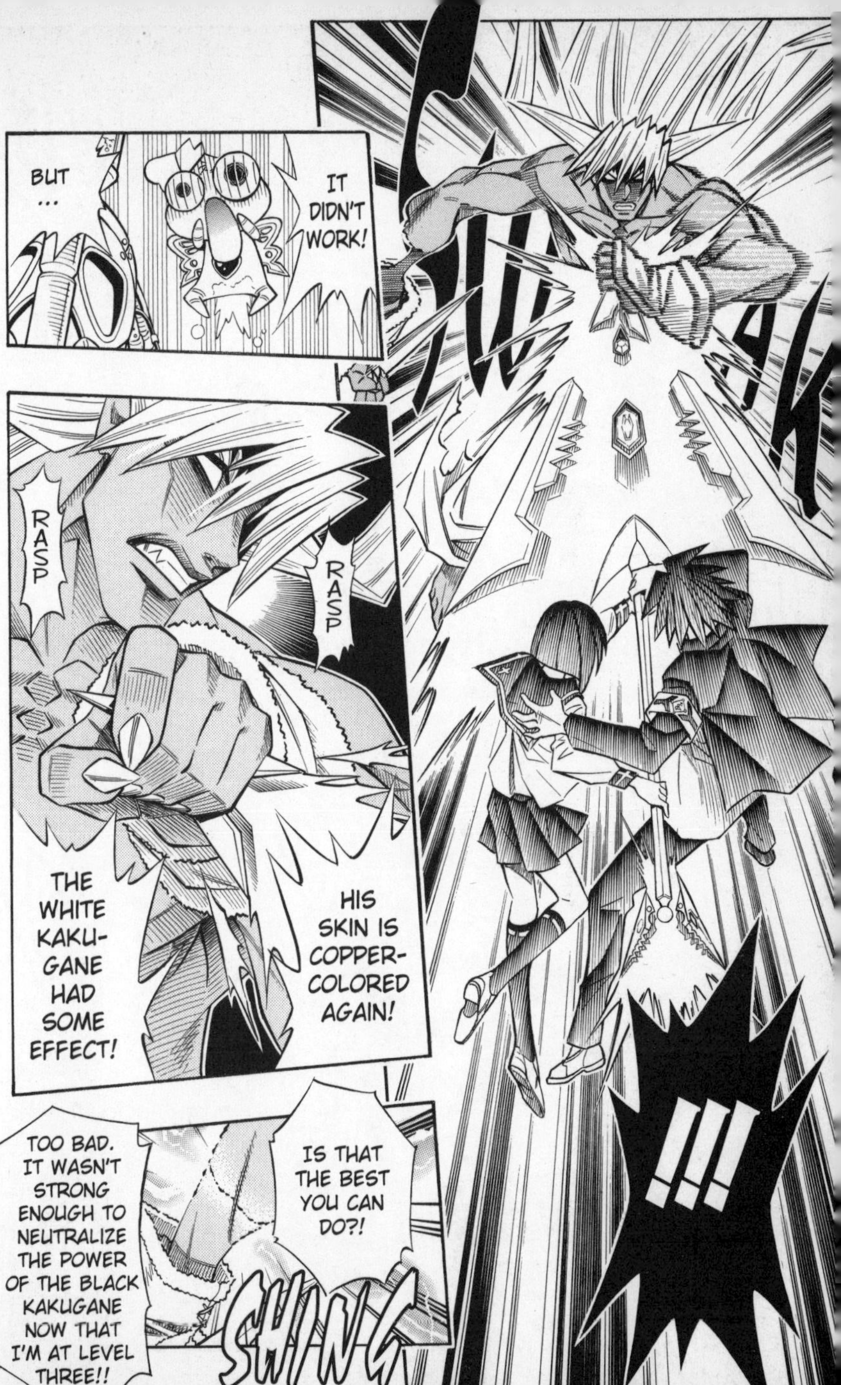
!!!
IT DIDN'T WORK!
BUT ...
RASP
RASP
HIS SKIN IS COPPER-COLORED AGAIN!
THE WHITE KAKU-GANE HAD SOME EFFECT!
IS THAT THE BEST YOU CAN DO?!
TOO BAD. IT WASN'T STRONG ENOUGH TO NEUTRALIZE THE POWER OF THE BLACK KAKUGANE NOW THAT I'M AT LEVEL THREE!!
SHING

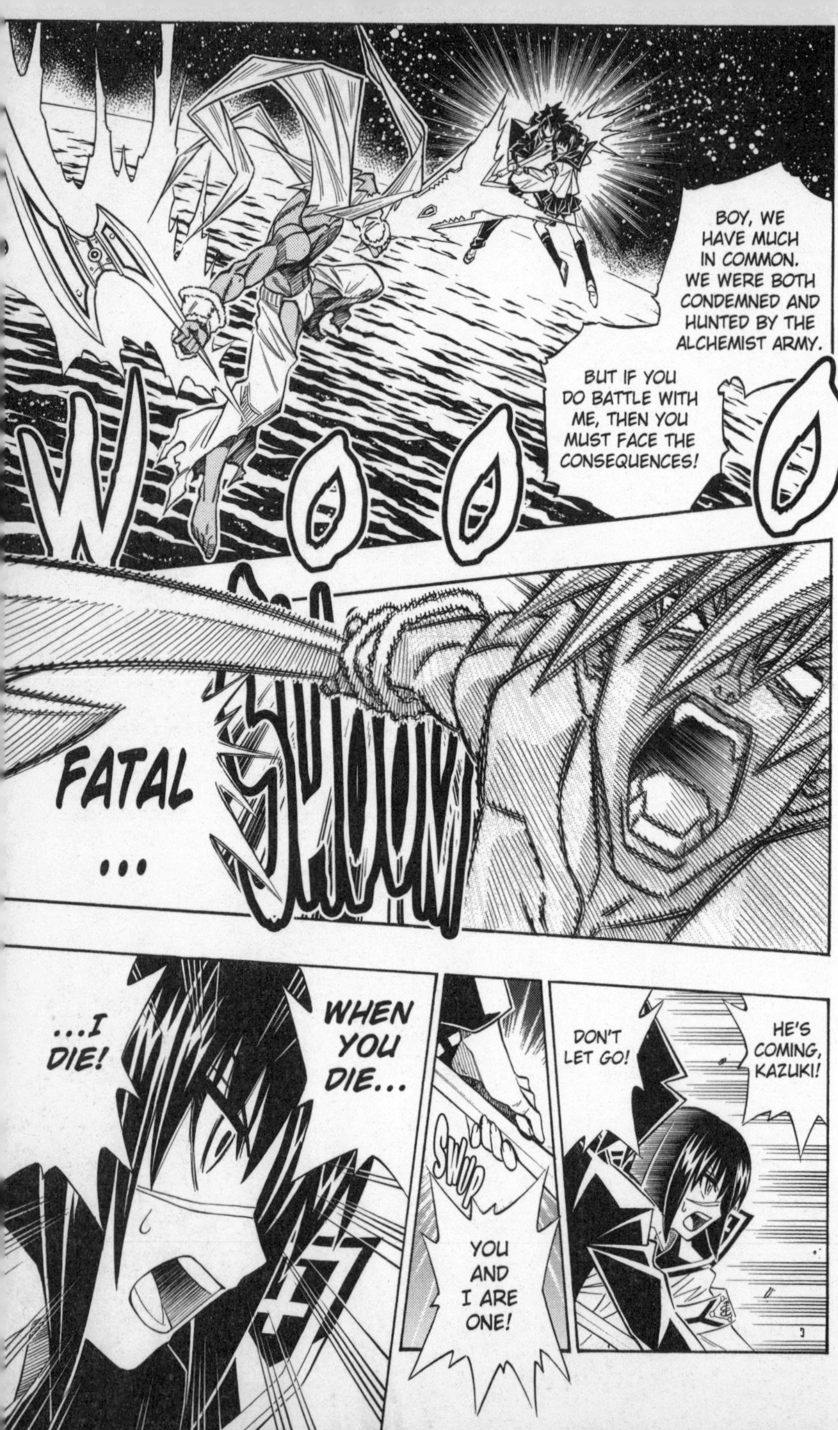
BOY, WE HAVE MUCH IN COMMON. WE WERE BOTH CONDEMNED AND HUNTED BY THE ALCHEMIST ARMY.
BUT IF YOU DO BATTLE WITH ME, THEN YOU MUST FACE THE CONSEQUENCES!
FATAL ...
HE'S COMING, KAZUKI!
DON'T LET GO!
SWUP
YOU AND I ARE ONE!
WHEN YOU DIE...
...I DIE!

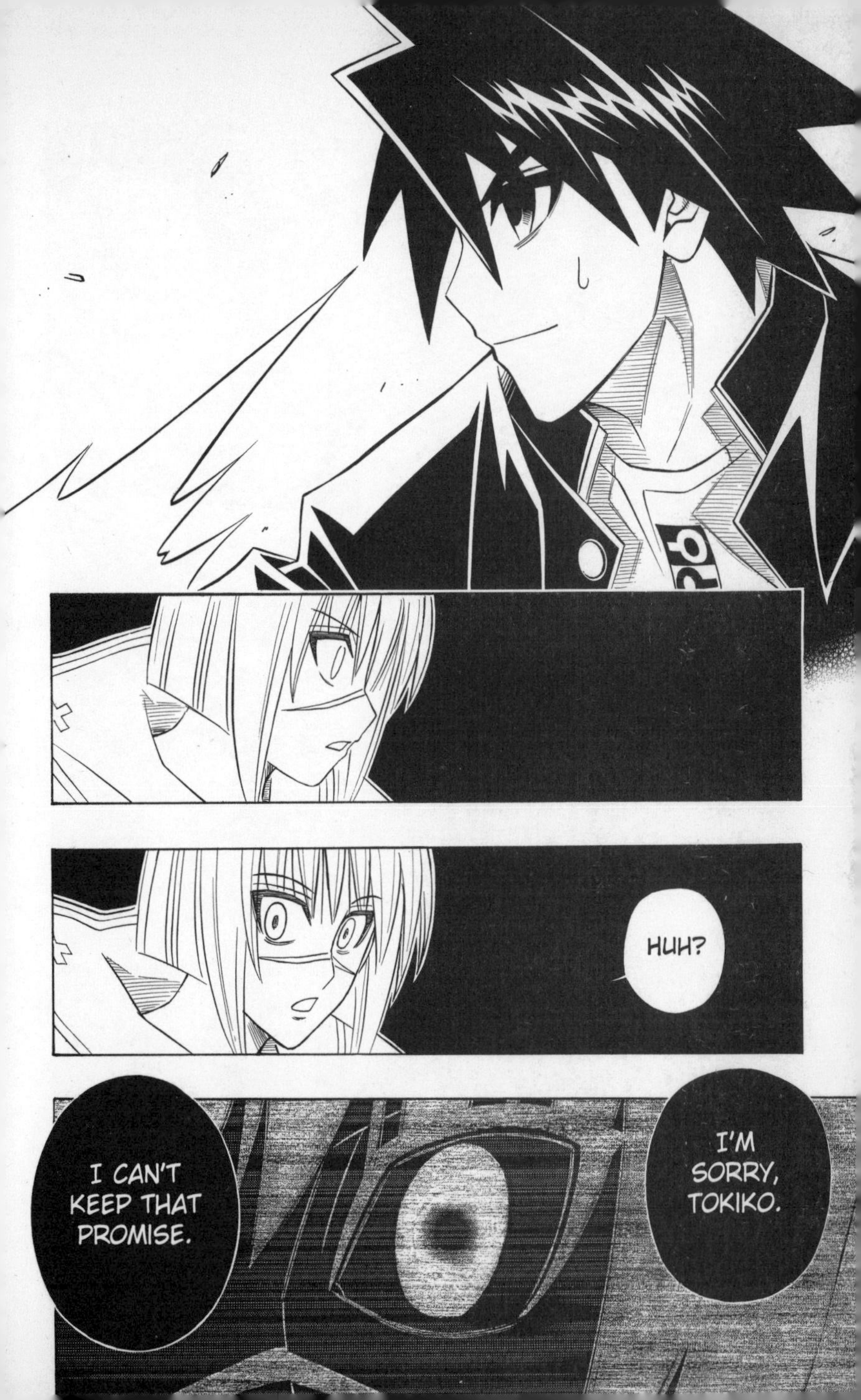
HUH?
I'M SORRY, TOKIKO.
I CAN'T KEEP THAT PROMISE.

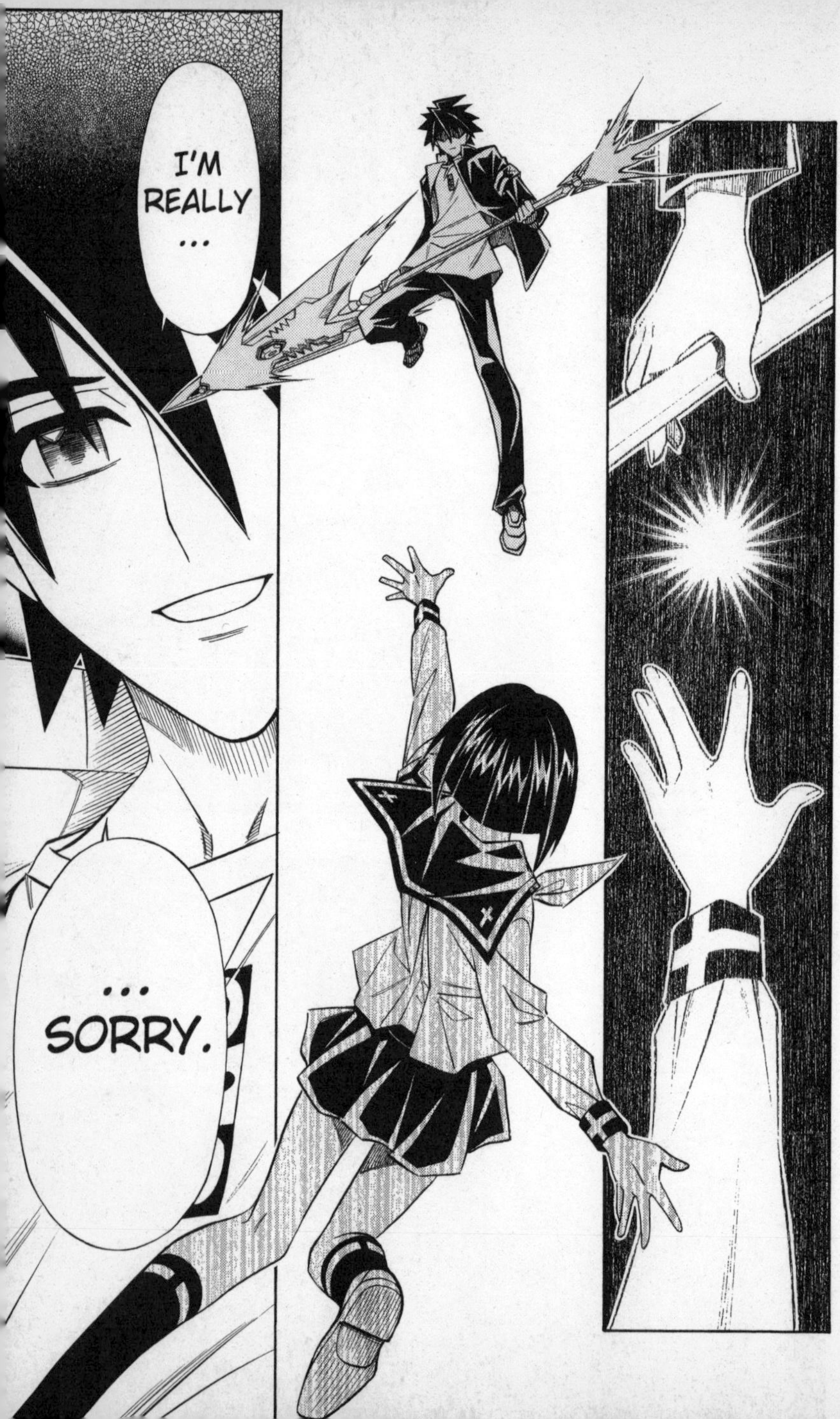
I'M REALLY ...
... SORRY.

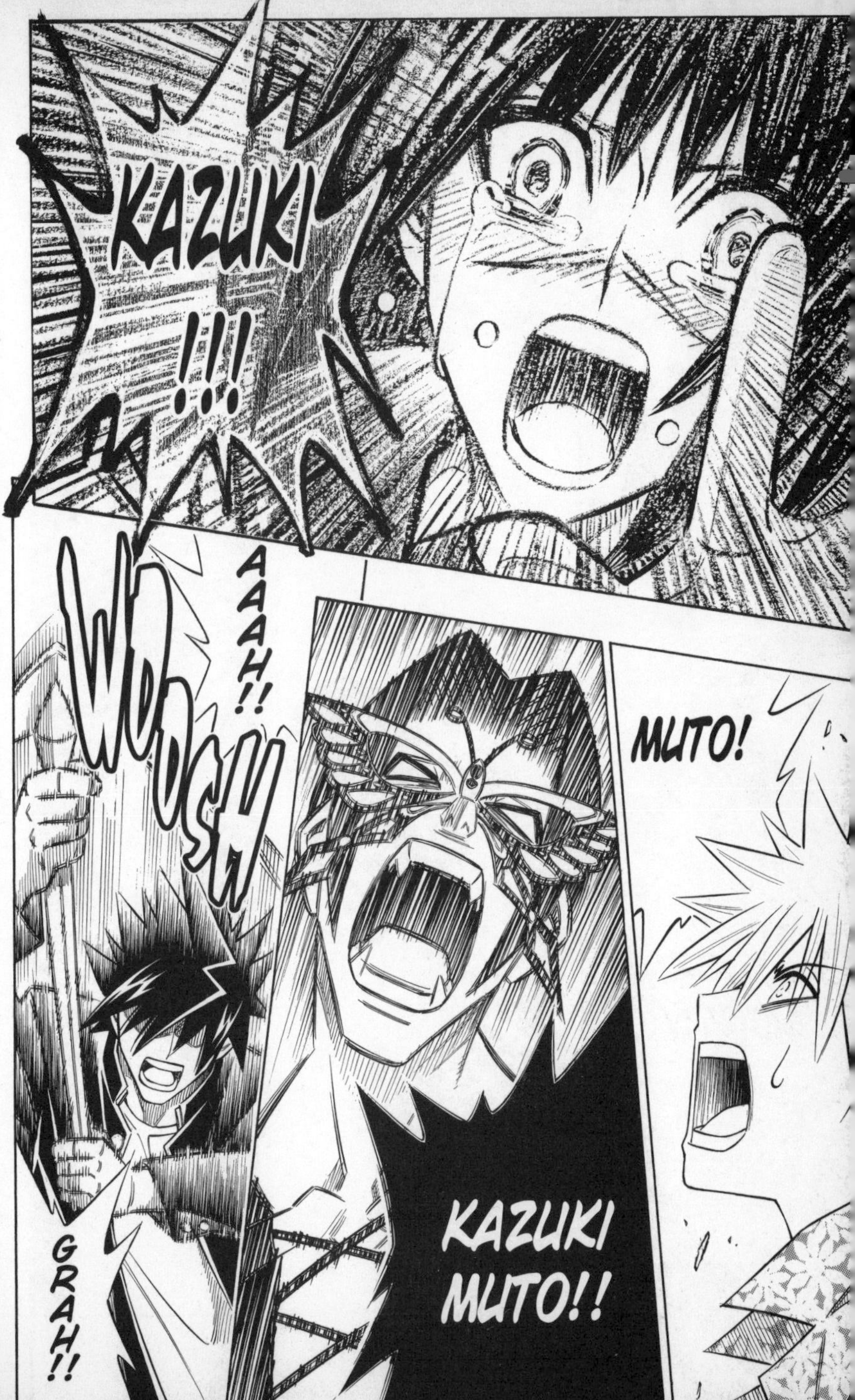
KAZUKI !!!
MUTO!
KAZUKI MUTO!!
AAAH!!
WOOOSH
GRAH!!

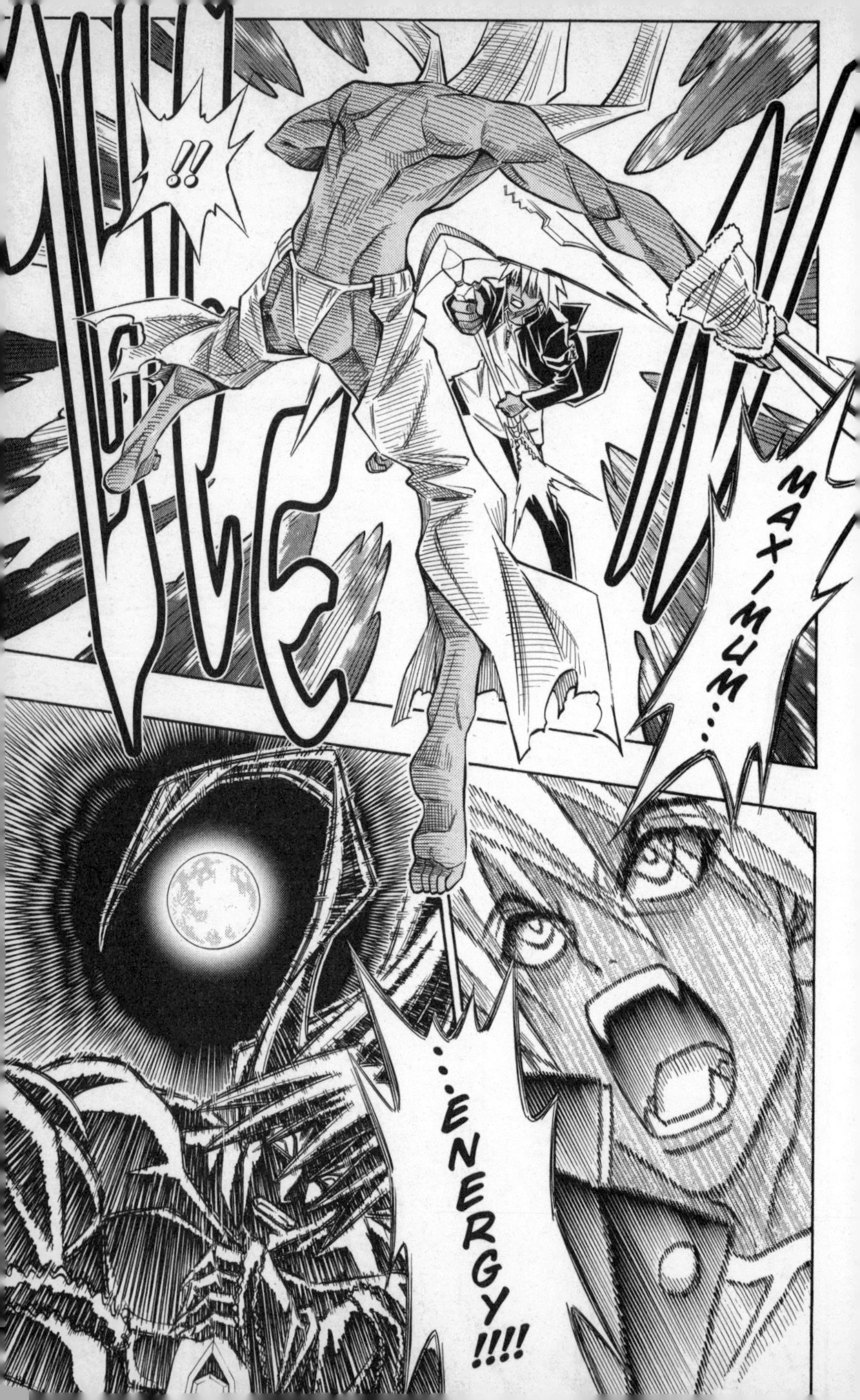
!!
MAXIMUM...
...ENERGY!!!!

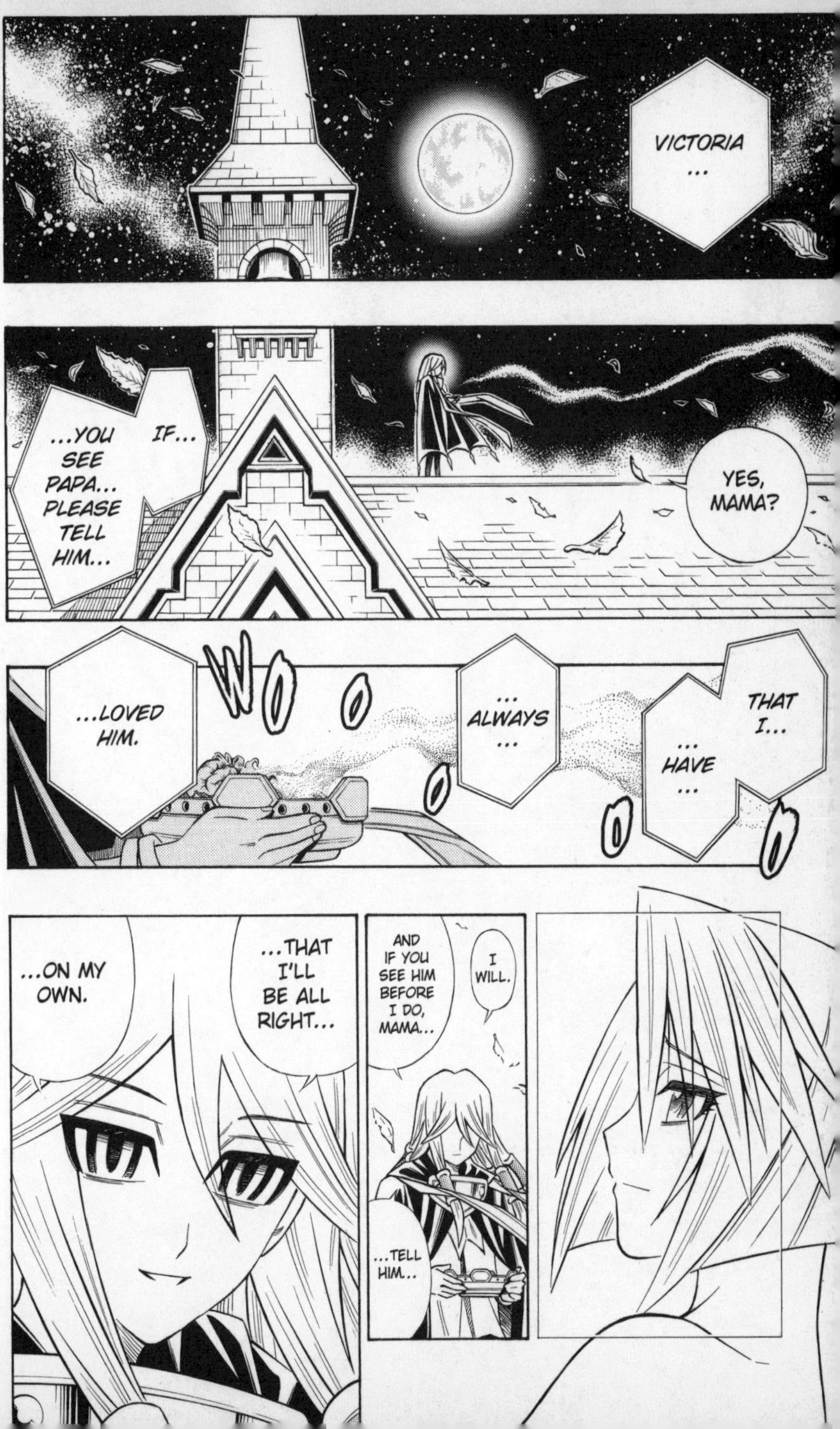
VICTORIA ...
YES, MAMA?
IF... ...YOU SEE PAPA... PLEASE TELL HIM...
THAT I... ...HAVE...
...ALWAYS...
...LOVED HIM.
I WILL.
AND IF YOU SEE HIM BEFORE I DO, MAMA...
...TELL HIM...
...THAT I'LL BE ALL RIGHT...
...ON MY OWN.

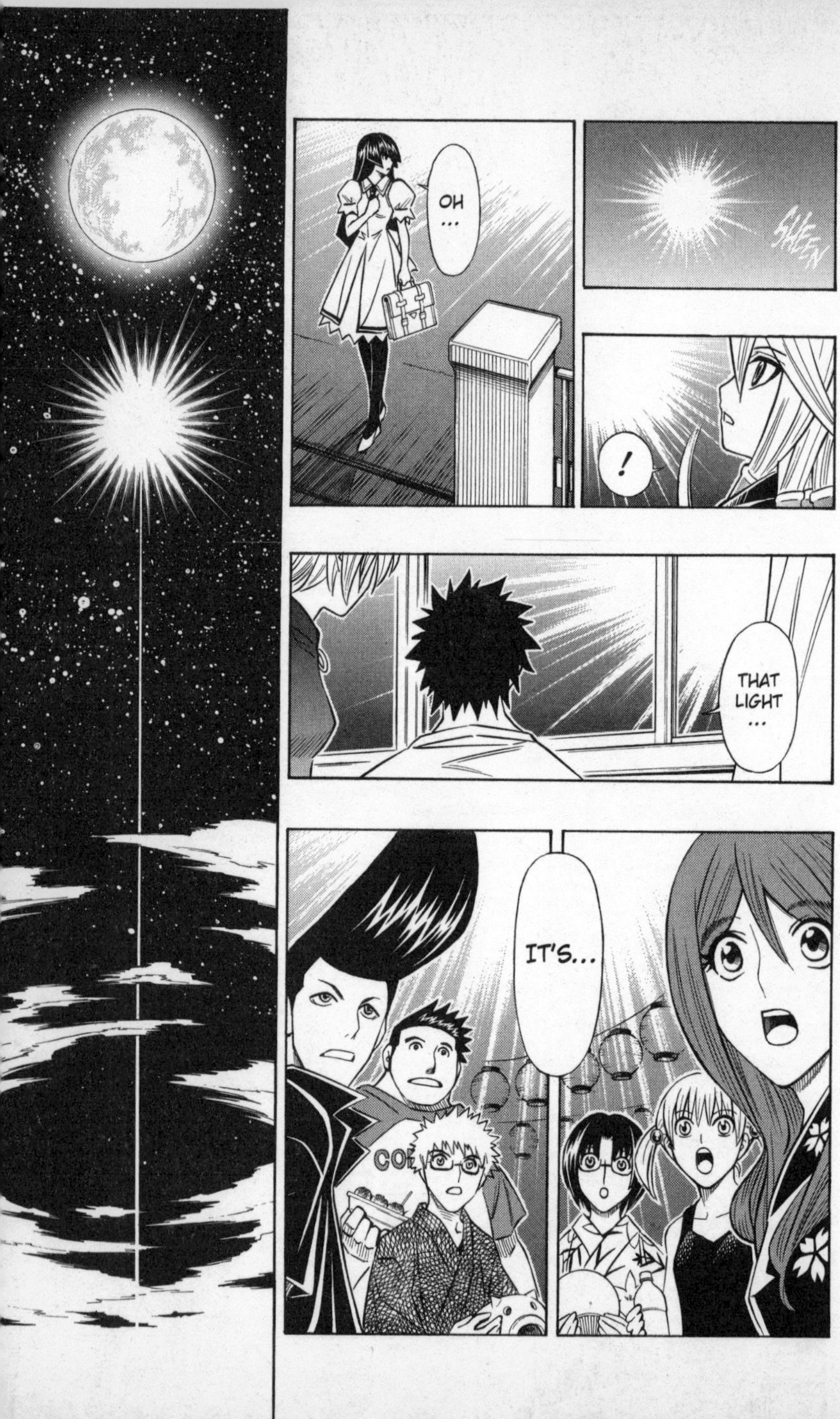
SHEEN
!
OH ...
THAT LIGHT ...
IT'S...

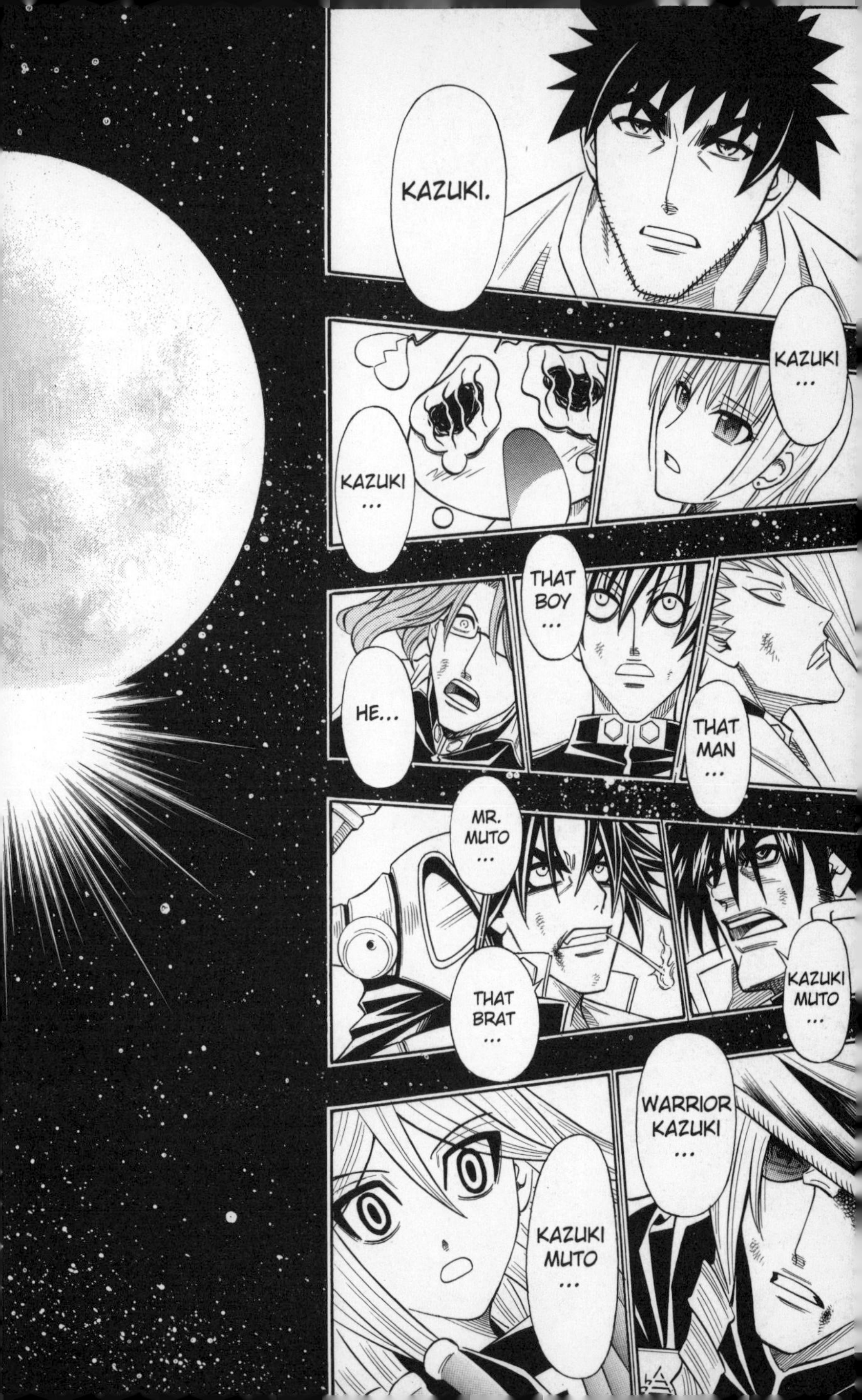
KAZUKI.
KAZUKI ...
KAZUKI ...
THAT MAN ...
THAT BOY ...
HE...
KAZUKI MUTO ...
MR. MUTO ...
THAT BRAT ...
WARRIOR KAZUKI ...
KAZUKI MUTO ...

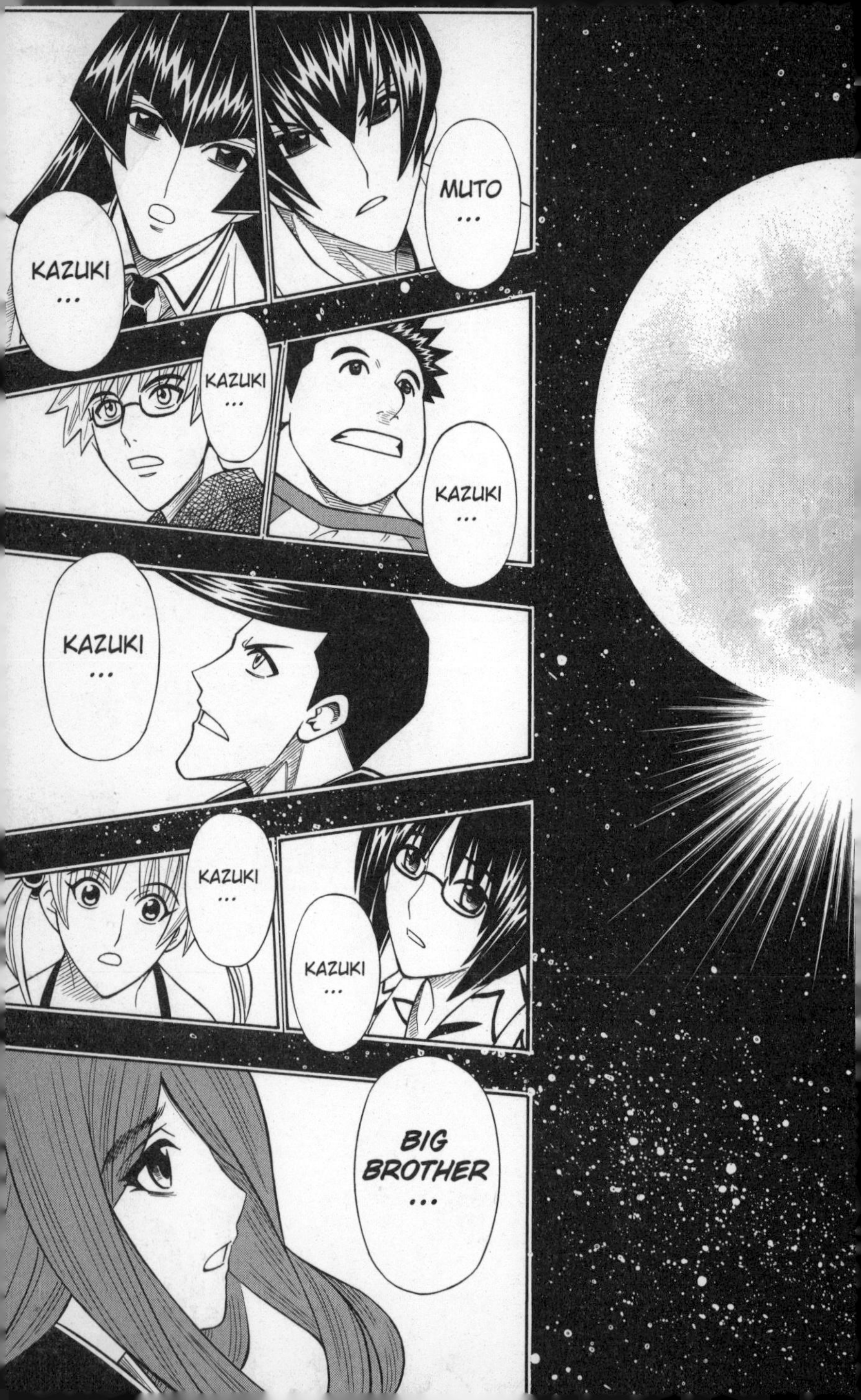
MUTO ...
KAZUKI ...
KAZUKI ...
KAZUKI ...
KAZUKI ...
KAZUKI ...
KAZUKI ...
BIG BROTHER ...

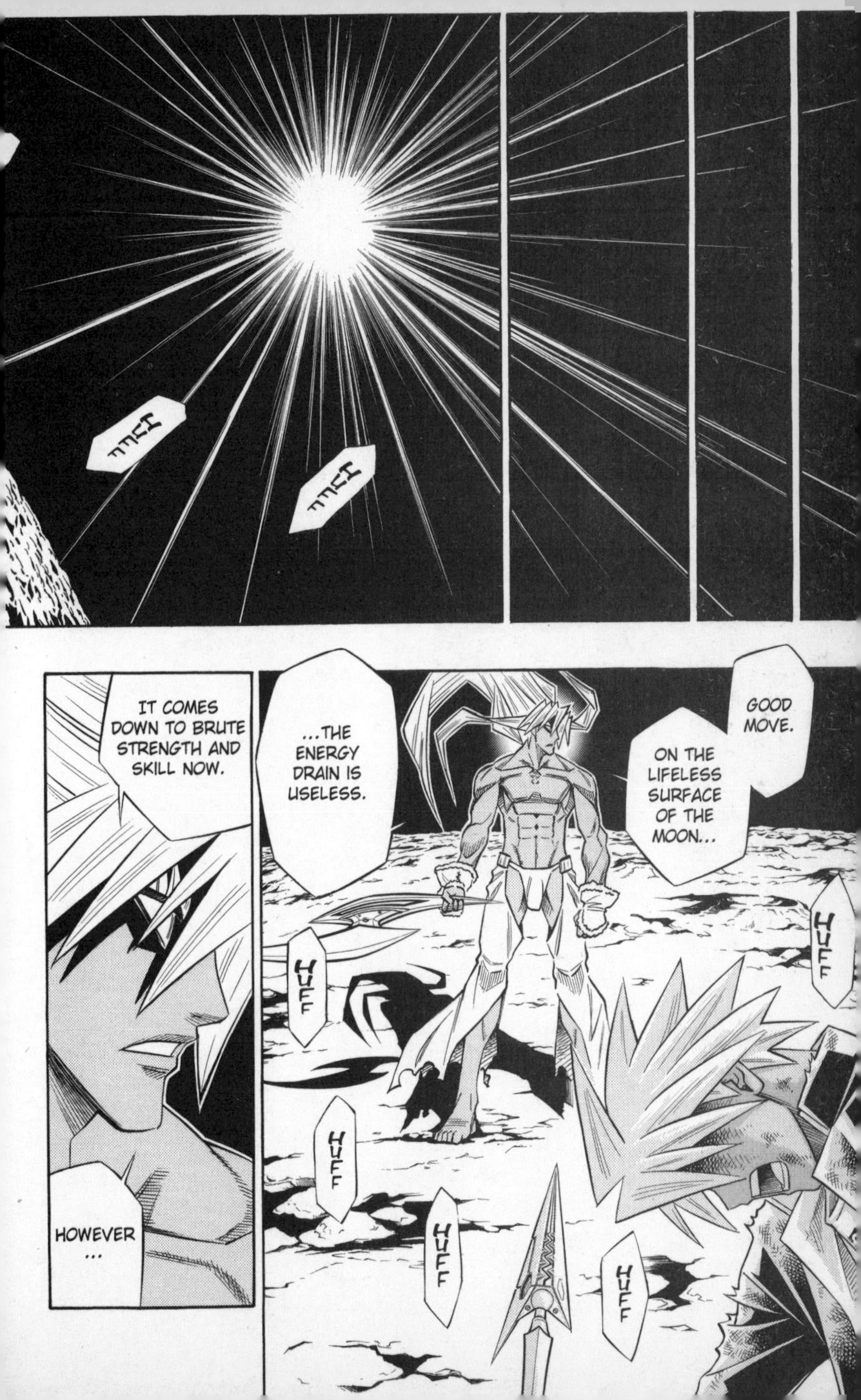
GOOD MOVE.
ON THE LIFELESS SURFACE OF THE MOON...
...THE ENERGY DRAIN IS USELESS.
HUFF
HUFF
HUFF
HUFF
HUFF
IT COMES DOWN TO BRUTE STRENGTH AND SKILL NOW.
HOWEVER...

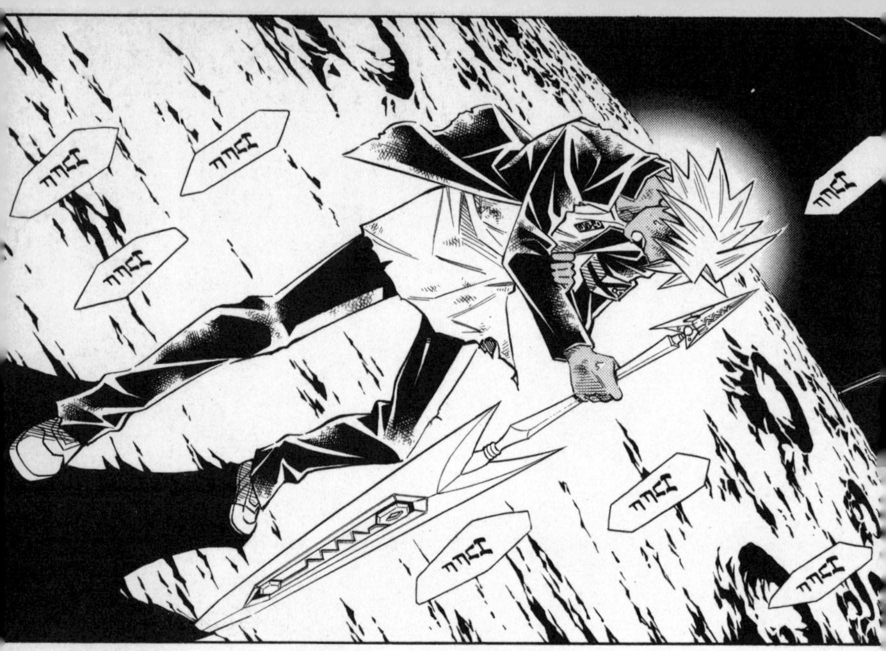

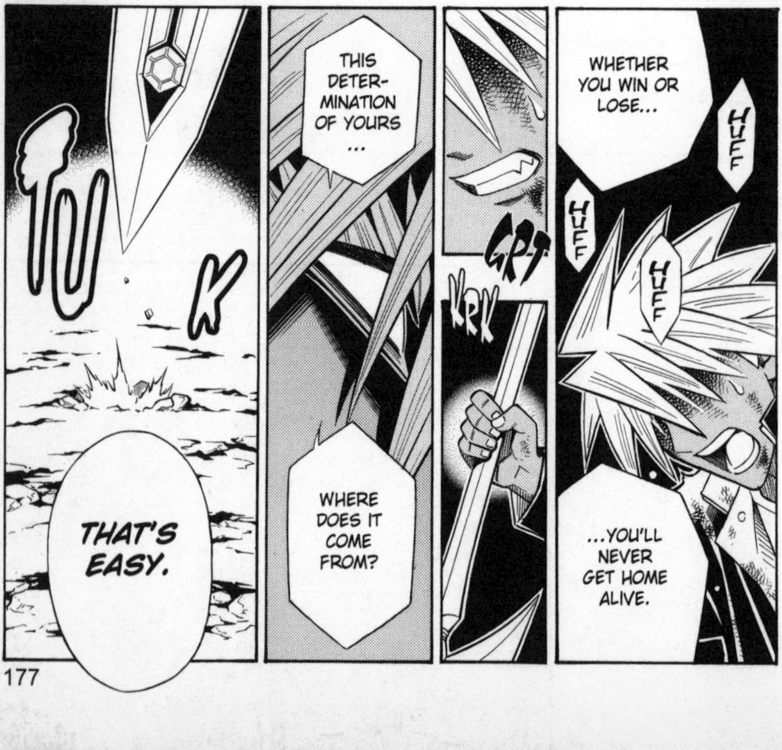
WHETHER YOU WIN OR LOSE...
HUFF
HUFF
HUFF
...YOU'LL NEVER GET HOME ALIVE.
GR-T
KRK
THIS DETER-MINATION OF YOURS ...
WHERE DOES IT COME FROM?
TUK
THAT'S EASY.

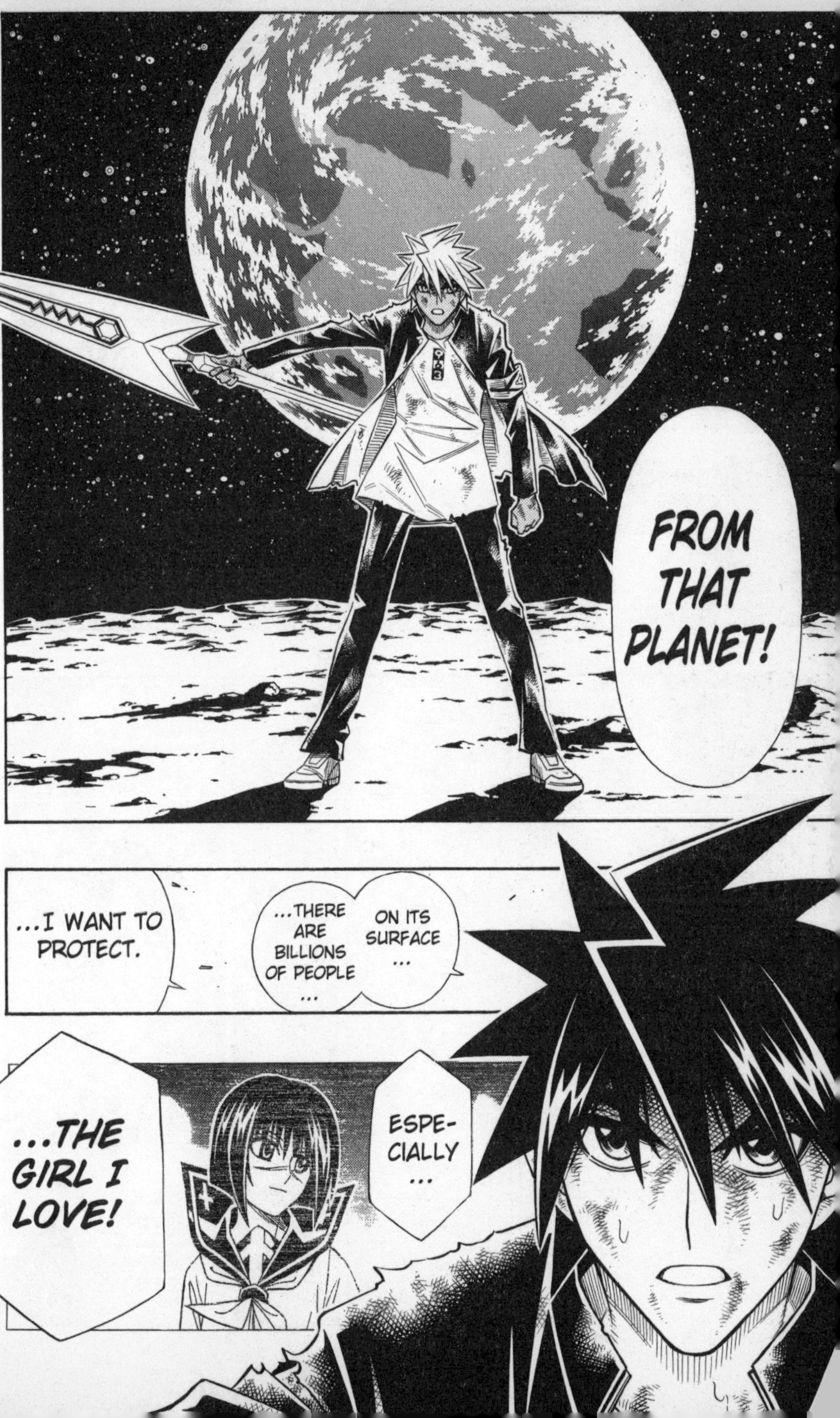
FROM THAT PLANET!
ON ITS SURFACE ...
...THERE ARE BILLIONS OF PEOPLE ...
...I WANT TO PROTECT.
ESPE-CIALLY ...
...THE GIRL I LOVE!

READ THIS WAY

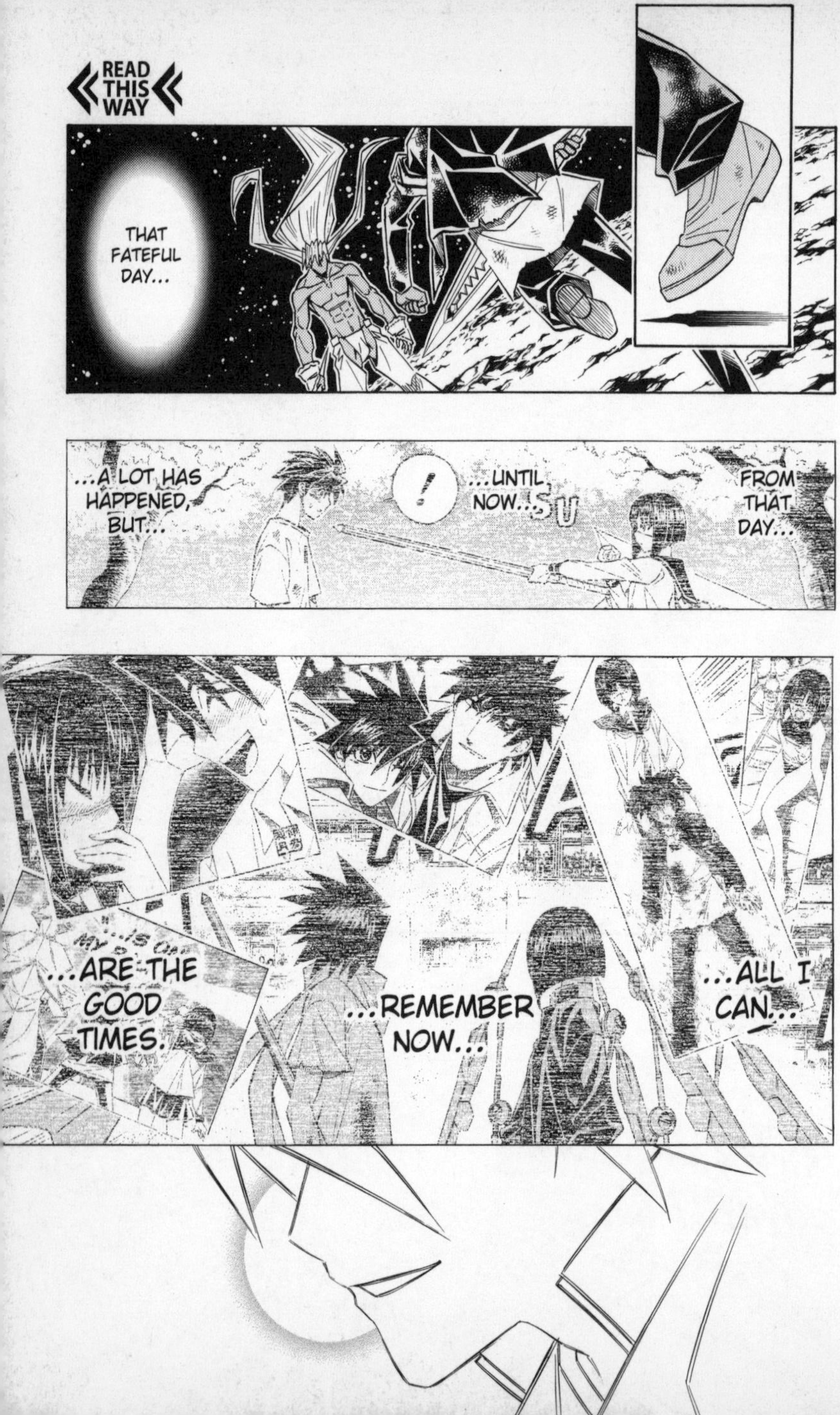
THAT FATEFUL DAY...
FROM THAT DAY...
...UNTIL NOW...
SU
!
...A LOT HAS HAPPENED, BUT...
...ALL I CAN...
...REMEMBER NOW...
...ARE THE GOOD TIMES.

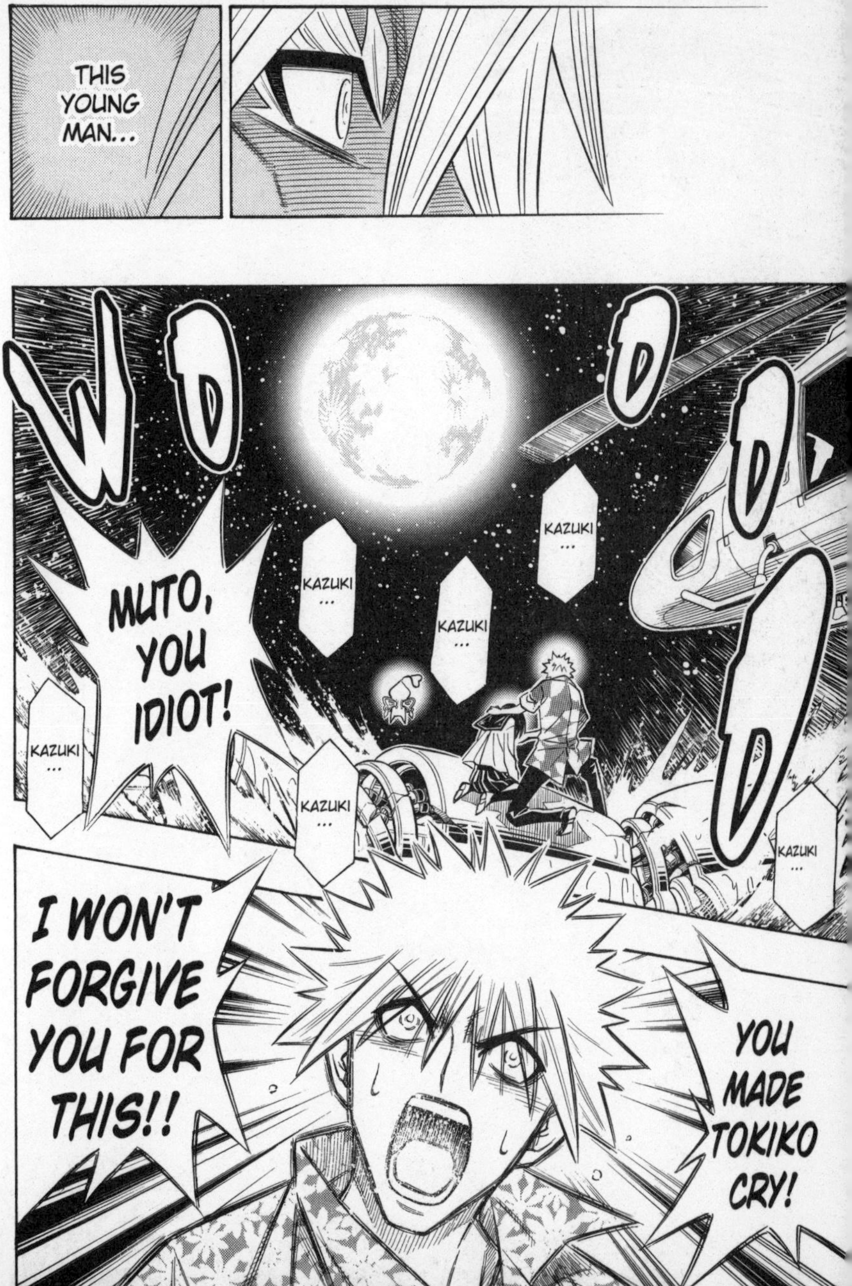
THIS YOUNG MAN...
MUTO, YOU IDIOT!
KAZUKI...
KAZUKI...
KAZUKI...
KAZUKI...
KAZUKI...
KAZUKI...
YOU MADE TOKIKO CRY!
I WON'T FORGIVE YOU FOR THIS!!

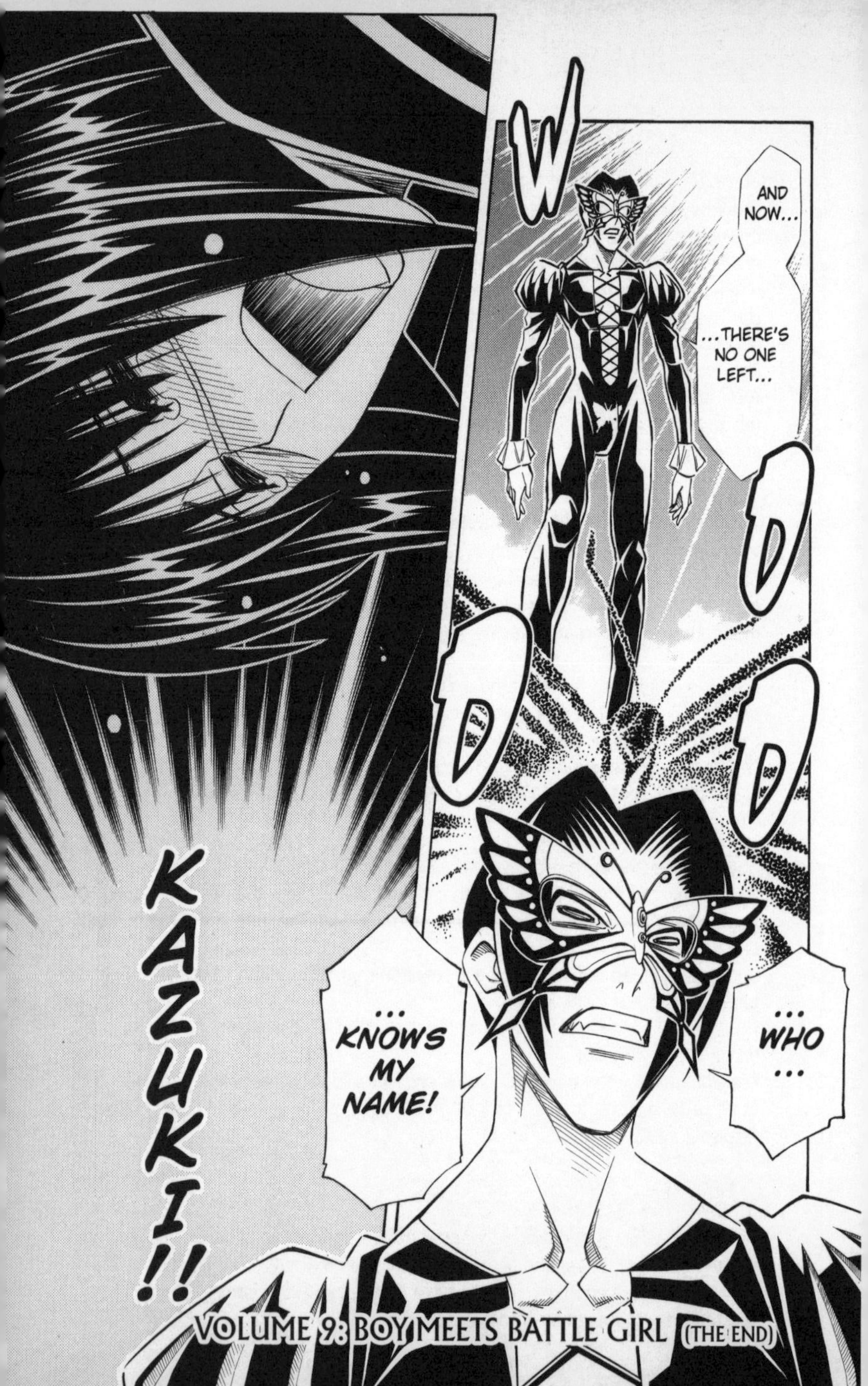
W
AND NOW...
...THERE'S NO ONE LEFT...
D D D D
... WHO ...
... KNOWS MY NAME!
KAZUKI!!

VOLUME 9: BOY MEETS BATTLE GIRL (THE END)

Liner Notes #74-Last Chapter

Chapter 74: The Two Final Battles

- The submarine Buso Renkin, Deep Breathing, was inspired by the *Nautilus* from the movie *League of Extraordinary Gentleman.* A submarine with a battering ram is just too cool. Not that it matters, but I think I like it even better than the original *Nautilus.* I'd like to be able to design more stuff like that.
- The re-extermination of Kazuki is put on hold. Kazuki seems happier for Tokiko and Gouta than for himself. I think this scene really shows what kind of person Kazuki is.
- You also get a hint of Hiwatari's motivations in this chapter. I wrote a little about this in the character file, but it's one of the things I'd really like to explore further someday.

Chapter 75: Infiltrating Newton Apple Academy for Girls

- After several chapters filled with mayhem, I wanted a little comic relief here. But comedy isn't really my forte. I always feel worn out afterward because of the extra effort it requires. After working on this series, I have new respect for comedians and comedic manga artists. The ability to make people laugh is amazing indeed.
- The logo I designed for Newton Apple Academy only appeared on the title page, but I think details like that make the world of the story more complete and I like the way it turned out.
- The academy was supposed to have a lot of history, but I don't think I really captured the feel of an old school. I still have a lot to learn.

Chapter 76: Secret of the Mask

- I really enjoyed depicting a battle that wasn't just a clash of brute force at the beginning of this chapter. I've really come to realize how useful the Motor Gears can be.
- On a whim, I decided to combine a sailor suit uniform with a cape. I'm really pleased with how well it worked.
- The scene where Kazuki worries about the safety of Tokiko and Victoria says a lot about his character.
- The array of tanks with cloned brains ended up looking more like one brain on a bank of TV screens. It was a lack of forethought on my part, and I was really disappointed.

Chapter 77: The Great Battle

- In Victor's flashback sequence, I wanted the scenery to look European. I tried to make mountains, trees, and fields in a totally different style, but it didn't really work (despite my efforts). I'd like to base a series in 19th-century Europe someday, but I guess I need to do more research.

- The ebony skin of Victor's Level 3 form was suggested by Hiroyuki Takei of *Shaman King*. When Victor first appeared, he said to me, "You should've had the guts to make Victor's skin black." So I ended up doing it here. I'm always amazed by Takei's sense of design.
- The first appearance of the Buster Baron. It's a reincarnation of the Armor Baron from my previous series *Gun Blaze West*. I'd wanted to do a giant robot Buso Renkin for a while, so here it is.
- Since he was fighting a giant robot, Victor had to match himself in size. I just love full-scale monster battles!

Chapter 78: Require a Decision
- This chapter had a lot of exposition, but it couldn't be helped.
- Gouta once again puts himself at risk for Tokiko. But after this scene, I'd hear Gouta talking like a girl every time Alexandria speaks.
- The first appearance of the octagon room. If you look carefully, the positions the characters are standing in are a bit unnatural.
- The first appearance of the white kakugane. Actually, in the planning stages, it was going to be a red kakugane. I'd planned to make the banner for the collection in the same gradation of red, but with all the work I put into the design of the octagon room, I didn't have time to apply the tone to the kakugane so it became the white kakugane. I thought, "Well, manga is black and white anyway." Then I found out the cover of the chapter was going to be in color. I should've taken the time to make it red.

Last Chapter: Boy Meets Battle Girl
- This was the last chapter of the weekly serialization. To all the fans that followed it week to week, I'm sorry. And thank you very much.
- By this point, it had already been decided that I was going to be given some pages in another magazine, but it was still the end of the serialization. I knew I couldn't wrap everything up, but I decided to cement Tokiko and Kazuki's relationship. *Buso Renkin* is also a story of first love, and I wanted the chapter title to reflect that.
- The title page shows Kazuki and Tokiko a moment after they kissed.
- The gang from school shows up again. The idiot trio and the girl trio are there. I'm glad I stuck to my original decision to not give any of them a Buso Renkin.
- Ouka appears again going about her normal and not-so-normal daily activities. Her personality is more multidimensional now. Perhaps it's a positive effect from being linked to Gozen. And again I have to say how much I like to draw him.

Liner Notes: Last Chapter-Buso Renkin Finale

- Bravo first appeared as Kazuki's trainer and mentor. But now that his own battle is over, he has warm feelings for the student who surpassed him. The passing of the torch is a fact of life and all I can say to Bravo is "well done!" I feel some regret that I couldn't show more of Bravo, Chitose, and Hiwatari's past, but maybe that wouldn't have been right for a boy's manga.
- Gouta acknowledges Kazuki as his ally. The ability to find common ground can be very helpful in overcoming conflicts. But I'm not finished with Gouta's story yet.
- Papillon's storyline will continue as well, of course. Even in the last chapter, he has better lines than the main character. His strange sense of style is part of his appeal, but for me Papillon is the dark hero of this series. That's why he often says things that I'd like to say myself. He's one of my all-time favorite characters.
- I'd always planned to have Kazuki say something like "I'm going to protect everybody, but who will protect me?" from the very beginning of the series. Will anyone come to his rescue? You'll find out the answer to that in the real climax of the series.
- Kazuki makes his decision and Tokiko decides to support him no matter what it is. They kiss and become as one. Again, I wish to thank everyone for their support of this series.

Buso Renkin Finale

- I'd never done a 60-page one-shot manga before. The sensation of drawing and drawing and never reaching the end was a new kind of hell for me, completely different from the hell of doing a weekly series. I guess the manga world has a lot of hells...
- Even with all the pages they gave me, it was still impossible to wrap everything up. So I begged the editorial office to let me do the climax in two installments. They took pity on me and gave me the go-ahead more easily than I expected.
- And so, this was the first of two installments in the conclusion of *Buso Renkin.* This was supposed to be the climax of the Victor storyline.
- When you're an adult, and a manga artist especially, the whole idea of a summer vacation is nothing but a distant memory. But I still remember how good it felt. I get nostalgic for the time when I could play day and night and ignore all the homework I should've been doing. I guess the mad rush to finish all the homework at the end of summer is a lot like what I go through to meet my deadlines.
- The Japanese headquarters of the Alchemist Army is shown for the first and last time. I like the way it turned out. It looks like an underground aquarium.
- The big moment between Kazuki and Tokiko. I did it here because the end of the chapter is one big battle. But it turned out more like a romantic comedy.
- I had a hard time developing Mahiro over the course of the series, but I'm really happy with the way she turned out. Originally I was going to have her be a dropout and a troublemaker, but I'll save that idea for another series.

- Although Bravo can't fight as an Alchemist Warrior anymore, his strength will still be needed.
- The Buster Baron and Victor battle in the sea like good movie monsters should. I had so much fun with this that I used up some of the pages I needed for the end of the chapter. But overall, I'm happy with how the battle turned out.
- The surprise return of Shusui. The Buster Baron's special ability is kind of a cheat, but it came in really handy so I went with it anyway. It also gave the members of the Re-Extermination Squad another moment in the spotlight. And the courage of the Great Warrior Chief is displayed too.
- Thruster packs and knuckle guards. I had a lot of fun with this battle, but in the end, they still lose.
- Kazuki's dilemma was caused by timing—two people needing something at the same time. So he found a way to get more time for himself. You can't always do this in real life, but it can be a good way to resolve problems.
- Gouta still won't shake Kazuki's hand. He accepts him for who he is, but there are some things he won't budge on.
- If you look carefully, page 156 is actually one whole image. That may not mean much to the readers, but I think it's definitely a major step in my development as an artist.
- Victor's "Rage! Rage is all I have left!" is one of my favorite lines in this chapter. But who wouldn't be mad if they were in Victor's shoes? Even a hundred years ago there were limits to what you could do to a child. I plan to touch upon this a bit more in the next installment.
- Kazuki and Tokiko's double attack. In the original plan, Tokiko's Valkyrie Skirt was going to hold the white kakugane while Kazuki propelled them with the Sunlight Heart Plus. But it was too confusing to draw it that way, so I dropped that idea. I'm kind of sad that the Valkyrie Skirt didn't get used in this installment.
- Kazuki breaks his promise to Tokiko and goes into outer space without her. This was kind of him, but cruel too. But I couldn't see Kazuki making any other choice here.
- Alexandria and Victoria say a last goodbye. I really wish I could've gone into more detail about this family.
- A bright sunlight-yellow light shoots toward the moon while all the characters look on. The final battle will be fought on the moon. I had all of this planned out a long time ago. A lot has happened with this series, but I'm really glad I got to do it.
- At the end of my life, I hope I'll look back at all the happy times. The ideal departure from this life is one where people seeing you off fondly smile as you pass.
- Victor grumbles, Gouta yells, Papillon mourns, and Tokiko sheds tears. Amid these outpourings of emotion, the story will finally come to an end in the next volume—the true climax. →

To be continued.

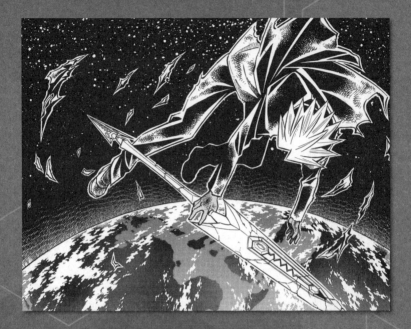

Coming Next Volume

Kazuki's stuck up on the moon with Victor! Papillon's up to his old tricks on Earth! How's it all going to end? Find out in the final volume of *Buso Renkin*!

Available in February 2008!

SERVING JUSTICE TO EVIL SPIRITS IS THEIR SPECIALTY! SJ

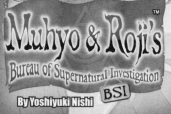

MANGA SERIES ON SALE NOW!

Muhyo & Roji's
Bureau of Supernatural Investigation
BSI
By Yoshiyuki Nishi

$7.99

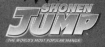

SHONEN JUMP
THE WORLD'S MOST POPULAR MANGA

On sale at:
www.shonenjump.com
Also available at your local bookstore and comic store.

RATED
FOR
TEEN
ratings.viz.com

VIZ
media
WWW.VIZ.COM

MUHYO TO ROZY NO MAHORITSU SODAN JIMUSHO © 2004 by Yoshiyuki Nishi/SHUEISHA Inc.

EYESHIELD 21

Gear up for the best bone-crushing slapstick football manga ever!

Manga on sale now!

$7.99

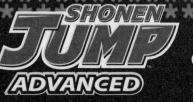

EYESHIELD 21 © 2002 by Riichiro Inagaki, Yusuke Murata/SHUEISHA Inc.

On sale at:
www.shonenjump.com
Also available at your local bookstore and comic store.

www.viz.com

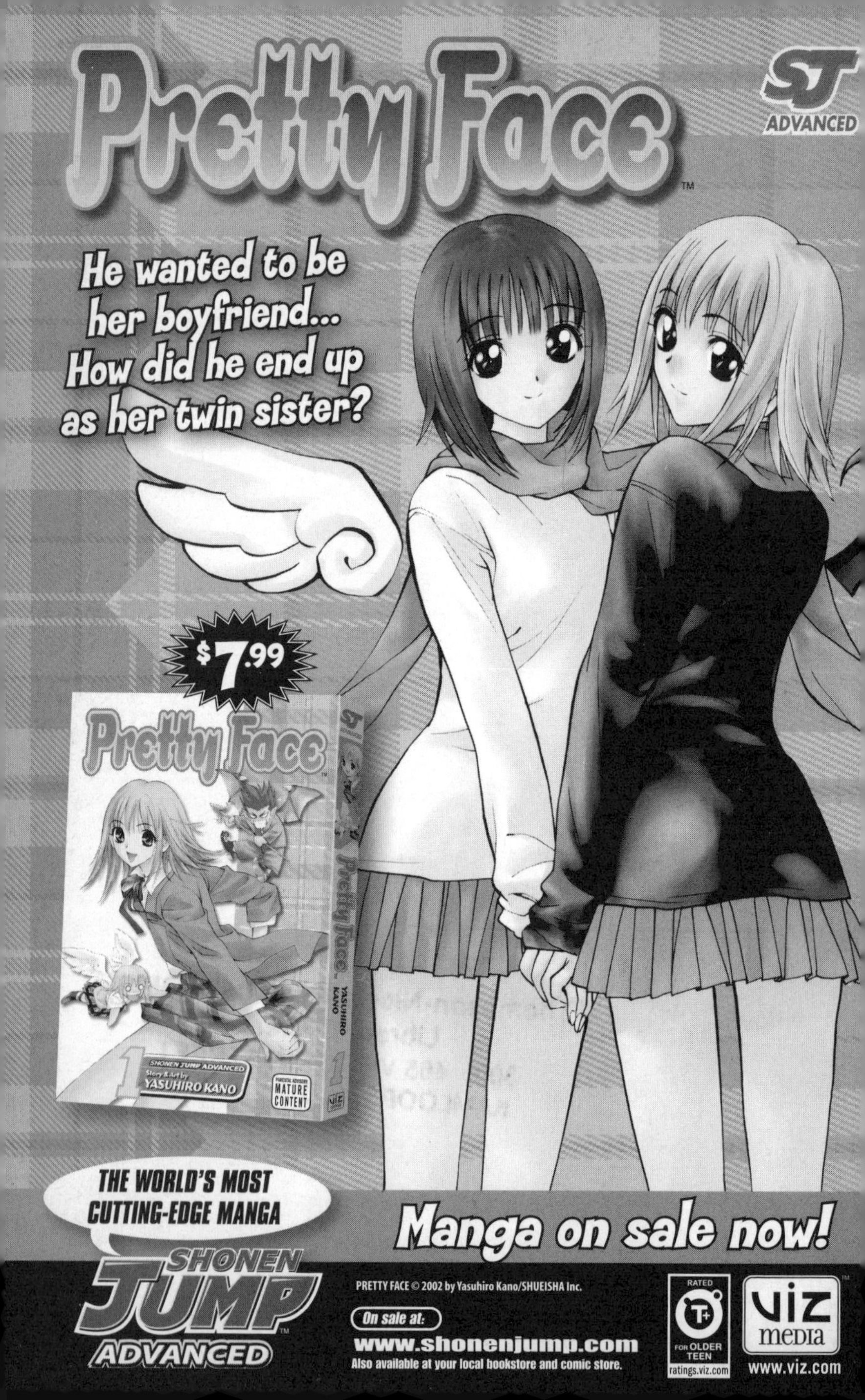
Pretty Face™
SJ ADVANCED
He wanted to be her boyfriend... How did he end up as her twin sister?
$7.99
Pretty Face
1
SHONEN JUMP ADVANCED
YASUHIRO KANO
MATURE CONTENT
THE WORLD'S MOST CUTTING-EDGE MANGA
Manga on sale now!
SHONEN JUMP ADVANCED
PRETTY FACE © 2002 by Yasuhiro Kano/SHUEISHA Inc.
On sale at:
www.shonenjump.com
Also available at your local bookstore and comic store.
RATED T+ FOR OLDER TEEN
ratings.viz.com
viz media
www.viz.com

3 5444 00036229 2

Tell us what you think about SHONEN JUMP manga!

Our survey is now available online.
Go to: www.SHONENJUMP.com/mangasurvey

Help us make our product offering better!

Thompson-Nicola Regional District
Library System
300 - 465 VICTORIA STREET
KAMLOOPS, B.C. V2C 2A9

THE REAL ACTION
STARTS IN...

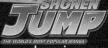

www.shonenjump.com

ADVANCED

BLEACH © 2001 by Tite Kubo/SHUEISHA Inc. NARUTO © 1999 by Masashi Kishimoto/SHUEISHA Inc.
DEATH NOTE © 2003 by Tsugumi Ohba, Takeshi Obata/SHUEISHA Inc. ONE PIECE © 1997 by Eiichiro Oda/SHUEISHA Inc.